UNITED STATES DISTRICT COURTS AND JUDGES OF ARKANSAS, 1836–1960

UNITED STATES DISTRICT COURTS AND JUDGES OF ARKANSAS, 1836–1960

EDITED BY

FRANCES MITCHELL ROSS

The University of Arkansas Press
Fayetteville
2016

Manufactured in the United States of America
ISBN: 978-1-55728-694-9
e-ISBN: 978-1-61075-580-1

20 19 18 17 16 5 4 3 2 1

Designed by Liz Lester

∞ The paper used in this publication meets the minimum requirements of the American National Standard for Permanence of Paper for Printed Library Materials Z39.48-1984.

Library of Congress Control Number: 2015960125

This project is supported in part by the United States District Court for the Eastern District of Arkansas and the United States District Court for the Western District of Arkansas.

Arkansas
Humanities
Council

This project is supported in part by a grant from the Arkansas Humanities Council and the National Endowment for the Humanities.

To the late United States district judge
Henry Woods

and the late United States circuit judge
Richard Sheppard Arnold

CONTENTS

ACKNOWLEDGMENTS

Many individuals contributed to this volume, most importantly the authors of the essays. The book's origin began some years ago when Judge Susan Webber Wright, then a UALR Law School professor and now a senior United States district judge, inquired of the editor's interest in participating in a federal court history project for Arkansas. Receiving an affirmative response, she communicated that to Judge Henry Woods and Judge Richard Sheppard Arnold, who guided various dimensions of the history project for many years. Both judges offered endless assistance as the numerous parts of the project took shape, aiding in arranging oral histories with other judges, participating as narrators for their own oral history interviews, facilitating research travel, defining the scope of this volume, and contributing essays to it. More recently Judge Morris Sheppard Arnold has played a crucial role in many ways in moving this book to the publication stage. Without the teamwork this reflects, no history would have materialized.

Images of Honorable Benjamin Johnson, Honorable Daniel Ringo, Honorable Henry Clay Caldwell, Honorable John Apps Williams, Honorable Jacob Trieber, Honorable John Ellis Martineau, Honorable Thomas Clark Trimble III, Honorable Gordon Elmo Young, Honorable Harry Jacob Lemley, and Honorable Jesse Smith Henley were all made available by the United States District Court for the Eastern District of Arkansas with permission to publish. The court likewise provided the image of the Richard Sheppard Arnold United States Courthouse in Little Rock with permission to publish. Much appreciation is due the court and James McCormack, clerk of court, United States District Court for the Eastern District of Arkansas, who arranged for and distributed these materials. James McCormack has also responded to numerous inquiries during the preparation of the manuscript.

This volume is equally indebted to the United States District Court for the Western District of Arkansas, which provided images of Honorable Isaac Charles Parker, Honorable John Henry Rogers, Honorable Frank Abijah Youmans, Honorable Heartsill Ragon, and Honorable John Elvis Miller and granted permission to publish. The court also made images available of these courthouses in Fort Smith: the historic US Courthouse and Jail; the United States Courthouse and Post Office, now razed, and the present Judge Isaac C. Parker Federal Building. The court granted permission to publish these courthouse images. Appreciation is extended to the court and to Christopher R. Johnson who, until his fall 2015 retirement, was clerk of court, United States District Court for the Western District of Arkansas. He coordinated and arranged delivery of this material and responded to countless requests. His successor, Douglas F. Young, has also provided helpful assistance.

The image of Judge William Story is in the public domain and hangs in the Benton County Courthouse in Bentonville, Arkansas. Jane Goble of Bentonville took the initial photographs of the Story image, followed by Deena Owens of the University of Arkansas Press, who did the final image. Access to the image was made available courtesy of Benton County, Arkansas. The *Arkansas Gazette* masthead is courtesy of the *Arkansas Democrat-Gazette*. The 1870s image of the State House building is courtesy of the Old State House Museum Collection. The image of the current United States Bankruptcy Court in Little Rock is courtesy of the Library of Congress. Thanks to Sheila Bell of Van Buren, who helped locate the sketch of the 1870s Crawford County Courthouse, located in Van Buren. This 1870s sketch of the Crawford County Courthouse by William Quesenbury was made available with permission to publish by the University of Arkansas Libraries, Special Collections, where it can be found in the Quesenbury Family Papers (MC 1003, box 1, folder 1).

The opening article, by Judge Richard S. Arnold and by Michael B. Heister, "The Structure of the United States District Courts in Arkansas," first appeared in 56 *Arkansas Law Review* 715 (2004) and is reprinted with permission of the *Arkansas Law Review* at the University of Arkansas. A version of the essay titled "Benjamin Johnson" by Professor Lynn Foster, UALR William H. Bowen School of Law, was prepared for and first published by the *University of Arkansas at Little Rock Law Review* in Volume 22, Issue 1 and is reproduced with its permission. The original article was titled, "Their Pride and Ornament: Judge Benjamin Johnson and the Federal Courts in Early Arkansas." Further information about the *UALR Law Review* is available at www.ualr.edu/lawreview. "Henry Clay Caldwell" by Judge Richard S. Arnold and George C. Freeman

III, was prepared for and first published by the *UALR Law Review* in Volume 23, Issue 2 and is reproduced with its permission. The article was originally titled "Judge Henry C. Caldwell." Further information about the *UALR Law Review* is available at www.ualr.edu/lawreview. Judge Gerald W. Heaney authored the essay titled "Jacob Trieber," which was prepared for and first published by the *UALR Law Review* in Volume 8, Issue 3 and is reproduced with its permission. The article was originally titled "Jacob Trieber: Lawyer, Politician, Judge." Further information about the *UALR Law Review* is available at www.ualr.edu/lawreview. Morton Gitelman, Distinguished Professor of Law Emeritus, University of Arkansas School of Law, authored the essay titled "Isaac Charles Parker," and first published a portion of that essay as "The Civil Side of Judge Parker" in 56 *Oklahoma Law Review* 129 (2003). It is reprinted with permission of the *Oklahoma Law Review*.

The United States District Court for the Eastern District of Arkansas and the United States District Court for the Western District of Arkansas partially underwrote the cost of publishing this book with donations from their library funds. Thanks are due to both of the district courts and to the Historical Society of the United States Courts in the Eighth Circuit for its work in facilitating the project. The book is a joint project of The Historical Society of the United States Courts in the Eighth Circuit, Eastern District of Arkansas Branch and Western District of Arkansas Branch.

The editor wishes to thank Kathryn C. Fitzhugh, reference and Special Collections librarian and professor of law librarianship, UALR William H. Bowen School of Law for her helpful responses and Crata Castleberry, branch librarian, US Courts Library Eighth Circuit, for valuable comments, materials, and detail checking. Without the able assistance of members of the court staffs, the University of Arkansas Press staff, and copyeditor Debbie Upton, a product with far less finish would have resulted.

PREFACE

Chief Justice Warren Earl Burger, United States Supreme Court, first called on the United States courts to preserve their histories and make them available to the public. Chief Justice Burger was also the first chairman of the Supreme Court Historical Society following its 1974 incorporation. The United States Court of Appeals for the Eighth Circuit, which includes the Arkansas federal courts, formed the Historical Society of the United States Courts in the Eighth Circuit in 1985 with Judge Henry Woods and Judge Richard Sheppard Arnold serving as members of the first board of directors. Among the circuit society's key accomplishments has been the sponsorship of a circuit history, *Establishing Justice in Middle America: A History of the United States Court of Appeals for the Eighth Circuit* by Jeffrey Brandon Morris, published in 2007. The circuit society has also encouraged each district court within the circuit to preserve and make available its own history. This publication of biographical essays of Arkansas district judges, which Judge Woods and Judge Arnold initiated for the two districts in the state, contributes to the overall circuit program.

Judge Woods identified and contacted authors for the essays, which focus on each judge commissioned to a United States district bench in Arkansas between statehood in 1836 and 1960. Both Judge Woods and Judge Arnold penned selections. Some of the authors have also published their essays as journal articles.

Coauthors Judge Richard Sheppard Arnold and his former law clerk Michael B. Heister introduce the subject with an in-depth discussion and historical overview of the Arkansas courts and jurisdictional changes that have occurred over time. The biographical essays begin with Benjamin Johnson, the first United States district judge in Arkansas. Professor Lynn Foster, of the University of Arkansas at Little Rock William H. Bowen School of Law, reviews Judge Johnson's background, his service on the state's territorial bench, and his work on the district bench from 1836 to his death in 1849. Logan Scott Stafford, Emeritus Professor of Law University of Arkansas at Little Rock William H. Bowen School of Law, continues with Daniel Ringo. Judge Ringo, a past chief justice of the state supreme court was confirmed to the United States district bench in 1850 after a recess appointment. When Congress formed the Eastern and Western Districts of Arkansas in 1851, he was reassigned to both of those districts. He continued to serve until the outbreak of the Civil War when he left the federal bench in 1861.

Toward the end of the Civil War the president named Henry Clay Caldwell to serve both of the Arkansas districts but in 1871 Congress reorganized the districts and created a new judgeship for the Western District and new seats for it. Judge Caldwell continued to preside in the then-smaller Eastern District. Judge Richard S. Arnold and his former law clerk George C. Freeman III provided the biography for Judge Caldwell from the time of his youth through service in the Union army to appointments to federal benches.

Beginning with Henry Clay Caldwell and William Story, who was appointed to the bench in the Western District after the reorganization of 1871, the essays treat the Eastern District judges first and then the Western District judges since the state has retained the two districts and separate judgeships since 1871. The career of Judge Caldwell may seem to somewhat contradict this organization. As noted, Judge Caldwell served for a few years as judge for both districts, then the Eastern only and for about a year as interim judge in the Western District after Judge Story resigned. During that time he continued full-time service in the Eastern District, his tenure lasting until 1890. Because his service was far lengthier in the Eastern District, Judge Caldwell's biography will be included with Eastern District judges. Much later Judge Jesse Smith Henley received a short recess appointment to the Eastern District before his regular appointment as a roving judge to both the Eastern and Western Districts. His biography will appear with the Eastern and Western District judges.

John Apps Williams followed Judge Caldwell on the Eastern District bench. After service in the Union army, Williams settled in Pine Bluff where he practiced law and for a time held a state circuit court judgeship. His United States district judgeship began in 1890 and continued until his death in 1900. Judge Henry Woods provided Judge Williams's entry. Jacob Trieber, immigrant from Prussia, Helena resident, lawyer, and United States attorney, replaced Judge Williams in 1901 after a recess appointment, and served until 1927. Judge Gerald W. Heaney, United States Court of Appeals for the Eighth Circuit, wrote Judge Trieber's biography. United States district judge for the Eastern District of Arkansas, Stephen M. Reasoner, authored the biography for John Ellis Martineau, tracing his career from teaching, to law school, to a state circuit judgeship, to the governorship, and finally to United States district judge in 1928 following Judge Trieber's death.

The year Judge Martineau died, 1937, the president named Thomas Clark Trimble III of Lonoke as the next Eastern District judge. Judge Trimble's career as attorney, his civic work, and his service as judge are recorded by his daughter, Elsijane Trimble Roy, United States district judge for the Eastern and Western Districts of Arkansas. Malvern native Gordon Elmo Young was confirmed to the Eastern District bench following Judge Trimble's death. His nephew, retired United States magistrate judge David Young, tracked Judge Young's career in law, public service, and civic work culminating with his appointment to the United States district bench in 1959. Judge Young served until 1969. His is the final essay for the Eastern District in this volume.

Entries for Western District judges take up with William Story, as previously noted. Story, a Wisconsin native, moved to Fayetteville in 1866 to practice law. He rose quickly to positions on the state bench with his career culminating in his appointment to the federal bench as Western District judge in 1871. By 1874 he faced impeachment hearings, resigned, and left the state for Colorado. Frances Mitchell Ross, faculty member emerita at the University of Arkansas at Little Rock, provided Judge Story's account.

Morton Gitelman, Distinguished Professor of Law Emeritus University of Arkansas School of Law, authored the next three essays for Western District judges: Isaac Charles Parker, John Henry Rogers, and Frank Abijah Youmans. Isaac Charles Parker, a St. Joseph, Missouri, resident, was commissioned to replace Story in 1875. He served until 1896. Judge Parker's work on the criminal side earned him designation as a firm administrator of justice although, as Professor Gitelman shows, Judge Parker carried a heavy civil workload as well. John Henry Rogers, a Mississippi resident, served in the Confederate army, studied law, settled in Fort Smith, won a seat in Congress, retired from Congress, and in 1896 was named to follow Judge Parker to the bench where he served until 1911. Missouri native Frank Abijah Youmans moved with his family to Arkansas in 1873 and established a law practice in Fort Smith in 1886. Following Judge Rogers's death in 1911, Frank Youmans was appointed to the bench and served until he died in 1932.

Heartsill Ragon, whose grandson, attorney Heartsill Ragon III, prepared materials for the essay on Judge Ragon, was an Arkansas native and practiced law in Clarksville. He served in the state legislature, as prosecuting attorney, and in Congress, from which he resigned to accept appointment to the federal bench in 1933 following the death of Judge Youmans. He remained on the bench until 1940. Susan Scafidi, Susie Margaret Ross, and Bradley J. Nicholson, former law clerks to Judge Morris S. Arnold, contributed materials for the essay on John Elvis Miller. In 1912 Miller, a Missouri native, moved to Searcy to begin his law practice. He later served as prosecuting attorney, congressman, United States senator, and in 1941 succeeded Judge Ragon to the bench where he served until 1967. Judge Miller then assumed senior status, a form of semiretirement that permits the judge to be selective about cases to take. The essay on Judge Miller concludes those for the Western District.

As the workload increased during the twentieth century, Congress authorized additional judges. For Arkansas, these were roving judges who were commissioned to both districts simultaneously. In 1990 the roving positions were assigned to the Eastern District. Essays for the first two judges who served as roving judges for both the Eastern and Western Districts were prepared by Susan Webber Wright, senior United States district judge for the Eastern District of Arkansas. Harry Jacob Lemley, a Virginia native, moved to Hope, Arkansas, following law school to practice law and to operate a plantation. In 1939 the president nominated him for a United States district judgeship as a roving judge. Judge Lemley served until he took senior status in 1958. Jesse Smith Henley, born in St. Joe, Arkansas, attended local schools and law school and served in several legal capacities at the local and federal levels before his 1959 appointment to the district bench as a roving judge to follow Judge Lemley. In 1975 the president elevated Judge Henley to the United States Court of Appeals for the Eighth Circuit. Judge Henley's biography concludes the essays in this volume.

While the essays reflect the service of each judge commissioned to a United States District Court position in Arkansas between 1836 and 1960, the tenures of some judges along with discussions and data in the essays will overlap that time frame. Readers will also note that, because of district reorganization, the terms of some early judges fit into the chronology of more than one district. Further, the end dates for sections III, IV, and V in the contents reflect only the end of the term of service of the last district judge considered in the section.

UNITED STATES DISTRICT COURTS AND JUDGES OF ARKANSAS, 1836–1960

CHAPTER 1

INTRODUCTION

The Structure of the United States District Courts in Arkansas

Richard S. Arnold and Michael B. Heister

The State of Arkansas came into being when the Twenty-Fourth Congress admitted the Territory of Arkansas into the Union in 1836.[1] It was admitted along with Michigan, its non-slave counterpart, as required under the Missouri Compromise of 1820.[2] At that time, Arkansas had one judicial district and one judge to run it.[3] That judge sat in Little Rock and acted as both a district court judge and a circuit court judge as the cases might require.[4] Thus, there were two federal courts in Arkansas: the district court of the United States for the District of Arkansas and the circuit court of the United States for the District of Arkansas. This ability to wear two hats would come and go as the state's federal courts assumed a more complicated structure.

A year later, in 1837, Arkansas was placed in the Ninth Circuit (there were only nine then) along with Alabama, the Eastern District of Louisiana, and Mississippi.[5] Thus, the District of Arkansas lost its circuit court jurisdiction.[6] In theory, the circuit court consisted of an associate justice of the Supreme Court and a district court judge.[7] The size of the

This article originally appeared in *Arkansas Law Review* 56 (2004): 715. Appreciation is extended to the *Arkansas Law Review* at the University of Arkansas for permission to republish the article. The authors thank Kris Albertus, Crata Castleberry, Todd Dill, and Justin Smith for their invaluable contributions to this work. Thanks are also due Dr. Jess Porter, University of Arkansas at Little Rock, for assistance with a map modification. New maps have been prepared that are suitable for this publication.

circuit and the limitations on travel made this difficult to accomplish. Not surprisingly, in 1842, John McKinley, the associate justice of the Supreme Court of the United States who was responsible for the Ninth Circuit, petitioned Congress for some relief from his obligation to travel ten thousand miles to hear cases in the course of a year.[8]

I. The Western District and the Indian Territory

Rather than paring back the workload in Arkansas, the Congress expanded it in 1844 by giving the District of Arkansas jurisdiction to hear cases arising out of the lawless Indian Territory, which was then primarily located in present-day Oklahoma, Kansas, Colorado, Nebraska, and Wyoming, all to the west of Arkansas.[9] As early as 1829, members of the Arkansas Bar suggested to Congress that it should divide Arkansas, still a territory at the time, into two districts and grant jurisdiction over the Indian Territory to a newly formed Western District.[10]

Little Rock, where the District of Arkansas held court, was not a convenient site to try cases that originated in the 100,000 square miles of the Indian Territory, and it quickly dawned on people that the structure of Arkansas's courts had to reflect this reality. Thus, in 1851, the small state got the unusual distinction of having a second district—the Western District of Arkansas.[11] Perhaps in recognition of the fact that this new court would sit in what was then a wilderness (or because no one wanted to travel that far), the circuit court jurisdiction that had been withdrawn from the District of Arkansas in 1837 was restored to the Western District.[12]

The newly minted Western District of Arkansas consisted of Benton, Washington, Crawford, Scott, Polk, Franklin, Johnson, Madison, and Carroll Counties and the Indian Territory.[13] Arkansas continued to have only one district judge.[14] He would sit twice a year in Van Buren (the county seat of Crawford County) with the Western District as both a district and circuit court and would otherwise sit in Little Rock as a district court for the rest of Arkansas, which was renamed the Eastern District of Arkansas.[15] The new districts meant new jobs in the form of a new United States attorney, a clerk, and a United States marshal for the Western District.[16] These jobs were considered patronage positions. At the time the district was created, these officers did not even have to live in the districts in which they served.[17]

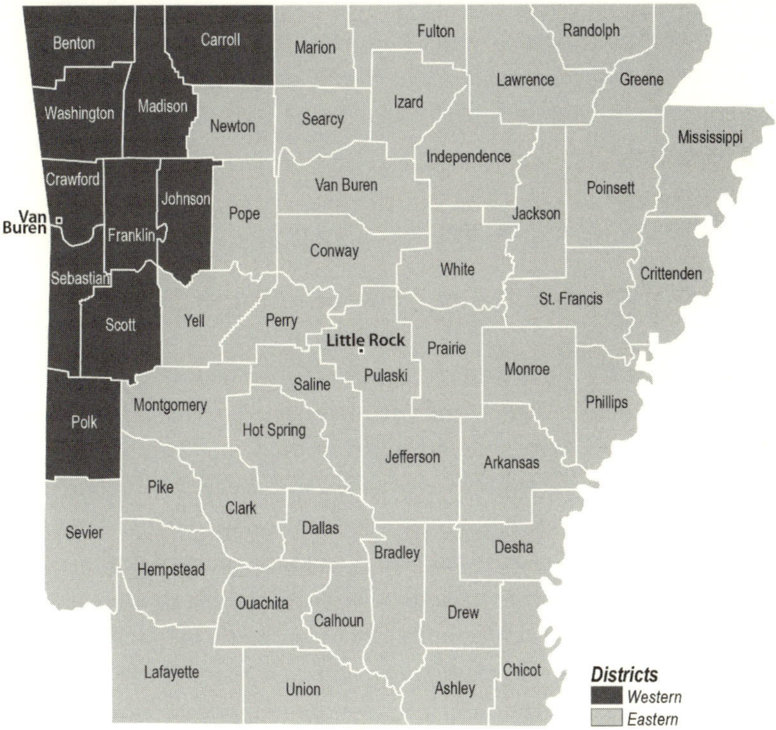

Arkansas in 1851. Cartography by Tom Paradise.

This new arrangement was not totally satisfactory. Holding court in Van Buren, and later in Fort Smith, the Western District still faced problems with transporting prisoners from the Indian Territory.[18] The commissioner of Indian Affairs, in 1872, proposed to solve the problem by having the Western District meet once a year in Okmulgee, in the Indian Territory.[19] This proposal was never adopted.

That may have been due, in small part, to resistance from Arkansans to the idea of holding court in the Indian Territory.[20] They based their opposition on, among other things, the lawlessness of the Indian Territory and the lack of qualified jurors.[21] One cannot help but wonder whether the fact that business would be lost if the court sat elsewhere also played a role in the citizens' opposition to this move.

Arkansas lost its claim to being the exclusive jurisdiction to enforce the law in the Indian Territory in 1883.[22] District courts in Kansas and

Texas were given jurisdiction over claims in their regions.[23] The jurisdiction of all three courts was withdrawn, and this unusual feature of the Western District came to a close by an act of 1895, when the federal government established federal courts in the Indian Territory, effective the following year.[24]

II. The Postwar Years

A decade after the creation of the Western District, the country was embroiled in the Civil War.[25] At that time, in 1862, Arkansas was moved from the Ninth Circuit to the Sixth Circuit, consisting of Louisiana, Texas, Kentucky, Tennessee, and Arkansas (all of which, with the exception of Kentucky, were then members of the Confederacy).[26] Toward the end of the war, attempts were made to have the circuit court meet an extra time in Arkansas but these efforts were defeated.[27] It is not clear why Arkansas was moved to the Sixth Circuit. It could be that, with the addition of Wisconsin to the Ninth Circuit that year, it was thought that the Ninth was growing too large and would be better off if the southernmost state, Arkansas, was moved into a circuit with states sharing similar economic and social conditions. It is more likely that, because armed conflict made it impractical for court to sit in these states, it made administrative sense to group them together in an inactive circuit.

In any event, it turned out to be a temporary arrangement. In 1866, one year after the war ended, Congress thought it best to have Arkansas in the Eighth Circuit, which also consisted of Minnesota, Iowa, Missouri, and Kansas.[28] The move may have been motivated by politics, ease of administration since at this time the rivers were still important highways, or, and most likely, a mix of both. In any case, the Eighth Circuit remains Arkansas's home to this day. Efforts were made in the 1970s to move Arkansas from the Eighth to the Fifth Circuit, on the theory that it would be more compatible with other southern states.[29] Interestingly, the Arkansas Bar stoutly resisted these efforts.[30] Apparently the lawyers preferred the devil they knew to the devil they knew not.

In 1871, Arkansas's federal courts underwent significant change. The Western District was expanded to include Phillips, Crittenden, Mississippi, Craighead, Greene, Randolph, Lawrence, Sharp, Poinsett, Cross, Saint Francis, Monroe, Woodruff, Jackson, Independence, Izard, Marion, Fulton,

Arkansas in 1871. Cartography by Tom Paradise.

and Boone Counties.[31] This expansion is puzzling because these counties made up much of the northeast part of the state—that is, much of the Western District now was in the eastern half of the state. The Western District continued to sit in the west, but at Fort Smith rather than Van Buren.[32] To make things easier on litigants, the Western District also began to sit twice a year at Helena.[33]

Court was held at Helena for reasons other than convenience to the litigants. By shortening the distance grand and petit jurors had to travel to court, the government could save itself a considerable amount of money.[34] This proffered rationale—that the government could save money by reducing the distance those who were being compensated by the government had to go to get to court—was constantly used to justify the creation of all the divisions that came about in Arkansas.[35] (The same argument is made today, and correctly so, to justify the location of a clerk's office of the United States Court of Appeals for the Eighth Circuit in St. Paul, as well as in St. Louis.) By combining this argument with the requirement that the host city provide accommodations to the court free of charge,[36] Arkansas's representatives could honestly argue that having additional sites for court was saving the government money. Of course, over time the free accommodations were no longer sufficient for the needs of the court, which meant new federal buildings had to be constructed. Given the propensity for government to expand, these secondary sites tended to turn into independent divisions that required more employees.

Interestingly, the bill that made all these changes failed on its first attempt.[37] It lost by two votes, twenty-two to twenty-four, in part because one of the senators from Arkansas was absent.[38] The opposition apparently suspected that the bill might be an attempt to lay the groundwork for a third district in Arkansas.[39] Such an attempt was in fact made in 1873, but without success.[40]

To accommodate this change in the court's structure, a judgeship for the Western District was created, and the judgeship that once covered both districts was made a judgeship for the Eastern District alone.[41] This addition was a long time in coming; Arkansas's congressional delegation had been trying to get the Western District its own judgeship since at least 1858.[42]

In 1877, the Eastern and Western Districts regained a geographically rational shape.[43] The Western District was now made up of counties in the west: Benton, Washington, Crawford, Sebastian, Scott, Polk, Sevier, Little River, Howard, Montgomery, Yell, Logan, Franklin, Johnson, Madison, Newton, Carroll, Boone, Marion, and the Indian Territory.[44]

The Eastern District took over duties in Helena and sat there twice a year in addition to its duties in Little Rock.[45] The Western District continued holding court at Fort Smith.[46] In a significant change, the Eastern District, when sitting at Helena, had circuit court jurisdiction restored to it.[47] Once again, both districts had circuit courts, which in theory could be held by a district judge, a circuit judge (a position created in 1869), or a district judge and a Supreme Court justice.[48] It should come as no surprise that neither Supreme Court justices nor circuit judges made it to Arkansas often.[49] Thus, Arkansas's district judges sitting in Fort Smith for the Western District or in Helena for the Eastern

Arkansas in 1877. Cartography by Tom Paradise.

District had an unusual amount of authority for the time. For example, they would sometimes hear appeals from their own rulings, which must have made for interesting discussions between the judge and the attorney appealing the decision.

III. The Partitioning of the Districts

To suit the growing state, the Texarkana Division of the Eastern District was formed in 1887.[50] Columbia, Howard, Hempstead, Lafayette, Little River, Miller, Nevada, Ouachita, Pike, and Sevier Counties were to have their disputes heard in Texarkana, rather than going to Little Rock (or Helena).[51] Note that Howard, Sevier, and Little River Counties had all been in the Western District prior to this adjustment.[52]

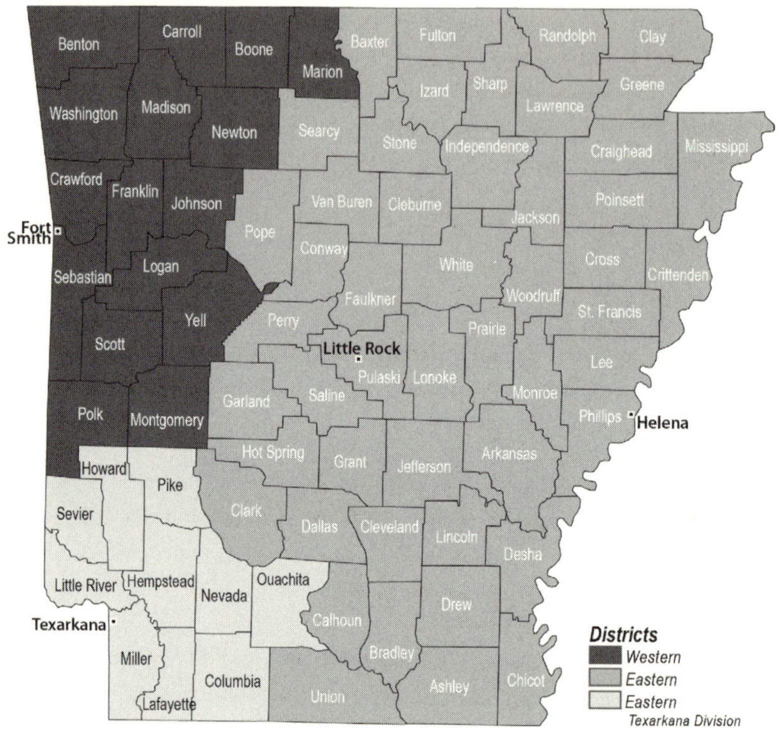

Arkansas in 1887. Cartography by Tom Paradise.

This expansion was opposed by the Senate Committee on the Judiciary.[53] Texarkana was 150 miles from Little Rock by direct rail.[54] And there were only sixty cases there in the prior year (1886).[55] The committee suggested that a cheaper solution to any inconvenience suffered by litigants in the southwest corner of the state would be to let the circuit court sit in Texarkana at its discretion.[56] Clearly, Arkansas's congressional delegation did not think this solution was adequate, and they carried the day (and brought more jobs) with the establishment of the Texarkana Division.[57]

Remember that since 1851, in the Western District, and 1877, in the Eastern District in Helena, the district judges had had the power, at least for trial purposes, to sit alone as a circuit court.[58] In 1889, multi-judge circuit courts began to sit in the Western District and at Helena in the Eastern District.[59] After this time, district judges could no longer sit as circuit courts to exercise appellate jurisdiction.[60] That function was exclusively assigned to multi-judge circuit courts, consisting, for example, of a district judge and a circuit judge.[61] Circuit judgeships had been created in 1869, though the Circuit Court of Appeals for the Eighth Circuit (as it was originally called), and the other regional courts of appeals, did not come into existence until 1891.[62]

The problem had been that a district judge's decision in criminal cases, while sitting as a circuit court, could not be appealed.[63] The creation of multi-judge appellate courts removed a serious anomaly in the structure of the federal system. In criminal cases, district judges, sitting alone as a circuit court, could review the judgments that they had previously entered at the district court.[64] To compound the problem, there was no further regular appellate review.[65] The Supreme Court had no appellate jurisdiction (except on habeas corpus) in criminal cases until 1889.[66] It is possible that this reform was made to subject the decisions of the famous "Hanging Judge" Parker in Fort Smith to review.[67]

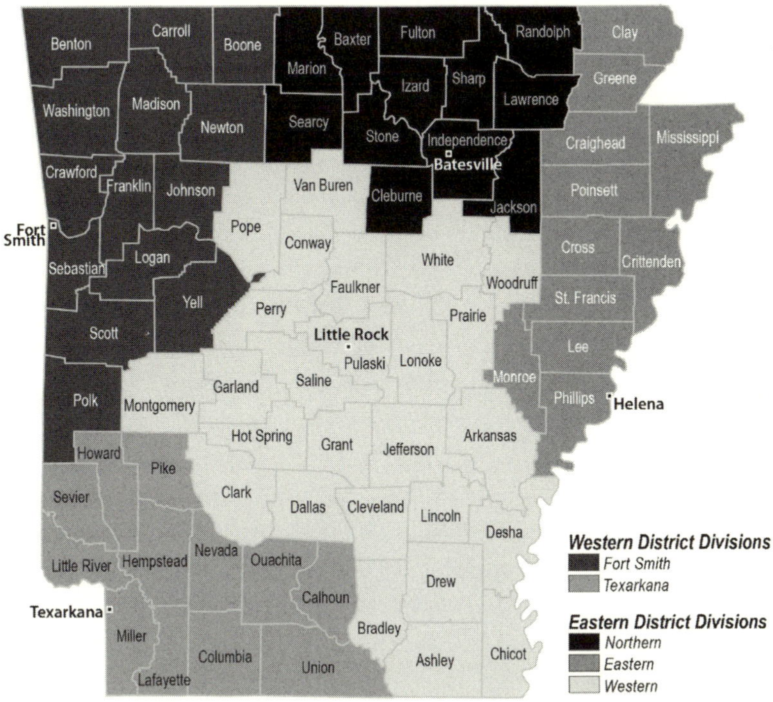

Arkansas in 1897. Cartography by Tom Paradise.

Eight years later, in 1897, Congress again amended the structure of Arkansas's federal courts.[68] These changes ostensibly reflected an attempt to allocate the courts' work into reasonable portions. The Western District had been created to handle work from the Indian Territory, and the withdrawal of jurisdiction over those cases took away the work that originally justified the district's creation.[69] Thus, there was a perceived need to shift some of the Eastern District's work to the Western District.[70] However, at this point Arkansas was still making do with only one district judge per district, so the workload in the Eastern District must not have been so great as to warrant a new judgeship.[71]

In this act, Marion and Montgomery Counties were shifted to the Eastern District and, in exchange, the Western District got the Texarkana Division of the Eastern District plus Union and Calhoun Counties.[72] Pike, Hempstead, Miller, Lafayette, Nevada, Columbia, Union, Ouachita, and Calhoun Counties all became permanent fixtures in the Western District.[73] Howard, Sevier, and Little River Counties returned to the Western District, after having spent ten years as part of the Texarkana Division of the Eastern District.[74] These twelve counties now made up the Texarkana Division of the Western District, while the remaining counties made up the Fort Smith Division.[75]

The changes did not stop here: the Eastern District was reorganized into three divisions.[76] These divisions were unhelpfully named the Western, Northern, and Eastern Divisions of the Eastern District. The Eastern Division was made up of Mississippi, Crittenden, Lee, Phillips, Clay, Craighead, Poinsett, Greene, Cross, Saint Francis, and Monroe Counties.[77] The court sat at Helena in Phillips County twice a year.[78] The Northern Division was made up of Independence, Cleburne, Stone, Izard, Baxter, Searcy, Marion, Sharp, Fulton, Randolph, Lawrence, and Jackson Counties.[79] The Eastern District sat at Batesville in Independence County twice a year as well.[80] The remaining counties constituted the Western Division, which sat in Little Rock in Pulaski County.[81] These names survived; today the Western Division sits in Little Rock, the Northern Division in Batesville, and the Eastern Division in Helena.[82]

To ease the administration of the courts in northwest Arkansas, the Harrison Division of the Western District was created in 1902.[83] Harrison, in Boone County, is 175 miles to the northeast of Fort Smith. Supposedly, this region generated most of the internal-revenue cases for

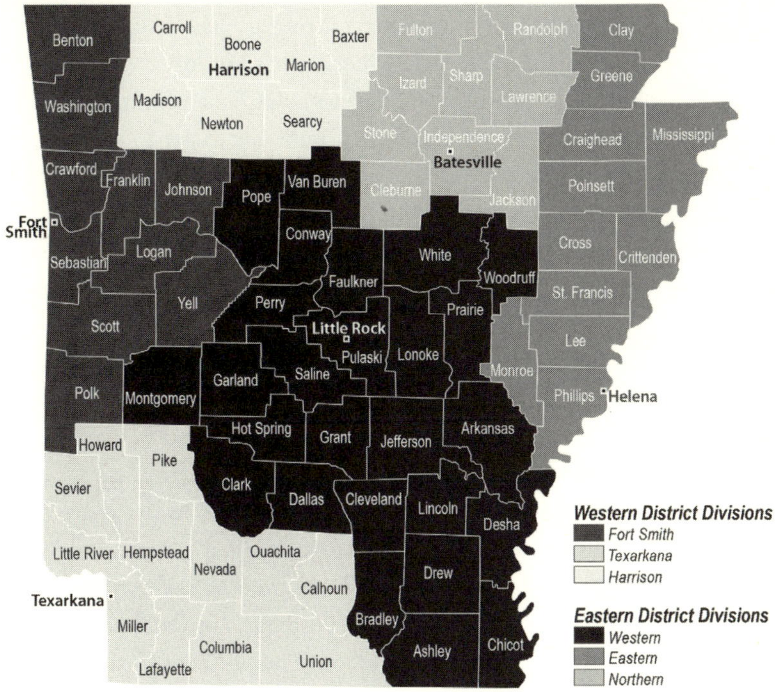

Arkansas in 1902. Cartography by Tom Paradise.

the Western District.[84] Also, the area was expected to grow rapidly due to the exploitation of zinc deposits that were being developed there.[85] This division consisted of Baxter, Marion, and Searcy Counties, which were simultaneously transferred from the Eastern District, and Boone, Carroll, Madison, and Newton Counties, which already resided in the Western District.[86]

One problem with the 1902 scheme was that the main federal jail was in Fort Smith.[87] Thus, prisoners were often kept there while awaiting trial in either Harrison or Texarkana. Transporting them back and forth was a nuisance. One solution was to allow criminal cases in either division to be transferred to the Fort Smith Division for the convenience of the parties.[88] The Federal Rules of Criminal Procedure permanently solved this problem by permitting a defendant to be tried where he is arrested and being held, so long as the United States attorney does not object.[89]

All this time, the population in northeast Arkansas was expanding rapidly.[90] The Eastern Division had been sitting at Helena since 1897.[91] In 1910, Congress required the Eastern Division to sit in Jonesboro as well.[92] Helena was in the far south of the division. An Arkansan in Jonesboro would have to use two or three different railroads to get to Helena and would have to stay there over night.[93] Roughly 200,000 Arkansans would have been spared this trip by the holding of court at Jonesboro. A plaintiff could file in Helena or Jonesboro, depending on which was more convenient. However, the clerk's office for the Eastern Division remained in Helena.[94]

Additional minor changes in the alignment of the districts in Arkansas were made in 1915.[95] Desha and Chicot Counties were detached from the Western Division of the Eastern District and moved to the Eastern Division.[96] This was probably a great relief to litigants from these counties. Now they would have to travel to only Helena, rather than Little Rock, to have their cases tried.[97] Perhaps to keep the workloads balanced, Yell County, formerly of the Fort Smith Division of the Western District, was given to the Western Division of the Eastern District.[98]

As in the past, this alignment ended up being short lived. In 1924, the Eastern District again underwent changes.[99] Portions of the Eastern Division and Northern Division were merged to create a fourth division in the Eastern District: the Jonesboro Division.[100] Note how patiently these expansions were accomplished. The groundwork was laid fourteen years earlier when Jonesboro became an alternate court site for the Eastern Division at virtually no cost to the government.[101] In fact, the arrangement was justified to Congress on the basis of how much it would save the government.[102] Now it was the site of a new division with a staff and, no doubt, future courthouse renovations.

This new division consisted of Fulton, Randolph, and Lawrence Counties, formerly of the Northern Division, and Clay, Greene, Craighead, Poinsett, Mississippi, and Crittenden Counties of the Eastern Division.[103] The Eastern Division also lost Chicot County, which was sent back to the Western Division.[104] In addition, the Eastern Division lost its distinction of having court in two places—it reverted to sitting in only Helena, as it had done prior to 1910.[105]

The Eastern District had been rearranged several times over the course of two decades.[106] However, the Western District remained virtually unchanged since 1902, when the Harrison Division was created.[107]

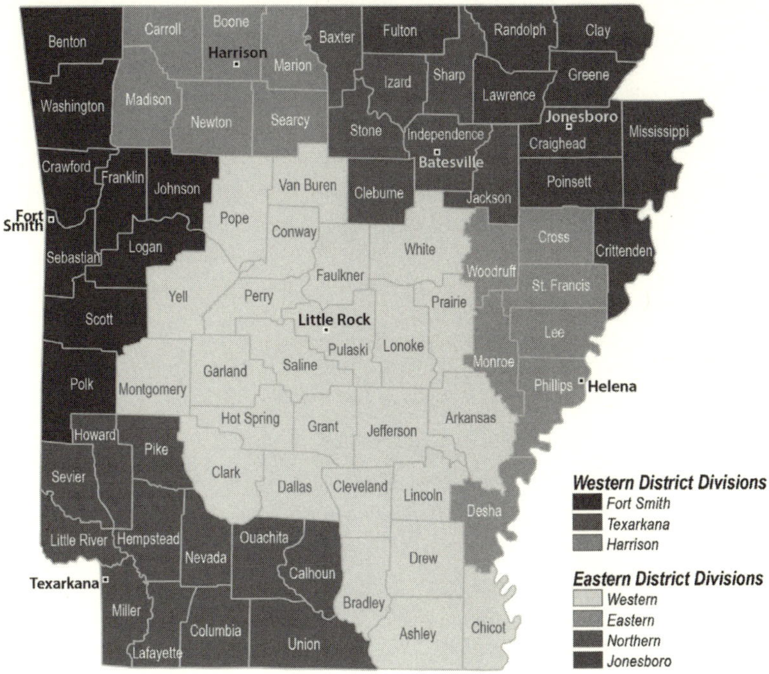

Arkansas in 1924. Cartography by Tom Paradise.

That repose was not to last because, among other things, oil was discovered in southern Arkansas in 1921.[108] In 1926, only two years after the creation of the Jonesboro Division, it was decided that the Western District needed a fourth division as well: the El Dorado Division.[109] Persons traveling from El Dorado to Texarkana encountered the usual difficulties experienced by travelers of that period. More importantly, the booming oil business was generating a lot of business for the courts.[110]

The El Dorado Division consisted of Columbia, Ouachita, Union, Ashley, Bradley, and Calhoun Counties.[111] The Texarkana Division gained no counties to compensate it for this loss.[112] The rest of the Western District remained as it was, as did the Eastern District.[113]

At this point it is worth recalling that within fifty years Arkansas's federal courts had gone from sitting in three cities to eight cities. The state's population had grown from roughly 480,000 people in 1870 to 1,850,000 people in 1930.[114] Despite the near tripling of the number of

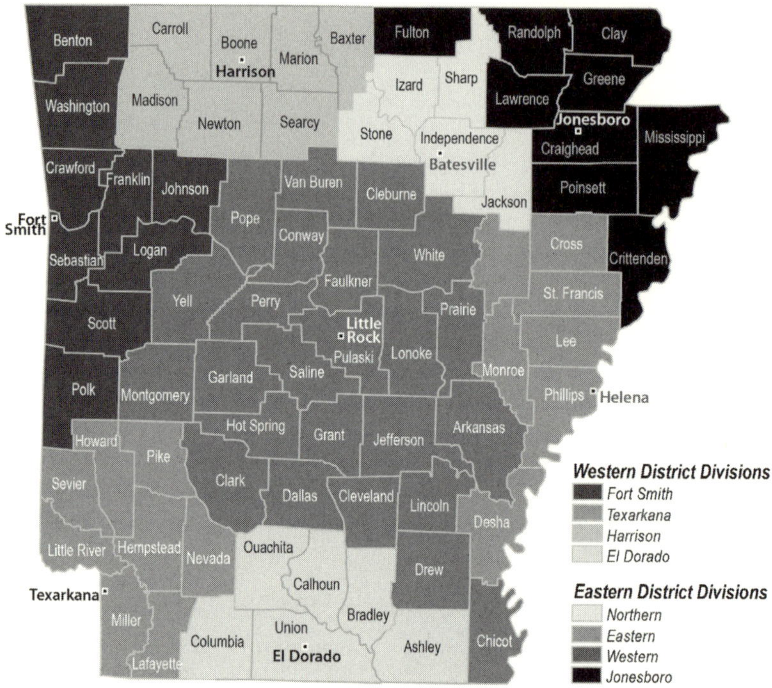

Arkansas in 1926. Cartography by Tom Paradise.

offices maintained by the clerks of court, and the near quadrupling of the population, there were still only two judges to handle the work.[115] This situation could not continue indefinitely.

Despite its need, when it came time in 1938 for Congress to create a batch of new judgeships, Arkansas was almost skipped over.[116] A theoretically nonpartisan group of congressmen recommended against the creation of a third judgeship in Arkansas.[117] Fortunately, the executive branch and the House of Representatives supported the move to create a judgeship, and that was enough to carry the day.[118] It was thought that neither district in Arkansas had a caseload to warrant a new judgeship.[119] Combined, however, they did. Therefore, a roving judgeship was created.[120] This judge heard cases in either the Eastern or the Western District as was necessary. The position was filled in 1939.

Meanwhile, the number of divisions in Arkansas continued to expand.[121] In 1940, two new divisions were added to the Western

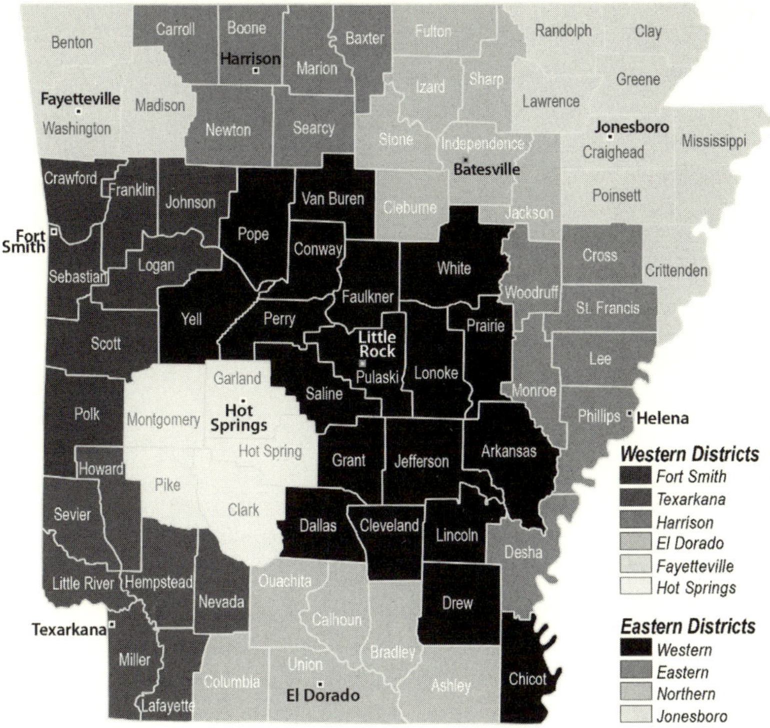

Arkansas in 1940. Cartography by Tom Paradise.

District.[122] Both divisions sat in the cities after which they were named. The Fayetteville Division was created out of Benton, Washington, and Madison Counties in the far northwest of the state.[123] The geography of the region, the Boston Mountains to the south and rivers to the east, made this a defensible expansion of the Western District.[124]

The new Hot Springs Division of the Western District combined Pike County and four counties that had been in the Western Division of the Eastern District: Clark, Garland, Hot Spring, and Montgomery.[125] The Hot Springs Division was created primarily to reduce the strain on the Western Division of the Eastern District, which heard the lion's share of cases among the divisions in Arkansas.[126] It also took some pressure off the Eastern District, which had more cases than the Western District.[127] It is easy to see why Pike County was included in the Hot Springs Division. There was a paved federal highway from Glenwood, which was probably Pike County's most populous city at the time, to Hot

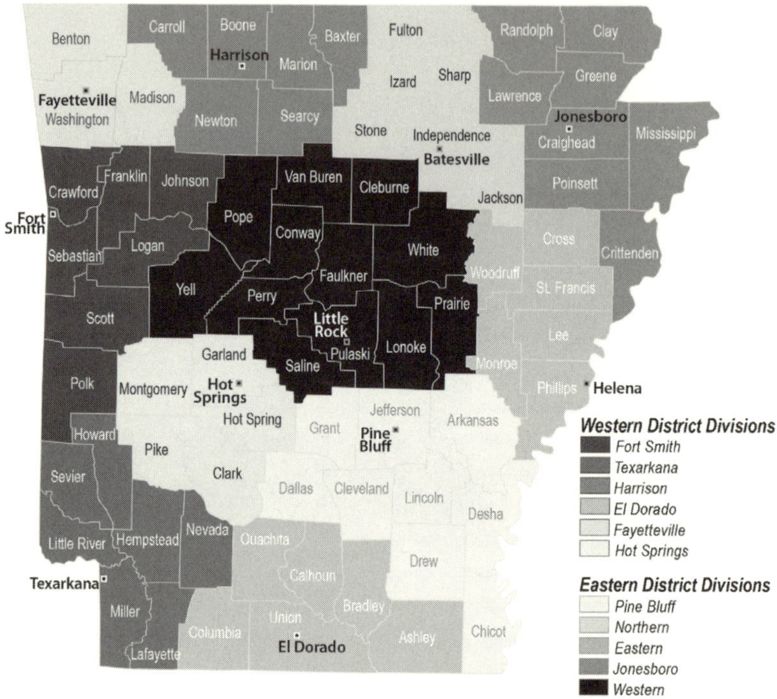

Arkansas in 1961. Cartography by Tom Paradise.

Springs, where court was held for the new division. By contrast, the trip to Texarkana involved forty miles of unpaved road—which significantly slowed travel and probably was quite uncomfortable.

This act also moved Fulton County from the Eastern Division of the Eastern District to the Northern Division of the Eastern District, which, geographically, made more sense.[128] Around this time, there were attempts to have the Eastern Division sit in Forrest City rather than Helena (where a district court had been sitting since 1871).[129] The idea was that Forrest City was more centrally located for the residents of the Eastern Division. However, the city was not well equipped to handle the court's business and this plan never came to fruition.

The Western Division was reduced again in 1961.[130] This was due to the creation of the fifth division in the Eastern District: the Pine Bluff Division.[131] This division consisted of Grant, Jefferson, Arkansas, Dallas, Cleveland, Lincoln, Desha, Drew, and Chicot Counties.[132] The court sat in Pine Bluff.[133] In this same act, Congress gave the Arkansas district courts another roving judgeship.[134] That change gave Arkansas two judges commissioned in both the Western and the Eastern Districts, so they could serve where the caseload demanded.[135] In 1978 the Eastern District gained another two judgeships, which raised its number of district-specific judges from one to three.[136]

A temporary judgeship was created for the Western District in 1984.[137] Temporary appointments are not filled when a vacancy occurs unless the appointed judge resigns or dies within a certain period of time, typically five years.[138] However, this position was quickly made permanent in 1990 with the passage of the Federal Judgeship Act of 1990.[139] At the same time, a new judgeship was created for the Western District.[140] Additionally, the two roving judgeships were made Eastern District positions.[141] Arkansas now has three judgeships for the Western District and five judgeships for the Eastern District.[142] The state has received no additional spots since.

IV. Conclusion

Over time, Arkansas's federal courts took on a remarkably complex structure given the relatively small size of the state. Missouri, our neighbor to the north, has eight divisions divided among its two districts.[143] Louisiana, with its three districts, sits in nine places.[144] Tennessee also has three districts with nine divisions.[145] In 2004, when this article was originally published, Tennessee and Missouri both had roughly 5.7 million people as compared to Louisiana's 4.5 million and Arkansas's 2.7 million people.[146] Arkansas has eleven cities in which a federal district court sits. Moreover, these are not merely pro forma locations, which are sometimes present in other states. In Arkansas, the district courts actually go to these cities and hold court. The bench, bar, and people of Arkansas seem satisfied with this arrangement. We suspect that any attempt to change it would result in the strongest opposition. The system can be criticized on efficiency grounds, but there is something to be said for showing the flag, and for bringing justice close to the people.

How did this happen? The primitive state of transportation in Arkansas, during much of Arkansas's history, is probably part of the answer. More divisions were needed than the state's population, considered alone, would ordinarily have justified. It is also true, and should be a source of pride, that Arkansas's senators and representatives have been exceptionally good at securing federal dollars and federal services for their voters.

United States District Judges of Arkansas 1836–2015, Years of Service

This list expands on the list in the published article to include all judges who had received commissions when the manuscript went to press. Except for judges who received recess appointments first, the dates given are for the periods of full-time service from the year of commission. Additional information about these judges can be obtained at the Federal Judicial Center website, available at www.fjc.gov.

Benjamin Johnson (1836–49) death

Daniel Ringo (1849) recess appointment;
(1850–61) resignation

Henry Clay Caldwell (1864–90)
appointment to another court

William Story (1871–74) resignation

Isaac Charles Parker (1875–96) death

John Apps Williams (1890–1900) death

John Henry Rogers (1896–1911) death

Jacob Trieber (1900) recess appointment; (1901–27) death

Frank A. Youmans (1911–32) death

John Ellis Martineau (1928–37) death

Heartsill Ragon (1933–40) death

Thomas Clark Trimble III (1937–57) Senior Status

Harry Jacob Lemley (1939–58) Senior Status

John Elvis Miller (1941–67) Senior Status

Jesse Smith Henley (1958) recess appointment;
(1959–75) appointment to another court

Gordon Elmo Young (1959–69) death

Oren Harris (1965–76) Senior Status

Paul X Williams (1967–81) Senior Status

Garnett Thomas Eisele (1970–91) Senior Status; 2011 retired

Terry Lee Shell (1975–78) death

Elsijane Trimble Roy (1977–89) Senior Status

Richard Sheppard Arnold (1978–80) appointment to another court

William Ray Overton (1979–87) death

Henry Woods (1980–95) Senior Status

George Howard Jr. (1980–2007) death

Hugh Franklin Waters (1981–97) Senior Status

Morris Sheppard Arnold (1985–92) appointment to another court

Stephen M. Reasoner (1988–2002) Senior Status

Susan Webber Wright (1990–2013) Senior Status

Jimm Larry Hendren (1992–2013) Senior Status; 2015 Inactive Senior Status

William Roy Wilson Jr. (1993–2008) Senior Status (Judge Wilson has continued service as Billy Roy Wilson since his legal name change in 2011.)

Harry F. Barnes (1993–2008) Senior Status

James Maxwell Moody (1995–2008) Senior Status; 2014 retired

Robert Toombs Dawson (1998–2009) Senior Status; 2015 Inactive Senior Status

James Leon Holmes (2004–present)

Brian Stacy Miller (2008–present)

Denzil Price Marshall Jr. (2010–present)

Paul Kinloch Holmes III (2011–present)

Susan Owens Hickey (2011–present)

Kristine Gerhard Baker (2012–present)

Timothy Lloyd Brooks (2014–present)

James Maxwell Moody Jr. (2014–present)

PART I

DISTRICT OF ARKANSAS (1836–51)

Arkansas Gazette masthead. This masthead, used by the newspaper during the early 1850s, shows the new State Capitol to the far right, facing the Arkansas River. Now known as the Old State House Museum, soon after the capitol was completed it became home to the United States District Court for the District of Arkansas with Judge Benjamin Johnson presiding. *Image used with permission from the Arkansas Democrat-Gazette.*

CHAPTER 2

BENJAMIN JOHNSON

1836–49

Lynn Foster

BENJAMIN JOHNSON served as a federal judge in Arkansas for twenty-eight years, spanning the time from Arkansas's creation as a territory to its early statehood. He was one of its first territorial judges, serving a longer term than any of the others, and its first federal district court judge. He was also one of the most prominent early Arkansans, and a member of what has been called "the Family," a political dynasty that wielded a great deal of power in antebellum Arkansas. This article discusses both the highlights of Johnson's judicial career and influence, and what he must have regarded as the most serious attack on his reputation and livelihood, the attempt to impeach him, set against the backdrop of early Arkansas history.

A version of the article about Benjamin Johnson was prepared for and first published by the *University of Arkansas at Little Rock Law Review* in Volume 22, Issue 1 and is reproduced with its permission. It was originally titled "Their Pride and Ornament: Judge Benjamin Johnson and the Federal Courts in Early Arkansas." Further information about the *UALR Law Review* is available at www.ualr.edu/lawreview. Author's note: Thanks to Judge Morris S. Arnold and Professor Emeritus L. Scott Stafford for their encouragement and their review of this article at the time it was originally prepared, and to Professor Emeritus S. Charles Bolton for his encouragement. Any errors are mine.

Benjamin Johnson. *Courtesy United States District Court for the Eastern District of Arkansas.*

I. Background

Benjamin Johnson was born in Scott County, Kentucky, on January 22, 1784, to Robert Johnson and Jemima Suggett, pioneers who had moved from Virginia. The Johnson family was one of the first to settle what is today Kentucky. Robert served as a captain in the militia, and in 1782 Jemima and the older children survived the terrifying Indian siege of Bryan Station, Kentucky. Robert and Jemima had a total of eleven children, of whom Benjamin's brothers James and John Telemachus served in the United States House of Representatives, and Richard Mentor held the offices of US representative and senator from Kentucky, later serving as US vice president under Martin Van Buren from 1837 to 1841. Johnson's siblings would become plantation owners of large tracts of land in Kentucky, Arkansas, and Mississippi.[1]

Benjamin Johnson married Matilda Williams in 1811, was admitted to the Kentucky bar, and served as a judge both in the Lexington Circuit and in the district court in the Lexington area, although he resigned prior to 1820 because of "considerations of a private nature." Johnson was involved in the ill-fated Yellowstone expedition of 1819, a Johnson family affair in which James Johnson supplied three of four steamboats, and Richard Mentor Johnson helped obtain the federal government financing. The purpose of the expedition was to transport troops and military supplies to Fort Lisa, north of present-day Omaha. None of the Johnson steamboats reached their destinations and the expedition failed.[2]

Meanwhile, the land that would later become Arkansas had passed from France to Spain in 1763, back again to France in 1800, and thence to the United States as part of the Louisiana Purchase in 1803, when Benjamin Johnson was nineteen years old. In 1812, when Louisiana achieved statehood, the District of Arkansas became the southern portion of the Territory of Missouri and its present-day southern boundary was set. In 1819, as Missouri prepared to enter the Union as a state, Congress changed the name of the remaining territory to Arkansas and set its present-day northern boundary, with the capital at the Post of Arkansas, "until the territorial legislature should direct otherwise." Thus by 1819 the northern, eastern, and southern boundaries of the territory of Arkansas corresponded to those of the present day, but the western territorial boundary was not fixed at its final location until 1828, when northwestern Arkansas was ceded by the Cherokees. This fluctuating western boundary did not facilitate the establishment of counties, judicial circuits, and the like. Ultimately, having the "Indian Country" as its western neighbor would win Arkansas the distinction of being a state whose western federal judicial district had jurisdiction over 74,000 square miles of Native American territory.[3]

The governmental structure of territorial Arkansas was, like that of most territories at the time, modeled after the type of government set out by the Northwest Ordinance. Territorial Arkansas was to progress through two stages of government. In the first stage, President Monroe appointed five officials: Governor William Miller, a brigadier general, hero of the war of 1812, and a resident of New Hampshire; the governor's second-in-command, Secretary Robert Crittenden, a native Kentuckian and brother of John Jordan Crittenden (who would serve as US senator, governor of Kentucky, and US attorney general during his career); and the three judges of the territorial superior court. These five were in addition to function as a legislature, until a general assembly could be formed. Andrew Scott of Missouri Territory, Charles Jouett of Michigan Territory, and Robert P. Letcher of Kentucky were appointed to be the first three territorial judges. The territorial government was to commence on July 4, 1819.

This stage lasted less than a year, and in fact ended, with elections for the General Assembly, before Governor Miller even arrived. The new government, meeting at the Arkansas Post, adopted all laws of the Missouri Territory not repugnant to the organic act establishing the Arkansas Territory and established two judicial circuits and circuit courts, replacing the courts of common pleas that had operated in the Missouri Territory. In August, Crittenden appointed circuit judges, attorneys, and other government officials.[4]

The superior court was slow to commence operations. Its first judicial session took place in January 1820 at the Arkansas Post, but Judge Scott presided alone, since Jouett and Letcher had left the territory the prior August. The territorial legislature complained in April that a prisoner had been languishing in a county jail for two years without trial because, with only one judge, the superior court was unable to hear capital cases; and complained again in October that the courts were "virtually shut." Meanwhile, Letcher resigned and Monroe appointed

Joseph Selden of Virginia to succeed him. Jouett resigned as well—the *Arkansas Gazette* claimed that "a swarm of Musquetoes" had driven him from the territory—and Monroe appointed John Thompson of Ohio as Jouett's successor. Thompson, however, never even set foot in the Arkansas Territory, changing his mind and turning back at Jackson, Mississippi.[5]

Monroe then appointed Benjamin Johnson to replace Thompson, in response to requests from the candidate's brother, US senator Richard M. Johnson, as well as other senators and prominent Kentuckians. Johnson arrived in time to sit with Andrew Scott at the second superior court session, held in June of 1821 at "the Little Rock."[6]

II. The Territorial Superior Court

Superior court judges were appointed for four years but were subject to removal by the president. In 1819, the superior court for the Territory of Arkansas had jurisdiction of all criminal and penal cases; exclusive jurisdiction of all capital cases; original civil jurisdiction concurrently with the inferior courts; and exclusive appellate jurisdiction in all civil cases involving amounts in controversy of $100 or more. One judge constituted a court of original jurisdiction, and two judges an appellate court. The combination of original and appellate jurisdiction was common at the beginning of the nineteenth century; courts had less business and jurisdictional lines were not so rigidly drawn as they are today. Over time, the original jurisdiction of the court was transferred gradually to circuit and justice of the peace courts, and the superior court's docket contained an ever-greater percentage of appellate cases.[7]

In the territories, one court system handled both "state" matters—such as most crimes, trespasses, and insolvency—and federal matters—such as trading with Indians without a license. In effect, the territorial superior court served as a combined state and federal appellate court. It was also the court of last resort, there being no appeal upward until 1828.[8]

Some of the opinions of the Superior Court for the Territory of Arkansas have been preserved for us through the efforts of Samuel H. Hempstead, who published them in 1856, in a volume also containing the opinions of the District Court for the District of Arkansas, and Ninth Circuit opinions arising in Arkansas. In the preface, he acknowledged his debt to Johnson: "The late Benjamin Johnson, of Arkansas, who sat in those courts for nearly thirty years, and was their pride and ornament, generally wrote out his opinions, and before his death placed such as had been preserved in my hands."[9]

Benjamin Johnson was clearly a dominant presence on the territorial superior court. He sat as a member of the bench in 112 of the 150 cases in which decisions were published. Of those 112, sixteen were actually written by him, seventeen were written by others, and seventy-eight were "per curiam" opinions—unsigned opinions agreed to by the entire court—in which he was present on the panel.

The early nineteenth century was a colorful, lawless time in Arkansas's history, and some of that atmosphere is preserved in the decisions, although much of it must be read between the lines, with a background knowledge of the contemporary persons and events. From what little we can glean through the frame of appellate law and archaic vocabulary of common law pleading, we are afforded a glimpse here and there of the way of life in the territory and early state of Arkansas. At the time of Benjamin Johnson's death in 1849, no railroad had yet come to Arkansas; no telegraph lines had been strung. No bridges spanned the Arkansas River. Arkansas was a slave state, with no industry to speak of. Pastimes were few and politics figured prominently, often becoming deadly.

Politics in antebellum Arkansas was in large part a contest between two factions. One faction (the "Family") consisted of the brothers Henry, James, and Elias Conway, their cousin Ambrose Sevier, the brothers Wharton and Elias Rector (also their cousins), Benjamin Johnson (Sevier's father-in-law), his sons Robert Ward and Richard H. Johnson, and prominent attorney and land speculator Chester Ashley. The other faction consisted of Robert Crittenden and his followers, including attorneys Robert C. Oden, William Cummins, Absalom Fowler, and Albert Pike. Prior to statehood there were no national parties in Arkansas; afterward, Family members by and large became leaders in the Democratic Party. Crittenden died young, two years before statehood, but those in his faction generally became Whigs. Most of these early political leaders were men of wealth and power, connected by complex business and personal relationships.[10]

The chief avenue to wealth and power on the cash-poor, agricultural frontier was land. The process of gaining ownership of land, however, was not necessarily easy. From 1686 to 1804, civil law had prevailed in Arkansas by virtue of its possession by Spain and France. As in other territory possessed by Spain and France, their cession of land to the United States left behind it a wake of myriad land grants and claims, both legitimate and fraudulent. This was certainly the case in Arkansas. Some early settlers claimed Spanish land rights; others, French. Indian holdings also complicated the picture. In 1804, Arkansas's indigenous tribes were the Osages, Caddos, and Quapaws, but additional treaty rights to Arkansas land were given by the US government to such tribes as the Choctaws, Chickasaws, and Cherokees, before they were ultimately displaced and moved to the Indian Territory. Finally, congressional actions affecting land rights were no less confusing. In 1812, Congress set aside two million acres of Arkansas as a "Military Tract" to veterans of the War of 1812. In 1815, in response to the severe New Madrid earthquakes of 1811 and 1812, Congress offered certificates in compensation to earthquake victims, which could be exchanged for public land. Finally, settlers who lived on and improved specially designated lands could purchase them later under "preemption" laws.[11]

Competing with these groups of claimants were the land speculators. William Russell, a founder of Little Rock, was one of the surveyors who plied his trade in what later became Illinois, Missouri, and Arkansas. Of him, an early settler wrote to a Land Office official, "It is easy for A crafty Surveyor to become A crafty Land Speculator." Thousands of acres passed through Russell's hands. Many attorneys were land agents and speculated in land. One such was Chester Ashley, one of the first attorneys to settle in Arkansas and a later US senator.[12]

These conflicting land rights caused a multitude of lawsuits in the territory and early state, some of which eventually reached the United States Supreme Court. Attorneys profited from these lawsuits as well. As will be shown, Benjamin Johnson played a major role in land disputes, deciding many of the most important claims.[13]

Three opinions from the first of Johnson's sessions on the bench appear in Hempstead's *Reports*. Of these, *Russell v. Wheeler*, written by Johnson, was an important link in the chain of events that would confirm the location and owners of the village of Little Rock. *Russell v. Wheeler* pitted claimants possessing New Madrid certificates against preemption claimants, and involved some of the most prominent early

Arkansans on both sides of the dispute. On one side, William O'Hara, a land speculator, obtained New Madrid certificates, used them to claim land that is now Little Rock, and assigned part interest in them to James Bryan and Stephen Austin (the same Stephen Austin who later became the "Father of Texas"). Unfortunately, the land they claimed partly overlapped land that was originally preempted in 1814 by an early frontiersman, and eventually was sold to William Russell and others. Speculative interest in Little Rock land grew as the Arkansas Territory was formed and discussions began about moving the capital away from the Arkansas Post to a more central location. During 1820, prominent persons purchased Little Rock land from either the O'Hara side or the Russell side.[14]

In October, the territorial legislature did indeed designate Little Rock the temporary seat of government beginning June 1, 1821. The New Madrid claimants had by now built on the disputed land. Amos Wheeler, acting on behalf of O'Hara and other New Madrid claimants, offered several sections to the territory for government use. Russell tried to enter the land, was rebuffed, and sued Wheeler for forcible entry and detainer. He won a favorable verdict from a jury in justice of the peace court. The Circuit Court of Pulaski County overturned the verdict, and Russell appealed to the superior court. Johnson, writing the superior court opinion in June of 1821, reversed the verdict (holding in favor of Russell) and remanded the cause to the lower court. In disputing the defendant's contention that the verdict below was "fatally defective" because it did not contain the correct wording, the court stated that if the meaning of the jury was clear, "yet the courts are bound to work and mould the verdict into form according to the real justice of the case." The court thus held in favor of the preemption holders. Immediately thereafter ensued, as one observer put it:

> a scene of true western life and character that no other country could present. First we saw a large wood and stone building in flames, and then about one hundred men, painted, masked, and disguised in almost every conceivable manner, engaged in removing the town. These men, with ropes and chains, would march off a frame house on wheels and logs, place it about three or four hundred yards from its former site, and then return and move off another in the same manner. They all seemed tolerably drunk, and among them I recognized almost every European language spoken.

> They were a jolly set indeed. Thus they worked amid songs and shouts, until by night-fall they had completely changed the site of their town. Such buildings as they could not move they burned down, without a dissentant [*sic*] voice.
>
> The occasion of this strange proceeding was as follows: The Territorial Court was then in session at Diamond Hill [today Crystal Hill], about thirty miles distant on the river above, and the news had reached Little Rock on the morning of our arrival that a suit pending in this Court and involving the title to the town, wherein one Russell of St. Louis was the claimant, had gone against the citizens of Little Rock and in favor of Russell. The whole community instantly turned out en masse and in one day and night Mr. Russell's land was disencumbered of the town of Little Rock. They coolly and quietly, though not without much unnecessary noise, took the town up and set it down on a neighboring claim of the Quapaw tribe, and fire removed what was irremovable in a more convenient way. The free and enlightened citizens of Little Rock made a change of landlords more rapidly than Bonaparte took Moscow.

A few months later, the two sides compromised, dividing the land between them.[15]

After the seat of territorial government moved to Little Rock, the court met in various buildings in town. During the court's first few sessions in Little Rock, it used the Baptist Meeting-House. In October 1825, the court met in Colonel Conway's frame house. For a while, the court met in a house owned by Chester Ashley. William Pope, who sometimes acted as court clerk, related an incident from Judge Johnson's court occurring at that time:

> On one occasion while the court was in session Judge Benjamin Johnson, one of the judges of the court, and who was at times very irritable, discovered Colonel Ashley in the act of whittling, with his pen knife, one of the wooden benches in the court room. Doubtless wishing for some object upon which to vent his ill-humor that day, he called out with some show of impatience, "Colonel Ashley, I wish you would quit cutting this court house to pieces!" To which Colonel Ashley replied good naturedly, "If it pleases your honor, I do not know who has a better right to do so; it is my property."[16]

Terms of the superior court were set by the General Assembly. At first there were two, in June and October. In 1820 the General Assembly attempted a restructuring of the lower courts, changing the circuit courts to courts of common pleas, each court to be administered by three judges. Circuit judges had to be "learned in the law"; however, the common pleas judges merely had to be "three respectable house-holders" appointed by the governor. The jurisdiction of the new common pleas courts was diminished, however; chancery jurisdiction was transferred to the superior court. "Chancery" or "equity" courts date back to medieval England. They were originally presided over by the chancellor and afforded different rules allowing for different types of pleading, and different remedies, to claimants whose cases did not fall within the rigid requirements of common-law pleading.

Finally, the judges of the entire superior court would now be required to ride one arduous circuit thus: February in Arkansas County, April in both Hempstead and Independence Counties, August in Arkansas County, and October in Hempstead and Independence Counties. For a territory with no bridges, no ferries, and almost no roads, this was a tall order. However, the legislature had immediate second thoughts because its very next act, passed on the same day, postponed the changes affecting the superior court for one year.[17]

A common means of political criticism in those days was to write a pseudonymous letter to a newspaper, and in August of the following year, a letter from "Sulpicius" was published in the *Arkansas Gazette*. Sulpicius complained that the law would make the members of the territorial superior court "judicial camels to carry her laws, through the deserts of her territory." He argued that neither Kentucky, Missouri, nor New York required their original judges to travel, at least not until bridges and ferries existed. He also criticized the requirement that the entire bench ride the same circuit together. Sulpicius's criticisms were heeded by the following legislature, which abolished the courts of common pleas, reestablished circuit courts, and changed the terms of the superior court to three per year in Little Rock. The nineteenth-century Sulpicius's identity is not known, but he was almost certainly one of the superior court judges.[18]

Early Arkansas was notable for the number of duels among its most prominent men, but nonetheless many Arkansans were shocked when in May of 1824 Benjamin Johnson's superior court brethren, Andrew Scott and Joseph Selden, engaged in a fatal duel. This account was told to William Pope by the son of Judge Scott:

> Soon after Judge Selden went upon the bench he and Judge Andrew Scott, also of the Superior Court, and two ladies, became engaged in a social game of whist at the residence of one of the ladies at the Post of Arkansas. In the course of the game one of the ladies, Judge Scott's partner in the game, remarked: "Judge Selden, we have the tricks and the honors on you." To which Judge Selden very abruptly replied: "That is not so, madam."
>
> The young lady, very much mortified at the ungracious reply, put up her handkerchief to hide her mortification, saying, "I did not expect to be insulted."
>
> Judge Scott remarked to Judge Selden: "Sir, you have insulted a lady, and my partner, and you must apologize for your rudeness."
>
> Judge Selden declined to apologize, saying: "I make no apology. She has stated what is not true."
>
> Judge Scott seized a candlestick, which was standing on the card table, and hurled it at Judge Selden. Parties who were present interfered, and prevented further difficulty at that time.[19]

However, the incident was not over. Scott challenged Selden to a duel. Several weeks elapsed, during which the court met, and according to the *Gazette*, the "variance" of the two judges toward each other interfered with court business. (Judge Johnson was not present at this term, being temporarily in Kentucky with his family.) Dueling was illegal in the territory at this time, and therefore, the judges met on the eastern side of the Mississippi. Scott shot and instantly killed Selden.[20]

Apparently Scott was not prosecuted, even though he and the seconds clearly broke the law, which the editor of the *Gazette* was outraged enough to reprint in the next issue. Henry W. Conway, who was by now Arkansas's territorial delegate to Congress, merely wrote the United States secretary of state that "I have learned today that Joseph Selden Esqr, one of the Judges of the Superior Court of the Territory of Arkansas, died on the 26th of last month," with no further explanation. (Ironically, Conway himself would be killed in a duel by territorial secretary Crittenden in 1827.) President Monroe appointed William Trimble to fill Selden's place. Scott remained on the bench until his commission expired in 1827. At that time the Senate did not vote to renew it because of the duel, and Thomas P. Eskridge was appointed in his place.[21]

The October 1824 term of the superior court featured a case of great interest. During the prior year, a hunting party of Arkansans had camped in Choctaw territory, in what is today Oklahoma. A band of Osage warriors, seeking revenge on some Caddos, encountered them and killed them on the spot. At the request of the US government, the five Osage leaders of the band surrendered themselves to stand trial in Little Rock. Two were found guilty. They moved the superior court for a new trial, and then an arrest of judgment on various grounds: that the court had no jurisdiction over Osages, that the verdict was contrary to the evidence, and that the indictment was deficient in several regards. The court denied both motions and Judge Johnson delivered the death sentence "in a very impressive manner." Hempstead relates that the Osages were executed, but in fact, the execution was postponed several times by the acting governor, and at the last the "unfortunate sons of the forest" were pardoned by President Adams and set free, to return to their country. The *Gazette* reported that when they reached their home "they gave a very ludicrous and amusing account of their trial, imprisonment and treatment, while they sojourned among us."[22]

During that same year of 1824, Judge Johnson was mentioned in the July 5 *Gazette* in connection with his appearance at the Fourth of July dinner in Little Rock. At the time, it was customary for gentlemen to gather on the Fourth of July for dinner, speeches, and toasts commemorating the War of Independence. At each dinner, a president and a vice president were chosen to preside. The president would read toasts submitted by the guests. The Fourth of July dinner attendees constitute a list of "who was who" in that long-ago Arkansas. Governor George Izard, Secretary Crittenden, US attorney Samuel Roane, territorial delegate Sevier, attorney Oden, and a number of others were present. Judge Johnson offered his toast to a fellow Kentuckian "Henry Clay—the ornament of the West."[23]

In 1827, the legislature finally prevailed in its efforts to require the superior court judges to ride circuits. Arkansas was divided into three judicial circuits, and Benjamin Johnson was assigned the second, consisting of Pulaski, Conway, Crawford, and Lovely Counties. During the same session, the legislature added a fourth circuit, and also allowed the governor to notify the president if a judge refused to ride the circuit.[24]

In 1828, Congress did indeed approve a fourth judge, James Woodson Bates, added the right of appeal from the Arkansas Superior Court to the US Supreme Court, and confirmed the requirement that the judges ride circuits. The aversion of the judges to riding the circuit can be partially explained by the following anecdote, told by an attorney to G. W. Featherstonhaugh, an English visitor to territorial Arkansas, who included his description in his travel memoirs:

> He stated that some years ago, after a hard day's ride, there was only one cabin at which they could stop, and that it was very important to reach it during the winter season. This cabin belonged to an old hunter, a pioneer in that part of the country, to whom the lawyers—in virtue of the extensive jurisdiction he had over the wilderness—had given the title of Governor Shannon; it consisted of one solitary room with a mud floor, and not a single article of furniture except an old log that he had hollowed out, and that he slept in at night, and sat upon at other times. Upon this mud floor travellers used to stretch themselves out in their blanket-coats, and there they pigged with the Governor, an old negress, and a team of dogs he kept to hunt the bars [bears], which were numerous around him. As there had never been a door—or any contrivance approaching it—to the cabin, the dogs used to come in and go out whenever they pleased: if they were all asleep, the barking of a wolf would rouse them, and out they would rush over the recumbent travellers, without being at all particular where they trod upon them. On their return, wet and covered with dirt, they made no ceremony of who they laid near, nor whom they laid upon, for dogs like to lie warm, and this was the reason why the Governor had made his bed in a log. It happened upon one occasion that a judge, who had never made this circuit before, favoured the governor with his company, and becoming at length outrageously annoyed at the stench and filth of the dogs, one of which had acted very irreverently to his Honor, called out to the Governor, that if he did not take the dog away he would kill him on the spot. Upon which his Excellency replied, that he "would be ____ ____ if the bl___d judges and lawyers of Arkansas hadn't slept with his dogs for seven years, and that if any man touched one of 'em, he would send him to sleep with the painters [panthers] in less than no time." The Governor was well known to be a resolute fellow, and as there was no other settler nearer than 30 miles, and "a pretty considerable sprinkling of bars and painters [panthers] about," the judge thought it best to put up with this slight upon his authority.[25]

Riding the circuit was not only uncomfortable and dirty. It could also be dangerous, as when Archibald Yell, later to be governor, almost drowned crossing the frozen Arkansas River while riding the circuit with some other attorneys from Fayetteville. Perhaps as a trade-off for the imposition of circuit riding, the legislature limited the superior court to appellate jurisdiction in civil and equity cases. Its original jurisdiction in civil cases was abolished.[26]

In October of 1828, a case involving territorial secretary Robert Crittenden came before the superior court. He had been indicted for sending a challenge to fight the duel in which he killed Family member and territorial delegate to Congress Henry Conway. However, the court held that the indictment was deficient in two ways: for stating "on or about" a time, rather than a specific time; and because the indictment did not conclude "against the peace and dignity of the United States." So saying, the court quashed the indictment and discharged the defendant.[27]

III. The Land Claims

Some of the most important cases decided by the superior court at this time involved Arkansas land claimed under supposed grants from the Spanish governor made at the close of the eighteenth century. Most land claims were decided by panels of commissioners appointed by Congress, but from time to time Congress would give courts jurisdiction over such claims. In 1824, Congress bestowed such jurisdiction on the territorial superior court.[28]

In November of 1827, "Bernardo Samperyac," acting through his attorney Robert Oden, filed a bill in the superior court asking the court to confirm his grant of 400 arpens from the Spanish governor Miro. US attorney Samuel C. Roane filed an answer stating that Samperyac did not exist, or if he did, that no one now living was authorized to file the bill, and asked that it be dismissed. On December 19, Roane moved to continue the cause until the next term. The court denied his motion. One John Hebrard appeared as a witness and gave testimony in open court, before judges Benjamin Johnson and William Trimble, that he had been *alcalde* [magistrate] in the Province of Louisiana, between 1789 and 1791, and commandant in Catahoola, from 1797 to 1803. He testified in full support of the claimants, stating that the grants from the governor were authentic, that he knew Samperyac, that fire had destroyed many records in New Orleans in the 1790s, and other information to that effect. Over one hundred similar cases, each for 400 arpens of land, appeared before the court in the five succeeding days, amounting to more than 60,000 acres of land. The court confirmed these grants in December 1827.[29]

The United States had one year in which to appeal; it did not. Roane had from the beginning expressed his doubts about the claims to US attorney general William Wirt, but did not send to Wirt the statements of the law in each case that the attorney general insisted he must have to file an appeal. A series of letters passed back and forth between William Wirt and Roane. Wirt believed the statute required Roane to send him copies of the Spanish laws and regulations, as well as a discussion of the rules, issues, facts, and reasoning of the court in each case. Instead, Roane sent him everything he had, which was the record.[30]

Meanwhile, in February 1828, Samperyac's claim transferred by deed to John J. Bowie, who in turn sold it to Joseph Stewart. The group of claims confirmed by the court in December became popularly known as the "Bowie claims." In October, the court authorized the claimants to withdraw their original papers. Many withdrew their papers, but originals from fifty-eight cases remained on file. In April of 1829, US commissioner of lands George Graham wrote the US attorney voicing his suspicions as to the genuineness of the Bowie claims, and asking that the original papers filed with the court be examined by an expert. In September, Acting Governor Fulton (who had replaced Crittenden as territorial secretary) wrote President Jackson that "most persons here, believe that those claims are fraudulent." It was imperative that the government act quickly, because the fraudfeasors would of course try to sell off their interests as soon as possible, and in most instances the person who purchases property for valuable consideration with no notice of any wrongdoing will usually win in court. First, the government postponed the issuing of patents (deeds from the United States). A handful had already been issued and the commissioner of lands wrote the US attorney asking him to annul them.[31]

Isaac T. Preston, the register of the Land Office at New Orleans, traveled to Little Rock in October of 1829. In a letter to the commissioner of lands, he pointed out the many problems with those Bowie claims left with the court that he was able to examine, including the obvious forged appearance of the orders of survey, the misspelling of Spanish words, the fact that many were written with the same ink and used the same witnesses, and more. "The toute ensemble to any eye accustomed to see ancient Spanish documents would produce the instant and undoubted conviction of their falsity." Preston was quite critical of both the 1824 act and of the court's decrees:

> [T]he law establishing the tribunal was a bad one as the result has awfully proved. And so are all laws establishing tribunals before which individuals may cite their government. The Government of a country should act for itself & is presumed to be just & even generous to individuals. Otherwise it should be dissolved. The Judges of such tribunals too often adopt the baneful principle, that as judges they may see through the lights of law & evidence that to be true, which as individuals they know to be false & to conceive that these lamps were given to lead them into darkness instead of illumination.[32]

The *Gazette* mentioned (but did not reprint) Preston's accusations, blandly protesting that if there was fraud, then it was fraud of the Bowies, and not the judges and lawyers of Arkansas. The *Gazette* also made its own count of the acres involved and claimed the total was 30,000, not 60,000.[33]

In November 1829 the president directed US attorney Roane to apply for a rehearing. In April of 1830, Roane filed a bill of review against Bernardo Samperyac and the other claimants, alleging fraud on the part of the claimants, and perjury on the part of Hebrard. Counsel (Ashley and Crittenden) filed a brief against allowing a bill of review. Richard Searcy, a prominent Batesville attorney assisting Roane, researched the law and to his dismay,

> the more I searched into the subject the more complicated and difficult I have found it to be. Since my return home I have examined the libraries at this place and in 20 vols of Vesey & 6 Vols of Johnsons Chy. Reports and some other Books I have not been able to find a single instance in which a Bill of Review has been sustained. It is now certain that in all of the libraries of the Territory no reported case can be found and it may well be doubted whether the court will proceed without authorities to decree the necessary relief.[34]

The composition of the court changed that month, as William Trimble was not reappointed to the superior court. In May, Edward Cross was appointed in his place. Also in May, Congress passed an act enabling the court to reverse or annul any former decrees it had made regarding land claims under the 1824 act and directing the Land Office to hold off from issuing patents until the original documents could be reexamined, and requiring the court to forward all documents, testimony, and reasons for their decision to the US Supreme Court if parties appealed. In August, Governor Pope expressed his displeasure with the US attorney and the court, stating in a letter published in the *Gazette* that "half in earnest" if it were true that the court had decided the original cases erroneously, if he were president, he would remove all of the judges without an investigation.[35]

The cause came up for hearing on January 26, 1831, and was heard by the court until February 1. Attorneys Chester Ashley, Robert Crittenden (the assignee of two of the annulled patents), and, surprisingly, ex-judge William Trimble (who had participated in the original decision) represented the Bowie claimants. US attorney Roane was assisted in court by Secretary Fulton. On February 4, the defendants moved that the question of forgery of the order of surveys be submitted to a jury, but the court overruled this motion. On February 7, the court reversed its previous decrees. Benjamin Johnson wrote the opinion, which basically defended the court's rights to reverse its decrees after so long a time, and to act with the full powers of a court of chancery, even though it had been given this particular, limited jurisdiction by an act of Congress. *Samperyac* was appealed to the United States Supreme Court, which affirmed the superior court in 1833. By this final act of the drama, Joseph Stewart was the lone appellant. He claimed to be a "bona fide purchaser" from John J. Bowie, ignorant of any fraud at the time of purchase, although on appeal he admitted that Samperyac was a fictitious person, Hebrard had committed perjury, and the evidence of title was forged. Thus on appeal, one of the issues was whether Stewart had any rights since he was not an innocent purchaser. The court held that he did not, expressed the opinion that he should not even have been admitted as a party, and affirmed the superior court.[36]

Josiah Shinn, an Arkansas historian, stated that "[w]hen the court reversed itself in 1831 the people were disgusted. Could there have been an election for Superior Court judges, there is little doubt but that, Eskridge, Trimble, Bates and Johnson would have gone down under an overwhelming vote of popular disfavor."[37]

Why did the court (Johnson and Trimble) make the mistake in the first place? Roane (in his own defense) stated that the forgeries were "so well executed, as to deceive the most skillfull [*sic*] persons we were able to procure for their inspection." However, Preston was quite scornful of the forgery, and believed that it was so obvious that the judges should have discerned it. Why did the court not grant a continuance? A possible reason is that at least one of the judges stood to gain from the Bowie claims. Suspicion certainly rests on Trimble, a friend of Crittenden, since Trimble, having been removed from the bench, argued the case on rehearing. However, Johnson had ties to Chester Ashley, who also argued the case on rehearing, and Johnson's son-in-law, Ambrose Sevier, was a party to some of the land transactions. Indeed, Sevier tried to prevent Congress from enacting a law to prevent frauds. Roane claimed that Richard Searcy was the "only Lawyer of reputation that is not engaged on the part of the claimants." Preston also agreed that a number of people were involved in the fraud. "Men of the deepest thought as well as the Bowies [!] are embarked in this business. I fear they are meditating some thing to increase and sanction their claims just as the law expires." Two letters from "Jaw-Bone" (probably Chester Ashley) published in the *Gazette* in 1830 accused Crittenden of profiting from the fraud at the expense of innocent purchasers. Territorial secretary Fulton accused Bowie, Ashley, and Crittenden of profiting from fraudulent sales. In fact, the territorial legislature memorialized Congress seeking patents for all innocent purchasers "who were told by the ablest of the Bench and of the Bar" that they had good title. (William Trimble, Speaker of the House, was one of the signatories.)[38]

As one might expect, similar Spanish and French claims cases arose in Louisiana and Missouri. Many of these claims involved the same parties who filed claims in Arkansas (Auguste Choteau, William Russell, Don Carlos de Villemont). Judge Peck, of the United States District Court of Missouri, repeatedly ruled against them. In 1826, Judge Peck decided a major case, *Soulard's Heirs v. United States*, in favor of the United States. (In fact, Roane had unsuccessfully argued from the precedent of this case before the Arkansas superior court in the 1827 Bowie claims cases.)

Powerful interests opposed the judge, and he was impeached in 1829, ostensibly for jailing a lawyer and abusing the contempt power, but the Senate failed to convict by one vote. Subsequently, Congress took the jurisdiction of land claims out of Peck's court and returned it to a board of land commissioners.[39]

Johnson's actions in the Bowie claims were characterized by Josiah Shinn, an early biographer, as "Judge Johnson's One Mistake." Shinn credited Johnson with "a graceful overruling of his own decision a few years later and greater caution throughout the rest of his long life in the investigation and application of precedents and legal authorities."[40]

IV. The Business of the Court

Other than land claims, the superior court decided cases in a variety of areas. Decisions involving property, both real and personal—including slaves—occupied much of the court docket. In 1831 the court issued an opinion written by Judge Cross ruling that ejectment, a cause of action to force someone in possession of real property to leave it, was indeed a valid cause of action in Arkansas, and tracing its history. The *Gazette* reprinted the text of that opinion in full. Ejectment was a useful legal tool in a territory whose land titles were as precarious as those of Arkansas.[41]

The poor monetary system during the nineteenth century also generated a number of cases before the court. Specie (gold and silver coin) was scarce, particularly on the frontier, but was nonetheless sometimes required for certain transactions, most notoriously land purchases, after President Andrew Jackson issued the unpopular Specie Circular in 1836. Paper currency was not yet printed by the United States government. As a substitute, bank notes and promissory notes circulated, but only to a limited extent. Bank notes were often not worth their face value, depending on the financial condition of the issuing bank. Bank failures were common. The following submission "To a Bank Note" in the *Arkansas Gazette* rendered poetical the riskiness of bank notes:

> I will not take thee, ragged elf,
> In payment for my labor—
> Your villainy's revealed itself,
> You've robbed myself and neighbor.

Your very face is all a lie,
Your promise but a bubble;
You raise the price on all I buy,
And plunge mankind in trouble.

And when we ask you for the cash
How well the matter's mended!
We find your Bank is "broke to smash,"
Or, hang you! You're suspended!

For banks the farmer grows his corn—
The laborer gives his earning;
The student, like a sheep, is shorn
In spite of all his learning.

The tension between the old common law, which limited the negotiability of such instruments, and the monetary needs of citizens in the new republic, particularly those living on the frontier, evinced itself in numerous court cases. Indeed, most of the cases decided by Judge Johnson involved debt in one form or another.[42]

Court procedure in the early nineteenth century differed mightily from that of today. The great reforms of the latter half of the nineteenth century existed nowhere. Instead, attorneys pleaded the old "forms of action"—account, assumpsit, covenant, debt, trespass, trover, and others. Pleadings were much more technical, and courts could, and did, seize upon defects in pleadings to impose rulings not justified by facts or substantive law, such as the quashed indictments of Robert Crittenden and the Osages discussed above. The relationship between judge and jury differed as well. Whereas today juries decide matters of fact (but not issues of law), in the nineteenth century they possessed more power. In criminal matters, as the *Gazette* reported, "the jury were constitutional judges in law as well as fact."[43]

Judges and lawyers of the nineteenth century, like the orators of the same period, were wont to extemporize at length. Certain speeches of judges could be read in the newspaper from time to time, particularly instructions to the jury and even more often, death sentences. Public hangings were common and were community affairs. In 1835, Benjamin Johnson, acting as judge of the Circuit Court of Pulaski County, presided over the murder trial of Morgan Williams, who was found guilty.

The *Arkansas Gazette* published the following sentence pronounced in open court by the judge:

> MORGAN WILLIAMS—You have committed a deed at which human nature starts; and the mind recoils with horror! You have shed the blood of your brother man, and the offended laws have pronounced your doom: "Whoever sheddeth man's blood, without cause, by man shall his blood be shed.
>
> The unpleasant task has this day devolved upon me, as the minister of the law, to pronounce this stern and solemn sentence. To die, when one is prepared to die, with a conscience void of offence towards God or man, is not, perhaps to be regarded as a very great calamity; for it is appointed unto all men once to die. But to be hurried from this world, to appear before the Great Judge above, stained with crime, and crimsoned o'er with guilt, is the greatest evil that can fall to the lot of man. Sitting in this judgment seat, we have no power to extend pardon to the guilty offender. But with God, there is mercy and ample stores of forgiveness. By deep repentance and sincere contrition, perhaps the mercy of heaven may reach your case, and your crimes, though red as scarlet, may be made white as wool.
>
> That you may employ your few remainint days in prostrating yourself before the throne of the Most High, and by sincere prayer and deep repentance, supplicate Him to pardon your crimes and blot out your offences—and that He may turn a listening ear to your supplications, and grant you full pardon, is my most fervent prayer.
>
> It now remains for me to pronounce the judgment of the law:
>
> MORGAN WILLIAMS—You have been arraigned before this Court on a charge of Murder—you have been heard in your defence, by Counsel appointed for you—you have had a fair and impartial trial by a Jury of your country, and that Jury have returned a verdict of GUILTY against you. It is my duty to pronounce the judgment of the law.
>
> You will be remanded to the prison of this county, in the custody of the proper officer, and there be imprisoned *until the 16th day of May next*; on which day, between the hours of 11 o'clock in the forenoon and 2 o'clock in the afternoon of that day, you will be taken by the Sheriff of this County, to the place of public execution, and there hang till you are *dead, dead, dead*.[44]

V. The Attempt at Impeachment

Article III federal judges hold their offices during "good behavior," or, usually, for life, and can only be removed by impeachment. However, territorial judges did not enjoy the life term, being appointed for four years at a time. In the autumn of 1832, probably inspired by the unsuccessful attempt to impeach Judge Peck discussed above, the Crittenden faction attempted to remove Benjamin Johnson from office by impeachment. The attempt began when a letter listing eight charges from William Cummins was published in the *Arkansas Advocate*, a Whig newspaper, on October 24. In January of 1833, Egbert Harris sent the charges, with the request for impeachment, to the Speaker of the House of Representatives.[45]

The first charge involved the murder trial of Charles Herod, one of three defendants who were tried separately before Judge Johnson. In the Herod trial, Johnson discharged the jury members after they had deliberated only one night and failed to reach a verdict. Cummins was assisting the prosecutor during this trial, and charged that such an early dismissal was "contrary to the settled practice of all criminal courts."[46]

The second charge involved Colonel John Dunlop, an employee and a member of the household of Judge Johnson, who had a grievance against John F. Sapp. Sapp had injured Dunlop in the past, and Dunlop had frequently stated his intent to kill Sapp in the hearing of the judge. In 1830, Dunlop shot at Sapp, on the porch of the courthouse, on two consecutive days. The second day, Sapp ran into the courtroom and claimed the protection of the court. "Judge Johnson, from the bench, answered his claim for protection, with a censorious, passionate, and violent reprimand." Dunlop was indicted for shooting John Sapp with the intent to kill. According to the charge, Judge Johnson pressured prosecutor Absalom Fowler to enter a nolle prosequi, which he did. Fowler later indicted Dunlop again and Johnson refused to try the case. As Sevier pointed out in his rebuttal, however, Dunlop was later killed by Sapp, while assisting a sheriff to arrest Sapp.[47]

The third charge against Johnson was that during 1829, he had, while intoxicated in the street, drawn his knife and threatened to cut the throat of Smith C. Moss, a campaigner for Richard Searcy, who was running against Johnson's son-in-law, Ambrose Sevier, for territorial delegate. Moss himself refuted this charge.[48]

The fourth charge against Johnson was that he frequently held court in an intoxicated state, specifically during the October 1827 term and also while the Bowie claims were being decided. "I have once seen him so intoxicated on the bench as to be, in my judgment, wholly unfit to perform the duties of judge." Other accusations of drunkenness alleged different locales: on a steamboat, at someone's house, in a tavern, in the street. Cummins charged Johnson with being so frequently drunk during the adjudication of the Bowie claims that Judge Trimble in effect sat alone.[49]

The fifth charge was that on the bench Johnson was "peevish, irritable, impatient, petulant and rude," disrespectful to all except a few of his friends. Regarding this charge, Orson Howell stated that in 1832, he was representing a plaintiff in a suit before the superior court in which Judge Johnson was one of the defendants. Cross was the judge. Howell made a motion, and while he was arguing it "Judge Johnson (then at the bar) said several times so as to be easily heard by Judge Cross, 'No Lawyer would make such a motion'—'He ought to be fined for making such a motion'" and other remarks of similar import."[50]

The sixth charge attacked Johnson's legal opinions as being vacillating, inconsistent and contradictory.[51]

The seventh charge was that eight years earlier, Judge Johnson had made a secret deal with James Lemon and two others, conductors of a "faro bank." Johnson then bet against Judge Selden, who thought he was betting only against Johnson, but unbeknown to him Johnson was dividing his profits from Selden with the bank. Ultimately, Selden lost about $300.[52]

The eighth and final charge was that Johnson improperly handled the case of Israel Embree. In 1827, Embree was indicted in superior court for murder. In 1828, jurisdiction over criminal cases was moved from the superior court to the circuit courts. Cummins accused Johnson of first voting with the other superior court judges to transfer Embree to the circuit court, and later improperly dismissing his indictment in the circuit court.[53]

In the opinion of at least one historian, Cummins's purpose in bringing the charges was to injure Sevier, then territorial delegate who was coming up for election, harm the Family, and aid Crittenden, who announced his candidacy for delegate in 1833.[54]

Johnson himself made no official response. By the time the charges had reached Washington, DC, President Andrew Jackson had reappointed him. Sevier defended Johnson on the floor of Congress, mainly by attacking the character of his accusers. Many prominent Arkansans wrote Congress in the judge's support, and the House Committee on the Judiciary issued a report stating that in its opinion territorial judges could not be impeached, and that even if they could, the evidence did not support the impeachment of Judge Johnson.[55]

However, his son, Robert Ward Johnson, nineteen or twenty at the time, was incensed by the attack on his father. He announced his intention to challenge Cummins and Fowler to duel, but his plans were interrupted by a trip to Kentucky. When he returned to Little Rock in August of 1833, he issued the challenges. Both men declined. Robert Ward then attacked Cummins on the street, after which both men were placed under peace bonds. Robert Ward next posted placards around town labeling Fowler a coward. After Fowler ripped down the placards, he exchanged pistol shots with Johnson at the corner of Main and Markham.[56]

VI. Federal Courts in Arkansas after Statehood

The year 1836, in which Arkansas became a state, marked the political zenith of the Family. Richard Mentor Johnson of Kentucky was elected to the vice presidency. James S. Conway was elected the first governor of the new state of Arkansas. Elias Rector was reappointed federal marshal. His brother Wharton served as US agent for the Creek tribe. Ambrose Sevier was chosen by the legislature to be one of the first two US senators. Statehood, of course, meant that Arkansas would become a federal judicial district with its own district court judge. Johnson, having served the longest term of all the territorial superior court judges, would have been an obvious candidate for the judgeship in any case. Andrew Jackson appointed him federal district judge in 1836.

The structure of the federal courts was different in 1836 than it is today. At that time the US Court of Appeals did not exist. The federal court system consisted of two inferior courts: the district courts, one in each state, and the circuit courts (later abolished in 1911). The circuit courts were presided over by district court judges and Supreme Court justices. They possessed both original and appellate jurisdiction, which waxed and waned as Congress repeatedly amended the Judiciary Act, but in general had original jurisdiction over diversity cases and criminal cases. Thus, as Arkansas's district judge, Benjamin Johnson rode the circuit, sometimes with Justice Peter V. Daniel of the United States Supreme Court, a fellow Democrat. An anecdote concerning the circuit court has come down to us:

> After Judge Johnson's appointment to the district bench, Mr. Justice Daniels [*sic*] came out upon the circuit. One day while a case was being argued, Judge Johnson expressed his opinion; whereupon the justice said with lofty dignity: "Judge Johnson, the court will first consult, and the associate justice of the supreme court will deliver the opinion of the court." The next day, when a case had been argued, the justice began to express his views, when Judge Johnson, seizing his arm, said in a stage whisper: "Justice Daniels, the court will first consult and then the justice of the supreme court can deliver the opinion of the court." The bar were immensely diverted, but Justice Daniels did not seem to enjoy the joke.[57]

In 1837, Congress amended the Judiciary Act, creating nine circuits, and placing Arkansas in the Ninth Circuit, along with Alabama, Mississippi, and the Eastern District of Louisiana. As district court judge, Johnson wrote twelve published opinions. As circuit court judge he wrote thirty-two published opinions alone and joined in six opinions with Justice Daniel.[58]

Shortly after statehood, the new capitol building (today the Old State House Museum) was finished. The US district court of Arkansas met in the north end of the west wing, on the first floor.[59] In the very first published decision of the new district court, *United States v. Ta-wan-ga-ca*, Judge Johnson significantly limited the court's jurisdiction. Ta-wan-ga-ca had been indicted for the murder of a white man in Indian Territory in the superior court of the Arkansas Territory; however, that court ceased to exist when Arkansas became a state. The question was whether Ta-wan-ga-ca could now be tried by the district court. First, Johnson ruled that the new district court was not a continuance of the territorial court. The new court had limited jurisdiction, fixed by Congress, which had neglected to continue over to the new court the business of the United States pending in the late superior court. Second, he ruled that the new district court had jurisdiction only over the state of Arkansas and not points west, that is, Indian Territory (74,000 square miles corresponding to present-day Oklahoma). Thus, he released Ta-wan-ga-ca. This decision of course would have serious effects on justice in Indian Territory west of Arkansas. Congress promptly remedied this problem by extending the jurisdiction of the federal district court of Arkansas to include "crimes, offences, or misdemeanors, which may be committed against the United States, in any town, settlement, or territory, belonging to any Indian tribe."[60]

Jurisdiction over Indian country came up again in April of 1840, when, sitting as a circuit judge, Benjamin Johnson decided two Indian Territory cases involving Moses Terrel as a defendant. In the first case, he was prosecuted for robbing a white man, John Ballard, in the Indian country. In the second, he and a second defendant were prosecuted for assault with intent to kill the same unlucky Mr. Ballard. (Interestingly, in the first case Terrel is described as an Indian, and in the second, as a white, although the court would have the same jurisdiction either way.) In both cases the jury found the defendants guilty, but Judge Johnson arrested judgment and discharged the defendants, ruling that there were no federal laws making robbery or assault crimes in Indian country.[61]

In April of 1844, the question of crimes in Indian country again was raised before the circuit court. During this term, Justice Peter V. Daniel of the United States Supreme Court presided over the court along with Benjamin Johnson. This time Moses Alberty was the defendant, alleged to have murdered a white man. The court analyzed several federal statutes relating to its jurisdiction and concluded, once again, that it had no jurisdiction over Indian Territory. Again, Congress tried to remedy this state of affairs by annexing Indian Territory to the State of Arkansas, and giving the district court the same jurisdiction over Indian Territory that the territorial superior court had possessed.[62]

An interesting twist in the Indian Territory cases came up in April of 1845. The grand jury of the circuit court indicted William S. Rogers, a white man, for the murder of another white man in the Indian Territory. Rogers argued that he had moved to the Indian country, joined the Cherokee tribe, married a Cherokee woman, and become a Cherokee in November of 1836, and that the victim had similarly joined the Cherokee tribe. Thus, since an "Indian" was alleged to have murdered an "Indian," the federal court had no jurisdiction. Judges Johnson and Daniel could not agree on a decision, and thus they certified the case to the United States Supreme Court for its decision. Weeks after the circuit court adjourned, Rogers escaped from prison and drowned several days later. Ironically, no one notified the Supreme Court, and Justice Taney delivered the now moot opinion, which was, in essence, once a white man, always a white man. The court held that Congress did not intend to exempt whites adopted as Indians from federal jurisdiction, since they "will generally be found the most mischievous and dangerous inhabitants of the Indian country."[63]

In 1847, Johnson discharged a prisoner indicted for being an accessory to the murder of an Indian "in the Indian country." Again, the basis for his decision was that the court had no jurisdiction because accessory to murder was not a federal crime. Also in 1847, another facet of the "who is an Indian" question was entertained by Justices Daniel and Johnson, when a Cherokee was indicted for the murder of "Billy, a white boy" in the Cherokee country. The defendant did not dispute his act, but rested his defense on the argument that Billy was an Indian because his mother was at least part Indian (her tribe was not known). Although the murder was "wanton" and "shocking," the weight of the evidence established that Billy's mother was indeed an Indian. The court cited precedent going back to Roman emperor Justinian's *Institutes* that a child inherited his mother's status. Billy was therefore an Indian, and the prisoner, not guilty as a matter of law, was discharged.[64]

Daniel and Johnson decided an interesting constitutional case in 1843, which does not appear in Hempstead's *Reports*, but was, luckily for later readers, published in the *Arkansas Gazette* and is discussed by John P. Frank. Arkansas had enacted a statute that forbade the tolling of statutes of limitations during the time defendants were out of the state. Thus, a prospective defendant could simply leave the state while the statute of limitations ran, and return, unable to be sued, at the end of the time period. The court held that this statute violated the nineteenth century's most favorite clause of the Constitution, the contracts clause, since it would impair the obligation of contracts.[65]

Land questions continued to dog the new state as they had the territory. In 1844, Congress extended the original 1824 act allowing claimants in Missouri and Arkansas to try the validity of their claims. In the late

1840s, a series of land claims cases was decided by Judge Johnson. In fact, of the twelve published district court decisions by Judge Johnson, seven concerned Spanish or French land claims. In 1846, he ruled that the district court could only confirm or reject the existence of a Spanish land grant claim against the United States, and not divide or partition the land. During the same year he rejected a suit involving a Spanish grant to the Baron de Bastrop, which lay mostly in Louisiana, stating that it should be decided by a court situated in Louisiana.[66]

In 1847, he was presented with a Spanish land claims case in which the land had been granted in 1793 to Don Joseph Valliere, the Arkansas Post commander. There was an actual survey, often a sticking point in the claims cases, and the grant had been timely recorded. However, Valliere died in 1799, and there was no evidence that he ever took possession, and nothing more had been done during the next fifty years except that a pamphlet was published in 1844 containing the legal opinions of Daniel Webster, James Kent, and other legal eminences that the claim was valid. Johnson denied it because of the lapse of such a long time between the grant and the suit, with no possession.[67]

The following year Johnson decided a French land claim case involving land granted in 1718 to the notorious John Law, the director-general of the Company of the Indies, by the king of France. John Law styled himself the "Duke of Arkansas" and instigated a huge speculatory scheme, in one of the first uses of paper money, which failed miserably, and was known as the "Mississippi Bubble." Johnson ruled that since Law had gone bankrupt, and his grant was transferred to the company, and subsequently back to the king, that the land passed from the king to the United States with the Louisiana Purchase, and that Law's heirs had no claim.[68]

The longest of the land claims decisions was *Winter v. United States*, involving a total grant of a million arpens from Baron de Carondelet to Elisha Winter, Gabriel Winter, and others, in 1797. Beginning in 1818, first the Louisiana Territory commissioner of land claims and later congressional committees investigated the Winter claims. In 1819, Joshua G. Clarke, one of the claimants, alarmed by federal surveying of the Winter land for military bounty purposes, protested to the president that the Winter group had recorded their titles and lived on the land since 1798, and that a House of Representatives select committee had reported in favor of their titles.[69]

The territorial legislature petitioned Congress to act on the Winter claims in 1820. In 1822, John Miller, one of the claim holders, wrote to Josiah Meigs, offering to "silence" the Winter claims if the United States would give him an island in the Mississippi plus a thousand acres on the Arkansas side.[70]

Winter's claim was stronger than many. The grant had been proven. Winter had erected a stone monument; thus rendering his claim "notorious." However, he did not possess a survey, often a sticking point with the land claims. Instead, he had a figurative "plot of survey," which he had presented to the board of commissioners, as required by US law, in 1808. Johnson began his opinion by praising counsel:

> This case has been thoroughly investigated by the counsel on both sides, and it gives me pleasure to add, that it has been argued by them with great zeal and uncommon ability, and which will the better enable me to form a correct opinion upon the questions which it is now my duty to decide.[71]

Johnson did not question the authority of Carondelet to make a grant of one million arpens; the issue was whether the land was "separated from the royal domain, so as to vest a right of property in the grantee." Citing Spanish law, Johnson noted the requirement of a survey for the grant to have taken place while Spain owned the territory. Thus he ruled against Winter's heirs. The petitioners appealed to the Supreme Court, which granted the appeal; but the petitioners then abandoned the cause and the case was never heard.[72]

The *De Villemont* case came before Judge Johnson during the same term of court. It, too, involved a grant of land by the Baron de Carondelet, in Chicot County, made in 1795 to Don Carlos De Villemont, the Spanish military commander of Arkansas Post from 1794 to 1802. The court found that the terms of the grant, which involved the grantees making a road and a clearing on the land, were not fulfilled. In addition, the precise location of the land could not be determined. Thus Johnson ruled against De Villemont and the other petitioners. [73]

The final land grant case, *Glenn v. United States*, involved a grant made in 1796 by Colonel Delassus, commandant of the post of New Madrid, to James Clamorgan, of over half a million arpens of land in Arkansas. Johnson ruled against Glenn, in a very brief decision rendered in April of 1849, the year that Johnson died, citing the same principles already handed down in the *Winter* and *De Villemont* cases: that the conditions of the grant were not fulfilled; that there was no survey; and that the grant was too vague to sufficiently specify the locality of the land. At the district court level, Albert Pike and D. J. Baldwin argued for the petitioners. The petitioners appealed to the Supreme Court, retaining as one of their counsel Daniel Webster. Attorney General Crittenden, the brother of Robert Crittenden, argued the cause for the United States. The Supreme Court affirmed Johnson, although it did hold that the terms of the grant sufficiently fixed its locality. Thus ended Benjamin Johnson's connection with the land grant cases, which consumed so much government time during the first half of the nineteenth century.[74]

VII. Conclusion

Benjamin Johnson died on October 2, 1849, at the Johnson family home at Great Crossings, Scott County, Kentucky and was buried in Mount Holly Cemetery in Little Rock. Of him, Albert Pike, who practiced in his court, said, "He was a man of excellent ability and of much reading in the law, reading a new volume of reports with as great a zest as a devourer of fiction reads the latest novel." Unfortunately, his judicial legacy has not been as great as it would have been had his opinions been published timely. "Remaining in manuscript for so many years, they have had but little influence upon the state's judicial history." Nonetheless, he was an important decision maker in the area of land claims and federal law. For reasons of brevity, this article has not discussed all of his opinions, nor has it revealed the other facets of his life: his involvement with the ill-fated Arkansas Real Estate Bank; his relationships with prominent early Arkansans; his family relationships; his founding and management of his huge plantation in Chicot County and his life as a planter and slave owner.[75]

After Johnson's death, the bar of the Supreme Court published a laudatory resolution that was printed in the *Arkansas Reports*. It is fitting that one whose life and work were so concerned with the law book should be remembered and honored in the pages of those same books.[76]

PART II

EASTERN AND WESTERN DISTRICTS OF ARKANSAS 1851–71

Scribner's engraving, about 1874, of the State House building. The capitol continued to serve as headquarters for the United States District Court for the Eastern District after the single District of Arkansas was divided into the Eastern and Western Districts in 1851. The Eastern District Court met in the capitol into the second half of the nineteenth century with Judge Daniel Ringo presiding until the beginning of the Civil War. *Courtesy of the Old State House Museum Collection.*

Crawford County Courthouse, Van Buren, c. 1870s, sketch by William Quesenbury. The Crawford County Courthouse in Van Buren, shown in this late 1870s image, was headquarters for the Western District Court from 1851 to 1871, during the tenure of Judge Daniel Ringo and for seven years of Judge Henry Clay Caldwell's tenure. *Courtesy Special Collections, University of Arkansas Libraries, Fayetteville.*

Crawford County Courthouse, 2012. The Crawford County Courthouse served the United States District Court for the Western District of Arkansas until Congress reorganized the district and moved the court to Fort Smith in 1871. *Courtesy Tommy McClain, Van Buren, Arkansas.*

CHAPTER 3

DANIEL RINGO

1850–61

L. Scott Stafford

DANIEL RINGO was the second judge to serve the United States District Court for the District of Arkansas (1850–51) and the first to serve the Eastern and Western Districts simultaneously (1851–61). Ringo was born in Kentucky in 1803 and came to the Arkansas Territory in 1820 at the age of sixteen. He stopped briefly at Batesville, in Independence County, which had a rather large colony of Kentuckians, before moving on to Little Rock. After living in Little Rock for five years, he moved to Arkadelphia, where he served as deputy county clerk and later county clerk of Clark County. During his years at Arkadelphia he studied law and was admitted to practice. He resigned his position as county clerk in 1830 and opened a law office in the Hempstead County town of Washington, which was then a jumping-off place for settlers headed for Texas. Sometime in the early 1830s he moved back to Little Rock and entered a law partnership with Chester Ashley, a prominent attorney and land speculator who would later represent Arkansas in the United States Senate.[1]

Arkansas was admitted to the Union in 1836.[2] Under the state's first constitution, supreme court justices were elected by joint vote of both houses of the General Assembly,[3] and in the fall of 1836 the legislature

Daniel Ringo. *Courtesy United States District Court for the Eastern District of Arkansas.*

selected Ringo as the first chief justice of the supreme court.[4] A turn-of-the-century biographical sketch contains an unflattering assessment of Ringo's response to the challenges he faced as the state's first chief justice:

> He had a great opportunity. A new commonwealth had been admitted into the Union. It had as yet no legal system of its own. A strong and sagacious man, with the authority which the position of chief justice always gives, would have been able to achieve a most enviable standing, laying the foundation of her jurisprudence broad and deep. Judge Ringo was not the man for this.[5]

Ringo was unsuited by temperament or training to the task of fashioning a legal system for the new state. Contemporary descriptions of the new chief justice portray him as a cautious, unimaginative jurist who reached decisions only after methodical deliberation.[6] As might be expected from a lawyer who learned his craft while serving as county clerk in a rural county, Ringo was more concerned with the law's form than its substance. According to Uriah M. Rose, a prominent Little Rock attorney who practiced before Ringo during the antebellum period, "Chief Justice Ringo . . . painfully sought out all of the technicalities that had ever existed in common-law pleadings through the ages, and . . . put them all in force at once."[7] Ringo's devotion to common-law pleading forms condemned Arkansas to a cumbersome system of justice in which cases were often decided on procedural points. The state would not break free from the procedural system established by Ringo until after the Civil War when the Reconstruction-era legislature finally adopted code pleading.[8]

Ringo's eight-year term as chief justice ended in 1844, when he was defeated for a second term by Thomas Johnson, the brother of United States district judge Benjamin Johnson.[9] Democrats controlled the Arkansas legislature, and Ringo made no secret of his support for the Whig Party.[10] His role in *Conway, ex parte*,[11] which the court decided in August 1842, may have also contributed to his defeat. In that decision a majority of the court, with Ringo dissenting, refused to interfere with an assignment by the state Real Estate Bank of all of its property to a group of private trustees. The court's decision outraged Archibald Yell, the state's popular governor. At the legislative session that convened in November 1842, Yell and his supporters retaliated against the two justices who voted in the majority in *Conway, ex parte*. One justice was defeated for reelection, and the second was targeted for impeachment. An impeachment resolution eventually passed the house but only after the governor's opponents attached an amendment calling for an investigation of the actions of the governor and Chief Justice Ringo with respect to the Real Estate Bank. The amendment effectively killed the impeachment resolution because neither side dared risk a trial in the senate. Although there is no evidence that Ringo acted improperly in the *Conway* decision, the controversy surrounding the case may have cost him votes when he came up for reelection at the 1844 legislative session.[12]

After leaving the state supreme court, Ringo quietly practiced law in Little Rock with his brother-in-law, Frederick W. Trapnell. He appears as attorney of record in three reported petitions for confirmation of Spanish land grants. In two of the cases he represented petitioners whose claims were rejected by US district judge Johnson.[13] In the third case his clients were the current owners of property who opposed the claims of the heirs of the former Spanish commandant of Arkansas Post and its districts.[14]

In 1849 United States district judge Benjamin Johnson died, and Whig president Zachary Taylor named Ringo to replace him, initially by recess appointment.[15] Since 1839 prominent Arkansans had petitioned Congress for the creation of a second judicial district in the state, and these efforts bore fruit shortly after Ringo's appointment when Congress divided Arkansas into an Eastern and a Western District. Ringo thereafter served as judge for both districts. The new Western District included the Arkansas counties of Benton, Washington, Crawford, Scott, Polk, Franklin, Johnson, Madison, and Carroll, as well as much of the Indian Territory that would later become the state of Oklahoma. The legislation establishing the Western District required Ringo to hold two terms of court annually at Van Buren in Crawford County, beginning on the second Monday in May and November. It also treated the Western District court as a circuit court for appeal purposes, which meant that decisions made by Ringo in the Eastern District of Arkansas were appealable to the Ninth Circuit Court while decisions he made in the Western District were appealable directly to the Supreme Court.[16]

Ringo's service on the federal bench was as undistinguished as his earlier stint on the state supreme court. During the twelve years he was a federal judge, Ringo authored only six reported opinions.[17] Ringo's opinion in *Roberts v. Pillow*[18] corroborates his reputation as a stickler for compliance with the formalities of law. Roberts brought an action to eject Pillow from land. Pillow's defense was that he owned the property under a tax deed from the sheriff and collector of Phillips County. Alternatively, Pillow claimed that he had adversely possessed the property for ten years under color of title based on the same tax deed. Ringo refused to permit Pillow to introduce the tax deed because he failed to show that the sheriff and collector had complied with the numerous formalities of the Arkansas statute regulating the sale of land for nonpayment of taxes. According to Ringo:

> [I]t is manifest that a party relying on such deed must in connection therewith, show such fact as in law vested in the collector authority to sell property . . . , before he can receive the advantages or entitle himself to the legal presumptions and effect declared by the statute as incidents to such deed. What particular facts may be sufficient for this purpose it is the business of the pleader to ascertain, and not the duty of the court to indicate or specify in advance.[19]

Pillow appealed the decision, and in reversing Ringo, the Supreme Court pointedly criticized his hyper-technical application of the Arkansas tax statute:

> It is easy, by very ingenious and astute construction, to evade the force of almost any statute, where a court is so disposed. We might say that the expression "deeds so made by the collector," means deeds made strictly according to the requirement of all the preceding sections of the revenue law, and decide that only deeds first proved to be completely regular and legal can be received in evidence; and thus, by qualifying the whole section by such an enlarged construction of these two words, and disregarding all the others, evade the obvious meaning and intention of the law. For if you must first prove the sale to be regular and legal before the deed can be received, what becomes of the provision that the deed itself shall be evidence of these facts? Such a construction annuls this provision of the law, and renders it superfluous and useless. The evil plainly intended to be remedied by this section of the act, was the extreme difficulty and almost impossibility of proving that all the numerous directions of the revenue act were fully complied with, antecedent to the sale and conveyance by the collector.[20]

Ringo's decision in a similar tax deed case decided three years later indicates that he may not have fully appreciated the nuances of the Supreme Court's reversal of *Pillow v. Roberts*. In *Overman v. Parker*[21] the purchaser of lands at a tax sale instituted legal proceedings in an Arkansas state court to confirm his title to the lands. Two persons, one a citizen of Tennessee and the other a citizen of Maryland, claimed the land in question, and they succeeded in removing the confirmation action to federal court based on diversity of citizenship. The two then argued that the purchaser's tax title should not be confirmed because the taxes on the lands in question had not been properly assessed prior to the tax sale.

Ringo confirmed title in the purchaser at the tax sale.[22] He apparently relied on the Supreme Court's holding in *Pillow v. Roberts* because the Supreme Court's opinion indicates that much of the argument before the high court was "wasted on the effect to be attributed to the recitals in the deed, and the decision of this court in *Pillow v. Roberts*."[23] In reversing Ringo, the Supreme Court distinguished *Pillow v. Roberts* as a collateral attack on a tax deed in which the burden of showing irregularity in the issuance of the deed was correctly placed on the party contesting the validity of the deed. The purpose of the confirmation proceeding in *Overman v. Parker* was to give other claimants the opportunity to contest the legality of the tax sale, and the court termed it absurd to make the tax deed, whose validity was in question, conclusive evidence of the legality of the tax sale.

Ringo also strictly applied federal procedural statutes. The Judiciary Act of 1789 permitted witnesses residing more than one hundred miles from the place of trial to testify by deposition before a magistrate.[24] In two reported cases decided in 1854 Judge Ringo insisted on literal compliance with the requirements of the statute. In *Marstin v. McRea*[25] Ringo suppressed a deposition because the magistrate certified that it was reduced to writing under the magistrate's direction instead of being reduced to writing by the magistrate himself or by the witness in the presence of the magistrate.

Ringo cited a similar error in suppressing depositions in *Ranier v. Haynes*.[26] There the witnesses had reduced their testimony to writing, but the magistrate's certificate failed to state that the reduction to writing took place in his presence. Ringo also deemed the certificate defective because it reflected that the witnesses were sworn to testify to the truth, which did not satisfy the statutory requirement that they be sworn to tell the "whole" truth.

The only reported criminal case in which Ringo participated was *U.S. v. Dawson.*[27] The defendant was indicted in the circuit court for the District of Arkansas in 1845 for the murder of a white man in the Indian Territory. He was not arrested until 1852, after Congress had split Arkansas into two districts and vested the Western District of Arkansas with jurisdiction over crimes committed against white persons within the Indian Territory.[28] The defendant filed a writ of habeas corpus with Ringo, in which he argued that he could not be tried in the Eastern District for a crime allegedly committed in territory annexed to the Western District and that he could not be tried in the Western District for a crime allegedly committed prior to the creation of that district. In January of 1853 Ringo, sitting as a district judge, dismissed the petition, ruling that the court sitting in the Eastern District was not divested of jurisdiction by the creation of the Western District and could proceed to try the defendant in the Eastern District. At the April 1853 term of the circuit court, the defendant renewed his motion before a panel consisting of Ringo and Associate Justice Peter Daniel of the Supreme Court. Ringo stuck with his conclusion that the court had jurisdiction, but Justice Daniel had a different opinion. The panel certified the question to the Supreme Court, which ruled that the creation of the new Western District did not affect the jurisdiction of the circuit court to try any criminal or civil cases pending at the time the change took place. The defendant also argued that trying him in the Eastern District violated his Sixth Amendment right "to a speedy and public trial by an impartial jury of the state and district wherein the crime shall have been committed," but the high court concluded that the quoted language applied only to offenses committed within the geographical limits of a state and not to those committed in other locations.[29]

Ringo was upheld by the Supreme Court in one other reported case. *Sessions v. Pintard*[30] was a complicated proceeding involving the liability of the sureties on an appeal bond. Pintard had originally obtained a decree against Goodloe for $10,552, to be satisfied by the sale of a certain tract of land. Goodloe appealed the decree to the United States Supreme Court, and, in accordance with the Judiciary Act, Goodloe posted a $12,000 appeal bond, which Sessions signed as surety. The Supreme

Court affirmed the decree, and Pintard sued Sessions on the appeal bond. At the same time Pintard procured an order selling the land specified in the original decree. Pintard applied the proceeds of the land sale to the original decree, which by the date of sale had grown to $16,875, and sought to recover the balance from Sessions. Sessions argued that the proceeds from the sale of the land should be applied to his $12,000 bond and that he was only liable for the balance due Pintard after such credit.

Ringo held for Pintard, and Sessions appealed to the Supreme Court, which affirmed. The report does not reflect Ringo's reasoning, but it probably corresponded to that of the Supreme Court. The high court concluded that Sessions had assumed liability for the entire amount of the appeal bond and only benefited from the proceeds of the land sale to the extent it reduced the amount owed on the original decree below the $12,000 limit of the appeal bond.

While serving on the federal bench, Ringo apparently had the time and money to engage in various commercial ventures. Along with his brother-in-law and former law partner, Frederick Trapnell, he acquired a plantation in Chicot County on the Mississippi River along with a sufficient number of slaves to rank among the state's largest slaveholders.[31] In 1853 he helped organize the Cairo and Fulton Railroad and subsequently served as vice president of the railroad and member of its board of directors.[32]

Arkansas seceded from the United States on May 6, 1861, and shortly thereafter Ringo resigned from the federal bench.[33] Prior to Arkansas's secession the Provisional Confederate Congress had passed a Judiciary Act creating one district court in each of the Confederate states.[34] On May 21, 1861, one day after it admitted Arkansas to the Confederacy, the Confederate Congress passed special legislation creating an Eastern and Western district of the Confederate district court in Arkansas that corresponded to the two districts of the former United States district court.[35] Confederate president Jefferson Davis immediately appointed Ringo as judge of both districts.[36]

Unfortunately, few records of Ringo's service on the Confederate bench have survived. He played a small role in the suppression of a pro-Union conspiracy in north Arkansas. In late 1861 Confederate authorities discovered that secret peace societies had been formed in the northern counties of Arkansas. They attracted not only pro-Unionists but also apolitical independent-minded mountaineers who wanted little to do with either side. Governor Henry Rector, a rabid secessionist, sent the militia to arrest large numbers of peace society members. About one hundred men were brought in chains to Little Rock where Rector planned to charge them with treason against the Confederate states. Ringo was apparently holding court at Van Buren when the men reached Little Rock because on November 28, 1861, Rector complained to Jefferson Davis that Ringo was not "at his post" to deal with the prisoners.[37] By the time Ringo returned to Little Rock, most of the prisoners had gained their freedom by joining the Confederate army.[38] Fifteen men, however, refused to enlist. Ringo convened a grand jury on January 20, 1862, but after taking evidence for ten days the grand jury declined to return a true bill.[39]

Van Buren fell under Union control in late 1862, and Little Rock was occupied in September of 1863. After the surrender of Little Rock, the Confederate state government retreated to Washington in southwest Arkansas, but there is no evidence that Ringo followed. Although contemporary news reports document the operation of the state supreme court in Washington, they fail to mention the Confederate district court. In all probability the Confederate district court in Arkansas simply ceased to function sometime in 1863.

The Civil War left Ringo impoverished. His slaves were emancipated, and his plantation in Chicot County was confiscated by the victorious Union forces.[40] He returned to the practice of law in Little Rock, but the adoption of code pleading as well as deteriorating health limited his ability to make a living.[41] He died on September 3, 1873, and was buried the same day in a family plot at Mount Holly Cemetery in Little Rock.[42] For almost a century Ringo's grave was unmarked. This was remedied in 1963 when the Arkansas Bar Association erected a stone at the gravesite.[43]

PART III

EASTERN DISTRICT OF ARKANSAS 1871–1969

United States Post Office and Courthouse, Little Rock, 1881. Completed in 1881, this building replaced the State House along with temporary space that was used by the Eastern District Court during the 1870s. In 1932, when the post office and courts moved to larger quarters, new uses for the building followed. Since its restoration in the 1990s, it has housed the United States Bankruptcy Court. United States district judges whose tenures coincided with the use of this courthouse were Judges Henry Clay Caldwell, John Apps Williams, Jacob Trieber, and John Ellis Martineau. *Library of Congress, Prints & Photographs Division, photograph by Carol M. Highsmith. LC-USZ62-123456.*

Richard Sheppard Arnold United States Courthouse. The 1932 United States Post Office and Courthouse, which replaced the 1881 building, is to the left in the photograph. While not all of these judges maintained chambers in Little Rock, judges featured in this volume whose tenures coincided with the use of this courthouse include Judges John Ellis Martineau, Thomas Clark Trimble, Gordon Elmo Young, Harry Jacob Lemley, and Jesse Smith Henley. In the 1990s the post office moved to new facilities. The courthouse was renamed for Judge Richard Sheppard Arnold in 2003 and the addition to the courthouse was completed in 2007. *Courtesy United States District Court for the Eastern District of Arkansas.*

CHAPTER 4

HENRY CLAY CALDWELL

1864–90

Richard S. Arnold and George C. Freeman III

HENRY CLAY CALDWELL was raised on the western frontier in largely Indian Territory, where he worked on his father's farm and was principally a self-educated young man. It is perhaps his early years that led him to develop a homespun populist philosophy and extreme sense of judicial fairness. Caldwell's career in public service began as a prosecuting attorney, which was followed by service in the Iowa House of Representatives and the Union army. Caldwell came to Arkansas while serving in the military and was appointed by President Abraham Lincoln to the United States District Courts for the Eastern District and for the Western District of Arkansas.

Although Caldwell came to Arkansas as an aggressor, as the colonel who led Union troops that took Little Rock during the Civil War, Caldwell became known as one of Arkansas's most admired and cherished friends.[1] Judge Caldwell served on the district court for the Eastern

This article was prepared for and originally published by the *University of Arkansas at Little Rock Law Review* in Volume 23, Issue 2 and is reproduced with its permission. It was originally titled "Judge Henry Clay Caldwell." Further information about the *UALR Law Review* is available at www.ualr.edu/lawreview. While the article focuses on Judge Caldwell's service to Arkansas's Eastern District, from 1864 to 1871 he also sat on the bench of the Western District.

Henry Clay Caldwell. *Courtesy United States District Court for the Eastern District of Arkansas.*

District of Arkansas until he was commissioned to the United States Circuit Courts for the Eighth Circuit in 1890.

Judge Caldwell was known to be a generous, kind, and virtuous man who had a strong understanding of the law. He was as active in civic affairs as he was in his courtroom. Judge Caldwell, who despised injustice and oppression, had a reputation for impartiality and saw the law as an instrument of substantive justice. Under his view of the law, no authority was necessary to justify doing what is right. Although Judge Caldwell usually sat without a jury upon the stipulation of parties who respected his pursuit of justice, he was a preserver of jury trials. He believed that the right of trial by jury was absolutely essential to preserve the rights and liberties of the people. Judge Caldwell's reputation as a jurist appears to be rooted in his notions that personal rights should prevail over property rights, and the common laborer constitutes the foundation of society. This article discusses Judge Caldwell's life and judicial career.

I. Early Years and Emergent Career in Public Service

Henry Clay Caldwell was born on September 4, 1832, to Van and Susan Moffet Caldwell. His father, Van Caldwell, an ardent Whig, named his son after the famous politician whom Van admired greatly.[2] Henry liked to be called "Clay."[3] Young Henry spent the first four years of his life on his father's farm in the Ohio River Valley in what was then Marshall County, Virginia, and is now Ohio County, West Virginia. Van and Susan Caldwell soon found the Ohio River Valley too civilized and too expensive.[4]

In 1836, they moved their family west to the Black Hawk Purchase in the territory of Wisconsin. Chief Black Hawk settled about half of a mile behind the Caldwells' cabin, and Van and Henry Caldwell visited the chief on at least one occasion.[5] The Caldwells initially settled along the Des Moines River in unsettled land still occupied by the Sac and Fox Indians, land that would later be called the Territory of Iowa. Van Caldwell obtained permission from the government and Indians to establish a ferry across the Des Moines River to carry passengers to and from the agency mill nearby on Salt Creek. Traffic to the mill failed to materialize, so Van moved to what would become Davis County and began to farm. Young Henry worked on his father's farm and essentially educated himself by reading whatever books he could find. As a young boy, he had attended the school in the Indian agency station for a few weeks during the time his father ran the ferry, but this was the only formal primary education he had. Caldwell went to Keosauqua, in Van Buren County, in late 1847 for some secondary schooling.[6]

A little more than a year later, Henry Clay Caldwell began an apprenticeship with the law firm in Keosauqua where he had been working as a chore boy to support himself through school. The firm was Wright and Knapp, and its founder, George G. Wright, would later become a United States senator and Iowa Supreme Court judge. The other founder, J. C. Knapp, who had been influential in getting Henry to come to town for school, was an Iowa district court judge for Van Buren County. Henry joined the bar in 1851 at the relatively young age of nineteen.[7] Three years later, he married Hattie Benton, George Wright's niece and Judge Knapp's sister-in-law.[8]

Henry Caldwell began his long career in public service when he ran for the office of prosecutor for Van Buren County in 1856 on the Republican ticket. He was the only victorious candidate on the new party's ticket in all of Van Buren County.[9] He served as prosecutor for two years and then ran for the Iowa House of Representatives. He again ran as a Republican and again won. During his first term in the House he was appointed chairman of the House Judiciary Commission. By 1860, he was ready for national politics. He made a trip to Chicago as a delegate to the Republican Convention being held in the "Wigwam" where he cast his vote for Lincoln.[10]

When the Civil War broke out, young Henry resigned from the Iowa Legislature to preserve the Union. He received a commission as a major in the Third Iowa Cavalry, which he had helped set up and recruit.[11] Major Caldwell was placed in charge of the Second Battalion (containing four companies). The Second Battalion was split from the rest of the regiment and sent south to Jefferson, Missouri. From there Caldwell carried out patrols and scouting parties. The Second Battalion met much resistance. It suffered more than 30 percent casualties in its first year of operation, but inflicted proportionally greater casualties upon the Confederate forces.[12] The Second Battalion stayed in southern Missouri conducting patrols, although it did fight in the battles of Pea Ridge in March of 1862 and Prairie Grove in 1862. Caldwell was promoted to lieutenant colonel in September 1862 to replace an officer who was severely wounded at Pea Ridge. In late 1862, his command was augmented by two more companies to assist him in patrolling the frontier between the Iron Mountains of Missouri and the Boston Mountains of Arkansas. In 1863, the Second Battalion moved south. Caldwell's troops joined Brigadier General Steel along the White River in Arkansas and moved in toward Little Rock to take the Arkansas capitol.

On the morning of September 10, Caldwell led the advance cavalry column that actually took Little Rock. His troopers crossed the Arkansas River east of the city and, after brief skirmishes, rode into the essentially evacuated city. Shortly thereafter, the infantry marched effortlessly through the abandoned Confederate lines. Mayor Charles B. Bertram formally surrendered the keys of the city to Colonel Caldwell. It seems the keys were safe in his hands. Caldwell organized a system of patrol for the city, which sixty years later an Arkansas paper would praise as never being duplicated:

> During the time that the city was in the hands of his troops[,] Colonel Caldwell day and night rode over the patrolled sections and saw that everything was in perfect order, and in that time there was not a single display of rowdyism or destruction on the part of his men or the citizens of the town.[13]

Caldwell's commanders later recommended that he be promoted to the rank of brigadier general, but Caldwell seems to have set his mind on civilian life. By early 1864, much of Arkansas was under control of the United States Army and civilian control was soon to follow. Colonel Caldwell knew that the seats for the United States District Courts of Arkansas were vacant, so he applied. He received the endorsement of Supreme Court justice Samuel F. Miller, who had practiced law in Iowa in the 1850s, and the Iowa congressional delegation.

The Third Cavalry meanwhile returned to Iowa for furlough after three years of duty. The regiment then packed up and headed for Memphis, Tennessee, where it remained throughout 1864. On May 4, 1864, Caldwell was promoted to colonel of the regiment, replacing the former colonel, who had become a brigadier general.[14] Apparently, Caldwell was also in line to become a general officer. Sometime shortly after Caldwell received Lincoln's nomination on May 2, 1864, he received a letter from his close friend James F. Wilson, who was at that time a congressman, that informed Caldwell, "You can be a Brigadier General or a United States Judge. Which do you prefer?"[15] On June 4, 1864,

Henry Caldwell resigned his commission with the United States Army and began his trip west to Little Rock where, sixteen days later, he took his oath as United States district judge for the Eastern and Western Districts of Arkansas. His commission to the Western District ended in 1871 following the appointment of a new judge for that district.

II. United States District Judge for the Eastern District of Arkansas

The Eastern District of Arkansas was typical of other federal districts. It had two trial courts, the district court and the circuit court. The jurisdictions of these courts were vastly different. The district court had jurisdiction over petty crimes and admiralty matters. The circuit court was the primary trial court in the federal judiciary, having jurisdiction based on diversity of citizenship. In theory, the circuit court was intended to have multi-judge panels made up of the district court judge(s) and the United States Supreme Court justice assigned to that circuit. In reality, the district court judges or judge for the district usually presided.[16]

Congress placed Arkansas in the Sixth Circuit in 1862, which included Texas and Louisiana, but four years later it placed Arkansas in the Eighth Circuit along with Iowa, Kansas, Minnesota, and Missouri.

Judge Caldwell held court in 1864, but did not hear cases. He merely swore in the marshals and clerks. He also spent the fall of 1864 reading and learning Arkansas cases.[17] In the spring of 1865, the federal courthouse in Little Rock opened its doors for business.

Judge Caldwell came to Arkansas both as an outsider and as a conqueror. As can be imagined, he was not instantly embraced by the local population. A local historian writing in 1877 sums up the spirit well:

> The young soldier-jurist, fresh from the victorious northern army, at that excited period when the intense prejudices engendered by the civil war were still at fever-heat, did not inspire the confidence of the southern people, who then knew nothing of his qualification or antecedents. The confiscation and other stringent Federal laws were to be administered by a soldier, who was supposed to be full of the pride and prejudice of the conqueror, with the tremendous machinery of a powerful government to sustain him. The old order of things had perished in the ruins of the revolution and a new *regime* was springing into power and crystallizing under the

> supreme dictation of the conqueror, whose limitation was controlled by nothing but his own sense of propriety.[18]

Judge Caldwell, however, was not one to hold back. He began his long career on the bench by launching a crusade against the practice of writ pleading in his court. His predecessor, Judge Daniel Ringo, had been chief justice of the Arkansas Supreme Court from 1836 until 1844 and the federal district judge, beginning with a recess appointment in 1849, until Arkansas seceded from the Union. Ringo had been instrumental in establishing a system of special pleading in both state and federal courts that was comparable only to the system that prevailed in England in the eighteenth century.[19] Reflecting upon this crusade a few years later, Caldwell himself summed up his feelings on writ pleading:

> There was a time in England and in this country when the fundamental principles of right and justice which courts were created to uphold and enforce were esteemed of minor importance compared to the quibbles, refinements and technicalities of special pleading. In that period the great fundamentals of the law seemed little, and the trifling things great. The courts were not concerned with the merits of a case, but with the mode of stating it. And they adopted so many subtle, artificial, and technical rules governing the statement of actions and defenses—for the entire system of special pleading was built up by the judges without the sanction of any written law—that in many cases the whole contention was whether these rules had been observed, and the merits of the case were never reached, and frequently never thought of.[20]

Needless to say the local bar, which had grown up under the old system, was less than receptive to these new reforms. A local historian recounts an anecdote about the mood in Judge Caldwell's early courtroom:

> The late Judge Watkins, then one of our honored legal luminaries, had a large practice in that court, and had prepared a large number of pleadings embodying these harassing obstructions, but he watched the indications closely to catch the practice before filing them. Finally his name was reached in alphabetical order on the roll, and he was politely asked by the court if he had any favors to ask. He rose slowly, and with dignified composure, said he had a bag full of pleas in abatement and demurrers prepared to file, but would graciously decline to do so—not desiring to promote and advance the cause of his adversaries.[21]

The effect of Judge Caldwell's quiet revolution took place in the context of an act of Congress that prevented anyone who had been disloyal to the Union from practicing before a federal court.[22] Local lawyers fought Judge Caldwell's imposition of code pleadings for several years until Justice Samuel Miller, who arrived in 1868 to sit on the circuit court with Judge Caldwell, affirmed the proceedings. With the exception of code pleading, however, Judge Caldwell seems to have quickly won the respect of the people of Arkansas.

During Reconstruction, Judge Caldwell proceeded cautiously and gently through the thorny political questions. It was said that "during the six years that the carpet-bag regime lasted, he was the greatest protection the people of the state had."[23] Judge Caldwell, however, was always a Union man. Although he opposed Governor Clayton's imposition of martial law, in which the governor sought to stem the violence attributed to the Ku Klux Klan, Caldwell later recanted, citing the measure's effectiveness in restoring order.[24] He also seems not to have shirked from his duties in enforcing the Fourteenth Amendment. In a resolution presented by George Rose of Little Rock before the Arkansas Supreme Court, Rose recounted:

> After having known the [black man] as a slave [the people of Arkansas] could not recognize his position as a freeman with equal rights before the law; and Judge Caldwell's strong insistence that the guaranties of the Fourteenth Amendment should be observed, gave offense to many.[25]

Judge Caldwell was also a die-hard Republican, but never let his political views interfere with his duties as a judge. The following article, written to show support of Caldwell to replace circuit judge McCrary[26] in 1884, shows how Caldwell was perceived during these times:

> When he first went upon the bench, now nearly twenty years ago, he had to deal with the acts of Congress confiscating the property of Confederates. These laws were designed to act upon the principle and follow the usages and procedure of Admiralty Courts, where no juries are allowed, and nothing was said in the act in regard to jury trial. Hence most, if not all, of the district judges, in administering these laws, held that causes under them were admiralty causes, and no trial by jury should be allowed. But Judge Caldwell, then newly administering Federal procedures, saw through the fallacy of this

> reasoning, and held that under the constitution they were common law causes, and their issues triable by jury; in which he was sustained by the United States Supreme Court. He then had to pass upon the perplexing question of the statute of limitations growing out of the closure of the courts during the war and the construction of the limitation act of Congress of 1863—in all of which he was correct, and his rulings sustained by the Supreme Court.

And then came before him the questions growing out of the "direct tax" laws of Congress of 1861, and their amendments; in these cases he was also sustained.

Then came the variety of questions of slave contracts, contracts arising from the purchase and sale of slaves, negotiable paper and conveyances of property based upon slave consideration, in which he was also sustained (except for one case).

Others were also issues involving contracts, agreements, and conveyances based on Confederate money consideration, and also contracts and conveyances dependent upon the legislation of the Confederate governments in the rebelling states and the decrees, judgments, and orders of their courts, and the action of their ministerial officers.

And later questions arose concerning the administration of the reconstruction laws, the election laws, and civil rights laws passed by Congress, all of which involved new issues and the new application of legal principles. Besides these, the administration and construction of the revenue and bankruptcy laws of the United States, both of which were new, produced difficult cases.

In the construction and application of this long array of new statutes, great caution, sound judgment, and clear, precise, and accurate knowledge of legal principles were necessary, for there were few, if any, precedents to guide the steps of the traveler in these then unexplored regions of the law. To evolve just conclusions for all these various and momentous issues required a clear intellect, great grasp of mind, and thorough familiarity with legal principles. Judge Caldwell, though sitting on the bench with such distinguished jurists as Justice Miller, Judge Dillon, and Judge McCrary, never appeared at a disadvantage in their august presence.[27]

Judge Caldwell was reversed by the United States Supreme Court only once in this period, in a case involving the enforcement of a promissory note for the purchase of a slave, *Osborn v. Nicholson.*[28] Given the extreme dearth of reported cases from this period, we cannot adequately assess his treatment of freedmen. This case, however, shows that the judge was neither sympathetic to slavery, nor afraid of voicing his opinion to that effect.

In *Osborn v. Nicholson*, the plaintiff had brought suit on a promissory note issued in early 1861, to be paid at the end of a year for a slave. The defendant had demurred on the grounds that the Arkansas Constitution explicitly prohibited the enforcement of contracts for the sale of slaves.[29] Judge Caldwell, in a passionate opinion, sustained the demurrer on the grounds that the Arkansas Constitution did not infringe on contract rights in violation of Article I section 10 of the United States Constitution. As for the argument that slavery was legal in Arkansas when the parties made the contract, Judge Caldwell replied:

> The law of the place where the thing happens does not always prevail. In many countries a contract may be maintained by a courtesan for the price of her prostitution, and one may suppose an action to be brought here upon such a contract, which arose in such a country, but that would never be allowed in this country. *Robinson v. Bland*, 2 Burrows, 1084.
>
> Now slavery contained in itself all the worst social evils, and the sale of female slaves for prostitution was only one of its many revolting features. Will anyone be so bold as to affirm that a slave contract entered into in a foreign country, and valued by the laws of that country, would now be enforced by the courts of this country, either state or nation. And if not, why not? Obviously because such a contract is against sound morals, and natural right, and opposed to the constitution and policy of our government. Now is there anything in our constitution and policy today by which the domestic slave trader is put in any better position before the courts of the country than the foreign slave trader would occupy?
>
> It is said slavery was once lawful in some of the states of the Union, and was tolerated by the constitution of the United States. Granted. But it has been abolished by the constitution of the United States, and of the several states, and that abolishment has been followed up by acts for the enfranchisement of the former slaves, and other legislation that indelibly stamps slavery and all contract and rights based on the slave code as illegal and void.[30]

He continues, citing *Dred Scott v. Sandford*[31] for the proposition that if the states' power over the institution of slavery was so absolute as to allow them to destroy Mr. Scott's marriage contract without violating the Constitution, then they must be able to abolish all contracts relating to it.[32]

The Supreme Court, however, disagreed. In an opinion written by Justice Swayne, the court ruled that contract rights had accrued before the statutes authorizing them were repealed and therefore the Arkansas Constitution violated the Contracts Clause, notwithstanding the Thirteenth Amendment.[33] The chief justice dissented, citing the main arguments made by Judge Caldwell.

In addition to the abundance of cases involving legislation stemming from the war and its aftermath, in both the district and circuit courts, Congress passed a new bankruptcy law that increased Judge Caldwell's workload. The Act of March 2, 1867, gave the district courts bankruptcy jurisdiction,[34] which markedly increased the pressure on district court judges. On the circuit court, however, Judge Caldwell received some assistance when Supreme Court justice Samuel Miller came to Little Rock for two weeks to join Caldwell on circuit court panels in both 1868 and 1870. Between these visits Congress also created nine circuit judgeships, one for each judicial circuit, to reduce the circuit riding of the Supreme Court justices to riding circuit every other year.[35] From 1870 until 1890, the Eighth Circuit's judge sat on the circuit court in Arkansas for one week per year, although the court was in session for over four months per year.[36] So while he was a district court judge, Judge Caldwell was a de facto circuit court judge.

The first circuit judge for the Eighth Circuit was John Forrest Dillon, who was chief judge of the Iowa Supreme Court when appointed to the federal bench. Judge Caldwell wrote letters of recommendation supporting Dillon's nomination. Dillon resigned in 1879 and was replaced by another Iowan, George Washington McCrary. McCrary had practiced law in Keokuk, Iowa, with Justice Miller, and had also been a pioneer in the Iowa Republican Party with Caldwell.[37] McCrary would resign in 1884, to be replaced by David Brewer of Kansas. Brewer went on to the United States Supreme Court in 1889 and was replaced by Henry Clay Caldwell. But we are getting ahead of our story.

In 1871, Congress created a new judgeship for the Western District, which was filled by William Story until he resigned and was replaced by the famous "hanging judge," Isaac C. Parker. The statute moved the terms of court for the Western District from Van Buren to Fort Smith, Arkansas, and set up a Helena division of the Western District despite the fact that Helena is in the extreme eastern portion of the state. Within six years, however, Congress removed the Helena division from the west and attached it to the Eastern District. At this time, however, it stipulated that the district court in Helena should have the jurisdiction of a circuit court, except for appeals. So the only circuit court held in Arkansas continued to be that in Little Rock.

On the circuit court, Caldwell's duties were compounded in 1875 by legislation that radically increased federal judicial jurisdiction. Luckily, Arkansas was spared from being inundated by cases brought under the Federal Enforcement Act of 1870, which flooded the other federal district courts in the South.[38] The Act of March 3, 1875, gave general federal-question jurisdiction—cases arising under the laws, treaties, or the Constitution of the United States—in addition to the court's former jurisdiction based on diverse citizenship of parties. The act also allowed certain cases involving a federal question brought in state court to be removed to the federal circuit court by the defendant. After this act, the jurisdiction of the federal courts would remain fairly stable until after Judge Caldwell was appointed circuit judge for the Eighth Circuit.

As Reconstruction weakened, Judge Caldwell actively supported returning Arkansas to home rule—eliminating federal supervision and allowing former Confederates to vote. When the Brooks-Baxter war broke out in 1874, Judge Caldwell actively supported Baxter and is credited with helping secure his recognition by the national government.[39] Later that year, the new Democratic government adopted a new constitution that superseded the Reconstruction constitution of 1868 and allowed Confederate officers once again to vote and hold office. President Grant saw this move as essentially a return to the state of affairs that had existed before the war, and asked Congress to reimpose reconstruction, that is, federal authority. Congress appointed an investigating committee and sent its members to Arkansas. Judge Caldwell informally intervened. He lobbied these congressmen, housing some in his home. He believed that the new constitution was not rebellious, but an exercise of popular sovereignty, and Arkansas should remain under home rule. The committee members agreed by returning with a favorable report. No action against the state of Arkansas was taken.[40]

With Reconstruction gone, Judge Caldwell's court began to take up the type of business that would continue to fill the federal reporters up through the turn of the century—railroad and labor cases. From the reported cases of Judge Caldwell during the 1870s and 1880s, we can see his judicial persona emerge. This persona would stay with him until his retirement. First, however, a more personal description is due.

Judge Caldwell seems to have reflected his upbringing on the frontier. He stood well over six feet tall, but was somewhat quiet. He had a large head with a broad forehead. He wore a beard, and the older he grew, the longer it grew. By the time he retired, his beard was very long and a bit unkempt—giving him the appearance of a trapper or mountain man. Henry Caldwell was also not known as a natty dresser. He was often described as being careless about his appearance.

Despite a rough exterior, he was a very upright and proper man. He was also characterized as being generous and kind. He was regarded as being a man beyond reproach; no one questioned his personal or judicial integrity.[41] Judge Caldwell had strong opinions and never hesitated to let people know them.[42] Yet he was said to be charming and was often asked to speak at public ceremonies throughout the Midwest on topics both related to law and not.

Judge Caldwell was very active in civic affairs during his years in Arkansas, and is credited with sponsoring or influencing legislative reforms in the late 1870s and 1880s. His crusade for code pleading extended beyond the chambers of his courtroom. When a law school was established in Little Rock, Judge Caldwell took the chair of pleading and practice. From the lectern he tried to imbue his students with his desire to disregard technicalities and go to the merits of each case. He is credited as being the father of code pleading in Arkansas.[43]

Judge Caldwell also led the fight to get married women individual property rights. Under Arkansas law, as he first found it, when a woman married the husband acquired all title to her personal and real property as long as she lived. Nor did a married woman who happened to work have any right to her earnings. Judge Caldwell proposed and helped secure the passage of articles in the Constitutions of 1868 and 1874, which provided married women with absolute ownership of their separate property free from the control of husbands and their creditors.[44] Judge Caldwell also supported women's suffrage, although he was less successful in winning over the Arkansas Legislature on this point.[45]

Judge Caldwell authored Arkansas's homestead and personal property exemptions. When Judge Caldwell came to Arkansas there were little to no exemptions allowed to insolvent debtors. Judge Caldwell actively recommended and supported the homestead exemptions and personal property exemptions. Again, these exemptions were ultimately incorporated into the Constitutions of 1868 and 1874.[46]

Other opponents in Judge Caldwell's crusades were Arkansas usury and mortgage laws. The Arkansas Constitution of 1868 had forbidden the legislature from passing any law limiting interest rates. Judge Caldwell is credited with getting the original usury section put into the constitution of 1874.[47] Later, corporations sought to get around the constitution by adding brokerage fees and attorney fees and other items that had the same effect as interest rates. Again Judge Caldwell came to the citizens' rescue. In 1887, he prepared and lobbied for an act, which passed, that allowed debtors to bring suits to vacate usurious mortgages without having first to tender the principal and interest of the loan.[48]

In 1886, Judge Caldwell gave a speech before the Arkansas Bar Association called "The Relation of Debtor and Creditor" in which he railed against Arkansas and farm mortgage practices.[49] The speech is wonderful in its emotion and vigor. It was printed with a cover picture that depicts an old man with a cane, his wife, and their dog walking down the road. As they walk they pass a sign pointing in the direction they travel on which is printed "Poor Farm." In the background is the homestead being plucked up by a spindly-clawed hand labeled "mortgage." Below the picture is printed: "The Usual Fate of Those who Mortgage their Homestead." Judge Caldwell began his speech by recounting how Solomon and Caesar had reformed their laws that punished debtors, but Arkansas and much of the Anglo-American legal community operated under the assumption that founded the debtors prison—"that all creditors were honest, and all debtors dishonest."[50]

This was an assumption, Caldwell quickly noted, "The converse of which would probably be never the truth."[51] He then launched out on a tirade against the "Anaconda Mortgage" employed by the landlord or planter to enslave the tenant farmer and small farmers of Arkansas, requiring them to obtain all credit and conduct all trade with the mortgagee. He ended his speech by recommending that the state prohibit all encumbrances on the homestead, and modify the act allowing mortgages on crops so that farmers might mortgage only what they had left after providing for their family. This speech, followed by another made before the Drew County fair that same year, was reproduced in the papers in the state and sparked considerable public debate.[52] In 1887, the Arkansas Legislature amended part of the act allowing mortgages of crops, to forbid mortgaging of any crop beyond those planted that year.[53]

Judge Caldwell was also a temperance man and constantly spoke out against the evils of alcohol. Although he was generally compassionate on the district court, he was ruthless on moonshiners, especially those who chose to operate in dry counties.[54] He authored the Arkansas Liquor Trafficking Law said to be the best, or strictest, in the nation.[55] Caldwell's feelings about liquor came out in a case he decided in the Circuit Court for the Eastern District of Arkansas after he had become a circuit judge.[56] In this case, the defendant, an agent for the Excelsior Brewery Company, challenged the constitutionality of a United States statute that provided that intoxicating liquors in interstate commerce shall, upon arrival, be subject to the laws of the state. Judge Caldwell upheld the statute as an exercise of Congress's power to regulate interstate commerce. In his recount of Congress's desire to make original package houses—houses dealing directly in interstate commerce, subject to state law[57]—Caldwell says:

> Liquor imported in packages of all forms and sizes, but all original packages, was sold in these houses. In this way the retail traffic in liquor was practically established. . . . Peaceful and quiet communities from which the sale of liquor had been banished for years were suddenly afflicted with all the evils of the liquor traffic. The seats of learning were invaded by the original package vender [*sic*], and the youth of the state gathered there for instruction were corrupted and demoralized, and disorder, violence, and crime reigned, where only peace and order had been known before.[58]

Another civil reform Judge Caldwell undertook, but upon the request of others, was the task of certifying a digest of Arkansas statutes. In 1874, Edward Gantt published *Digest of the Statutes of Arkansas*[59] under the authority of the General Assembly. Caldwell was chosen to examine and approve the work as being authentic. Not only is this quite a testimonial to the General Assembly's and the legal community's perception of Judge Caldwell's ability, but it shows his reputation for impartiality. After all, it would seem most logical to get a state court judge to certify this type of work, and the fact that the legislature chose Caldwell shows he had something unique to add.

Judge Caldwell was as active in his courtroom as he was in his community. He hated what he perceived as injustice and oppression, especially under the law. In a memorandum written in his honor by the Little Rock Bar, the authors noted that:

> it might not be too much to say that on occasion he did not hesitate to stretch the judicial power to the limit—to defeat the operation of any rule of law, or practice, under which an advantage not consonant with his ideas of right and justice might be gained to the injury of a litigant.[60]

Judge Caldwell usually sat without a jury upon the stipulation of the parties because "the litigants knew that they would get from Judge Caldwell the same substantial justice which they hoped for at a jury's hands, and partly because his personality was so dominating that the jury was merely the mouthpiece of his views."[61] However, Judge Caldwell was a protector of jury trials and stated that trials by judge and jury are "immensely superior to any other mode of trial that the wit of man has ever yet devised, or is capable of devising."[62]

Judge Caldwell was active in asking questions of counsel and would often suggest corrections to defective pleadings. He would also ask questions of witnesses to seek the truth in determining their credibility.[63] He was reputed not to allow a lawyer's inexperience to lose a case with merit, as illustrated by the following anecdote:

> On one occasion, some years ago, Judge Yonley, a gentleman of ability and local distinction, with much ingenuity was about to defeat a good cause represented by a young adversary at the bar; but [Caldwell] came to the stripling's relief and saved him from disaster. Judge Yonley left the courtroom tearing his disheveled hair in a rage, and swearing in vociferous oaths that he would rather have Rufus Choate, Reverdy Johnson, and William M. Evarts as opponents in the trial of a cause before Judge Caldwell than one d—n fool stripling.[64]

Local attorneys regarded Judge Caldwell as being very polite and courteous to all counsel. He also had a practice of coming down from the bench, greeting counsel, and shaking hands. Moreover, when Judge

Caldwell served on the Court of Appeals for the Eighth Circuit, it is noted that after a lawyer from Arkansas had argued before the court, Judge Caldwell would always come down from the bench after argument and take the lawyer back to his chambers for a friendly talk.[65]

While serving on the district and circuit courts in the Eastern District of Arkansas, Judge Caldwell gained a reputation as a sound jurist. He was even asked to sit on circuit court panels in other districts. In 1876, he alone held a three-week session of the circuit court for the Eastern District of Missouri, and in 1880 held circuit court for the District of Kansas.[66]

Judge Caldwell's reputation as a jurist seems to be rooted in his notion that personal rights should prevail over property rights, and that the common laborer is the foundation of society. In his later years as a district judge, Caldwell developed several unique approaches to railroad receiverships that made him famous. The first of these practices was making claims for operating supplies preferential to bondholder's mortgages. He explained how he came to this practice, called "Coonskin Cap Law," in a response to a toast given to him at a Colorado Bar Association Meeting in the 1890s, which was later reproduced in its entirety in Volume 37 of the *American Law Review*.[67]

His response was essentially a story that began with a tale of a poor timber cutter living on the Mississippi River bottom making railroad ties for an Arkansas railroad company. The man worked for the railroad for four long years, but the railroad, always being short on cash, never fully paid him. Then the woodcutter became ill and was laid up for over a year. As soon as he recovered, he learned that the railroad was in receivership and he went to court to file his claim. The man appeared personally before the young Judge Caldwell wearing a "coon-skin cap, with the tail hanging down the back, coarse cotton shirt, and pants and shoes to correspond."[68] The cutter explained how he should be paid his claim because whenever he supplied wood to the steamship companies, he always received a lien superior to all mortgages. The judge knew that the Supreme Court had not found that such a rule applied to railroads, but of course, railroads were relatively new. While the timid judge had found some authority for treating claims for supplies preferentially when they had accrued within four months, he was willing to stretch this time out to six months only.

The short of the story is that the court did not grant the man his claim and the poor man hanged himself. Caldwell explained:

> Nothing is a lesson to us if it doesn't come too late. The specter of that man of honest toil hanging from that tree, the vision of that cap, and an uneasy and alarmed conscience, imposed upon that judge the burden of prayerfully inquiring whether the judgment that produced this awful tragedy was just, and upon making that inquiry he found that there was a close analogy between ships and railroads; that both were instruments of commerce; that neither could perform their functions or be of any utility to the public, or of any value as a security, unless they were kept running, and that they could not be kept running without labor, materials and supplies, that were not and could not be paid for at the time they were procured or purchased; and that every one taking a mortgage on such property knew this, and must therefore be held to have impliedly consented that such claims should have preference over his mortgage.[69]

He found that there was just as much law for saying that such claims were valid if they accrued within six years, as there was for saying that they must have accrued within six months; that the length of time depended on the length of the chancellor's foot; in a word, that all the law on the subject was judge-made law; and that he thereupon determined to measure out equity according to the length of his own foot—not a small one—instead of that of some other judge, and to make a little judge-made law himself, and he then and there made it a rule of his own court that no railroad receiver would be appointed except upon the condition that all claims for labor, supplies, and materials necessary to keep the road in operation, and all claims for damages resulting from its operation that were not barred by the statute of limitations, should have preference over mortgages. And this rule is what the toastmaster has been pleased to call the "Coon-skin Cap Law." This rule was without any precedent to support it, but it was sublimely just, according to Judge Caldwell. It was its own precedent, and it would be happy for mankind if all judicial precedents had the same everlasting and impregnable foundation. Since the adoption of that rule no citizen of Arkansas has had occasion to commit suicide for the same reason the "coon-skin cap man" did.

This explanation also gives us some notion of how Judge Caldwell saw the law—as an active vehicle of substantive justice. Under his view of the law, one needed no authority to do what was right. Receiverships were an equitable proceeding, and Judge Caldwell's philosophy seemed to echo greatly that "equity delights in doing justice and not just by halves."

Dow v. Memphis & L.R.R. Co.[70] is the first reported case in which we see "Coon-skin Cap Law" employed. This is the first case where Caldwell required, as a condition to the appointment, that parties requesting the appointment of the receivers agree to allow the receivers to pay preferentially all future claims of suppliers in cash. The appointment of a receiver in a suit to foreclose a mortgage was up to the chancellor's discretion. The practice was controversial.[71]

Although the Supreme Court upheld the general principle of a court's placing conditions upon the appointment of a receiver in *Fordick v. Schalls,* [72] twelve years later Justice Brewer harshly criticized the practice in *Kneeland v. American Loan & Trust Co.*[73] In dicta, which some members of the Eighth Circuit bar said was aimed specifically at Judge Caldwell,[74] Justice Brewer said:

> Because in a few specified and limited cases this court has declared that unsecured claims were entitled to priority over mortgage debts, an idea seems to have obtained that a court appointing a receiver . . . could rightfully burden the mortgaged property for the payment of any unsecured indebtedness. Indeed, we are advised that some courts have made the appointment of a receiver conditional upon the payment of all unsecured indebtedness in preference to the mortgage liens sought to be enforced. Can anything be conceived which more thoroughly destroys the sacredness of contract obligations?[75]

Another practice that Caldwell is credited with creating is the practice of allowing receivers to be sued at law in state courts, especially for torts committed by the railroads. He allowed plaintiffs to bring these suits without leave of court. The first case in which this is reported is *Dow.*[76] In *Dow,* the plaintiffs, as a condition to reappointment of a receiver, had to agree that the receiver would allow the plaintiff to bring tort actions against the railroad and that the receiver would pay all judgments against the railroad. In explaining his condition, Judge Caldwell noted:

> The general license to sue the receiver is given because it is desirable that the right of the citizen to sue in the local state courts, on the

> line of the road, should be interfered with as little as possible. It is doubtless convenient, and a saving and protection to the railroad company and its mortgage bondholders, to have the litigation growing out of the operation of a long line of railroad concentrated in a single court, and on the equity side of that court, where justice is administered without the intervention of a jury. But, in proportion as the railroad and its bondholders profit by such an arrangement, the citizen dealing with the receiver is subjected to inconvenience and expense, and he is deprived of the forum, and the right of trial by jury, to which, in every other case of legal cognizance, he has the right to appeal for redress.[77]

This procedure was also a controversial one. In 1887, however, Congress explicitly authorized federal courts to allow suits at law in receivership.[78]

Through these railroad receivership cases, Caldwell, as district court judge, developed a reputation for standing up against the railroads and their powerful bondholders—a reputation that continued beyond his service on the district court. Seymour Thompson, who would later write the treatises *Thompson on Negligence* and *Thompson on Corporations,* wrote in a law review article published in 1893:

> Mr. Circuit Judge Caldwell when Judge of the United States District Court for the Eastern District of Arkansas, and *ex officio* Circuit Judge, persistently refused to allow his court to go into the general railroad business, and granted receivers of railroads on a principle of necessity, and then, only upon equitable terms. . . . The Supreme Court approved his policy. One of the equitable conditions imposed by him on bondholders soliciting the appointment of a receiver, was that they should consent in advance, that the receiver might be sued in the State Court, and that they should appoint an agent within the jurisdiction, on whom the process of said court might be served. His decision in *Dow vs. The Memphis, etc., R. R. Co.* (20th Fed. Rep., 260), is one of the best judgments that has ever been delivered on the subject of railway receiverships. One cannot read it without acquiring the impression that if other Judges had pursued the same policy, the disciplinary Act of Congress, passed in 1887, authorizing actions against receivers of railroads appointed by the Federal Courts to be brought without obtaining leave of court, would not have become necessary. . . .
>
> One cannot read the decision of this eminent Judge without feeling regret that he has not long before this been transferred to a seat on the highest Federal bench. His long experience as a Federal

> Judge, his clear perception of legal principles, his strong sense of justice, his well-known firmness of character, and especially the entire absence of any unsteadiness in his judicial work, point to that place as his proper sphere.[79]

It is clear that Judge Caldwell's service on the district court bench had a great influence on Arkansas law and the rights and legal powers of Arkansans. However, the legal legacy of Judge Caldwell was not yet complete; for, as stated previously, he went on to serve as the first chief judge of the Eighth Circuit Court of Appeals.

III. United States Circuit Judge for the Eighth Circuit

When President Harrison offered Judge Caldwell the circuit judgeship for the Eighth Circuit on February 27, 1890, Caldwell did not immediately accept. Judge Caldwell had not solicited the position.[80] He was, however, chosen from a pool of at least twenty-seven nominees whom the Justice Department had screened. This pool included famous jurists such as Caldwell's brother in the Western District of Arkansas, Judge Parker, and his future brothers on the court of appeals, Walter Sanborn and Amos Thayer.[81] Again Justice Miller, who would pass away later that year, supported fellow Republican and Iowan Henry Caldwell. Some people also seemed to think that Caldwell's wartime friend, the man who took his place as colonel of the Third Iowa Cavalry and who was secretary of the interior to Harrison, John W. Noble, had some part in the nomination.[82]

Apparently, Judge Caldwell was hesitant to leave his home and live the life of a "tramp" wandering all over the vast territory that made up the Eighth Judicial Circuit.[83] At that time the Eighth Circuit included one-third of the territory of the United States and had a population of over 11 million people.[84] As mentioned earlier, Caldwell had some experience with the size of the circuit because he had served as a circuit judge by assignment in other districts. Caldwell, however, accepted the position and was sworn in as United States circuit judge for the Eighth Circuit on March 13, 1890.

Judge Caldwell spent his first year as a circuit judge traveling throughout the circuit and holding court in various districts. On March 3, 1891, however, the Circuit Court of Appeals Act became law, and

Judge Caldwell's duties changed drastically. The Circuit Court of Appeals Act of 1891 came about as an attempt to relieve the overburdened federal judicial system, especially the Supreme Court, from a crushing workload. The Act of 1869 had intended for circuit courts to have a panel of two judges, one being either the circuit judge or circuit justice, and the other a district judge. By the late 1880s, none of these ideals was met—circuit riding by the justices had for all intents and purposes ceased, and eight-ninths of all cases in circuit courts were heard by single judges, almost always district judges. The situation was worse in the Eighth and Ninth Circuits, principally because of the vast geographical areas. The problem was exacerbated by the circuit court's appellate jurisdiction; while circuit courts were the primary trial courts in the federal system, they were also the appellate courts for district courts. As a result, it was common for a single district judge to sit on the circuit court and hear an appeal from his own decision in the district court. An ABA report made in 1890 characterized the situation as follows: "Such an appeal is not from Phillip drunk to Phillip sober, but from Phillip sober to Phillip intoxicated with the vanity of a matured opinion and doubtless also a published decision."[85] This problem was compounded by the fact that the decisions of the circuit court were final in all cases involving less than $5,000.

A district judge alone in a district, like Judge Caldwell, who held circuit court in his district, enjoyed an enormous amount of power. The Act of 1891 created a circuit court of appeals to hear cases on appeal from the district and circuit courts. The primary impulse had been to relieve the overburdened Supreme Court, and the act transferred cases from the Supreme Court docket to these new courts of appeals. The Supreme Court, however, retained direct appellate jurisdiction over particular types of cases.[86] The circuit courts lost their appellate jurisdiction but remained, along with the district court, a court of first instance. The act created a second circuit judge for each circuit and designated that the courts of appeals would be made up of three-judge panels with one district judge sitting with the circuit judges.

The Court of Appeals for the Eighth Circuit was organized in St. Louis, Missouri, on June 16, 1891, with Circuit Justice Brewer and Judge Caldwell attending.[87] The court heard its first case on October 12, 1891. Judge Caldwell presided over the three-judge panel, which also included District Judges Amos M. Thayer of St. Louis and Moses Hallet of Denver.

The Eighth Circuit was the busiest circuit in the country between

1892 and 1901 (see table 1). Luckily, Chief Judge Caldwell was joined by Walter H. Sanborn of Minnesota on April 4, 1892. The workload on these two was so great, however, that in 1894 Congress authorized a third circuit judge position for this circuit. On August 20, 1894, Amos Madden Thayer of Missouri joined the Court of Appeals for the Eighth Circuit. About this same time, the court began to hold an annual spring term in St. Paul, Minnesota, in addition to the fall term in St. Louis. In 1900, the court would add a third term in Denver, Colorado.

Hearing 150 plus cases in addition to sitting on circuit court (trial) panels obviously kept Judge Caldwell busy. In his twelve years on the court of appeals he wrote 306 opinions, thirty dissents, and one concurring opinion. In addition, he wrote twelve reported cases on the circuit court.[88]

TABLE 1. Court of Appeals Caseload 1892–1901

ALL CIRCUITS					EIGHTH CIRCUIT			
YEAR	NEW CASES DOCKETED FOR YEAR PENDING JUNE 30	CASES DISPOSED	CASES PENDING JUNE 30	NEW CASES APPEALED TO SUPREME COURT	DOCKETED FOR YEAR ENDING JUNE 30	CASES DISPOSED	CASES PENDING JUNE 30	CASES APPEALED TO SUPREME COURT
1892	841	403	438	207*	120*	87		
1893	704	542	438	29	163*	145*	99*	17*
1894	766	684	510	21	182*	156*	125*	9*
1895	866	870	510	43	170	189*	112*	15
1896	815	824	501	56	157*	152	117*	21*
1897	775	729	547	33	151*	133*	135*	10
1898	806	833	521	35	127	182*	81	5
1899	907	856	572	38	193*	147	127*	8
1900	952	917	607	41	174*	191*	110*	11
1901	901	937	571	46	168*	165*	113*	21

NOTE: *Asterisk denotes category in which the Eighth Circuit led the other circuit courts of appeals. The attorney general's reports throughout the period are not necessarily accurate since they were based on incomplete reports from other circuits.[89]

Ironically, Judge Caldwell's dissents are the court of appeals opinions that generated the most commentary. One of these dissents was from a majority opinion written by Judge Sanborn in *McMaster v. New York Life Insurance Co.*[90] The United States Supreme Court heard the case on writ of certiorari and reversed the court of appeals, adopting the grounds articulated by Judge Caldwell.[91]

The case essentially came down to which terms would prevail—the express terms of an insurance policy or the terms of the insured's application that were later changed without his knowledge or consent. The insured had bought several life insurance policies that could be renewed annually. Upon delivery and payment of premiums for these policies, the insured asked whether the policies would insure him up to thirteen months from that day, December 18, 1893. The agent replied that they would. The buyer then took the policies and stored them without reading them. If he had read them he would have seen that the agent had changed the terms of the preprinted policy, so that renewal payments were due on December 12, 1894. Since the policy offered a grace period of one month, the terms of the policy provided that the insured was covered thirteen months from December 12, 1893, not December 18, as the agent had promised. The insured did not pay a premium in 1894, and he died January 18, 1895. The administrator of his estate brought an action to collect on the policy in the Circuit Court for the Northern District of Iowa, which, after making findings of fact, dismissed the action. The plaintiff then appealed to the Court of Appeals for the Eighth Circuit.

Judge Sanborn, writing for the court, affirmed the circuit court. He found that the terms of the written policy were plain and unambiguous and therefore previous parol (extraneous) evidence could not be brought in to change those terms. The application contained proposed terms to which the insurance company was free to object in part or entirely. It did reject one term, which insurer failed to note because he failed to read the policy. Judge Thayer concurred in a separate opinion reasoning that the provisions of the policy were clear, and that the insurer is presumed in law to have consented to those terms by his acceptance and retention of the policy.

Judge Caldwell, of course, dissented, arguing characteristically:

> The right decision of this case does not depend upon any technicality of law. It is a case in which common sense and common honesty and legal sense and legal honesty are at one. It arises upon a contract of life insurance, which must be interpreted according

> to the settled canons for the construction of such instruments, and the determination of the rights of the parties thereunder. In every contract of insurance, the law prescribes to each party the observance of the strictest integrity and truthfulness. Insurance law, when rightly expounded, is always in harmony with honesty and sound morality. At the very beginning of insurance law in England there was infused into it, through the influence of the civil law, a different spirit from that which prevailed in other branches of the common law. Neither the maxim caveat emptor nor its spirit has found a lodgment in the law of insurance.[92]

Judge Caldwell continued by reasoning that the terms of the contract were formed when the defendant received the insured's application. The insurance agent's subsequent insertion of the challenged clause was an illegal act, if not fraud. The court should recall that where the construction of an insurance contract is doubtful, it should be settled in favor of the insured. In closing, Judge Caldwell launched into an attack on the rule created by the majority:

> The rule of the Court obliterates all distinction between truth and falsehood in the dealings of men. It establishes the doctrine that the law has no partiality for truth, and no prejudice against falsehood. It applauds and approves an end obtained by falsehood and fraud, as a high exhibition of business tact and skill, and reserves its censures for the innocent and trusting victim of the fraud, because, forsooth, he accepted as true the word of the man he was dealing with; and it permits the party who made the false representation to avail himself of his own falsehood, to the prejudice of the man who trusted him. It makes confidence and bunco games respectable, and elevates the sharper who practices them to a plane of equality with honest and reputable business men. It is a rule at which all rascaldom will rejoice, and all honest and trustful men take alarm. It stimulates falsehood and deceit by the grant of impunity, and destroys confidence among men. It converts written contracts, which were designed to prevent fraud, into the most powerful agencies for the perpetration and protection of fraud. In this case the insurance company, in effect, receives a reward of $5,000 for its falsehood and fraud, and a penalty of $5,000 is imposed upon the beneficiary named in the policy, because the insured trusted in the truth of the company's representations.[93]

> It is undoubtedly true that a written contract is presumed to express the agreement of the parties, but this is not a conclusive presumption, and the exceptions to the rule are as well understood and clearly defined as the rule itself. No writing, however solemn, can be made a vehicle for fraud, or convert a mistake into verity. The case at bar, upon the facts found, falls within the well-defined exception to the rule, as shown by all the authorities. No apology is made for demonstrating the truth of this assertion by somewhat extended quotations from controlling authorities.[94]

The case was heard by the United States Supreme Court on writ of certiorari. In an opinion written by Chief Justice Fuller, the court reversed the court of appeals and held for the plaintiff, essentially upon those grounds stressed by Judge Caldwell.

Judge Caldwell's most famous case on the court of appeals was also a dissent and would gain him further fame as a protector of labor and a preserver of jury trials. *Hopkins v. Oxley Stave Co.*[95] was an appeal of an interlocutory injunction granted by the Circuit Court for the District of Kansas.[96] The court had enjoined the local Coopers Union from boycotting the products of the company unless it discontinued the use of hooping machines. Judge Thayer, writing for the court of appeals, affirmed the lower court. The court of appeals was not persuaded by the defendants' argument that their acts were legitimate, because they sought to prevent the future decline of wages and gain more employment for coopers. It found that the Oxley Stave Company did not threaten to decrease wages, and only one member of the combination worked there. It then held that the group was a conspiracy formed to incite violence and could be enjoined by the circuit court.

Judge Caldwell dissented in a lengthy and spirited opinion that espoused the right of workers to assemble peaceably. He began the dissent by attacking the court's characterization of the Coopers' actions as a "conspiracy," a term he claimed was wrought with evil purpose:

> From the earliest times the word has been used to denote a highly criminal or evil purpose. Thus, in Acts xxiii. 12, 13, it is said: "And, when it was day, certain of the Jews banded together, and bound themselves under a curse, saying that they would neither eat nor drink till they had killed Paul. And they were more than forty which had made this conspiracy."

☆ ☆ ☆

> The "conspiracy" charged upon the defendants consisted, then, in the Coopers' Union and the Trades Assembly agreeing not "to purchase or use any commodities that were packed in machine-hooped tierces and barrels, which came in competition with the hand-hooped barrels," which were the product of their labor (and the bill charges no more); and the "threats" consisted in giving the complainant and certain packing houses formal notice of this purpose.[97]

Caldwell challenged the court's jurisdiction over the matter even assuming the majority's characterization of the gathering by stating, "a federal court of chancery cannot exercise the police powers of the state of Kansas, and take upon itself either to enjoin or to punish the violation of the criminal laws of that state."[98] He then launched into a theme we have seen before with railroad receiverships, the threat he saw emanating from a growing tendency to resolve legal matters on the equity side of the court because of a growing mistrust of the jury. Noting the provisions in Article III and Amendment V preserving the right of jury trial, he wrote:

> Undoubtedly, it is the right of the people to alter or abolish their existing government, "and," in the language of the Declaration of Independence, "to institute a new government, laying its foundations on such principles, and organizing its powers in such form as to them shall seem most likely to effect their safety and happiness." It is competent for the people of this country to abolish trial by jury, and confer the entire police powers of the state and nation on federal judges, to be administered through the agency of injunctions and punishment for contempts; but the power to do this resides with the whole people, and it is to be exercised in the mode provided by the constitution. It cannot be done by the insidious encroachments of any department of the government. Our ancestors, admonished by the lessons taught by English history, saw plainly that the right of trial by jury was absolutely essential to preserve the rights and liberties of the people, and it was the knowledge of this fact that caused them to insert in the constitution the peremptory and mandatory provisions on the subject which we have quoted.[99]

He then went on to compare this case with that of William Perm and William Mead, noting that in that case it was the jury's determination not to bow to the desires of the court that kept a travesty of justice from occurring. A large amount, but small proportion, of this dissent is provided below because of the insight it affords to us of Caldwell:

> This proposition, that it is unlawful for men to do collectively what they may do, without wrong, individually, was enunciated more than a century and a half ago, when all manner of association and cooperation among men, offensive to the king, or not in the interest of despotic power or the ruling classes, or not approved by the judges, were declared by the courts to be criminal conspiracies. It was promulgated at a time "when," in the language of Mr. Justice Harlan in his opinion in *Robertson v. Baldwin*, 165 U.S. 288, 17 Sup. Ct. 333, "no account was taken of a man as man, when human life and human liberty were regarded as of little value, and when the powers of government were employed to gratify the ambition and pleasure of despotic rulers, rather than promote the welfare of the people," and when laborers had no rights their employers or the courts were bound to respect. The idea of the power of men in association has always been abhorrent to despots, and to those who wish to oppress their fellow men, because its free exercise is fatal to despotism and oppression. The strength it imparts carries its own protection. In all ages those who seek to deprive the people of their rights justify their action by ancient and obsolete precedents, and by coining definitions suited to their ends. . . . What each individual member of a labor organization may lawfully do, acting singly, becomes an unlawful conspiracy when done by them collectively. Singly, they may boycott; collectively, they cannot. The individual boycott is lawful, because it can accomplish little or nothing. The collective boycott is unlawful, because it might accomplish something. People can only free themselves from oppression by organized force. . . . The doctrine compels every man to be a stranger in action to every other man. This is contrary to the constitution and genius of our government. It is a doctrine abhorrent to freemen. It is in hostility to a law of man's nature, which prompts him to associate with his fellows for his protection, defense, and improvement. Under its operation every religious, political, or social organization in the country may be enjoined from combined action, if their religious faith or political creed or practice is obnoxious to the judge. It was originally designed for this very purpose.
>
> . . . The asserted rule has no boundaries or limitations other than the chancellor's discretion. Whatever combined action he

wills to permit is lawful. Whatever combined action he wills to prevent is a conspiracy.

. . . While laborers, by the application to them of the doctrine we are considering, are reduced to individual action, it is not so with the forces arrayed against them. A corporation is an association of individuals for combined action; trusts are corporations combined together for the very purpose of collective action and boycotting; and capital, which is the product of labor, is in itself a powerful collective force. Indeed, according to this supposed rule, every corporation and trust in the country is an unlawful combination; for while its business may be of a kind that its individual members, each acting for himself, might lawfully conduct, the moment they enter into a combination to do that same thing by their combined effort the combination becomes an unlawful conspiracy. But the rule is never so applied.

. . . It cannot be the law that the men and women who do the work of the world, and who produce its wealth, have no rights against the wealth they create, and no right to prefer and promote by lawful and peaceful means the sale of the products of their labor, to secure for themselves continued employment. The "irreparable damage" suffered in business by a vanquished competitor at the hands of his successful rival constitutes no cause of action, either at law or in equity. It is the result of the law of competition, to which all men are subject. They take their chances, and must abide the result, whether it bring fortune or failure.

. . . All capital seeks to increase its power by combination, and to that end assumes the form of corporations and trusts. The plaintiff in this case is a corporation. It represents a number of persons associated together for the very purpose of combined and collective action. Many of these combinations are on a gigantic scale. Their power and influence are well nigh irresistible. They are the employers of the great mass of the laborers. They are formed solely for pecuniary profit, and know no other law than that which promotes their pecuniary interests. They defy all social restraints that would have a tendency to lessen their dividends. What the stockholders want is more dividends, and the best manager is the man who will make them the largest. The struggle is constant between the laborers, whose labor produces the dividends, and those who enjoy them. The manager is tempted to reduce wages to increase dividends, and the laborers resist the reduction, and

> demand living wages. Sometimes the struggle reaches the point of open rupture. When it does, the only weapons of defense the laborers can appeal to is the strike or the boycott, or both. These weapons they have an undoubted right to use, so long as they use them in a peaceable and orderly manner. . . . Let the person and property of every citizen be securely protected by fixed laws, and speedy punishment follow the commission of crime. Let the constitutional mode of trial remain inviolate. The necessity for this is illustrated in this case. No American jury could be found who would say these defendants were guilty of a "conspiracy," or of making "threats" to injure any one. Like the jury in the Penn Case, they would say, "Guilty of refusing to purchase the plaintiffs barrels and the commodities packed in them, only," and the common sense of all mankind would respond that that creates neither criminal nor civil liability on any one. The decree of the circuit court should be reversed, and the case remanded, with instructions to dismiss the bill.[100]

The case was not reviewed by the Supreme Court. Judge Caldwell's dissent did, however, catch the attention of labor organizations, who went so far as to try to get him nominated for the presidency.[101] He was a Republican from the days of the party's inception and continued to be one all of his life.

This was not the first time Henry Caldwell had been mentioned in national politics. In 1896, he had been mentioned as a possible Republican presidential and vice presidential candidate.[102] That year the *American Law Review* printed an article by Caldwell on railroad receiverships and also wrote a sketch of the judge that seems to be a political endorsement of him. The article compares Caldwell to Lincoln and informs the readers that there is a movement under way to nominate Caldwell for the presidential (Republican) ticket:

> In stature, mind and heart, Judge Caldwell greatly resembles Abraham Lincoln. Like Mr. Lincoln, he stands at the remarkable height of six feet four. Like Mr. Lincoln, he carries on his tall frame a very large and massive head. Like Mr. Lincoln, he comes from Virginia ancestors. Like Mr. Lincoln, he has remained, through every elevation of official station, in touch and in sympathy with the common people. So extensive have the public acquired a knowledge of his character in this respect, that there is at the

> present time a strong, though quiet movement on foot, to make him a candidate for the presidency; and there are well informed politicians who do not hesitate to predict that if those who favor the free coinage of silver put in the field a separate candidate, Judge Caldwell will be the man.[103]

The judge was never one to hold his tongue, so his political opinions were well known. The article mentioned above notes that Judge Caldwell was at that time in favor of the free coinage of silver. He wanted Congress to pass a law providing that all debts be dischargeable in either silver or gold and making void all contracts by which the debtor waives this option. He firmly believed that the general government should supply only paper currency.[104] Finally, the article notes that Caldwell "is in favor of the passage and enforcement of just and wholesome laws, protecting the people against monopolies and trusts, and controlling to this end, the exercise of the corporate franchises."[105] Similarly, a Chicago politician wrote a personal letter stating the following:

> There was a gentleman in my office to-day, who has been in correspondence with a number of prominent men in the West on political matters in general; and he tells me that in every instance Judge Caldwell's name was the one name placed above all others. The silent mutterings that are now abroad in our land are surely going to break forth by the time the St. Louis convention comes together.[106]

Judge Caldwell did not, however, receive the Republican presidential nomination. One commentator notes that the very things that made Caldwell popular with the rank and file of the party made him unpopular with the party leadership, especially in the East.[107]

In 1892, the Republican Party nominated William McKinley and adopted a platform endorsing a single gold standard. This put Caldwell at odds with his party. In fact, Judge Caldwell's support of a double silver/gold standard was well known enough to attract the attention of the Democrats, and it seems that William Jennings Bryan was interested in having Judge Caldwell on his ticket.[108] Edward Stiles, in a chapter on Caldwell in his *Recollections and Sketches of Notable Lawyers and Public Men of Early Iowa*, quotes "the press of the time" on the subject:

> The Associated Press correspondent called on Judge Caldwell today and said to him: "An Associated Press dispatch from Minneapolis

> is authority for the statement that you have declined to permit the use of your name for Vice President. Is the statement in the above dispatch true?"

The judge replied:

> Yes. Several weeks ago I received letters from some of the leading and influential members of the party intimating that it might become desirable to nominate me for Vice President. I paid no attention to the previous loose talk on the subject, but learning from these letters that the matter of my candidacy was assuming somewhat of a serious aspect, I immediately advised these gentlemen by letter that I could not under any circumstances consent to the use of my name for that position. A brief extract from one of these letters will disclose my reason. "No federal judge should become a candidate for any political office and continue to hold his judicial office. It would subject him to merited criticism, and impair his influence and usefulness as a judge. Moreover, I esteem the office of United States Circuit Judge of equal dignity with that of Vice President, and of more practical importance and authority. The Vice President has nothing on his mind except the state of the President's health, and nothing to do but to be the guest of honor at big dinners that kill. He is more ornamental than useful. The position would not suit me."[109]

It is interesting that Caldwell did not seem to object to the party affiliation. Perhaps he split off from the Grand Old Party for good.

Some sources say that Judge Caldwell was also considered for the Supreme Court of the United States, but there is much less documentation on this rumor. Theodore Fetter, in his *A History of the United States Court of Appeals for the Eighth Circuit*, asserts that both Presidents Cleveland and Harrison considered appointing Caldwell to the Supreme Court.[110] In 1915, *Case and Commentary* published an article on Judge Caldwell that described him as "famed in the judicial and political world as the only man who refused an appointment to the office of Chief Justice of the United States Supreme Court because he felt himself unfitted for the task."[111] Later in the article the author elaborates:

> Judge Caldwell was the principal in one of the political secrets that stirred the nation. Because of his great ability and his high standing in the South, Judge Caldwell was selected by President Cleveland

> to become chief justice of the United States Supreme Court, and a representative of the President called on the judge to ask him if he would accept. To the amazement of the political world, Judge Caldwell refused the appointment, and gave as his reason the simple statement that he felt he was unfitted for the office, that he did not have the proper mental equipment and training.[112]

We are unable to confirm the account with another source. Yet no matter how accurate one finds the article in *Case and Commentary*, it is obvious that Judge Caldwell's homespun populist philosophy and his extreme sense of fairness struck chords with people all over the nation and in both parties.

On June 2, 1903, Judge Caldwell, writing from his summer home in Wagon Wheel Gap, Colorado, tendered his resignation to President Roosevelt.[113] The president, in a letter dated June 8, replied:

> Sir: It is with sincere regret that your resignation as United States Circuit Judge for the Eighth Circuit, to take effect June 4, 1903, is hereby accepted as tendered.
>
> I desire to take this occasion to congratulate you upon your long and faithful service upon the United States bench with such distinguished usefulness, and to assure you of the high esteem which your ability and integrity have always commanded. The impartial administration of law and justice which has marked your judicial career should bring a serene satisfaction to you in your remaining years which I trust will be many and full of health and happiness.
>
> Sincerely yours,
> Theodore Roosevelt[114]

Judge Caldwell's health had been declining. Also, the wear and tear of moving from St. Paul to Denver to St. Louis every year, and occasionally sitting on circuit courts throughout the circuit, began to take its toll on the judge despite the addition of a fourth circuit judge.[115] In fact, many people had believed that he was going to retire a year earlier when he became seventy, but he held out another year.[116]

Judge Caldwell retired on full pay ($7,500 per year)[117] and with the longest term of active service on the federal bench—thirty-nine years—a record he took to his grave in 1915.[118] After a brief sojourn in the tropics to get rid of a spell of grippe, he briefly returned to Wagon Wheel Gap and then moved permanently to Los Angeles, California. There he spent the rest of his life reading and tending to his garden. While there, he was approached by people from the East in the hope of getting him to represent them, but he refused. It is said that he was once even offered $50,000 to go to Kansas and defend a corporation. Again, he refused.[119]

In his eighty-second year, 1914, Caldwell made a trip back to what he considered his real home—Little Rock, Arkansas—to celebrate his sixtieth wedding anniversary. The City of Little Rock greeted "the man who captured it" as one of their own, claiming that for forty years he was the "most prominent citizen of Little Rock."[120] However, Judge Caldwell went back to California, where on February 15, 1915, he passed away at the age of eighty-three. He left behind a widow, a son, two daughters, four grandchildren, three great-grandchildren, and forty-seven years of public service. On February 20, Colonel John M. Moree, Judge Jacob Trieber, Fay Hempstead, W. W. Dickerson, George B. Rose, D. H. Cantrell, W. P. Field, and Durand Whipple carried a large casket to a site in Oakland Cemetery in Little Rock. There lies Judge Henry Clay Caldwell, United States district and circuit judge, and colonel, United States Army.

CHAPTER 5

John Apps Williams

1890–1900

Henry Woods

JOHN APPS WILLIAMS, Judge Henry Clay Caldwell's successor on the Eastern District bench in 1890, was born May 1, 1835, in Remsen, New York, but moved, while a youth, to Waukesha County, Wisconsin. He was a merchant in Delafield, Wisconsin, in 1860 and served as clerk of the Waukesha County Court in 1861. When the Civil War began, he raised a company and was elected captain in the Twenty-Eighth Wisconsin Infantry, serving from 1861 to 1865. Williams mustered out at Pine Bluff, Arkansas, where he decided to settle and enter the law practice. He formed a partnership in 1866 with Ed W. Martin of Pine Bluff. Later law partners included Richard H. Stanford, W. E. Hemingway, John M. Clayton, who was assassinated during a contested congressional campaign, and M. A. Austin.[1]

Williams was elected as a delegate from Jefferson County to the Arkansas Constitutional Convention of 1874, the convention that formulated and adopted the constitution that is still in force in the state. Shortly afterward, he was selected judge for the Eleventh Judicial Circuit Court of Arkansas, comprised of Jefferson, Arkansas, Lincoln, and Desha Counties. He resigned this position in 1882 to reenter the practice of law.[2]

John Apps Williams. *Courtesy United States District Court for the Eastern District of Arkansas.*

In September of 1890, President Benjamin Harrison nominated Williams as judge for the United States District Court for the Eastern District of Arkansas. He succeeded Judge Henry Clay Caldwell, who had been appointed judge for the United States Circuit Court for the Eighth Circuit. The United States Senate confirmed Williams on September 22, 1890, and he took the oath of office, administered by Judge Caldwell, on October 6, 1890.[3]

Judge Williams was prominent as a Republican campaign orator and was especially influential during the period of Radical Reconstruction in Arkansas. Although he was a diligent partisan in politics, he was able to maintain pleasant personal relationships with prominent Democrats. He was a man of expansive personality and was much in demand as a toastmaster at banquets.[4]

Judge Williams published fifteen opinions, most dealing with routine matters of little precedential value. One decision, however, was especially noteworthy. It involved title to land that comprised the business and much of the residential property in Hot Springs, as well as the entire Hot Springs National Park. In *Muse v. Arlington Hotel Co.*,[5] the plaintiff claimed this property based on succession to a Spanish land grant made in 1788 to Don Juan Filhiot. In the Louisiana Purchase Treaty of 1803 with France, the United States had agreed to recognize all valid land grants. Judge Williams rejected the plaintiff's claim in a lengthy and scholarly opinion. He first noted that Spanish land grants were governed by regulations promulgated by Governor O'Reilly in the Province of Louisiana in 1770. These regulations provided that title would not be confirmed in the grantee until a survey of the grant was conducted in a particular manner. Williams held that the survey was not so conducted and the land grant was, therefore, void. He advanced, as an additional basis for voiding the claim, an Act of Congress of June 1, 1870, known as the "Hot Springs Act." The act gave all persons claiming title to the "Hot Springs Reservation" an opportunity to institute claims against the United States in the Court of Claims. The suits, however, must be filed within three years or they would be forever barred. The claimants in *Muse* had never filed such a suit. Judge Williams also found that the United States had purchased the property from the Indian tribe that had previously occupied it. His final ground for dismissing the claim was that the predecessors in title to the present claimant had instituted a suit under an 1824 act. That suit was dismissed for noncompliance with an order to produce the original papers.

C. F. Simmons Medicine Co. v. Simmons[6] was another interesting case. The defendant manufactured and sold a medicine to which he gave a name similar to the name of the complainant's medicine, including the name of the inventor. Defendant Simmons placed on the wrappers of his medicine a picture of a bust and an autographed signature, similar to signs that had long been used by the complainant's medicine and which were familiar among an ignorant class of purchasers. He issued directives that were almost a literal copy of the complainant's and he published a card in which he described himself as the son and successor of the inventor of the complainant's medicine. Judge Williams held that the defendant was guilty of unfair competition, which he enjoined. He held that the medicines of the defendant "were so dressed by him with the intent to deceive the public and lead the ignorant class of the purchasers . . . to believe that they were purchasing complainant's medicines, which had been established for over fifty (50) years and had become well and favorably known to the purchasers."

In re Massey[7] reflected the turbulent politics in the South after the Civil War. With respect to an election in Conway County, Judge Williams held that the laws of the United States concerning elections at which congressmen are elected are paramount. The judge wrote that Mansfield's *Digest Arkansas*, which provided that "the judges of elections shall securely envelop all the ballots which may have been received under seal and return the same to the clerk of the proper county, which in no event shall be opened except in the case of a contested election," cannot be held to justify the clerk's refusal to produce the ballots before a United States grand jury, pending an investigation into alleged violations of federal laws.

Judge Williams, as a staunch defender of federal power, rendered two significant tax decisions. *Humes v. City of Little Rock*[8] involved selling trading stamps that were redeemable by the seller in merchandise at their face value. The stamps were given to cash customers as a premium. This was a lawful and legitimate vocation, not injurious to the public. Williams ruled that a city ordinance imposing a license tax of $50.00 per week on such occupation was void as unreasonable and an infringement upon the constitutional liberty of the citizens.

In re Rozelle[9] was another tax case. Judge Williams held that a municipal ordinance that imposed a license tax on every merchandise broker who maintained a warehouse or office within the city limits was void when applied to a broker whose sole business was making contracts by sample for the sale and delivery of merchandise to citizens of the state. At the time the contracts were made the property belonged to citizens of other states and was situated in other states. Further, the tax on the brokers involved interstate commerce and contravened the provision of the federal Constitution that vested power to regulate such commerce exclusively in Congress.

In a number of published opinions, Judge Williams only stated well-settled legal principles. For instance, *U.S. v. Niemeyer*[10] consisted solely of his charge to the jury in a case involving illegal timber cutting on public land. In *Gordon v. Jackson*,[11] he ruled that an action at law in ejectment, and not an action to quiet title in equity, was proper to try plaintiff's title and remove defendant from land claimed by plaintiff. In *Farmers' Loan & Trust Co. v. Stuttgart & A.R.R. Co.*,[12] he found that a mortgage given by a railroad was superior to a lien for the later purchase of rails.

The following rulings illustrate other types of cases Judge Williams heard. When an injunction stayed an action, sureties on the bond were responsible for the entire penalty and did not receive credit for money paid on the judgment when the unpaid balance on the judgment exceeded the amount of the bond penalty.[13] The one-year statute of limitations for special actions on the case applied to an action brought against the directors of a national bank under Revised Statute 5239.[14] Proof was insufficient to establish that homestead rights were surrendered by writing between the lines of the instrument after execution of the mortgage and acknowledgment.[15]

Several of Judge Williams's decisions reflected the mores of his time and would be decided differently today. He held, for example, that a mortgage was void because it was executed on Sunday in violation of Arkansas statutes.[16] In *Franz v. Wahl*,[17] Williams permitted removal of a proceeding to probate a will from state to federal court. Removal was justified, he wrote, because the appellant "cannot get justice in the state courts because of the local prejudice and undue influence of the proponent of the will." In *Little Rock & M.R. Co., v. St. Louis, I.M. & S. Ry.*

Co.,[18] Judge Williams held that a railroad company was not required by the Interstate Commerce Act to furnish to competing carriers equal facilities for the interchange of traffic when equal facilities involved the use of track by such carriers. He continued that the company may still permit such use by one carrier to the entire exclusion of the others.

Williams served ten years on the federal bench. He died suddenly and unexpectedly of heart failure on July 7, 1900, while vacationing in Manitou Springs, Colorado. His wife and one son, Weatherford, survived him. Williams was buried in Oakland Cemetery in Little Rock, Arkansas, on July 12, 1900.[19] His obituary in the *Pine Bluff Graphic*[20] stated that:

> He was an able judge with a heart as kind and tender as that of a woman. The members of the bar here and throughout the old eleventh circuit were all his personal friends, and the same is true of the lawyers in his federal district. He was possessed of fine judiciary attainments and great strength of mind. In disposition, he was blessed with a lovely character. He did not harbor malice against one who had done him a wrong and was overflowing with gratitude to one who had been his friend.

CHAPTER 6

Jacob Trieber

1901–27

Gerald W. Heaney

Prologue

On July 26, 1900, President William McKinley appointed Jacob Trieber of Helena, Arkansas, to a recess appointment as United States district judge for the Eastern District of Arkansas. He was renominated in December and confirmed and commissioned the following January. That he deserved the appointment was conceded by Republicans and Democrats alike. He was a man of intelligence, compassion, and integrity, a brilliant lawyer with a reputation for hard work, an active, committed Republican with an unequaled record of service to the party and, most of all, an Arkansan who worked on every worthwhile civic project

This article was prepared for and first published by the *University of Arkansas at Little Rock Law Review* in Volume 8, Issue 3 and is reproduced with its permission. The article was originally titled "Jacob Trieber: Lawyer, Politician, Judge." Further information about the *UALR Law Review* is available at www.ualr.edu/lawreview. The author gratefully acknowledges the Adler-Rosecan Foundation, which made possible the research efforts of Melanie R. Carlson and Henry G. Watkins III, students at the University of Arkansas at Little Rock School of Law. He also acknowledges J. Marshall Trieber, Carolyn LeMaster, and the Arkansas History Commission for the valuable information they provided; his secretaries, Elda E. Ignatius and Mary L. Bibbey; and his law clerks, Gary R. Ostos-Irwin, Colleen V. Short, Ann L. Iijima, and Dean A. Rindy, for their assistance in research and writing.

Jacob Trieber. *Courtesy United States District Court for the Eastern District of Arkansas.*

at the state and local level. The appointment was, however, a miracle of no small proportions: he was a Prussian immigrant of modest means, with no college or law school training, a member of a two-man law firm in a small Arkansas town, and a Jew aspiring to a position that no Jew in the history of the United States had held and in a state where the Jewish voting population was minuscule. But appointed he was, and the appointment brought credit to President McKinley and to the political and bar leaders who supported him. The appointment was particularly well received by the general populace, who were pleased that for the first time since the Civil War, one of their own, rather than a northerner, had been named to this important position.

Jacob Trieber served as judge for twenty-seven years and became one of the nation's most distinguished jurists and renowned constitutional scholars. Perhaps his most significant opinion came in 1903 in the infamous *Whitecapping* (Ku Klux Klan) case in which he became the first judge to squarely hold that federal law protects blacks from racial discrimination in employment. The Supreme Court reversed him, paving the way for decades of discrimination by holding that federal law provides blacks with no such protection. Judge Trieber's view was vindicated sixty-five years later, in 1968, when the Supreme Court overruled its *Whitecapping* opinion. The article that follows highlights Jacob Trieber's career as a lawyer, a politician, and a judge, and examines some of his more important opinions.

Raschkow to Helena (1853–76)

Morris and Blume Trieber found conditions improving in the tiny village of Raschkow, Prussia (now Germany), by 1868. Nevertheless, it was in that year that they decided to leave. Immigration to America would not be easy, but after months of talking, praying, and worrying, they were firm in their resolve: their youngest son, Jacob, would grow up as an American.

The decision was a difficult one. Morris and Blume had strong and long-standing ties to their community and country. They had a good home in the village of Raschkow. Blume's father, David Brodeck, and his father before him had been respected rabbis and community leaders. The Trieber family's religious roots and exemplary living brought them the friendship and respect of their neighbors. Their wholesale linen business in nearby Breslau provided a modest living. More important, the two middle children, Conrad and Johanna, were unwilling to leave Prussia.[1]

Powerful forces, however, drew Morris and Blume to America. They longed to be with their eldest son, David, who had immigrated a few years earlier and settled in St. Louis, Missouri, where he operated a retail business. Their principal concern, however, was their thirteen-year-old son Jacob. He was an exceptional child. Born on October 6, 1853, he was an intelligent and conscientious student who had done better in the gymnasium (high school) than any of their other children. Although in good health, he was small of stature. Morris and Blume dreaded the day that he would be drafted into the Prussian army and assigned to an infantry company, the fate of most Jewish conscripts.

Further, even though life for Prussian Jews had improved considerably since the liberalizing revolutions that took place in Western Europe beginning in 1848, employment opportunities for Jewish youths from middle-class families were still very limited.[2] In all probability, Jacob would be restricted to his family's mercantile business or to teaching. Moreover, Jews were excluded from judicial, administrative, and other offices that were connected with the Christian character of the state.

Conrad and Johanna argued that conditions would continue to improve for Prussian Jews, but Morris and Blume would not be convinced. Prussia was in a constant state of political flux. The chancellor, Otto von Bismarck, governed Prussia with little regard for its constitution. A militaristic Germany did not offer the future that the Triebers hoped for.[3] To the contrary, America was the land of opportunity. Lincoln had freed the slaves and proclaimed the principle of equal opportunity for all. Certainly, Jacob would be able to develop his talents to the fullest in the United States. With these thoughts in mind, the Triebers sold their business, gathered their belongings, and immigrated to America. They were reunited with their son, David, in St. Louis on June 1, 1866. Eleven years later, on March 15, 1877, Jacob Trieber became a United States citizen.

The Triebers stayed in St. Louis for two years and worked with David in his retail business.[4] Jacob enrolled in high school. He quickly realized that he was ahead of his schoolmates in all subjects except English. He struck a bargain with one of his teachers: German lessons in exchange for English lessons. To help support his family, he worked evenings and weekends as a newsboy and a theater usher.

In 1868, the Trieber family moved to Helena, Arkansas. Helena promised more opportunities for immigrants than St. Louis. It was a growing Mississippi rivertown, and many believed that it would soon rival Memphis as a center for trade. Moreover, there was a small but growing Jewish population in that community, and it was important to the Triebers that they continue to participate in the religious life of their people.[5]

In Helena, Morris and David Trieber opened a dry-goods store. Jacob helped support himself by keeping the store's books. He wanted to be a lawyer, however, and eventually a judge. The opportunity came in 1873 when, at the age of twenty, he made an arrangement to "read the law" with Marshall L. Stephenson of Helena, a former justice of the Arkansas Supreme Court. He worked in Stephenson's office during the day and during nights as an assistant to the clerk of the circuit court. Typewriters were unknown at that time so Jacob became an expert scrivener, preparing copies of legal papers. Eventually, he mastered the English language and the law. In 1876, he was admitted to the Arkansas Bar and soon thereafter formed a partnership with L. C. Stephenson, Marshall's brother. In 1878, L. C. Stephenson moved to Colorado, and Marshall returned to Helena and resumed the practice of law with Jacob Trieber. It was from this platform that Jacob Trieber launched his career as lawyer, banker, businessman, politician, and judge.

The Helena Years (1876–97)

The law firm of Stephenson & Trieber was successful from the start. The firm not only had a good commercial practice, but the partners were kindred souls—both loved the law, business, and politics.[6]

Involving himself in business ventures, Jacob bought and sold real estate, lent small sums of money, and undertook, with his friend Harry Tappan, the construction of the Tappan Building on the main street of Helena. His most important venture came in 1885 when he and several friends organized the First National Bank of Helena. In 1893, he became its first president.

From the beginning, Jacob Trieber's ambition was to be a federal judge. He recognized that he could only realize that goal if he established himself as a good lawyer, an active participant in community and fraternal affairs, and a committed Republican. His partner supported him in that ambition by sponsoring him for the Masons, encouraging him to participate in civic activities, and supporting his extensive political activities.

Jacob Trieber joined the Masons in 1874, and participated actively in the affairs of that organization until his death. In 1906, he was elected grand master and served in that position for two years. He was involved in most community projects undertaken in the city of Helena and in civic projects on a statewide level. Indeed, between his busy law practice, his Masonic responsibilities, and his civic activities, it is a wonder that he had any time for Republican politics. However, convinced it was his only route to fulfill his ambitions, he gave the party his greatest effort and energy.

He joined the Republican Party in 1874. A Republican by choice rather than by inheritance or environment, he admired Abraham Lincoln and Ulysses S. Grant, and revered Theodore Roosevelt to the point of fashioning his appearance after him. He believed in the policies of the Republican Party of his day: a strong union, the primacy of the United States Constitution, a high protective tariff, and greater opportunities for blacks. He was also at home with the Republican Party's pro-business policies.

Referred to by newspapers as "the perpetual candidate,"[7] Jacob Trieber was a hard-working, plainspoken, highly partisan grassroots Republican, who was willing to serve in any party position, to campaign for any Republican candidate, and to run for any elective office. In 1882, he was elected to the Helena City Council and quickly gained a reputation as "alert and careful, and always on the side of economy in public expenditures."[8] Ten years later, he was elected treasurer of Phillips County. He served in both offices until 1897 when he became the United States district attorney for the Eastern District of Arkansas.

His first venture into national politics came in 1880, when his party efforts earned him a seat as a delegate to the Republican National Convention in Chicago, Illinois. His political mentor and the leader of the Republican Party in the state, General Powell Clayton,[9] supported him for the position. He went to Chicago hoping that Ulysses S. Grant, who had already served two terms as president of the United States, would be renominated.

There was little or no debate on the three-and-one-half-page platform, which extolled the Republican Party for having ended slavery, built railroads, and increased foreign trade. There was even less debate over the sections of the platform that declared that constitutional questions were to be decided by federal rather than state courts, which carved out a role for the federal government in public education, and which called for a constitutional amendment to prohibit state aid to sectarian schools.[10] The closing paragraph of the platform mirrored Jacob Trieber's political beliefs:

> The equal, steady and complete enforcement of laws, and the protection of all our citizens in the enjoyment of all privileges and immunities guaranteed by the Constitution, are the first duties of the Nation. The dangers of a solid South can only be averted by a faithful performance of every promise which the Nation had made to the citizen. The execution of the laws, and the punishment of all those who violate them, are the only safe methods by which an enduring peace can be secured and genuine prosperity established throughout the South. Whatever promises the Nation makes the Nation must perform. A Nation cannot safely relegate this duty to the States. The solid South must be divided by the peaceful agencies of the ballot, and all honest opinions must there find free expression. To this end the honest voter must be protected against terrorism, violence or fraud.[11]

At the convention, Jacob Trieber and the Arkansas delegation cast their twelve votes on every ballot for Grant. After thirty-six ballots, however, the convention nominated James A. Garfield and Chester A. Arthur for president and vice president. By voting for Grant on every ballot, Jacob Trieber, at age twenty-seven, the youngest delegate at the convention, became identified as one of the "Old Guard."[12]

Jacob Trieber was again elected as a delegate to the Republican National Convention in 1884, where James G. Blaine was nominated for president. Blaine was narrowly defeated, however, by Democrat Grover Cleveland in the November election. In that same election year, Trieber ran for attorney general of Arkansas and was badly defeated. He was not a delegate to the Republican National Convention in 1888, but he campaigned in Arkansas for Benjamin Harrison, who was subsequently elected president. He was rewarded in 1890 by being named supervisor of the census for the First Congressional District. In 1891, he was the unsuccessful Republican caucus nominee for the United States Senate.

In the fall of 1892, Jacob Trieber ran for Congress against P. D. McCulloch. The two candidates debated in every county and major city in the district. The major issues were the use of federal troops to supervise elections in the state (the "Force Bill"), the treatment of blacks, the tariff, and "free silver."[13] On November 6, the *Forrest City Times*, a Democratic newspaper, reported one of the debates:

> Although the weather was very inclement, rain pouring and mud slushing, there came together a large number of citizens of all shades of political opinions, yesterday afternoon at the court house to hear the great McCulloch, and Hon. Jacob Trieber. . . . Mr. Trieber . . . made a very excellent speech the striking feature of which was that he admitted that he was not in sympathy with his party on the National bank and Force bill issues, and appealed to the people to lay aside prejudices and vote as patriots. . . . Mr. Trieber stole much of the usual democratic thunder. He paid the people of Arkansas many nice compliments, and in a large measure surprised the writer by the absence of the usual republican outcropping of venom. It is true he accused the Democratic party of a good many ugly things, but he seemed to do so simply for the reason that it was usual and expected of him and not that there was "anything in it" or that he had any interest in his thrusts. When his time expired Hon. G. P. Taylor introduced "Hon. P. D. McCulloch our next congressman." Little Mac's first words stirred the hearts of every white man present and reawakened the old love which the people have for him. He spoke of the grand old Democratic party's age and of the adversities which it had conquered, and made plain the fact that it is the greatest of all parties and one that can never die. . . . [T]he little giant in a thirty minutes talk uttered the most beautiful and at the same time the most scathing denunciation of the infamous Force bill[14] and its authors and advocates to which it has ever been our pleasure to listen. . . . The fact is that Trieber is no match for McCulloch in debate, and the latter's flow of beautiful language comes as natural as the bubbling water from the woodland spring; such words could only emanate from the pure in heart.[15]

Trieber predictably lost the election, 16,679 to 9,541, but carried Helena and Phillips, his home county, by virtue of a large black vote.

In 1896, the Republican State Convention was held in Little Rock, Arkansas, and Jacob Trieber played a dominant role. He was a member of the committee on resolutions and the State Central Committee. The resolutions were moderate in tone for Arkansas Republicans: "No mention of ballot-box stuffing, free bills or bloody shirts. . . . Powell Clayton had the entire aggregation in the hollow of his hand and directed its every movement."[16] Trieber was elected as a McKinley delegate to the national convention at St. Louis. Additionally, for the second time, he was rumored to be the congressional candidate for the First District:

> With his "well-known weakness for politics, his popularity with his Democratic friends, his absolute control of the colored contingent and his recently developed weakness for the downtrodden white metal, Mr. Trieber is the only Republican in the district who could make the slightest showing against the candidate of the Democratic party."[17]

The unexpected happened when Mr. T. O. Tucker of Clover Bend, Lawrence County, was nominated instead of Trieber.

The big issue at the national convention in St. Louis was free silver. Although Jacob Trieber was a free silverite, he voted for the gold platform after he saw there was no hope for the silver platform. In the 1896 elections, Trieber ran for chief justice of the Arkansas Supreme Court but used that forum primarily to campaign for William McKinley. Both Trieber and McKinley lost the state, but McKinley won the presidency, and Trieber's hard work put him in line for a position in the McKinley administration.

Trieber as United States District Attorney

Jacob Trieber's reward was not long in coming. On April 6, 1897, he was named United States attorney for the Eastern District of Arkansas. Republicans agreed that Jacob Trieber was the best man for the job. The Democrats, for the most part, also gave him their endorsement. In newspaper accounts he was praised as "one of the very ablest and most conservative Republicans of the state and has at all times labored for the true principles of Republicanism,"[18] and as "an astute and successful Republican politician, and socially one of the most urbane gentlemen in the world. . . . A better selection could not have been made. Mr. Trieber is a lawyer of ability, a financier of recognized prominence and a clever gentlemen socially and otherwise. *The World* rejoices in his good luck and hopes he will make his way to the front as rapidly as his merits justify."[19]

As United States attorney, Jacob Trieber was responsible for the enforcement of federal law and was obligated to represent the government in civil cases. The civil calendar was light, being limited, for the most part, to Indian land disputes, railroad matters, and land condemnation cases. But the criminal calendar was an active one. The "moonshining" district lay in the Eastern District of Arkansas, and Jacob Trieber was responsible for controlling the illicit distilling of "mountain dew." Indeed, he spent much more of his time in this endeavor than he would have liked.

Unlike some Arkansans who considered moonshiners to be as foul a breed as murderers, Jacob Trieber felt compassion for them: "The moonshiners as a rule are good citizens in every way except that they will break the law in making whiskey. In this they do not believe that they are committing any wrong and they are otherwise honest."[20] His attitude prompted some moonshiners to voluntarily comply with the law. One day, twenty-six moonshiners from Cleburne County and forty from Pope County simply walked into his office at Little Rock and surrendered. The *Helena World* praised Trieber: "Our Jake must be as persuasive with the mountain-dew folks as he was wont to be with all manner of people before he went away from us. This district has never had a more efficient, industrious and painstaking official."[21]

During the years that Jacob Trieber served as United States attorney, he also held the office of vice chairman of the Republican State Committee. In that position, he became the principal spokesman for the party,[22] and the eyes and ears of General Clayton, who, although he was serving as minister and as ambassador to Mexico, remained the behind-the-scenes leader of Arkansas's Republican Party.[23]

Jacob Trieber played a key role in the 1898 campaign. He was a speaker of marked ability, with a charming, engaging style. Because of his command of facts, he was described as "that walking encyclopedia of Republicanism from Helena."[24] He was a Republican of enormous popularity. Wherever he went, Republicans gathered, interrupting his speeches with applause. In fact, when mentioned as a potential candidate for governor of Arkansas in 1898, one newspaper account acclaimed: "Should the republican party see fit to name him as the standard-bearer, he would poll a vote which would be so great as to be a matter of astonishment. He is the ablest Republican in Arkansas."[25] Every day for two months, he met a Democrat in debate on the political issues. Such able Democrats as ex-governor James P. Clarke and Joseph T. Robinson (later to become United States senator and candidate for vice president on the Alfred E. Smith ticket in 1928) were, according to some, outdone by the grand oratorical skills of Jacob Trieber.

In the campaign of 1898, Jacob Trieber spoke of the Democratic Party as a party of the past with a dismal record. He stated that there had been eighteen months of prosperity under the McKinley regime, but declared that "Arkansas has not been able to participate in this prosperity, . . . simply because the democratic party is in control."[26] He questioned: "[W]hat in its twenty-four years of power has the democratic party done to justify its continuance?"[27] The state had not been developed as it should have been—"the curse of the democratic legislation was responsible for keeping Arkansas back."[28] He was charismatic, possessed by the idea that Republicanism was the answer to Arkansas's ailments.

He attacked the state election laws because he believed they disenfranchised black voters. This, he argued, was disastrous for Republican candidates because many Republican voters in Arkansas at that time were black. He complained that "[t]oo many [white voters] are prone to vote the Democratic ticket regardless of who were its nominees because of that party's anti-black policies."[29] He questioned: "Are you free men under this election law? Can you expect good government unless the sanctity of the ballot is maintained?"[30]

Trieber's opponents spent much of their time defending themselves against his attacks. In one debate, Democratic ex-governor J. P. Clarke supported the state election laws:

> [T]hey were intended, among other things, to break up the practice in eastern Arkansas and elsewhere of political tycoons and negro preachers standing around the polls and handing blue and red tickets to voters. . . . It puts every voter on his own responsibility and puts a stop to one man controlling 500 votes.[31]

Clarke also attacked Trieber, stating that he did not "think it surprising to hear Trieber boast of [national] prosperity since he is enjoying a nice cozy $4,000 job. A few are doing well, but they are not down here raising cotton."[32]

Jacob Trieber had a sharp tongue and pen when it came to the Democratic Party. He wrote that the Democratic Party could be subdivided into four groups, some being more palatable than others:

> [T]here are so many different branches of "Democracy" that a fellow, if he is a democrat, must be careful and not be taken for some other kind of a democrat. Now there are the "Randall Democrats," quite respectable and sound on the tariff issue, but rotten to the core on every other issue.
>
> Then there are the "Sound Money Democrats," patriotic on the subject of finance and bitterly opposed to any repudiation or depreciation of the money, yet on other subjects all wrong. Then we have among us the "Yellow dog Democrat" who votes anything labeled democratic regardless of men or principles. As you are not one of those . . . I feel safe that you'll not attempt to convert me into that kind of a thing. And last is the swamp Democrat, whose sole platform is "D—— the Nigger." I am sorry we have so much of the latter in Arkansas, but I honestly believe, it is the most popular platform for a Democrat, and carries more of them into office, than any other, silver not excepted.[33]

As sharp as his attacks on the Democratic Party were, he did not attack his Democratic opponents personally. As a result, he was respected by the Democrats, and when the time came, many of them supported him for the judicial appointment.

Trieber was often asked to give speeches outside the political arena. One memorable oration was delivered on Memorial Day, May 30, 1898, in Little Rock. In that address, Trieber gave his view as to the meaning of the Civil War, views that paralleled those of the admired Teddy Roosevelt:

> It was a war of necessity. It might have been postponed, but it could not have been averted. The antagonisms existing could never be finally settled short of an arbitrament of blood. Political compromises could delay, but compromises stand no longer than the interests of those making them dictate.

> The seeds for that late war were sown and began sprouting with the adoption of the Constitution. Are we a nation composed of sovereign states, indissoluble and indivisible, or a mere confederacy, with the right of withdrawal from the Union reserved to each state? . . . The election of Abraham Lincoln, the grandest figure of the nineteenth century as president, although in the manner prescribed by the constitution, precipitated this crisis. . . . The god of war, the tribunal from whose decision no appeal lies, has determined that this Union cannot and never will be dissolved. That this flag, emblematic of the union of states shall never cease to waive triumphantly where it was once planted; that the stars on it are as indestructible as those on the firmament of heaven itself; that as it does this day it shall forever and ever float as a beacon light, and a haven of refuge to the oppressed of the world and a protector of every nation on the Western hemisphere whose liberty or independence is threatened by foreign foe or foreign interference.
>
> Disunion is a thing of the past; to prevent it no loss of life could be too great and no sacrifice too large.[34]

On July 7, 1900, John A. Williams, the United States district judge for the Eastern District of Arkansas, died. Speculation among politicians as to his successor was rife. The names being tossed around included John McClure, W. G. Whipple, and, of course, Jacob Trieber. "No formal scrabble will be engaged in until after the burial of Judge Williams," reported the *Arkansas Gazette* on July 8. "No matter how much any of the prospective candidates may deprecate an unseemly struggle for such an exalted place, there will nevertheless be no little diligence exercised by their respective friends."[35]

While saddened by Judge Williams's death, Jacob Trieber turned all his energies toward securing this prize.[36] He wrote letters to everyone he thought could help him secure the appointment. Trieber was humble, yet confident, in his persistent requests for support:

> My friends and the bar generally have honored me by presenting my name for appointment to this high position, and while I am not unmindful of my inability to come up to that standard, which such judges as Caldwell and Williams have established in this District, I have been persuaded, that perhaps I am the best that can be obtained from the material on hand.[37]

Trieber received countless endorsements—some solicited, some unsolicited—some written immediately upon the news of Judge Williams's death. Five Democratic justices of the Arkansas Supreme Court wrote endorsement letters to the president. He was endorsed by the local bar association and by prominent Democrats who wanted the president to know that the appointment was satisfactory to them.[38] Meanwhile, at the July 8, 1900, Republican State Convention, Trieber nominated his old friend, Colonel H. L. Remmel, to be the Republican candidate for governor.

Upon learning of Judge Williams's death, General Clayton left Mexico City for Washington to take up the question of successorship. After holding several conferences in that city, he left for Little Rock, arriving on July 14, 1900. He immediately went into conference with Republican leaders to assert his authority over the appointment. The *Arkansas Gazette* reported on July 15 that:

> [I]t is understood that he favors Judge Jacob Trieber and has used his influence with President McKinley for his appointment. His approval is deemed so strong toward appointment to any position in the gift of the president that a local Republican leader who is in a position to know what transpired during the day said last night: "We expect the appointment of Judge Trieber Monday."[39]

On the sixteenth, the Republican State Committee met and recommended Jacob Trieber for the judgeship.

On July 21, 1900, Colonel Remmel met with President McKinley in Canton, Ohio. Also present were Senator Mark Hanna of Ohio, who had engineered the president's nomination in 1896, and Judge William R. Day, circuit judge for the Sixth Circuit (appointed by President Roosevelt to the Supreme Court on February 23, 1903). Remmel wrote to Trieber later that night:

> The President greeted me by saying—How are you Remmel and who do you want for Judge? This gave me my opportunity in the presence of all these gentlemen and I used it, I assure you, with I think their hearty approbation. I then gave the President the brief of your endorsements and he read them aloud. I then took up your religious faith. He referred to his recent action in appointing a [Jewish] Judge for Puerto Rico. I assured him your appointment

> would be appreciated as the very highest compliment to your people.
>
> He is especially solicitous regarding your ability as a lawyer, your integrity, and your private life all of which of course I enlarged upon.
>
> Senator Hanna . . . said further your age was just right. I impressed the President of the importance of prompt action, the Receiverships to be named and that I would like appointment made before the 30th. He said I will wire Griggs at once. What is done will be done before the 30th. Of course, I could not press him for a promise as I would not have gotten it.[40]

The letter indicated that Remmel expected Trieber to serve as an active advisor for the remainder of the 1900 campaign.[41] He concluded by writing: "This was a most satisfying visit. The result is certain."[42] Five days later, the president signed an order giving Jacob Trieber an interim appointment as United States district judge. Jacob Trieber received the notice in the early afternoon of August 1, 1900. He immediately called his wife and a few close friends and asked them to come to the courthouse for the swearing-in ceremony.

The *Arkansas Gazette* deemed him a good choice, even though a Republican:

> Judge Trieber is a republican, but not an offensive one. He is a man of broad-gauged ideas, cool and level-headed, an able lawyer, an untiring student, and one who is capable of filling the position of a federal judgeship to the supreme satisfaction of all lovers of justice. Judge Trieber is as thoroughly identified with the best interests of Arkansas as any man born and reared in the state. His appointment will be a deserving one. He is well equipped for the position. There is no member of his party in this state more worthy of being the successor of Judge John A. Williams. The selection of Judge Trieber will meet with no objection from any democratic source in Arkansas.[43]

Jacob Trieber was flooded with congratulatory letters from his friends and admirers. The one he relished most came from his former law partner, L. C. Stephenson, who wrote on August 2, 1900:

> Dear Jake:
>
> I just saw in the paper that you had knocked the persimmon—

got the Dist. Judgeship, and I hasten to extend the congratulations of both Harriet and myself.

We both feel glad, because it is "Jake's" good fortune, and we both are confident that the mantle will fall in graceful folds upon you. Outside of a purely financial view of the matter, it must be a satisfactory reflection that one is "out of the cold, the sleet and the reach of the winds of adversity" for life.

You are the right man for the place. . . .[44]

Jacob Trieber—The Judge

Jacob Trieber went right to work. The docket in the Eastern District of Arkansas was not current and, to him, that was a grievous sin. He immediately scheduled cases for trial and by the time he came up for confirmation in January of 1901, he had brought his docket up to date. In his total of twenty-seven years on the bench, Jacob Trieber not only kept his docket current but often found time to serve as a district judge in the Western District of Arkansas, the Eastern and Western Districts of Missouri, and the Southern District of New York.

He also sat by special designation on the United States Court of Appeals for the Eighth Circuit on a regular basis from 1913 until his death.[45] In that period, he heard more than 350 Eighth Circuit cases and wrote the opinions in more than two-thirds of them. Indeed, his appellate workload matched that of some of the less active members of the court.[46] Notwithstanding Judge Trieber's busy court schedule, he still found time to teach at the Arkansas Law School, to write several articles on law and banking,[47] to promote his ideas on constitutional and judicial reform (the most important being that proposed amendments to the Constitution should be submitted directly to the people),[48] and to serve as president of the Arkansas Bar Association.

Judge Trieber's caseload reflected the times in which he lived. The large number of bankruptcy cases evidenced the hard economic times suffered by the nation during much of his tenure.[49] The frequent litigation of Indian land disputes mirrored the opening of Indian Territory to white settlers,[50] and the numerous cases concerning violation of liquor laws on Indian reservations were a measure of the evil that liquor brought to the tribes.[51] The labor cases grew out of the increased industrialization and the concomitant growth of the labor movement in the Southwest.[52]

Although many of Judge Trieber's opinions deserve further study, this article focuses on a select few cases that best reflect his fundamental beliefs and that have had the greatest impact on the development of the law. In the area of civil rights, Judge Trieber announced several innovative interpretations of law, including the first decision to hold that blacks are entitled to equal employment opportunities. The two migratory bird cases provided a unique opportunity to explore the boundaries of the federal government's legislative power. The railroad cases reveal Trieber the capitalist who believed that Arkansas's full potential lay with enlightened industrialization. The United Shoe Machinery Company cases established several foundational principles of antitrust law. Finally, his criminal law opinions demonstrate his belief that although laws should be promptly and strictly enforced, justice also requires that sentences be short and that prisoners be treated humanely.

Discrimination against Blacks in Employment and Voting

The first significant cases to come before Judge Trieber concerned discrimination against blacks in employment and voting. On October 6, 1903, Judge Trieber impaneled a grand jury to investigate the infamous "whitecappers" (Ku Klux Klan) who had for so long terrorized blacks and their white sympathizers throughout Arkansas.[53] The whitecappers had been a blight on the state since he had arrived there as a young boy. In 1892, the year he ran for Congress, the whitecappers orchestrated a "race war between the whites and blacks" in Calhoun County, Arkansas.[54] An article in his "hometown" newspaper, the *Helena World*, reported that "this county . . . is afflicted with a gang of irresponsible men who have been terrorizing the defenseless negroes of that vicinity until they have actually succeeded in driving the majority of them out of the neighborhood."[55]

That same day, as reported in the *Arkansas Gazette*, "Ed McCollum, a negro, was taken from the county jail . . . by a masked mob and tied to a tree in the courtyard and his body riddled with bullets."[56] Judge Trieber had long believed that these all-too-common lynchings were not only a tragedy for blacks, but a tragedy for the whites of Arkansas as well. He lamented in one letter that "people wouldn't know there is anything in Arkansas except murders and demagoguery. . . . This country is growing by leaps and bounds . . . while Arkansas is asleep . . . despite her great natural resources."[57] He recalled his childhood in Prussia and how discrimination against Jews consumed that country; he feared for the future of any country that permitted discrimination, and hoped that, somehow, Arkansas could steer a different course.

Although Judge Trieber had never really been an outspoken advocate for civil rights, he had often espoused his view "that the demagogue is the worst foe of our free institutions. . . . Let us try to enthrone reason and eradicate prejudice and follow the precepts laid down in that divinely inspired instrument, the Declaration of Independence."[58] As one of the quintessential self-made men of his generation, he was deeply confident in the power of good example. He sought to communicate—through his own life and deeds and his commitment to equal justice—that racism was detrimental to the people of Arkansas, and that only when the race problem was laid to rest would that state's great potential be achieved. In a June 1900 letter, he wrote:

> Of course the prejudice which is still to be found among many people is not easily overcome, and in my opinion, instead of attempting to overcome it by force or abuse, it is the better part of wisdom to act along conservative lines and remove the prejudice by acts of wisdom. Of course, it takes a longer time to accomplish a great deal along that line; at the same time, we are more sure of success. . . . Free discussion without bitterness of feeling, appealing to the justice of the people instead of trying to arouse their prejudices and passions, are bound to succeed in the end, and my efforts shall always be along that line.[59]

The whitecapping cases presented a critical opportunity for justice and reason to prevail over prejudice. Because of his widespread identification with the best interests of Arkansas and his unquestioned integrity and ability, Judge Trieber was uniquely well positioned to ameliorate racial tensions through the southern strategy of gradual persuasion. The Arkansas press had described him as a "staunch friend of equal and exact justice,"[60] and stated that "Mr. Trieber . . . impresse[s] all his hearers with a feeling of fairness seldom exhibited."[61] Ultimately, after twenty-five years on the bench, he would describe his judicial philosophy as follows:

> All courts are established for the same object . . . the protection of the rights of the people, for the protection of the lives, property

> and those rights, either guaranteed by the constitution and laws of the nation and the state, [or] are inherent in every free man under a democratic republican government such as ours.[62]

The *Arkansas Democrat* commented that:

> Proclaimed by many jurists of the land, such facts would have seemed platitudinous, almost hollow, but voiced by Judge Trieber, they became a code of ethics, a system of jurisprudence in which he believed with the passion of a man whose sincerity at no time in all his distinguished career had been questioned. . . . Judge Trieber declared that certain rights are inherent in every free man and the records of his court gave evidence that the man ruled as he believed . . . [his] knowledge and his vast learning in the law made his court a truly American institution where men could come to ask justice but could find no preference.[63]

Now that the whitecappers had finally been brought into court, Judge Trieber was required to apply a lifetime of learning to ensure that equal justice was meted out. The whitecapping cases had captured great public notoriety all year. The cases began in the spring of 1903 when the whitecappers posted notices on farms throughout Poinsett County warning all blacks to leave the county "or else." The whitecappers had been burning down homes and crops and lynching blacks in an attempt to ensure total white supremacy. They were enraged by a number of blacks who had purchased or leased farms in Poinsett County and were achieving economic success rivaling or exceeding that of the white farmers in the county. Many of the prominent white planters, however, were opposed to the whitecappers' mob rule and were fearful of losing the black laborers they depended upon. Moreover, the whitecappers had warned white planters against selling land to blacks, thus preventing the planters from disposing of their property as they saw fit. In February of 1903, the planters hired several detectives from Memphis, Tennessee, to investigate and, they hoped, "capture" the whitecappers. In March of 1903, however, the whitecappers murdered detective J. F. Brown while he was investigating a recent whitecapper attack at the home of a black family.

Meanwhile, a new sawmill opened in nearby White Hall, Arkansas. Davis & Hodges Co. had hired eight black workers to help operate the mill. On August 17, 1903, at least fifteen whitecappers, with torches and firearms, converged on the mill and demanded that all blacks be fired and replaced by whites. Davis went to Justice of the Peace John Harrington, but Harrington "not only refused to help keep the peace, but joined the mob."[64] Davis then discharged all of his black workers.

In the fall of 1903, the United States attorney sought conspiracy indictments under the Civil Rights Act of 1866,[65] and the Civil Rights Act of 1870,[66] against fifteen of the whitecappers involved in the Davis & Hodges mill incident (*United States v. Hodges*)[67] and against twelve of the whitecappers involved in the Cross County terrorism (*United States v. Morris*).[68] The cases posed difficulties from both a practical and legal standpoint. Practically, as the *Helena World* commented, "It is difficult to secure proof against [the whitecappers]. When a gang of hoodlums circle around the back end of large plantations at the hour of midnight and fire into negro cabins and then disappear, it is difficult to swear who did the nefarious work."[69] The *Arkansas Gazette* noted that the whitecappers' victims give "very unwilling testimony, apparently being afraid of the consequences that may be visited on them after they have returned to their homes."[70]

The cases also posed one of the most contentious legal issues of the day. The whitecappers were growing in number each year, and Judge Trieber often expressed his fear that mob rule might prevail over law and order. If anything had been proved since the Civil War, it was that the state of Arkansas was unwilling and unable to prevent whitecapper violence and racism. Moreover, of late, the state had acted in haste to pass numerous laws requiring racial segregation and discrimination, and now the only bulwark against entrenched racism was federal law.[71] However, the Supreme Court had ruled that the Fourteenth Amendment did not reach private conduct,[72] and although the Thirteenth Amendment did reach such conduct,[73] the scope of that amendment and the accompanying civil rights statutes was unsettled. Judge Trieber had researched the question thoroughly and had formulated a grand jury charge, which he was confident reflected the correct state of the law.

Judge Trieber entered the courtroom, the grand jury before him. He charged the jury that the

> matters . . . before you . . . are somewhat extraordinary and of great importance. Under the laws of the United States . . . it is a serious offense "for two or more persons to conspire to injure, oppress, threaten or intimidate any citizen in the free exercise or

> enjoyment of any right or privilege secured to him by the constitution or laws of the United States." . . . Since the adoption of the thirteenth amendment to the constitution of the United States, slavery has ceased to exist in this country and every citizen is entitled to enjoy those rights which are inherent in every free man. Without enumerating what all of these rights are, it is sufficient to say that among them are, in the language of the Declaration of Independence, the cornerstone of our republican form of government, the following: "That all men are created equal; that they are endowed by their Creator with certain inalienable rights; that among these are life, liberty and the pursuit of happiness. . . ." The right to own, hold, dispose, lease and rent property, either real or personal, and to perform honest work for the support of himself and his family are natural rights belonging to every free man, without any statute or written law. Deprive a man of these rights and he ceases to be a free man. Congress, in order to leave no doubt on that subject, has enacted statute[s] [protecting these rights]. . . . Under these acts, the court charges you . . . that it is unlawful for two or more persons to conspire for the purpose of preventing by force, threats or intimidation any citizen of the United States from renting lands and cultivating the same, or performing any honest labor, when hired to do so, on account of his being a . . . citizen of African descent.[74]

Two days later, the grand jury returned indictments against the twenty-seven defendants. The defendants then moved to dismiss the indictments on the ground that the federal statutes under which the indictments were made were unconstitutional. Judge Trieber overruled the demurrer and, the next day, announced his celebrated opinion in *United States v. Morris*,[75] in which he held that:

> In my opinion, Congress has the power, under the provisions of the thirteenth amendment, to protect citizens of the United States in the enjoyment of those rights which are fundamental and belong to every citizen, if the deprivation of these privileges is solely on account of his race or color, as a denial of such privileges is an element of servitude within the meaning of that amendment. . . . That the rights to lease lands and to accept employment for hire are fundamental rights, inherent in every free citizen, is indisputable.[76]

Judge Trieber then continued the cases until the next term and set separate trial dates for the *Hodges* and *Morris* cases.

In the meantime, Judge Trieber learned that the whitecappers in the *Hodges* and *Morris* cases would be defended by two of the most prominent attorneys in the state, one of whom was the lieutenant governor of Arkansas and the other a popular candidate for prosecuting attorney. The whitecappers also remained busy in their campaign to eliminate blacks from the state's workforce. For example, in El Dorado, Arkansas, a band of whitecappers forced several black workers to quit their jobs at a construction site.[77]

The *Hodges* case came on for trial on March 16, 1904, and Trieber, as usual, was well prepared. At the close of the evidence on March 17, he instructed the jury that:

> [I]t is a question of whether a man shall be permitted to employ whom he pleases to employ, or whether he shall be compelled to employ those whom others with whom he has no relations wish him to employ. It is a question that strikes at the fundamental principles of our government, that of the right of every citizen, be he white or black, to work for a living, to engage in the pursuit of happiness and a livelihood. It is a question of whether right and law should prevail or the unlicensed mob.[78]

After four hours of deliberation, the jury returned guilty verdicts against the three "ringleaders in the conspiracy" and found the remaining defendants innocent.[79] The jury recommended mercy for the defendants and the *Arkansas Gazette* commented that, "the general opinion is that the sentence will be a light one, the men being ignorant rather than vicious."[80] Judge Trieber sentenced two of the defendants to one year and one day in prison, plus a $100 fine. The third defendant received sixty days in the county jail plus a $100 fine.

The convicted men were released on bond pending appeal, their lawyer "propos[ing] to test the constitutionality of the federal statute . . . claiming that under this statute the negro citizen is granted a protection in the federal courts that is not given to white men."[81]

Meanwhile, on March 17, 1904, trial commenced in the *Morris* case. The defendants were charged with conspiracy to force blacks to give up their farms and to leave the county, and were also charged with conspiracy to hinder the investigation of these incidents by murdering detective J. F. Brown. Establishing the identity of the perpetrators was difficult: detective Brown was "shot several times through a window"[82] by masked whitecappers, the attacks on farms owned by blacks had been perpetrated by masked whitecappers, and the victims were reluctant to testify because of threats of violence against them. After less than two hours of trial, the United States attorney dismissed the complaints against four of the defendants because he was unable to prove his case against them. Judge Trieber denied demurrers by the remaining defendants who claimed insufficiency of the evidence. After a short attempt to adduce additional evidence, however, the United States attorney believed he had not proven his case beyond a reasonable doubt and dismissed the complaints against all remaining defendants.

While the appeal in *Hodges* was pending, Judge Trieber expressed, in a letter to United States district judge Thomas G. Jones of Montgomery, Alabama, the significance and hope he found in the whitecapping cases and their probable impact on racism. Judge Jones had asked for Trieber's comments on his charge to the jury in a pending lynching case.[83] Trieber wrote:

> [I]t is such action on the part of Federal Judges, especially by one like yourself, who is a native of the South, has served in the Confederate Army, and whose former political views cannot be questioned by the people of the South, which will arouse public opinion to the enormity of the crime. . . . The responsibility for this unfortunate condition we have in this section is in part due, I think, to the spirit of some of the gentlemen connected with the press of the South. They seem to think that any criticism of any of the acts of irresponsible mobs is a stab at the South, when in fact it is for the benefit of the good people of the South.
>
> I do not know the conditions existing in your state, but in our state the rabble seems to have obtained absolute control of the politics of the state, and what is worse than anything else is the fact that their supremacy has been obtained solely by appealing to the prejudices existing in the minds of many against the negro. The true representative of our section, that is, those who are intelligent, have most at stake, and the greatest interest in the welfare of our section, are practically barred from participation in the administration of the affairs of our state.
>
> I sincerely believe that this race question could be solved to the lasting benefit of our country and in conformity with the spirit of this civilized age, provided those well meaning Northerners could be induced to keep quiet and trust the good people of the South

> with the solution of this problem. When I tried the whitecapping cases here the jury which convicted the parties was composed exclusively of natives of the South; yet there was no trouble to secure a righteous verdict. This shows that the rabid expressions found in many of our leading newspapers, and so freely indulged in by petty politicians, do not express the sentiment of the better class of people. To awaken their conscience and supply them with the moral courage necessary to give expression of their views on the subject is all that, in my opinion, is necessary to influence a patriotic adjustment of the negro question.[84]

Judge Trieber's opinion in the *Hodges* case was surprisingly well received by the Arkansas press and the public, and it appeared for a while that employment opportunities for blacks in Arkansas would be improved. This was not to be, for on May 28, 1906, the Supreme Court overruled *Hodges*, holding that the federal courts lacked jurisdiction to protect blacks from racially motivated discrimination by private individuals, no matter how severe. The Court reasoned that the ability to earn a living was not a fundamental right of citizenship protected by the Thirteenth Amendment, and that extending protection to blacks against racial discrimination would be a form of improper reverse discrimination against whites. The Court further stated that the punishment of such wrongs as were charged must be sought in the state courts.[85]

Judge Trieber immediately saw the folly in this position. The Supreme Court in *Hodges* failed to note that the mill owner had first sought help from the state justice of the peace, but that officer had instead joined the mob in demanding that the black workers be discharged. Additionally, in the years since *Hodges*, no state charges were ever brought. Indeed, the new state prosecuting attorney had been aided in his election by the fact that he had been defense attorney for the whitecappers. Jacob Trieber hoped that state authorities might, in the future, have the courage to use the state's Reconstruction-era civil rights law[86] to quell the spread of whitecapper violence. However, the Arkansas Legislature shortly repealed that law, leaving blacks no access to federal or state courts for protection of their basic civil rights.[87]

Judge Trieber was soon confronted with the abject tragedy of the Supreme Court's *Hodges* decision. The year 1906 was marked by some of the bloodiest race riots in this nation's history, but the federal government would no longer assist in quelling the violence.[88] Moreover, as the years went by, the whitecappers' forces and their violent racism grew exponentially; they were formally reorganized into the Ku Klux Klan in 1915. By 1923 that organization would reach a record national membership of six million and would engage in open displays and parades of proud racism.[89] "[F]or almost fifty years . . . the *Hodges* case . . . became the rod and staff of those who denied that the federal government had the authority to intervene in race relations."[90] Blacks would be denied protection from racial discrimination in employment until the late 1940s when a few states and municipalities passed the first barebones fair employment laws. Comprehensive protection against racial discrimination in employment was not provided until the enactment of the Civil Rights Act of 1964.

In 1968, Judge Trieber's interpretation of the Thirteenth Amendment and the Civil Rights Act of 1866 was at last vindicated when the Supreme Court[91] overruled *Hodges.* The Court adopted Judge Trieber's reasoning in *United States v. Morris*[92] and held that the Civil Rights Act of 1866,[93] by authority of the Thirteenth Amendment, reached private, racially motivated interference with fundamental rights.

In the years following *Hodges,* Judge Trieber was faced with two other significant civil rights cases. In January 1905, trial commenced in a case that challenged the validity of the Arkansas poll tax amendment. The underlying events began in 1890, when the United States House of Representatives passed an election rights bill sponsored by Representative Henry Cabot Lodge. The "Force Bill," as it was called, permitted federal officials to supervise balloting for congressional candidates in the South to prevent election fraud and disenfranchisement of black voters.[94] Although the bill had been defeated in the Senate in 1890, the possibility of the bill's reintroduction was an issue in Trieber's race for Congress in 1892. He told an audience that he was generally opposed to the bill because, "while fraud [is] sometimes perpetrated in our elections [I] would much rather have a ballot box stuffed by our people than have toughs from Massachusetts, New York, Ohio and Illinois come down here and stuff it to suit them."[95] Although the bill ultimately was defeated, southern politicians realized that methods other than force and fraud were necessary to suppress the black vote. Mississippi led the way in 1890 by adopting a constitutional amendment requiring the payment of a poll tax as a suffrage prerequisite.[96] In 1893, the Arkansas Legislature submitted a poll tax amendment to the voters; the amendment passed by a 75,940 to 56,601 vote, and was declared adopted even though it did not receive a majority of the total vote of 156,192.[97]

Judge Trieber was now called upon to decide a case that arose when the black plaintiff attempted to vote in the November 1904 congressional election, and was barred from voting on the sole ground that he had not paid the Arkansas poll tax.[98] Plaintiff sought damages, claiming that the interference with his voting rights was unlawful and that the poll tax amendment was invalid because it had not been adopted by the majority of the total votes cast at the election, as arguably required by the Arkansas Constitution, rather than the total votes cast on the poll tax issue alone.

The case presented two significant legal issues: first, whether a federal court has jurisdiction to determine whether a state constitutional amendment is properly adopted,[99] and second, whether, under Arkansas law, a constitutional amendment must secure a majority of the highest number of votes cast in the election or a majority of the number cast on that one question. Judge Trieber held that because the question concerned the right to vote in a congressional election, the federal court had jurisdiction.[100] He went on to hold that the poll tax amendment was invalid because it had not secured a majority of the votes cast in the election.[101]

The right of Arkansans to vote in federal elections without paying a poll tax was short lived. In 1909, the Arkansas Legislature enacted a second poll tax amendment, identical to the first. It was approved by a vote of 88,386 votes for and 46,835 votes against.[102] The validity of the poll tax was not again challenged in Arkansas during Judge Trieber's tenure.[103]

In 1905, Judge Trieber confronted another civil rights issue. In the spring of that year, the United States attorney charged several individuals with keeping blacks in a state of peonage and with arresting and returning them to a condition of peonage when they attempted to leave their plantations.[104] These indictments, "the first of the kind ever known in Arkansas,"[105] marked an attempt to end the widespread peonage system in Arkansas. Judge Trieber knew this system well, having lived in Phillips County where over three-quarters of the population were black and worked as virtual slaves in the cotton farming areas of the east Arkansas delta. Typically, white planters would advance cotton seed and supplies at inflated prices to black sharecroppers, who would then sell their cotton at a below-market price to the white planters. Because the black sharecropper would usually be in debt to the white planter, and since no black could leave the farm until his debts were paid, he was held in economic bondage, or peonage. Judge Trieber knew that the white planters had prevented blacks from trucking their cotton to Helena or Memphis where they might obtain a fair price.[106] He also recalled the recent Cross County whitecapping cases where the whitecappers became enraged when former black sharecroppers saved enough money to purchase or lease lands that they could farm as independent planters.

Judge Trieber realized that it would be difficult to secure indictments and convictions because it was widely believed that peonage was not unlawful.[107] His challenge was to explain to the jury how peonage was unquestionably unlawful despite its widespread acceptance in the state. He informed the jury that:

> [I]n the case of peonage, to protect the poor laborer against the exactions of the wealthy employer, compelling him to agree to work in many instances for a mere pittance for a loan made to relieve his most necessary wants, this law has been enacted. . . . If the evidence which is laid before you satisfies you that some men in this district have entered into contracts of that kind with some laborers, and that afterwards, before the debt was paid, the laborer wanted to quit, and he was prevented from doing so by force, threats or intimidation, or if he has left, and was arrested either on some trumped-up criminal charge or without any warrant of law, and returned for the purpose of compelling him to carry out his contract and work until his debt was paid off, then it is your duty as grand jurors to find an indictment against such person or persons. . . . This law is, no doubt, one of the most salutary statutes in existence, but it is wholly immaterial what your or my individual views as to the wisdom of the enactment of this law may be.[108]
>
> The grand jury returned a sixty-count indictment against nine persons. Although the *Arkansas Gazette* predicted a significant legal battle, it never occurred because seven of the men pled guilty before trial, one pled guilty after a short trial, and one man, Justice of the Peace John McElwee, was discharged by Judge Trieber for lack of evidence. McElwee's only role had been to issue a warrant for the arrest of a black laborer who had left the farm of a wealthy black planter.

Shortly after these cases were concluded, the Supreme Court, in *Clyatt v. United States*,[109] upheld the constitutionality of the anti-peonage laws. It overturned Clyatt's conviction for enslaving a black, however, on the highly suspect ground that, although he had enslaved the black, he had not *returned* him to peonage, as alleged by the indictment, because the black had not previously been held in peonage.[110]

The Supreme Court's ruling and other factors permitted the peonage system to continue in Arkansas. Ultimately black dissatisfaction with this system led to the infamous and bloody "Elaine Race Riots" in 1919. This historical event has been so well reported that it is not necessary to reiterate the details here.[111] In short, black sharecroppers in Phillips County were attempting to organize a union and, allegedly, a rebellion against the peonage system. When white planters and local authorities learned of this and tried to prevent blacks from organizing, a "race war"[112] broke out, resulting in dozens of injuries and the deaths of at least "five whites and eleven negroes . . . although many times that number probably were killed."[113]

One hundred twenty blacks were indicted and, ultimately, after short trials orchestrated by a lynch mob, fifty-four were sentenced to prison and twelve sentenced to death.[114] With respect to the twelve (who received a forty-five-minute trial), there were several state court appeals and habeas corpus petitions and petitions for certiorari to the United States Supreme Court.[115] Finally, six were discharged and six sentenced to death. On September 21, 1921, two days before the scheduled executions, the six filed a petition for a writ of habeas corpus in the federal district court for the Eastern District of Arkansas. Judge Trieber granted the writ and set a hearing date, but disqualified himself because of his long years of residence in Phillips County. The case was then assigned to Judge John H. Cotteral of Oklahoma City, Oklahoma. Judge Cotteral sustained a demurrer by the State of Arkansas and dismissed the case. However, Judge Trieber, although he had previously recused himself, certified that there was probable cause for appeal.[116]

The Supreme Court accepted certiorari and in *Moore v. Dempsey*[117] sustained Judge Trieber's initial grant of the writ of habeas corpus. It ordered a hearing to determine whether the six had been accorded a fair state trial. Justice Holmes reasoned:

> [I]f . . . the whole proceeding is a mask—[if] counsel, jury and judge were swept to the fatal end by an irresistible wave of public

> passion, and [if] the State Courts failed to correct the wrong, neither perfection in the machinery for correction nor the possibility that the trial court and counsel saw no other way of avoiding an immediate outbreak of the mob can prevent this court from securing to the petitioners their constitutional rights.[118]

In the end, the hearing was never held, as counsel for the six agreed to dismiss the petition for writ of habeas corpus if the death sentences were commuted to twelve years.

During the period that Judge Trieber was deciding the whitecapping, peonage, poll tax, and Elaine Riots cases, he publicly voiced his support for equality of opportunity in several speeches.[119] For example, in April 1914, in a speech before the "Political Equality League," he stated that, "a woman is a person and should be entitled to all the rights guaranteed by the constitution to a male person."[120] He accurately predicted that, within ten years, women in every state would have the right to vote.[121] In a 1916 speech on the Constitution, he "warn[ed] against the dangers from radicals and demagogues attempting to influence the weak and ignorant [and] appealed to . . . lawyers to do all in their power to create a greater respect for the Constitution as the foundation of our liberty."[122]

In sum, Judge Trieber decided several far-reaching civil rights cases, but, in his lifetime, the influence of these decisions was greatly limited by Supreme Court reversals—reversals which that Court subsequently recognized as unwise. In the final analysis, his greatest contribution to the cause of equality of opportunity was provided through his own personal example. As the *Arkansas Gazette* wrote,

> His life is a high example of the victory that may be won over adversity by unending labor, based upon the fundamentals of sound character and worthy ambition. By his conscientious loyalty to his convictions and his clients, and by the charm of his address, he has succeeded in overcoming various adversities and prejudices that threatened his early progress.[123]

Similarly, as the *Helena World* commented upon his appointment to the federal bench:

> It was long given in Arkansas that no Republican, foreigner or Jew could hold office in that state. This time-honored aphorism has just been discredited—and for the first time—by the appointment

> of the Honorable Jacob Trieber . . . as judge for the United States District Court for the Eastern District of Arkansas.[124]

Migratory Birds

Jacob Trieber had a profound interest in the question of state/federal relations under the Constitution. Early in 1914, he became involved in the first of two cases that would give him an opportunity to explore that question. The migratory birds provision of the Appropriation Act for the Department of Agriculture of 1913 allowed the Department of Agriculture to set aside closed seasons for migratory game and birds.[125] Harvey C. Shauver was indicted for a violation of this provision, a federal misdemeanor. The case stirred a bitter controversy. On one side were the hunters who wished to protect their traditional hunting practices; bird migrations in spring, one of the targeted seasons, provided an especially bountiful source of sport and food. On the other side were the conservationists, concerned about the "merciless slaughter of wild life,"[126] the farmers who needed the birds to control crop-destroying insects, and the farsighted sportsmen who realized that conservation was necessary to ensure continuing game availability. Shauver argued that the migratory bird provision was unconstitutional.

Judge Trieber's sympathies lay with the conservationists and farmers, but he agreed with Shauver.[127] In so agreeing, he was one of the first federal district judges to hold a federal statute unconstitutional.[128] He held that the Constitution did not authorize Congress to regulate the shooting of migratory wild game. He pointed out that Congress possessed only those powers granted by the Constitution expressly or implicitly, and that the court must declare void any statute beyond those powers.[129] He reasoned that although the federal government had power over its own property, it could not regulate migratory birds, which were owned by the states in their sovereign capacity as representatives of their people.[130] He also held that the United States had no implied power to exert control even if the states were incapable of such control, there being no general police power not supported by a specific constitutional provision.[131] Judge Trieber stated: "It may be, as contended on behalf of the government, that only by national legislation can migratory wild game and fish be preserved to the people, but that is not a matter for the courts. It is the people who alone can amend the Constitution to grant Congress the power to enact such legislation as they deem necessary."[132] Denying a motion for rehearing, he pointed out that, according to the Supreme Court, the commerce clause did not give the federal government power over migratory game, as game was internal state commerce, not interstate commerce.[133] He then added:

> For this court to disregard these decisions of the highest tribunal of the land would be an assumption of authority not only unwarranted, but improper. The Supreme Court is the only tribunal which possesses that power, and it exercises it very sparingly. Fortunately, this question can be reviewed by that court on error, and it is hoped that the government will take proper steps to have it done.[134]

Judge Trieber also stated that "although in full sympathy with all measures tending to preserve the wild game for the benefit of all the people, the court can find no valid reason for changing the conclusions reached at the former hearing."[135]

The reaction to Judge Trieber's opinion in *Shauver* was immediate and mixed. One incensed reader wrote to the *Kansas City Star* that the opinion supported "the soapbox decisions of learned spring shooters of wild fowl who never even saw the national constitution."[136] The letter continued:

> The friends of birds need feel no alarm over this incident, nor anything more serious than mild interest. . . . The side of the people and the birds will be taken care of, if need be, by a hundred able lawyers, who are fully convinced that the law is constitutional and that its stability can be demonstrated to the satisfaction of any open and logical legal mind.[137]

Other writers were able to see beyond the immediate results of Trieber's decision:

> The principle involved is of considerable importance. If the bird law rests simply on the conservation of natural resources, why might not the federal government follow it up with a forest law and prescribe the conditions on which a farmer might fell a tree on his own land? The bird law is generally agreed except by pot-hunters to be a good law, but many of those who believe in it heartily are a

> little uneasy in regard to the invasion of state rights involved, and a decision by the supreme court will be welcome. If that is adverse the bird lovers will have to renew their campaign in the states; if it is favorable it is the states which will have to keep jealous watch against the use of the precedent for a further invasion of their prerogatives by the central government.[138]

A supporter of the statute, Colonel J. H. Acklen, president of the US game commissioners and counsel for the United States in *Shauver*, stated:

> Judge Jacob Trieber is admittedly one of the ablest judges on the federal bench. Furthermore, he is a man of remarkable attainments in matters outside of the law. He is an ardent advocate of game and bird protection. He knows both from study and observation the importance to the agricultural interests of the country of protecting our insectiverous birds and the inadequacy of most state laws to protect our migratory wild fowl from threatened extermination. These facts add great weight to his conclusions, which I am sure he regretted to have to reach, but as an able lawyer and conscientious judge he felt undoubtedly constrained to declare the act unconstitutional.[139]

The United States appealed to the Supreme Court. Meanwhile, it sought another means of obtaining the desired results. In 1916, it negotiated a treaty with Great Britain for the protection of migratory birds.[140] Pursuant to this treaty, Congress enacted the Migratory Bird Act of July 3, 1918.[141] Subsequently, on January 7, 1919, the Supreme Court dismissed the appeal on the government's motion.[142]

An opportunity to test the new act arose soon thereafter. E. N. Thompson was accused of a violation of this act. Like Shauver, Thompson demurred to the accusation, arguing the unconstitutionality of the act.[143] Judge Trieber disagreed.[144] He initially noted that the Constitution expressly gave to the federal government, through the president and Congress, the power to make treaties, and expressly denied this power to the state. He then stated that the treaty power of the federal government was broader than Congress's power to enact statutes, pointing out that while the legislative power is limited to the enumerated powers, the treaty power was limited only to the "authority of the United States." He concluded by saying:

> While this court is of the opinion that the power to declare treaties void, if clearly violative of some provision of the Constitution . . . exists, it should . . . "never be exercised but in a very clear case indeed."
>
> To make treaties is one of the highest attributes of every sovereign government, and if the United States does not possess it to the fullest extent it would not be invested with the powers which belong to independent nations, and the rights of our citizens in their intercourse with foreign nations, or their right to the protection of life, liberty, and the enjoyment of property in foreign countries would be at the mercy of foreign nations, as the states are without authority to enter into treaties. It is impossible to conceive that the framers of the Constitution overlooked a matter of such importance, and intended to deprive the people of protection in foreign lands, which can only be secured by treaty.
>
> To say that by the exercise of that power the people of the states may be deprived of their liberty is to reflect, not only on those who by the Constitution are invested with that power, but on the people themselves, for a treaty can only be made by the President and the concurrence of two-thirds of the Senators, all elected by the people, and their servants.
>
> In the opinion of the court, the power to make the treaty in controversy exists, and the act of Congress to carry it into effect was in discharge of a moral obligation assumed by the nation, by the convention with Great Britain.[145]

Judge Trieber's decision in *Thompson* went unchallenged.[146]

United Shoe Machinery Company Cases

Two years after Judge Trieber became involved in the migratory bird cases, Chief Justice Edward Douglass White of the United States Supreme Court asked him to become involved in a complex antitrust case involving the United Shoe Machinery Company. In the early 1900s, United Shoe manufactured and leased more than 95 percent of the shoe-manufacturing machinery in the United States. The leases contained "tying clauses" that restricted the lessees' rights to use machinery or supplies made by other companies.[147]

These tying clauses had been a target of the federal government's antitrust campaign. In December 1911, the United States filed suit against the company,[148] claiming that the leases violated the Sherman Act.[149] Three months after the *United Shoe* suit was filed, the Supreme Court, in *Henry v. A. B. Dick Co.*,[150] held that the Sherman Act did not forbid tying arrangements.

Reaction to *A. B. Dick* was strong. Many were concerned that the tying arrangement exception to the Sherman Act punched a dangerous hole in antitrust protection.[151] Consequently, in 1914, Congress passed the Clayton Act.[152] During congressional debates, United Shoe's tying arrangements were specifically condemned.[153]

Meanwhile, the suit against United Shoe under the Sherman Act continued. In 1915, the United States District Court for the District of Massachusetts held that the lease clause did not violate the Sherman Act.[154] The Supreme Court affirmed in a 4–3 decision.[155]

Shortly after the Clayton Act was passed, the United States tried once more to enjoin the tying arrangements of United Shoe, this time under section 3 of that act. This case initially came before Judge David P. Dyer, United States district judge for the Eastern District of Missouri.[156] On November 15, 1915, he granted the motion of the United States for a preliminary injunction.[157] The United States Court of Appeals for the Eighth Circuit reversed this order without prejudice on May 16, 1916, when the government abandoned its claim to a preliminary injunction.[158]

When Chief Justice White asked Judge Trieber if he would be willing to take over the case,[159] he agreed to do so without hesitation, even though he knew that it meant months away from his family, and that he would be required to keep his own calendar current. There were important questions of antitrust law to be addressed, including the constitutionality of the newly passed Clayton Act. The matter was of great economic importance. The case was complex—precisely the type of litigation upon which his disciplined mind thrived. Moreover, his extensive business experience would be of value in deciding the issues.[160]

The case proved to be as complex as Judge Trieber had anticipated. It first came before him on United Shoe's motion to dismiss, a motion that he denied. A trial on the merits followed.

Judge Trieber initially held that section 3 of the Clayton Act was within Congress's powers under the commerce clause. He started with the basic premise "that courts are slow to declare the acts of co-ordinate departments of the government . . . void, and unless it appears beyond a reasonable doubt that the act is violative of the fundamental law of the United States the courts will uphold it."[161] He acknowledged that leases as a mode of commerce may not have even existed when the United States Constitution was written, but stated:

> The fact that the question has never been before the courts, or that the power has never been exercised by Congress, is no proof that the Constitution does not authorize it.
>
> It may be conceded that every lease is not commerce, but that is not conclusive that none may be. Each case must be determined from the peculiar facts shown to exist in that case. When a corporation with millions of capital, doing an annual business amounting to millions of dollars, sees proper to conduct its business by only leasing its chattels, instead of selling them, why is it not as much engaged in commerce as if it sold them outright?[162]

His decision on the commerce clause foreshadowed the broad reach later Supreme Court decisions[163] would give to the commerce clause:

> It is sufficient to say that as new methods of transacting business are devised, if they are found to be in effect methods of carrying on commerce in any business, and the means for commercial transactions between the owner of the article on the one hand, and the person who wants to deal in it or use it in carrying on his business on the other hand, whether it be manufacturing, selling, trading, leasing, transportation, communication, or information, and it is sent or transported from one state to another, it is interstate commerce, and therefore, subject to be regulated by Congress under the commerce clause of the Constitution.[164]

The trial on the merits continued for nearly four years. In 1920, Judge Trieber found that the Clayton Act did not constitute an unconstitutional taking of patent rights: "In short, individual rights, whether claimed under patents or otherwise, must be subordinated to the public good, and, unless clearly arbitrary and unreasonable, courts will respect the acts of the legislative department."[165] He concluded:

> [W]hile Congress cannot deprive a patentee of the exclusive use of the patent, or reduce the time for which it is granted by existing law, without violating the Fifth Amendment, a patentee has no

> vested right in conditions of contracts for use, license, or lease of his patented invention, which Congress may not prohibit, if in its judgment they are injurious to the public welfare, though he may have possessed that right under the common or municipal law, as theretofore construed by the courts.[166]

He also held that the tying provisions did violate the Clayton Act:

> Can it be doubted that these provisions are not only within the spirit but the letter of the statute? What is the natural, direct, and necessary effect of these conditions? There can be but one answer to this: To compel the lessees to use defendants' machinery and material, regardless of whether the terms granted by the defendants are as favorable as can be obtained from other manufacturers of some of the machines or dealers in some of the materials.[167]

Judge Trieber refused, however, to apply the act to leases and contracts entered into before the enactment of the provision.[168] He did so notwithstanding the fact that four federal courts, including the United States Court of Appeals for the Second Circuit held that section 3 should be given retrospective construction.[169]

The Supreme Court affirmed.[170] It noted that "[t]he record embraces twenty-seven volumes of printed matter and four volumes of exhibits. . . . [W]e may add that . . . the opinion gives evidence of careful and painstaking research."[171]

To this day, Judge Trieber's opinions in *United Shoe Machinery Co.* continue to be among the most cited cases in antitrust law.

Railroads

During his entire term of office, Jacob Trieber was involved in many aspects of railroad litigation. As an unabashed supporter of economic development in Arkansas, he believed that the expansion of the railway system in the state was essential. In the 1900 campaign, he argued,

> there [are] some things upon which we all should agree, viz, to develop the resources of the state and build up a home market . . . so far as Arkansas [is] concerned, it should be considered the great garden spot of the United States because of its wonderful resources . . . yet . . . the state [has] not been developed as it should be.[172]

He criticized the Democrats' "policy of the past few years [which] has been to antagonize new enterprises and keep them out."[173] His Democratic adversary, Governor Joseph Clarke, mockingly retorted that, "while he was in the governor's office, a New England party of capitalists came into the office and said there was no outlook for factories in Arkansas because we have but one railroad system and they couldn't distribute their product at a fair rate of freight."[174] He attacked Trieber's suggestion that Arkansas should encourage railroads and manufacturers to come to the state through tax breaks and promises of profitability and stated, "the right of railroads to charge rates must be limited" and advocated the formation of a railroad commission.[175]

A railroad commission was indeed created and in subsequent years, this commission would attempt to limit railroad rates, and to impose special taxes and public improvement obligations on railroads. These activities and other public laws regulating railroads led to numerous lawsuits in Judge Trieber's court. In 1907, the Arkansas Legislature passed an act, aimed at foreign railroad corporations, which prohibited a foreign corporation from removing to federal court any suit brought against it in state court and which required the payment of a substantial reincorporation fee. The Chicago, R.I. and P. Railway Company brought suit in Judge Trieber's court to enjoin enforcement of the law. Judge Trieber held that the suit was not barred by the Eleventh Amendment and enjoined enforcement of the act on the ground it impaired the franchise of the railroad in violation of the contract clause of the federal Constitution and several provisions of the Arkansas Constitution.[176]

On February 9, 1907, the Arkansas Legislature passed an act fixing the maximum passenger fare within the state on certain lines at two cents per mile. On June 4, 1908, the Arkansas Railroad Commission similarly limited railroad freight rates. Several railroads then filed an action that alleged that the rates were confiscatory and unreasonable. Judge Van Devanter of the United States Court of Appeals for the Eighth Circuit, sitting as a district judge, granted a preliminary injunction in favor of the railroads[177] and the case was set for trial in Judge Trieber's court. After a lengthy trial, Judge Trieber agreed with Judge Van Devanter's view that the two-cents-per-mile rate was confiscatory and unreasonable, but he also found that the rate increases which the railroads had initiated after the preliminary injunction had been granted were "extortionate."[178] He wrote,

> [t]herefore, not only to prevent a multiplicity of suits, but to require complainants who seek equity do equity, this court is justified in prescribing such maximum rates as may be just to the railroads as well as the public. . . . The railroads are entitled to reasonable profits on their investments, and the public to reasonable rates or to express it differently, the rights of the public and railroad companies are reciprocal.[179]

Judge Trieber adopted a temporary tariff that allowed the railroads to charge 3 cents per mile for passengers and 2.67 cents per mile for freight.[180]

To avoid appeal, the parties agreed to try for eighteen months a rate of 2.5 cents per mile for freight and 3 cents per mile for passengers. At the end of this period, both parties were dissatisfied; the state wanted the 2-cents-per-mile rate and the railroads wanted the 3-cents-per-mile rate. When the parties were unable to agree, the railroads brought suit, seeking a permanent enjoining of the 2-cents-per-mile rate. Judge Trieber issued a long and detailed opinion holding that the 2-cents-per-mile rate was confiscatory and unreasonable.[181]

The Supreme Court reversed on the ground the data submitted by the railroads was inadequate.[182] Not to be dissuaded, the railroads again brought suit. This time they submitted more complete data. Judge Trieber again ruled that the rates were confiscatory and set a rate which allowed the railroads a profit.[183] He noted that railroads in recent years had been saddled with new costs associated with a variety of remedial legislation, and stated that rail rates must be set high enough to allow railroads to pay for these obligations. Praising Trieber's "careful discussion," the Supreme Court affirmed, agreeing that the Arkansas rates were "unduly low."[184]

In subsequent years, Judge Trieber decided a number of similar cases involving railroads in which he agreed that rate limitations or special taxes or obligations on railroads were confiscatory or in violation of the state or federal constitutions. In *Mudge v. McDougal*,[185] he granted an injunction prohibiting Saint Francis County from taxing the property of the railroad plaintiff at a rate twice that of the property of other corporations or individuals.[186] In *Hines v. Clarendon Levee District*,[187] he held unconstitutional a special act of the Arkansas Legislature that required the plaintiff railroad to build up a certain section of its railbed to prevent flooding and to serve as a levee for the town of Clarendon.

He wrote, "[i]t is impossible to escape the conclusion that the real object of the act is to require the railroad to protect, at its expense, the town of Clarendon from overflow."[188] Quoting the United States Supreme Court,[189] he explained, "'[t]he business of a railroad is transportation, and to supply the public with conveniences not connected therewith is no part of its ordinary duty.'"[190]

Although Judge Trieber was criticized in the press for being a "friend of the railroads," [191] he commented in an interview:

> There is a different view taken of railroads in courts than is taken by the people and the legislature. The general public thinks that the principal purpose of having railroads is to enact acts to raise wages, put up beautiful structures in every town for stations, to reduce hours of labor, to pay all taxes on road improvements and to make them liable for damages. . . . The principle of damn the railroads doesn't apply in court any more than the principle so largely practiced by the railroads of damn the public did. [192]

Notwithstanding his belief that railroad expansion should be encouraged, he also supported the view that railroads should be regulated to ensure fair and safe working conditions. In *Spain v. St. Louis & S.F.R. Co.*,[193] he upheld the constitutionality of the Federal Employers' Liability Act (FELA), which he viewed as a desirable step toward humanitarian treatment of labor. He expressed his philosophy with respect to employees' rights before the Arkansas Bar Association:

> [FELA] is a recognition by Congress of the broad humanitarian views of the right of employees now prevailing, instead of the narrower one established by the common law at a time when the workingman was accorded but few privileges, and considered but little better than a serf; when property rights were recognized as paramount to personal rights. It expresses the twentieth century conception of human rights instead of that of preceding centuries, a view now generally recognized by all civilized Nations.[194]

Shortly thereafter, however, the Supreme Court, in a badly divided 5–4 plurality opinion, held the act unconstitutional on the ground that the language of the act could be construed to cover intrastate traffic and employees injured in such traffic.[195]

After Congress passed an amended act limited to interstate traffic,

Judge Trieber became the first federal judge to uphold its constitutionality. He wrote:

> The object of Congress in the enactment of the law was to protect the men employed in this hazardous occupation, in which thousands are annually killed or maimed without any fault of the master himself, but by the negligence of other employees, over whom the servant has no control, and in whose selection he had no voice. The legislation is neither new nor revolutionary.[196]

In stating that Congress clearly had the constitutional authority to pass the act, he noted that such legislation not only advanced safety for workers, but also improved the safety of railroads for all customers and improved the productivity of labor. This time the Supreme Court agreed.[197]

In *United States v. Kansas City Southern Railway Co.*,[198] Judge Trieber upheld the constitutionality of an act of Congress (the Hours of Service Act) which limited the maximum working hours of railroad employees to sixteen hours a day. United States district judge Rogers had directed a verdict for the defendants on the grounds that the unlawful overtime was excusable because of unavoidable accident, an act of God, or unforeseeable cause. The government had then moved for a new trial. In the meantime, Judge Rogers died, and Judge Trieber was assigned to the case. Judge Trieber granted the motion for a new trial, holding:

> [A]ll the delays shown to have occurred could have been prevented by the exercise of reasonable diligence or at least anticipated, and the court is unable to find, after a careful reading of all the testimony, that any delays were caused by casualty, unavoidable accident, or act of God, or by any cause which could not have been foreseen.[199]

Similarly in *St. Joseph & G. I. Railway Co. v. United States*,[200] Judge Trieber, writing for the United States Court of Appeals for the Eighth Circuit, rejected the contention of the railroad that the Hours of Service Act did not limit the working hours of an employee on a "work train" operating wholly within one state. "In our opinion, this is too narrow a view of this act, which was intended . . . to be a remedial statute . . . to promote the safety of employees and travelers on trains moving in interstate commerce, and should be liberally construed to effect its purpose."[201]

Not only was Judge Trieber a vigorous advocate of railroad expansion, but he also made other important contributions to the economic development of the state of Arkansas. He was an early advocate of a Uniform Commercial Code and played a key role in the drafting of Arkansas's first banking law.[202] He wrote several articles and speeches on banking, commercial law, and economic development in Arkansas,[203] was a member of the Little Rock businessmen's club, and took part in many economic development projects, including the restoration of Arkansas's first state capitol.

Criminal Justice and Court Reform

In 1925, Jacob Trieber completed a difficult and thought-provoking task at the request of the *Arkansas Democrat*: to reflect upon and write about the twenty-five years he had served on the district court bench. He decided not to discuss specific cases, even though he had, over the years, compiled a list of what he considered his most important decisions. Instead, he devoted one article to a general discussion of criminal law and another to court reform.

When it came to criminal cases, he believed that:

> Before a man can be punished, his case must be plainly and unmistakably within the statute. At the same time, even penal statutes must be naturally construed according to the legislative intent as expressed in the enactment; the courts refusing, on the one hand, to extend the punishment to cases which are not clearly embraced in them, and on the other hand, equally refusing, by any mere verbal nicety, forced construction, or equitable interpretation, to exonerate parties plainly within their scope.[204]

Occasionally, of course, a case arose where the language of the statute would have allowed prosecution of the defendant, but common sense dictated to the contrary. One such case involved a young man who had spent the night with his girlfriend in a hotel fifty yards outside of their home state. The young woman's irate father had the man brought before Judge Trieber on charges of transporting a woman across a state line for immoral purposes. Judge Trieber dismissed the case, stating that the difference between a felony and a sin must be greater than fifty yards.[205]

Judge Trieber's philosophy of strict construction of criminal statutes compelled him to release defendants when their actions, even though reprehensible, did not fall precisely within areas forbidden by law.[206] Conversely, there were times when, although his heart went out to the defendants and their families, the law required him to impose sentence:

> Judge Trieber wept and seemed to be almost choking several times while he was announcing the penalty. The wife and mother of the prisoner were also in tears. . . . Judge Trieber told [the defendant] that he would have been glad to give him a lighter sentence if the law permitted it.[207]

He stated in the *Arkansas Democrat* article that:

> Few laymen realize the feeling of a judge, when compelled to inflict punishment which in many instances causes as much, and in some greater suffering to the innocent wives, children and other members of the family of the guilty party, than on the violator of the law. Nor is this feeling confined to criminal cases. . . . Yet, under his oath, a judge must suppress these feelings of sympathy and decide in accordance with what he conceives to be the law, regardless of the suffering his decision may cause.[208]

His sentencing philosophy, as expressed in the article, also reflected his compassion for the defendants:

> As I do not believe in severe sentences, I rarely ever sentence a person on more than one count, or if I do I make the sentences on each count concurrent, which is equivalent to a sentence of one count. In my opinion it is not the severity of punishment but the certainty of it, with no likelihood of the pardon which deters those inclined to violate the law from doing so. This, of course, does not apply to habitual criminals, who must be sentenced for long terms for the protection of society.[209]

One of his reasons for giving short sentences was his disapproval of prison conditions. He often expressed the view that the Arkansas state prisons were especially inhumane and in need of improvement. On May 19, 1902, he wrote to F. F. Kitchens, sheriff of Phillips County, to discuss the unsatisfactory condition of the county jail there: "It is an old, filthy place with no sewage connections and . . . a bad smell. The jail here [in Little Rock] has modern improvements. [Accordingly, I will continue to send prisoners to Little Rock and will not send them to

Phillips County] . . . if I can possibly avoid it."[210] On October 23, 1902, he wrote to Marshall Ford, sheriff of Lee County, stating:

> [I]t is my intention . . . that the prisoners are treated properly. . . . I understand that there are three and four prisoners in one cell and the cells are rather small. That ought not to be. I do not want the prisoners to get sick; besides they are human beings and ought to be treated humanely. They ought also to have a little fresh air every day, and if you can arrange it so as to give them an hour or two of exercise without too much expense to yourself in guarding them, I wish you would do it. There will probably be other prisoners sent to you for safe keeping to await trial, provided they are properly treated. If this is not done, they will all have to be brought here to Little Rock.[211]

On January 3, 1912, he wrote to H. M. Jacoway, of the United States House of Representatives, and said:

> A Federal jail is an absolute necessity in this district. The best jail in the district is that in Little Rock, but it is usually so crowded with state prisoners that the Federal prisoners have to be crowded in and the place cannot be kept clean. [Our prisons are so bad that] [i]n a number of instances persons have asked to be sent to Atlanta for a year and a day rather than spend six months or more in one of our jails. . . . It is a great injustice to put [many of the federal prisoners] in such a jail. Aside from that the health of the prisoner is seriously affected. . . . Several hundred dollars are annually spent in this District for medical bills which would not be incurred if they were kept in a clean, wholesome prison.[212]

In his second article for the *Arkansas Democrat*, Judge Trieber discussed a few of his ideas on court reform, focusing primarily on judicial efficiency. He believed: that a judge should take a firmer hand in jury selection and do much of the questioning of prospective jurors himself, thus avoiding many of the attorneys' irrelevant questions; that the number of peremptory challenges allowed should be reduced; that a judge should take a more active role during the trial because "[a] judge should be something more than a moderator to decide on objections. He should be responsible for correct results[.]"[213] He also proposed that the rules of evidence should be liberalized and made uniform because the old rules were developed in times when defendants had no rights to counsel or to testify.[214]

Judge Trieber had additional ideas about court reform that he did not discuss in his article, principally, the establishment of lower courts which could relieve the district courts of some of their more mundane, yet time-consuming, cases:

> [T]he dignity of the federal district courts has been to a great extent destroyed by the requirement that all criminal cases, no matter how trivial, can only be tried in those courts, and to a jury. The motley crowds seen now in those courts, as defendants or witnesses is nauseating. Lawyers, whose practice was heretofore confined to police and magistrates' courts, who were never seen in a federal court, now crowd them, defending parties charged with violations of the national prohibition law and similar offenses of a petty nature, who, if charged with violations of petty offenses of the laws of the state would only be tried in inferior courts.[215]

The quantity of prohibition cases Judge Trieber heard tried his patience.[216] On one occasion, upon seeing an all-too-familiar face before him, he delivered a reprimand:

> "What is the matter with you people in Saline County," Judge Trieber asked of the attorney who had represented R. D. Baxter, an old offender of that county. "What can be done to stop the manufacturing of liquor down there? It seems to me that in spite of the penalties I assess, the violators continue to thrive in Saline county. That county is the worst in the state, it has even exceeded the record made by Garland county several years ago for liquor violations.
>
> "I believe that the churches are not doing their duty. They should send missionaries into Saline county instead of sending them into Africa and other foreign countries, and educate the people to obey the laws.
>
> "What are the people coming to? They come into my court here after getting into family rows and swear falsely against their neighbors without any apparent fear that there is a God!"[217]

Friendship with him provided no refuge for offenders. In 1924, the *Jonesboro Daily Tribune*, calling him "A Just Judge," reported:

> When forty-two citizens of Jackson county, some of whom were good friends of the justice, were brought before him on the charge of buying booze, the judge fined the whole "pot and biling" without discrimination or favortism. Among the number who faced the jurist was a fellow practitioner at the bar, who had been a warm

> personal friend for twenty years. There was no bar of friendship to stand in the way of justice and no fixing of things by sympathetic fellow lawyers. They all received what they were entitled to under the law.[218]

Another time, "Grandma Wirges," an elderly North Little Rock woman who ran a dairy, dropped in on Judge Trieber and presented him with a bottle of her homemade wine. Although he accepted the gift, he affectionately admonished her, "Grandma, you know the law of the land. And you know I will uphold the law. If you are ever brought into my court for violating the prohibition law, I will sentence you just like anyone else." He knew that Grandma Wirges loved to tell that story, and that she always ended by saying, "and the old goat would have done it, too!"[219]

Looking back on the twenty-five years, Judge Trieber was reasonably satisfied with the workings of the criminal justice system, despite its failings, as justice seldom miscarried:

> [T]he instances of convictions in criminal cases of persons, who were not guilty, are rare. I can recall but two such instances, although I make it a rule to investigate independently after the conviction, if my attention is called to matters which were not brought out at the trial.
>
> In both instances I immediately, after ascertaining the facts, recommended pardons, which were at once granted.[220]

He also noted in his article that, similarly, there had been few instances where juries had returned verdicts of not guilty when the defendant's guilt had been established beyond question. Nevertheless, he continued his campaign for court and prison reform; he knew that love of and respect for the law were fully consistent with a desire to improve conditions.

The Later Years

Jacob Trieber celebrated his seventieth birthday on October 6, 1923. His wife, family, and close friends used the occasion to renew their requests for him to take senior status or, at the very least, to decline further assignments to the court of appeals and other district courts. They knew that he had regular angina pains and that he tired more easily than in the past. He would have none of it. He loved the law and would continue on active status until his health would no longer permit or until he died. As for accepting outside assignments, he would not give them up. He enjoyed the companionship of the judges at the court of appeals, and the stimulation of serving in other districts. Moreover, he felt that it was his duty to respond to requests by the chief justice of the United States Supreme Court to help out in other districts. Jacob Trieber's reputation was national in scope.

In the fall of 1923, Chief Justice William Howard Taft asked Judge Trieber to spend some time in the Southern District of New York. That district was then experiencing a serious backlog because political leaders were unable to agree on appointments for three vacancies. Judge Trieber was unable to accept the designation at that time because of the press of business in the Eastern District of Arkansas and prior commitments to the court of appeals, but he cleared his calendar so that he could spend several weeks in New York in the winter and spring of 1925. The *New York Times*, in an unusual editorial, chronicled his work in the city:

> Arkansas has sent the perfect judge to this metropolis in the person of Federal District Judge Jacob Trieber . . . Judge Trieber, previously unknown to a great many jurists and attorneys of prominence in New York, has attracted considerable attention and been the subject of approval from everyone who has come in contact with him.
>
> During his first few days in court, he gave the local legal talent and prosecutors a very direct intimation of his ability to administer and propound the law. It happened that a young assistant federal attorney was late in appearing before Judge Trieber, and had held up the orderly procedure of the day's business. The visiting jurist delivered a very pertinent lecture on timeliness, and declared his attitude in this regard in such a way that there was not any doubt about how he felt when government officers are late to work.
>
> He has made such a hit with the associate judges that he is unable to keep up with the list of social activities such as luncheons and visits which they have arranged for him.
>
> In the first mail fraud case which was called before the Arkansas judge, the five defendants stayed on trial two days. After their attorneys found out what an extraordinary jurist they were appearing against, the clients were advised to ask leave to change their pleas from not guilty to guilty.

The case involved a notorious scheme of "bucketing brokerage" firms which had failed for more than $1,000,000. He sentenced them less than 15 minutes after their counsel asked him to accept a plea of "guilty."

It is the zippy way in which Judge Trieber disposes of the business before his court that has made him an instantaneous success as a visiting jurist in this city. He is much more alert on the law, some attorneys contend than a large percentage of the regular district judges. It is conceded that he is the most perfect out-of-town judge who ever presided in the big town.

The mail fraud case which he tried smashed all records in the Southern district. Heretofore, some of these cases have taken up the trial time of from three to seven weeks.

The distinguishing characteristics of the Arkansas jurist as seen by casual observers in his court may be substantially outlined as follows:

He is a keen student on all pivotal decisions of federal law. He calls off United States Supreme Court decisions and cites cases without any recourse to reference books. Only in one instance was he known to have taken one doubting attorney to his chamber and pointed out the particular decision. He speaks with confidence and leaves those whom he addresses perfectly satisfied that he is right and they are wrong. This finality phase of Judge Trieber is not a mannerism, New York attorneys admit. It is a finality which is strongly fortified by fact and authority. It is a finality which has been developed by a keen student of the law.

Judge Trieber has shown New York courts how to move through a trial expeditiously. The irrelevant matters, the repetitions, the long regiments of witnesses all testifying to the same points are chopped out. During the mail fraud case, the judge told one of the defense counsel who had called witnesses for repetition, that he should concede "some intelligence to the jury."

☆ ☆ ☆

His court room is dignified and possessed of that atmosphere of orderliness for which the English courts are noted. This typifies the administrative ability of Judge Trieber. It is a frequently discussed fact among lawyers that some of our best American judges know the law and procedure perfectly, but fail miserably as admin-

> istrators of order and respect in their court rooms. Judge Trieber combines these two excellent qualities.
>
> There is no pounding of a gavel or shouting while Judge Trieber is on the bench. The usual turmoil which frequently starts off a New York criminal trial is absent. The visiting jurist proceeds in a dignified and businesslike manner with the problems of the day. Neither side is allowed to become oratorical or qarrulous.
>
> He apparently has little consideration for poor lawyers. It has not taken him long to separate the goats from the sheep, during his visit.[221]

Others were similarly impressed. Augustus N. Hand, the chief judge of the Southern District of New York, wrote, "You taught me some new law to which my attention had never been called in the opinion which you sent. . . . [B]efore the spring you might make a judge out of me. [You are] the best teacher I have seen in a long time. . . . You did us a lot of good and I want to get you again as soon as possible and for as long as possible."[222] United States attorney for New York, Emory R. Buckner, wrote to Trieber, "I have not given up our hope to entice you to visit us again, even for a short time."[223]

In November of that year, Chief Justice Taft again wrote to Judge Trieber on behalf of Judge Hand: "He says you like to come and can do about twice the work of an ordinary Judge. I am sure that when you are so much appreciated, you will feel like going to New York."[224] Trieber reluctantly declined because he had only been back in Arkansas for a few months. He would have liked to return for two reasons, to serve in the busy, challenging New York district, and to spend some additional time with his daughter Bess and his grandson, who lived in Scarsdale, New York.

In April of 1927, Judge Hand wrote to Trieber: "How about your coming up here and giving us a little legal education this summer?"[225] Chief Justice Taft joined in the invitation. He wanted Judge Trieber to take over the important and complex *Journeymen Stone Cutter* case which was then pending. Ida Trieber tried to dissuade him, telling him he should take his regular summer vacation in a cooler climate. Nevertheless, Judge Trieber accepted and went to New York in August and plunged into his calendar. The weather was hot and the work hard. In September his arteriosclerosis worsened, and he developed an infection in his hand. He had no alternative but to suspend his work. He was taken to his daughter's home where he became progressively worse, and died on Saturday, September 17.

In honor of Judge Trieber, flags were at half-mast over the state capitol and all federal buildings in the Eastern District of Arkansas. Moreover, all federal offices in the district closed.[226] Governor John E. Martineau, United States senators, Thaddeus H. Caraway and Joseph T. Robinson, and Judge Trieber's old opponent, Edgar A. McCullough, all sent letters of condolence to Mrs. Trieber. The eulogy in the *Arkansas Gazette* was typical of those throughout the press:

> Judge Trieber's respect for the dignity of his profession was a part of his devotion to it. His court was conducted with high regard for the importance and the seriousness of its functions. He was an austere as well as a wise judge. But when he left the bench he dropped his austerity as one might drop a cloak. His kindness, his quick wit and his polished mind won him many friends without as well as within his profession. He was a charming conversationalist because his love of study had given him an unusually broad range of information.
>
> Judge Trieber found his greatest pleasure in his home, which was constantly the object of his tenderness and thoughtfulness. He was always a loving husband and an affectionate and helpful father. And he was a kind and thoughtful neighbor. He will be sadly missed by many laymen who enjoyed a friendship that was always sincere and loyal.[227]

Funeral services were held at the Trieber home with burial at Oakland Cemetery in Little Rock. The final eulogy was delivered by William H. Martin, United States district attorney, Masonic brother, and maternal grandfather of Judge G. Thomas Eisele, chief judge for the Eastern District of Arkansas from 1975 to 1991. Ironically, Martin, the judge's closest friend and an ardent Democrat, was campaigning for Democrat Al Smith in rural Arkansas when he was notified of the death. Martin eulogized:

> His life is a high example of the victory that may be won over adversity, by unending labor, based upon the fundamentals of sound character and worthy ambition. His great prominence in his profession, rounded out by an illustrious career on the bench,

> is known by all men. He equipped himself splendidly to meet the demands of high office, and brought to bear upon their discharge a storehouse of knowledge acquired throughout his industrious life, and to this he added that lofty uprightness which had already marked him as one to be trusted under all conditions. With such a man it is not strange that his record contains no scar or blotted page or that the finger of doubt or suspicion never pointed his way. To those privileged to know him well his life was an ever present inspiration, and his gentle manliness and broad charity bound him to us with ever-increasing strength. He was never a disappointment. He hoped his friends might be always right, but this did not prevent his commiserating with them when they were wrong.
>
> And so his was a full life. Full of labor and high endeavor, fully compensated by a distinct degree of success, by the love of his friends, by the development of his family along lines and in a way that made his life very content.[228]

Thus ended the career of the young Jewish immigrant, the self-educated small-town lawyer, the Republican politician from Helena, the federal judge who admonished the nation in 1903 that black men and women were entitled to equal treatment in the workplace, a man whose integrity and competence inspired the respect of all who knew him.

CHAPTER 7

John Ellis Martineau

1928–37

Stephen M. Reasoner

JOHN ELLIS MARTINEAU, United States district judge for the Eastern District of Arkansas from 1928 to 1937, was born December 2, 1873, in Clay County, Missouri. He was the son of Gregory and Sarah Hetty Lamb Martineau, who settled in Clay County in 1871. The Martineaus moved to Concord, near Lonoke, Arkansas, in 1875 and settled on an eighty-acre farm where the children grew up. As a youth John Martineau was acquainted with Joseph Taylor Robinson. Like Robinson, Martineau taught school beginning at the age of sixteen. Teaching enabled both men, who were lifetime friends, to attend the University of Arkansas.[1]

After the university, Martineau went to Argenta, later renamed North Little Rock, to teach. He also attended the Law Department of the University of Arkansas, located in Little Rock, and received a bachelor of laws in 1899. He was admitted to the bar that year. Elected to the Arkansas House of Representatives in 1902, Martineau served two terms and in 1907 was appointed chancellor in the first chancery circuit where he served for twenty years. On May 1, 1919, Martineau and Mabel Erwin Thomas, who had both been widowed, married.[2]

As chancellor, Martineau helped Scipio Jones, an African American attorney, achieve prominence at an out-of-state convention Jones was to

John Ellis Martineau. *Courtesy United States District Court for the Eastern District of Arkansas.*

attend. Asked by Jones for a letter of introduction, Martineau suggested an alternative that he thought would bring more recognition to Jones at the convention. Martineau proposed to disqualify himself on the next day divorces would be heard in his court and have Jones "elected by the attorneys present to hear a Negro divorce suit." When the day arrived for Jones to preside, the press was there and Jones received such attention that he was well received at the Chicago convention.[3]

Judge Martineau was elected governor in 1927. During Martineau's brief tenure as governor, he actively promoted better roads, using the slogan "Better Roads to Better Schools," and he succeeded in getting the first comprehensive highway measure adopted that placed the cost of the roads on the user rather than on the land. The measure was generally known as the Martineau Road Law.[4]

While Martineau was governor, massive flooding swept much of Arkansas, brought on by heavy and constant rains throughout the Mississippi Valley that began in January of 1927. By mid-to-late April all rivers and streams were out of their banks and half of Arkansas was estimated to be under water. Three feet of water stood in the North Little Rock business district and five hundred people were marooned on a bridge near Pine Bluff. Water poured upstream in the Arkansas River from the Mississippi into Arkansas City to a depth of ten feet. Inland seas formed over farmland making it possible for side-wheelers to leave riverbeds and steam across flooded fields and over treetops to rescue the stranded. A heard of steers disappeared in a whirlpool and over 50,000 animals had to be burned or buried when the waters receded. Flood losses along the Arkansas River exceeded $43 million in addition to the millions lost by the three major railroads that served the state. The Baring Cross Railroad Bridge between Little Rock and North Little Rock washed away as did all levees on the Arkansas between Fort Smith and Little Rock.[5] Secretary of Commerce Herbert Hoover headed flood relief work at the national level. Hoover was sufficiently impressed with Martineau's relief work at the state level that he helped persuade Republican president Calvin Coolidge to appoint Martineau, a Democrat, to the federal bench when Judge Jacob Trieber died in 1927. Democratic senator Joe T. Robinson, Martineau's longtime friend, had also intervened with the president on Martineau's behalf. The appointment met with strong protests from Republican leaders. Martineau was one of the few Democrats whom Coolidge appointed. Associate Justice E. L. McHaney, whom Martineau had appointed to the Arkansas Supreme Court to fill a vacancy, administered Martineau's oath of office.[6]

During Judge Martineau's nine-year tenure on the bench, six of his opinions were published, either as written by him or as reviewed by the Eighth Circuit Court of Appeals. Several are discussed here. Two were railroad cases. In one of these, *St. Louis-San Francisco Ry. Co., Missouri Pacific R. Co. and Chicago, R.I. and R. Ry, v. Board of Directors of St. Francis Levee District,*[7] the St. Louis-San Francisco Railway Company and the Missouri Pacific Railway brought suit against the Board of Directors of the St. Francis Levee District to stop collection of the board's proposed tax assessments against the railroads for the years 1929 and 1930. Specifically, the railroads alleged that the assessments against their property were arbitrary and violated both the due process and equal protection clauses of the Fourteenth Amendment. The levee district contained roughly 1,600,000 acres, 4,000 acres (or 1/400th) of which was owned by the three railroads that were involved. The total assessment against all property was $500,000, $80,000 (or 1/5th) of which was on the parcels owned by the railroads.

Judge Martineau held that any scheme of assessment by a levee district that places approximately one-fifth of the burden on one-four-hundredth ownership of property is clearly inequitable and invalid. On appeal, the Eighth Circuit reversed Judge Martineau on grounds that the district court erred by entertaining the suit. The Eighth Circuit held that the railroads had neglected to exhaust the administrative remedy provided by the levee district, which allowed the railroads a hearing before the board of directors to attack the validity of an assessment.

A second railroad case, *Missouri Pacific R. Co. v. Norwood*[8] decided in 1932, involved the Arkansas "full crew" law that was enacted in 1907. Judge Martineau, one of three judges on the panel that heard these arguments, wrote the opinion. The law was intended to regulate the railroad industry by requiring a crew of three brakemen to work on freight trains with twenty-five or more cars. A similar law of 1913 required three switchmen at certain busy crossings. The railroads challenged the validity of these laws contending that the third men were unnecessary. The railroads contended that in the years since the laws were passed conditions in the railroad industry had improved, the dangers the statutes addressed had decreased or been eliminated, and the statutes were unnecessary and arbitrary under the due process clause of the Fourteenth Amendment. Writing for the Court, Judge Martineau held that although considerable safety improvements had occurred, perils remained and so did the necessity for the "full crew" laws. The Court, thus, upheld the "full crew" laws.

In *Williamson v. Chicago Mill and Lumber Co., et al.*,[9] Judge Martineau's opinion addressed plaintiff's quiet title action concerning two islands deeded to him in 1929 by the State of Arkansas under an Arkansas statute, the "Island Act." Judge Martineau found (a) that the Island Act had not been repealed; (b) that the lands in question were islands since they were surrounded by water at ordinary stages of the Mississippi River; and (c) that the defendant's prior payment of taxes on these "islands" could not deprive the State of Arkansas of its title by adverse possession. Judge Martineau found for the plaintiff. On appeal, the Eighth Circuit affirmed the lower court's award of title to the plaintiff. In addition, it allowed plaintiff to recover damages for defendant's cutting and removing of timber from plaintiff's islands. Judge Martineau had dismissed this claim.

Oklahoma-Arkansas Telephone Co. v. Southwestern Bell Telephone Co.[10] was a case involving a local telephone company that owned and operated a telephone line from Poteau, Oklahoma, to Fort Smith. Bell also operated a line between Poteau and Fort Smith, as well as lines throughout the Southwest although it did not have a switchboard in Poteau where calls could originate. In 1923, the two companies entered into a working "traffic" agreement, which governed the routing of calls among the respective lines. In 1928, Bell legally terminated this contract and refused to allow Oklahoma-Arkansas to use Bell's lines. Bell also established its own switchboard in Poteau. This effectively rendered Oklahoma-Arkansas lines inoperative, requiring that any calls destined for points beyond Fort Smith had to be carried from Poteau to Fort Smith on Bell's lines.

Oklahoma-Arkansas sought by injunction a reconnection or restoration of its lines with the Bell system as the 1923 contract had provided. Judge Martineau reasoned that this controversy essentially involved two telephone companies competing for long-distance business between Poteau and Fort Smith. Because Bell alone had ample facilities to handle all public business between the points, the public interest did not compel reconnection. One telephone company could not, where public interest was not affected, compel a connection with its competitor solely upon the ground that a failure to obtain such a connection would cause it loss. The Eighth Circuit Court of Appeals affirmed the decision.

Judge Martineau sat on other district benches during his tenure in Arkansas, particularly in New York, Brooklyn, and St. Louis. He was a member of the Quapaw Club, the XV Club in Little Rock, and Kappa Sigma fraternity. Judge Martineau was noted as a liberal in his views and as a humanitarian in his rulings. He died of complications from the flu on March 6, 1937, at age sixty-three, and was buried in Roselawn Memorial Park Cemetery in Little Rock. A newspaper editorial published the day after his death noted that "He possessed in unusual degree judicial temperament and poise. It might be said that he was born a judge, as others have been born poets or musicians or physicians or engineers. He was noted among his professional brethren in the law for the clearness and range of his judicial vision. With this acute and luminous perception he had an innate sense of justice. He was always ready to cut through anything that seemed to stand in the way of justice. Under other geographical circumstances he might have become a nationally famous judge."[11]

CHAPTER 8

Thomas Clark Trimble III

1937–57

Elsijane Trimble Roy

THOMAS CLARK TRIMBLE III was nominated on June 17, 1937, by President Franklin Roosevelt to be United States district judge for the Eastern District of Arkansas. The Senate confirmed him on June 18, and he received his commission that same day to the seat that had been vacated by John E. Martineau. Trimble was chief judge from 1948 to January 14, 1957, when he assumed senior status. His service ended with his death on July 6, 1965.[1]

As part of the nomination process, Trimble conferred with Arkansas senator Hattie Caraway, and he had the strong support of Senator Joe T. Robinson, a former law partner. United States attorney general Homer S. Cummings recommended Trimble to President Franklin Delano Roosevelt, who sent Trimble's name directly to the full Senate floor. The speed of the nomination process showed the confidence that both the attorney general and the president had in Robinson, who was one of the Senate's most powerful members.[2]

The author of *Arkansans of the Years*,[3] referring to Senator Robinson's death on July 14, 1937, wrote that "It was not his privilege to see how widely acclaimed this appointment came to be. Even in the National

Thomas Clark Trimble III. *Courtesy United States District Court for the Eastern District of Arkansas.*

Conference of Judges generally held annually in St. Louis, Judge Trimble is a leader and is regarded as a judge of exceptional ability and discretion."

Trimble was born August 27, 1878, in Lonoke, Arkansas, and resided there until his death. His parents, Thomas Clark Trimble Sr. and Sally Henderson Chapline Trimble, moved to Arkansas from Holly Springs, Mississippi. The senior Trimble was also an attorney who served as prosecuting attorney and as circuit judge. Tom Trimble III grew up in Lonoke, graduated from Lonoke High School, and received an LL.B. from the Law Department of the University of Arkansas, located in Little Rock, in 1902. He then practiced with the law firm of Trimble and Robinson[4] in Lonoke. The firm name soon changed to Trimble, Robinson and Trimble. Trimble III apparently found it difficult in the beginning to try cases because the firm's clients wanted to hire either the elder Trimble or Joe T. Robinson. After a few months, however, Trimble III came into his own, began to develop a substantial client base, and was eventually recognized as one of the best trial lawyers in the state.

By 1915, Tom Trimble III had a well-established practice. In that year he married Elsie Jane Walls, also a native of Lonoke County. They had a happy marriage and five children, three of whom became practicing attorneys. One daughter followed her father into the judiciary and was appointed to the federal bench in 1977. Trimble was elected president of the Arkansas Bar Association in 1933. A few years later, he received an honorary doctorate of laws from the University of Arkansas. He served as special judge on the Arkansas Supreme Court and received a distinctive award from the Arkansas Bar Association for outstanding service to the judiciary and bar.

Judge Trimble's civic activities included serving on the Lonoke City Council, heading the Red Cross, and serving as president of the Lonoke Baptist Church. He was also a founder and president of the local Kiwanis Club. Trimble was very active in Democratic Party politics and assisted in the campaigns of Senator Joe T. Robinson and other state and local officials. He served on the state Democratic Committee for a number of years and was elected a delegate to the Democratic National Convention in Houston, Texas, when Franklin Delano Roosevelt was nominated for his first term as president of the United States.

Early in his career, Judge Trimble proposed that federal probationers be made responsible to the probation officers of the court in whose jurisdiction they might move, even if different from the court of original jurisdiction. This recommendation, which was adopted by statute, produced savings for the taxpayers. The Judicial Council commended Judge Trimble for this suggestion.

Many of Trimble's cases were jury trials that were not appealed and many of his decisions were not published. For these cases there is no written record to review, yet his published opinions show that he heard a wide variety of issues, both civil and criminal.

Two important issues that Judge Trimble tried continued to resurface into the 1990s. In 1933–34, the Arkansas General Assembly enacted a tax on interstate carriers that required those who used Arkansas highways to pay what was intended to be a fair share of the costs to maintain them. The effect of the statute was to tax all gasoline over twenty gallons in any vehicle that was driven on Arkansas highways. The statute also provided the method and manner to collect the tax. This issue was presented to Judge Trimble in the 1938 case of *Dixie Greyhound Lines v. McCarroll*.[5] Judge Trimble resolved this issue in favor of the state and held as follows:

> The statutes, prohibiting operation of any automobile carrying over 20 gallons of gasoline without payment of a state tax on the excess gasoline, are constitutional and constitute proper exercise of the state's taxing authority, as proceeds of such tax are devoted entirely to construction and maintenance of the state highway system. . . .
>
> Interstate commerce must pay its own way and pay for facilities furnished it by various states, if charges therefor are reasonable and bear a fair degree of relationship to facilities afforded.

The Eighth Circuit Court of Appeals reversed and held that the tax would constitute a burden on interstate commerce.[6] In 1940, the United States Supreme Court affirmed the Eighth Circuit in *McCarroll v. Dixie Greyhound Lines*,[7] with one justice concurring and three dissenting. During the 1990s, the state legislature continued to seek appropriate methods to fairly tax interstate truck traffic for the maintenance of Arkansas highways.

In *Hoxie School District No. 46 v. Brewer*[8] Judge Trimble heard one of the first Arkansas cases on school integration. In this case, the school district sought a declaratory judgment and injunction alleging that it had made administrative findings that the school should be opened to both white and Negro children on an integrated basis. The district alleged that the defendants conspired to prevent the district from carrying out the integration plans. The defendants filed a motion to dismiss the pleadings. In overruling the motion to dismiss, Judge Trimble held that "it must be stated that there are now no valid segregation laws of the State of Arkansas, for they have, in effect, been declared unconstitutional and void by the Supreme Court of the United States."[9]

Thereafter, the Eighth Circuit Court of Appeals entered a detailed opinion discussing many aspects of integration in the schools and affirming the district court's findings in all particulars.[10] Since the 1950s, integration matters and related issues have continued to be litigated in the courts of Arkansas and other states.

The unpublished case of *United States v. Baker*[11] attracted national interest. Baker, who was not a physician, headed a hospital in Eureka Springs and claimed to have a cure for cancer. The indictment charged that Mr. Baker had used the mails to defraud in falsely advertising a cure for cancer. After a fifteen-day trial, the jury found Baker guilty on all counts. Mr. Baker was reported to have attended court every day dressed in a white or lilac-colored suit with matching tie and silver-rinsed hair. He made a flamboyant figure and tried to take control of the courtroom until Judge Trimble reprimanded him. Several able counselors assisted Baker and diligently attempted to get reversible error in the record.[12] In *Baker v. United States*,[13] however, the Eighth Circuit affirmed the lower court on all issues raised in the appeal. In that opinion, the court noted that the defendant's brief had sixty-six pages devoted to "Assignments of Error Intended to be Urged," but that no error was found. This case was particularly important because the American Medical Association wanted to stop Mr. Baker's quack medical practice. Judge Trimble imposed a four-year prison term and a $4,000 fine on Baker.[14]

In a series of West Memphis civil rights cases, the chief of police, the Crittenden County sheriff, other local officials, and a prominent attorney were indicted for depriving certain citizens of their rights to a fair trial. The indictment charged that certain officers would make false arrests, mistreat those who were arrested, force them to hire a particular lawyer, and then require them to appear in a kangaroo court where exorbitant fines were exacted from them. The police chief and the attorney were both convicted, but the sheriff died shortly before his trial was set to occur. The trial and the sanctions imposed on the guilty attracted publicity and called attention to the bad conditions in that area. Local residents quickly acted to restore legal rights to the public, including fair trials and fair treatment from law enforcement officers.[15]

The unpublished case of *United States v. Wakelin*[16] was one of the most difficult cases Judge Trimble heard. Joe Wakelin, chief of police at Hot Springs, Herbert Akers, chief of detectives, Grace Goldstein, operator of the notorious Hatterie Hotel, and others, were indicted for harboring one of the nation's most notorious gangsters, Alvin Karpis, who was designated as Public Enemy No. 1. Mr. Karpis would fly into Hot Springs, spend money from a robbery, remain openly in the city where he was welcomed by some city officials, fly out, pull another job, and return to Hot Springs. At trial, the government proved convincingly that the officers were well aware of Karpis's presence and that they, along with Grace Goldstein, harbored him. The case took several weeks to try and resulted in convictions of Wakelin, Akers, and Goldstein, who all received substantial sentences.[17]

Following her trial for willfully harboring known criminals, Mrs. Goldstein was then tried for violating the Mann Act by transporting her niece to Hot Springs for immoral purposes. She was quickly convicted and received an additional sentence for that offense. This case grew out of the Karpis trials and packed the courtroom. According to Judge Trimble, people would not go home to eat.[18]

Judge Trimble was known for his sense of humor and as a raconteur. He enjoyed telling anecdotes about incidents that occurred during his service on the bench. A favorite of his stories involved a violation of the Migratory Bird Act. The defendant was brought before Judge Trimble, who asked the United States attorney Leon B. Catlett to state the charges. The attorney stated in legal terminology that the defendant did pursue, hunt, take, capture, kill, and possess a duck out of season, all in violation of the statutes of the United States and a treaty between the United States, Canada, and Great Britain that protected migratory birds. From the bench, the judge asked the defendant how he pled to the charges. Hesitating for a moment, Smith, the defendant, replied, "Well, I'll tell you, I shot the damned duck, but I didn't have nothing to do with that treaty thing!"[19]

A similar case arose when a Yell County farmer was brought before

Judge Trimble on charges of permitting his dogs to enter into and run on a game refuge. The defendant pled that they simply got loose and ran a deer to the refuge. Judge Trimble said, "Now Mr. Jones, it is your duty to keep your dogs off the refuge. It is no trouble. That line is plainly marked. Doesn't it have signs up there saying, 'This is a game refuge'?" The defendant said, "Shore, Judge, it says that, but them dogs can't read."[20]

After two decades on the bench, Judge Trimble took senior status. At that time, and again when he died at age eighty-six, many editorials and comments were published about his judicial career. This excerpt from the *Arkansas Democrat*[21] illustrates:

> Judge Thomas Clark Trimble sat in judgment of many important cases while he was on the bench of the federal district court for the Eastern District of Arkansas for more than 20 years. He presided over cases involving the late John R. Brinkley, who had a couple of hospitals in the area for operations involving goat glands, and his decision contributed materially in putting an end to the doctor's career. He also was on the bench at the trial of some of Hot Springs' police officials charged with conspiracy to hide Alvin Karpis, a notorious underworld character. Judge Trimble's court also dealt with a highly publicized cancer cure scheme of Norman Baker, who was charged with using the mails to defraud. His work on the bench drew plaudits from bar groups and he was awarded an honorary doctorate of law degree by the University of Arkansas.

CHAPTER 9

Gordon Elmo Young

1959–69

David Young

GORDON ELMO YOUNG was born in Malvern, Arkansas, April 26, 1907. By the time he graduated from high school others had begun to recognize his legal acumen. The Malvern High School annual, *The Mal—1925*, described him as both the class orator and class lawyer. While attending Hendrix College in Conway, Arkansas, from 1925 to 1927, he met his future wife, Elizabeth Gregg. After he finished at Hendrix, Young went to law school at the University of Texas for two years while debating the merits of remaining in Texas to practice law or returning to his native state. Concluding that he wanted to practice in Arkansas, Young transferred to the University of Arkansas where he completed law school in 1931. In a letter to his family shortly before Christmas in 1930, he noted that his academic performance had been of such quality that he was to receive the first bachelor of science in law as well as a bachelor of law with honors.

Young and Elizabeth Gregg maintained their courtship from the time they met at Hendrix in 1925. While he attended law school in Texas and at Arkansas, Gregg completed her legal education at the Arkansas Law School, a forerunner of the University of Arkansas at Little Rock

Gordon Elmo Young. *Courtesy United States District Court for the Eastern District of Arkansas.*

William H. Bowen School of Law. After he obtained his law degree, Young returned to Malvern to practice in 1931, and Elizabeth Gregg began her practice in the same year. This was in the midst of the Great Depression. Young shared an office with the late Senator John L. McClellan, beginning a friendship and mutual admiration that lasted until Judge Young's death in August of 1969. Young supplemented his practice by serving as deputy prosecuting attorney for Hot Spring County and also as Malvern city attorney. After practicing law in Malvern, Young moved to nearby Pine Bluff, Arkansas, in 1939, where he practiced law until his appointment to the federal bench in 1959. As a general practitioner, Young had a broad and varied practice in Pine Bluff and was known for his attention to all details. The late chief justice of the Arkansas Supreme Court Carleton Harris said of Young that "[a]s a lawyer, Gordon Young was as thorough in the preparation of a lawsuit as any attorney I have ever known."

Despite a rapidly growing law practice, Gordon Young became vigorously involved in civic work. His tenure as president of the Pine Bluff School District probably provided Young with insights into issues he later faced as he presided over school desegregation cases. After he was appointed to the federal bench and began to hear school desegregation cases, it must have seemed ironic to Young that in 1954, shortly after the *Brown v. Board of Education*[1] decision, he submitted a resolution for the Pine Bluff School Board's adoption pledging the board to respect and follow the *Brown* decision.

In August of 1959, President Dwight Eisenhower nominated Gordon Young to the Eastern District bench to succeed J. Smith Henley, who held a recess appointment and who had subsequently been appointed to the Eastern and Western Districts. The Senate confirmed Young on September 2, and he received his commission September 10, 1959. Judge Young's keen sense of civic responsibility contributed to his desire and willingness to serve on the federal bench. At a portrait-hanging ceremony that posthumously honored Judge Young, United States district judge John E. Miller of the Western District related a personal exchange he had had with Gordon Young at the time Young was debating whether to accept the nomination. Young had traveled several hours from Pine Bluff to Fort Smith to seek Judge Miller's counsel. Miller shared his own personal experience with Young for two hours and explained the duties

Young would be accepting. At the portrait-hanging ceremony Judge Miller said that Young's response to the discussion was that he would be unfair to himself, to his family, to his people, and to his state if he did not accept the challenge. At his investiture on September 25, 1959, Judge Young described himself as a "country lawyer." A member of the bar confirmed the accuracy of this description stating that Judge Young "never lost interest in common people." The headline in the following day's newspaper reflected the new judge's standing before the bar—"'Lawyer's Lawyer,' . . . Takes Oath as U.S. Judge."[2]

While Judge Young was on the bench, attorneys described him as demonstrating a unique combination of wisdom, warmth, sympathy, sternness, courage, and compassion. He also possessed a keen sensitivity for judicial economy and efficiency, which surfaced in his dismissal of one frivolous lawsuit on the ground of "silliness." A more private and humorous demonstration of Judge Young's predilection for quickly disposing of routine, trivial issues in order to concentrate on more complicated matters can be found in a letter sent to Judge Young by a local attorney. In his first letter to the judge, the lawyer had inquired as to whether he should attend this conference. The lawyer's second letter, responding to the judge's reply, outlined the history of the pending case, noted the scheduling of the pretrial conference and set forth Young's answer to his inquiry. It gives one a glimpse of Young's inclination to dispose of matters expeditiously:

> The full text of your letter, written in reply to [my inquiry as to the necessity of attending a scheduled pretrial conference], was limited to one word: "No." Some years ago I filed a $1,000 brief and transcript (supporting my petition for *certiorari*) with the Supreme Court of the United States, and this Court disposed of my massive contentions in two words: "Writ denied." I thought this ruling of the higher tribunal was exceedingly terse; but its tersity can't compare with yours. As compared with your ruling, the ruling of the Supreme Court was prolix.

Photographs found in Judge Young's office and home showing young persons whom the judge had made United States citizens at naturalization ceremonies captured best the part of his judgeship that he enjoyed the most. With a big grin on his face, he would be embracing four or five recently naturalized youngsters who were proudly waving miniature United States flags. Newspaper accounts of his death in 1969 noted that, in contrast to these inspiring naturalization ceremonies, Judge Young found it very depressing to preside over the draft resistance cases of the 1960s. Privately, it was reported, Young said the sentences he meted out to those persons were among the most difficult he ever had to give.

As with many judges of this district, Judge Young grappled with difficult cases involving the desegregation of the public schools, the constitutionality of the treatment inmates received who were incarcerated in the state penitentiary system, and legislative reapportionment. He also presided over a significant case involving an indigent defendant's right to representation by counsel. In *Gideon v. Wainwright*[3] the court was faced with resolving the issue of what type of offenses required that counsel be afforded to indigent defendants. In *Winters v. Beck*[4] Judge Young dealt with this issue in the context of a federal habeas corpus proceeding challenging a state court conviction for "immorality," a misdemeanor. The federal petitioner had been sentenced to a term of 30 days in jail and a fine of $254.00. Superficially, this charge and punishment would not seem to warrant the services of appointed counsel, Judge Young observed. The case was complicated by an archaic Arkansas statute that provided that indigent misdemeanants could be required to serve one day per dollar of fine that a defendant was financially unable to pay. In this case, the defendant's indigency led to his being sentenced to serve 284 days in jail. Focusing upon the "seriousness" of the charge that set the punishment at 284 days in jail, Judge Young held that the petitioner should have been apprised of his right to court-appointed counsel. The United States Supreme Court sustained Young's decision shortly before he died, and the case established a national precedent on this issue.

It is somewhat ironic that the report of Young's investiture in 1959 shared the same newspaper page with an article dealing with an ongoing integration dispute in a local school district since Young presided over several school desegregation cases. One desegregation issue he faced demonstrated the manner in which good faith, racially neutral policies of the past became impediments to genuine desegregation efforts. The issue was addressed in *Rogers v. Bd. of Education of the LR Ark. Sch. Dist.*[5] For a number of years, the governing bodies for junior and senior high school athletes in white schools had a policy that read as follows:

> [W]here two senior high schools or other schools of secondary grade are located in the same city or district a pupil who attends one may not transfer to the other without a corresponding change of residence, without losing his eligibility for competition in athletics until he has attended the new school for one calendar year.[6]

Black schools belonged to a governing body with a similar rule, and there was no evidence that either body had adopted the rule for racially discriminatory reasons. Rather, the rule had been enacted to avoid the possibility that athletic "recruiting" would take place in areas that had more than one school. Despite the nondiscriminatory motive and laudatory goal, Judge Young held that enforcement of this policy would have a detrimental effect upon black students who desired to transfer from a predominantly black to a predominantly white school. This case illustrates the difficult issues and subtle forms of racial discrimination that can spring from a racially neutral motivation.

As in the school desegregation area, the federal courts in the Eastern District have played an active role in determining the manner of treatment inmates may be subjected to in a state prison. In *Jackson v. Bishop*[7] Judge Young and United States district judge Oren Harris permanently banned the use of a "crank telephone," which had been used to apply electrical shocks to the anatomy of prisoners. The decision also prohibited application of corporal punishment to the bare skin of prisoners, but it did not ban corporal punishment per se. The evidence of abuse this case produced was the forerunner of more searching judicial review of prison conditions.

The political process also came under scrutiny in the federal courts, and early in his tenure Judge Young had occasion to consider a congressional reapportionment issue. After the 1960 census the Arkansas congressional delegation was reduced from six to four. The legislature undertook to realign the congressional districts from six to four. The plaintiff in *Park v. Faubus*[8] contended that the four districts diluted her vote.[9] Judge Young concluded that one vote in the Second District was not worth as much as another vote in the Third District and that the districts were not based upon population "as nearly as practicable." Judge Young therefore held that the legislative reapportionment was unconstitutional. These sorts of reapportionment cases were not particularly unusual after passage of the Voting Rights Act in 1965. However, in more recent cases, race has played a major factor in determining whether congressional lines have been properly drawn. *Park v. Faubus* is also unusual because, rather than imposing a court reapportionment of the congressional districts, Judge Young "merely place[d] the State and petitioner in the same position that they stood before the passage of any act at all." This meant, according to federal statute, that congressional elections would be at-large statewide. Just a week before *Park v. Faubus* was decided, Judge Young sat on a three-judge district court panel that held that the reapportionment of legislative districts within the state was similarly unconstitutional.[10]

In July of 1960, the first arrests were made in the Eastern District of Arkansas under a new law making it a federal offense to transport explosives across a state line for the purpose of damaging property. Federal Bureau of Investigation agents found dynamite that was set to detonate in an empty building on the campus of a then all-black college. Because it was in the midst of a controversial political season, much speculation surrounded possible motives of the arrested defendants. Attorney General Bruce Bennett, challenger to incumbent Governor Orval Faubus, implied that the governor was capable of resorting to some form of sensational act such as that for political benefit. Faubus denied any such conspiracy as "stupid," but *Newsweek* magazine reported that:

> . . . the most astonishing political development in the case came in a revelation by a Justice of the Arkansas Supreme Court, Jim Johnson. Johnson, a political crony of Faubus, asserted that he knew [two of the three men arrested] well, and considered both "very fine people." Not only that, Johnson said, but he and his family had spent the preceding Saturday night in [one of the defendant's home].[11]

Reflecting his earlier described knack for concentrating on the issues at hand without becoming embroiled in extraneous matters, Young commented: "This bombing business in Arkansas has got to stop. People have to realize that we will not live in a state of anarchy."

On a lighter note, Judge Young had occasion to preside over the trial of two criminal defendants charged with engaging in a counterfeit operation in rural northern Arkansas. The defendants were detected passing this currency at a number of locations, one of which was a local brothel.

Two of the women engaged by these men testified in a very colorful fashion how their services had been wrongfully procured by some of this counterfeit currency. Judge Young's courtroom deputy clerk at the time related that this testimony brought an unusual measure of comic relief to what otherwise would have been a rather routine case.

An overview of Judge Young's cases reveals a theme of recurring issues that confronted the federal courts both before and after his tenure. A memorial resolution adopted by a local bar association at the time of his death shows the lasting impression he left on litigants and attorneys. "Judge Young was an example of a Judge who conducted the affairs of his Court without fear or favor, but at the same time recognized the responsibility any Judge has to the persons appearing in his Court, and his duty to preserve a government of law and not by men."

PART IV

WESTERN DISTRICT OF ARKANSAS 1871–1967

US Courthouse and Jail, 1888, Fort Smith. Following its relocation to Fort Smith, the Western District court first met in rented space in the Rogers Building with Judge Story presiding. Because of an 1872 fire the court moved to a building that was part of a recently abandoned United States Army fort. This became the courthouse from which Judge Story and Judge Parker presided. It is now part of the Fort Smith National Historic Site. *Courtesy United States District Court for the Western District of Arkansas.*

US Courthouse and Post Office, Fort Smith, 1889. The 1889 courthouse and post office replaced the previous building but was razed in 1937. For the last years of his tenure, Judge Parker, followed by Judges Rogers, Youmans, and Ragon presided from this courthouse. *Courtesy United States District Court for the Western District of Arkansas.*

Judge Isaac C. Parker Federal Building and Courthouse, formerly known as the Fort Smith US Post Office and Courthouse, 1937. This 1937 courthouse and post office building, renamed for Judge Parker in 1996, is the headquarters office for the United States District Court for the Western District of Arkansas. In the 1990s the post office relocated. Of the judges featured in this volume, the building served Western District judges Ragon and Miller. Roving judges Lemley and Henley would, upon occasion, have heard matters in the building. *Courtesy United States District Court for the Western District of Arkansas.*

CHAPTER 10

William Story

1871–74

Frances Mitchell Ross

WILLIAM STORY, the second of six children of Wisconsin farmer and sawmill owner John Patton Story and his wife, Elizabeth Quarles Story of Brookfield, Waukesha County, was born April 4, 1843.[1] He attended schools in Brookfield, in Salem, Massachusetts, near his father's original home of Marblehead, and graduated from the University of Michigan Law Department in 1864. With war under way, Story joined the Thirty-Ninth Regiment Wisconsin Volunteer Infantry as a sergeant. This was one of several "Hundred

Special thanks to Judge Morris Sheppard Arnold for assistance with an opinion search for Judge Story; to Dr. Rodney Ross, Center for Legislative Archives National Archives Washington, DC, for his many years—even decades—of assistance with materials for this essay and related projects; to the late Dr. C. Fred Williams, Professor of History Emeritus and director of the Center for Arkansas Studies University of Arkansas at Little Rock; to Professor Carl Moneyhon, Department of History, University of Arkansas at Little Rock; to Dr. David Ware, historian, Arkansas secretary of state; to the Ouray County Historical Society, Ouray, Colorado, and the Colorado Historical Society for quickly responding to requests for materials; to J. Todd Ellison, former archivist and professor, Fort Lewis College, Durango, Colorado, and to his daughter for their assistance in making papers from collections in the archives available; to Linda Pine, former archivist at the University of Arkansas at Little Rock; to the Arkansas History Commission; to Special Collections, Mullins Library, University of Arkansas and to the Division of Rare and Manuscript Collections, Cornell University Library for additional materials.

William Story. Photograph of the original image by Deena Owens. *Courtesy Benton County, Arkansas.*

Days Regiments" that was obligated for one hundred days of Civil War service. Organized in June of 1864, the Thirty-Ninth left Wisconsin for Memphis where it performed guard duty around the garrison and railroad and picket duty around the city. The regiment assisted in repulsing a Confederate raid led by General Nathan Bedford Forrest in the Second Battle of Memphis on August 21. It saw no other hostile action and returned to Wisconsin to muster out on September 22.[2] After military service, Story may have done additional reading in law at a Milwaukee firm and he did practice law at the Milwaukee office of Carter, Pitkin and Davis. By the age of twenty-three Story had completed his education, he had done military service, and he had begun a professional career in Milwaukee. Then he left.[3]

Lafayette Gregg, a leading Republican from northwest Arkansas, invited Story to practice law with him in Fayetteville, although how they initially made contact is uncertain. Story accepted and in 1866 arrived in Fayetteville. Republicans were in power, Reconstruction under way, and advancement came fast for William Story. He gained the attention of politicians and in 1867, Governor Isaac Murphy appointed him to the bench of the state's Eighth Circuit Judicial District in northwest Arkansas.[4] After the adoption of Arkansas's 1868 constitution and Powell Clayton's election as governor, Clayton named Story to a six-year term on the bench of the Second Judicial Circuit in eastern Arkansas. An out-of-state newspaper later criticized this appointment claiming that Story had never "had a case or seen the face of a client."[5] In 1869, however, attorneys of the Second Circuit Bar published a commendation giving Story high marks for the manner in which he had conducted his first court in Woodruff County.[6] Such commendations, it should be noted, were a common form of recognition from attorneys about judges. Toward the end of 1868, Clayton appointed Story special chief judge of the state supreme court. Story's role in this capacity was to write opinions in cases when the chief justice had to recuse because of involvement with those cases in lower courts. Lafayette Gregg could have had a hand in this appointment since Gregg at that time was a justice on the state supreme court. These judicial accomplishments suggest that Story had positioned himself well for future success, and all of this by the age of twenty-five.[7]

After he moved to eastern Arkansas to take up his circuit judgeship, Story also engaged actively in politics. He supported Arkansas's

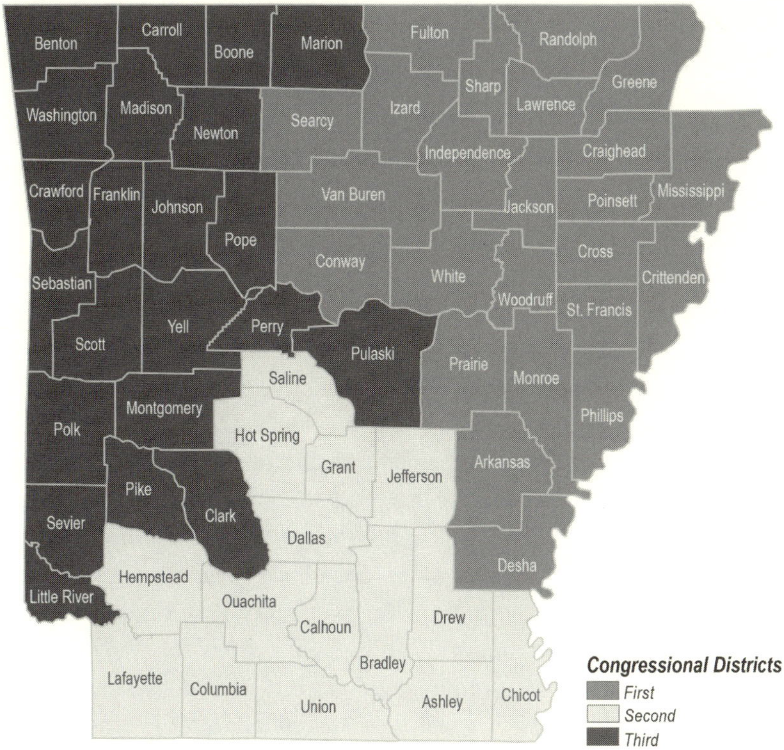

1870 Arkansas Congressional Districts. Cartography by Tom Paradise.

First District congressman Logan Holt Roots in Roots's 1870 campaign for reelection. Roots and Powell Clayton, Story's patron, were both Republicans but by 1870 the Republican Party in Arkansas had split into bitter factions. Roots and Clayton belonged to opposing sides.[8] Since he allied with Roots, Story no doubt alienated Clayton but he was well placed to benefit from the Roots connection should an opportunity present.

While Roots won the 1870 Republican Party nomination from the First Congressional District,[9] he lost in the general election to a candidate of yet a third Republican faction that had allied with Democrats. Nor did Roots's Republican faction fare well elsewhere in the state.[10] The Powell Clayton faction picked up strength, although charges of fraud surrounded the elections. Since Clayton's opponents fared poorly in this electoral season, they sought another way to stop him. By the time Roots's term ended in March of 1871, he and Arkansas senators Benjamin Rice and Alexander McDonald had successfully promoted legislation to reorganize the United States District Court for the Western District of Arkansas and to create a new judgeship for it. On March 3, the last day of the session, Senators Rice and McDonald along with Congressman Roots also endorsed William Story's application for the judgeship. As Erwin Surrency noted in his *History of the Federal Courts*, by the end of the nineteenth century the only qualification for a federal judgeship was loyalty to the party in power.[11] In Story's case, it would be loyalty to the faction of the political party in power. Street talk had also suggested that Story had been expected to marry Senator McDonald's daughter. President Ulysses Grant nominated Story and the Senate approved him, all on March 3. Story's swearing in took place on April 4, the new judge's twentieth-eighth birthday. This appointment may have seemed part of a family tradition to William Story since his great-uncle was the eminent legal scholar Joseph Story, who for twenty-four years sat on the United States Supreme Court. Family connections such as this were also important assets for aspiring judges.[12] Outgoing congressman Roots soon joined Judge Story as marshal of the reorganized Western District and if testimony given in later investigations was correct, Roots's brother P. K. (Philander Keep) was expected to be made clerk and deputy at Helena.[13] That testimony, however, may just have been speculation since evidence has not surfaced to show that P. K. served in those capacities.

William Story's three-year career as United States district judge was inseparably bound to Reconstruction-era politics, politicians, and their plans for the Western District. While Story figured prominently in the plans of the faction that secured his judgeship, that group lost power to the Powell Clayton faction and the fortunes of the initial officeholders changed accordingly. An overview of events of the time will provide context for the period of Story's judgeship.

The Arkansas politicians in Congress who promoted a restructured Western District in 1871 argued that it would help contain lawlessness in the Indian Territory, over which the one judge of the state's Eastern and Western Districts had long had jurisdiction. Since 1851, the Western District had included the western counties of Arkansas and the Indian Territory. The judge held court in Van Buren.[14] But what was the shape

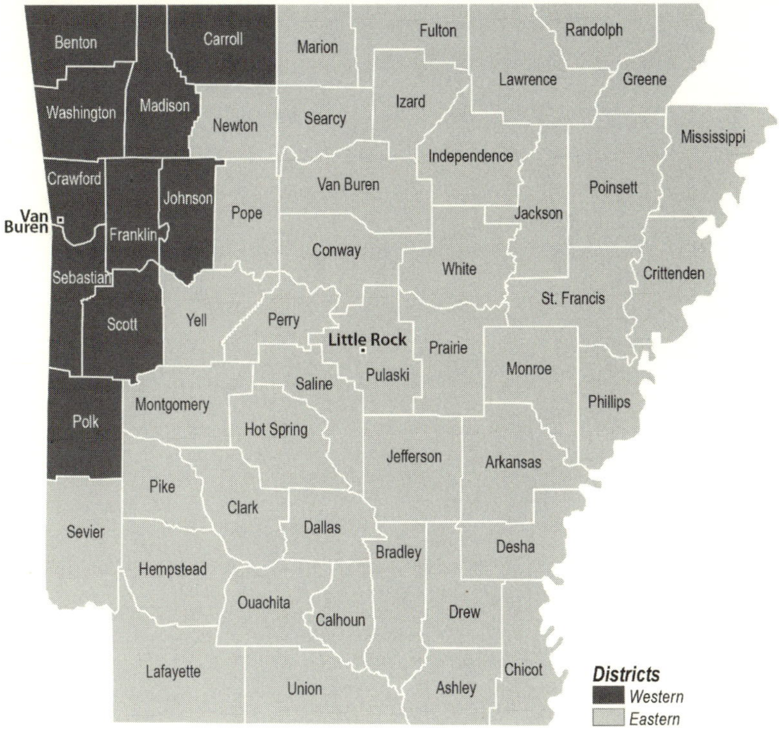

1851 United States District Court for the Western District of Arkansas. Cartography by Tom Paradise.

of this new Western District? In the name of law and order in the Indian Territory, the politicians had drawn up a district that still included the Indian Territory and the same western counties but with a new judgeship, a new seat in Fort Smith,[15] a northern corridor, the better part of the First Congressional District and a second seat in Helena on the Mississippi River.[16]

Through this designer district they had provided jobs for their own and they had positioned themselves to use recent Reconstruction legislation, the Enforcement Acts passed by Congress in 1870 and 1871, to stage a political comeback for their Republican faction. The Enforcement Acts gave federal court officials—the judges, marshals, and US attorneys—broad powers to enforce voting rights in federal elections. The acts moved trials of election officials to federal courts and set out punishments for

1871 United States District Court for the Western District of Arkansas. Cartography by Tom Paradise.

election officials who either prevented qualified voters from registering or who permitted the unqualified to register to vote.[17] With the right men in place and the law behind them, anti-Clayton politicians intended that Arkansas's new Western District court would provide the political ammunition to challenge Clayton's Republican faction in the 1872 elections. This Republican Party infighting was part of the power struggle within the party that eventually played out in the 1874 Brooks-Baxter war in Little Rock, which hastened the end of Republican rule and of Reconstruction in the state.

After the 1871 reorganization, Judge Henry Clay Caldwell, a Republican who had been the sole judge of both Arkansas districts until the 1871 redrawing, was left with a significantly reduced Eastern District and claimed no allegiance to any faction. Caldwell viewed the reorganization as a "gross fraud on the government & the people of the districts. Not a man in the state (out side the two or three in the secrets) knew a word of the measure until it had become a law. It was gotten up by Rice and Roots for purely personal and political ends & appointments made & the court run accordingly. Roots who was just going out of Congress was to be (& was made) marshal & the district was to be made to furnish the sinews of war for the political combination then formed." The motivation behind the redistricting, Caldwell said, was "not a moral reason for legislation in reference to U.S. Courts."[18]

Did the plan work? Changes in the Arkansas political landscape doomed it to fail. In 1871, the year of the court reorganization, the state legislature elected Powell Clayton to the United States Senate to replace Alexander McDonald, who did not stand for reelection. Although Clayton faced ongoing challenges from the opposing side, federal officials who were allied with Clayton's opponents were soon seeking other jobs. Clayton had Roots and Story in his sights and the senator's supporters mounted a campaign to oust them. In early 1872, for example, a letter from a Fort Smith writer appeared in a pro-Clayton Little Rock paper that accused Roots of misusing the marshal's force. The writer accused Roots of dispatching deputies to round up voters to vote for his candidates in a recent local election. The writer also criticized Judge Story, accusing him of allowing the court to be run as a political machine.[19]

While charges against Roots continued to flow from the opposition presses in the state, Senator Clayton and his allies proposed measures in Congress to alter the Western District, if not abolish it. Senator Lyman Trumbull of Illinois, who was chairman of the Senate Judiciary Committee and a Roots ally, likewise proposed a measure to redraw the district. Roots objected, writing to Trumbull that his proposal would be judicially ineffective for Arkansas and that it would nearly legislate Judge Story out of office before the next election. That would only help the Claytonites, Roots wrote. Other proposals Roots had seen he believed were equally dangerous to his interests.[20] Informing Trumbull of the rumor that Clayton wanted control of the marshal's job,[21] Roots wrote that these "reports are very discouraging to the men of this state who are looking forward with some little hope to having an untrammelled vote counted as cast—at the next election . . . the state courts here are so run that no villainous outlaw of the State Administration stands in the least fear of prosecution in them for the grossest frauds that he may commit." He continued, "The people, however, have had some hope that with the jurisdiction of this United States Court, and the Enforcement Act, a wholesome influence would be exerted towards intimidating the State Officials from wholesale fraud in elections."[22] Roots's intent to use the court and the Enforcement Acts to achieve election results fit the pattern of the period. Historian Stanley Kutler has written that legislation to remove elections to federal courts was part of the Republican pattern to tailor the judicial system to the needs of section and party and the 1871 enforcement act almost entirely circumvented state courts.[23] Like Roots, Judge Story also expressed reservations about the proposed reorganization plans but explained that his goals for new legislation were to improve court administration and to reduce expenses in the district.[24]

Roots felt certain that Clayton supporters wanted to remove Story before the 1872 elections. About reports that the president might remove him as marshal, Roots wrote that he considered "this matter of vital importance to the future prospects of the state, as I know the ballots cast will be for honest and upright government, and I am sincerely anxious to have them so counted." Roots and Story proposed a revised and smaller Western District within the state, but different in configuration from ideas coming from Washington. Roots could accept a downsized district within the state, he said, because "the immense amount of criminal business in the Indian Territory makes my emoluments constantly all that I am allowed by law." Both Roots and Story agreed that a rearranged district would make possible a more efficient court operation.[25] The stakes were high in the struggle to control the United States District Court for the Western District of Arkansas.

While saving the district, the judge and the marshal were critical to Roots, Story, and their allies, only two of the three survived the season. The district remained intact and the judge in office but on June 19, 1872, Roots was out as marshal amid reports of massive frauds and soaring expenses in the marshal's office. The US attorney general later explained that the suspension came because the department believed expenditures in the district "were unreasonable and extravagant," possibly illegal. Reports defending Roots countered that the charges of fraud were politically motivated.[26] Expenses had begun to increase even before the Roots-Story years, when they escalated and continued to be high for many years.

WESTERN JUD. DIST. ARKANSAS

Original caption: Present Limits, Black Lines.—Includes Indian Territory, Fort Smith & Helena
Present map: [see bold outline of WD in Indian Territory extending east through the state]
Original caption: Proposed Limits, Black & Red Lines.—Includes Indian Territory & Fort Smith
Present map: [see bold outline of WD in Indian Territory to bold north-south line through the state]

Existing and proposed Western District, 1872. Sketch by Logan H. Roots. Associated with HR 2204, A Bill Establishing a United State District Court in the Papers of the House Judiciary Committee (HR39A-F 13.12); 39th Congress: Records of the US House of Representatives, Record Group 233, National Archives.

The dramatic rise in expenses, along with reports of many other activities that were considered to be illegal or fraudulent, did stir talk of abolishing the district. The Western District survived, but remained one of the most expensive districts to operate in the country for most of the rest of the century. Conditions that caused some of the expenses could best have been remedied by congress but were slow in coming.

Replacing Roots was his immediate predecessor, a Clayton man, William A. Britton,[27] just in time for the fall elections. In the 1872 elections Britton, assisted by many deputy marshals, claimed success by bringing in the Republican ticket Clayton wanted although a flood of complaints about election tactics followed. The complaints prompted Britton to write the United States attorney general that "We are peculiarly situated in this state as to politics. Very little difference here in a political campaign and war."[28] Because so many people lodged complaints about election irregularities, however, the United States House of Representatives formed a select committee headed by Congressman Luke Poland of Vermont to investigate. The committee returned two reports.[29] Along with these complaints the ghost of fraudulent practices in the marshal's office resurfaced. Adding to Britton's problems were ongoing reports of ever-higher expenses in the Western District. The United States Senate did not confirm Britton as marshal, and John Sarber, also allied with Clayton, replaced Britton in 1873.[30] Problems in the marshal's office continued under Sarber, who resigned under fire on July 1, 1874.[31] Three marshals went down in three years.

Meanwhile, what of Judge Story and his work? Spring 1871 newspaper accounts of the new court administration glowed with positive descriptions, reporting that the judge was "giving entire satisfaction" and that Roots, too, was "doing things up in apple pie order."[32] According to accounts printed in the *Arkansas Gazette*, the court moved in smooth and orderly fashion, pleasing court officers and members of the bar who attended.[33] Although Story left no published opinions, he held court at Helena and Fort Smith. After the May 1871 term ended he left Fort Smith, probably for Wisconsin, and in October of 1871, he married. His wife, Ada Belle Olin, was not Senator Alexander McDonald's daughter, as earlier rumors had suggested. Rather the judge's bride was born in Waukesha County, Wisconsin,[34] and lived in Milwaukee where the wedding took place. In February of 1872 Mrs. Story became ill. While she accompanied Story to Helena for the March court session, because of her continuing illness he took her to be with her parents in Milwaukee and returned to Arkansas until the court session ended in July. Off to Milwaukee again, Story and his wife came back for the fall court terms. Mrs. Story apparently went to Helena for the court session that fall, although neither of the Storys was well at the time.[35] Some of Mrs. Story's illness could have been related to pregnancy, since the Storys had a daughter during their time in Arkansas.

Since criminal work far surpassed civil litigation in Story's court and because most of the criminal cases came from the Indian Territory, Fort Smith was the busier office. Trials, convictions, and hangings took place,[36] but the early and positive picture of the Story court vanished as management problems surrounded the court, which officials found difficult to solve. Roots wrote in 1872 that at a recent term, "witnesses were kept more than fifty days, and yet the Judge averaged right straight along over nine hours a day upon the bench." In a recent three-day murder case, Roots said, the judge was on the bench eleven hours in one day trying to finish. Both the marshal and the judge agreed that more frequent terms of court would help.[37] But critics blasted the Story administration for actions of court officials. United States commissioners, who were appointed by judges and could be removed only by the judge who appointed them, came under fire.[38] The commissioners, whose duties included issuing arrest warrants and conducting preliminary investigations of those who were arrested, were said to dismiss criminal charges after the accused paid the fees. Critics also claimed that Judge Story frequently continued cases from term to term and that the marshal's office dismissed jurors and witnesses who had been called, sometimes without pay. They raised questions about Story's handling of murder cases, especially his decisions to grant bail for a convicted murderer and to bail a man who had been indicted for murder. Some insinuated that money might have changed hands in those cases, and rumors circulated that Story had offered to sell his office. These rumors seemed to feed each other and may have reached points of exaggeration. In later testimony Story offered explanation for his actions in the murder cases, but his critics used the decisions to question his management ability and his judgment. Nor were congressional committee members who later heard charges against the judge convinced by his account.[39] As was the case with some of the expenses in the marshal's office, certain types of complaints about court administration represented problems that went on for decades and that proved to be beyond the ability of court officials to remedy.

A group of Fort Smith attorneys, both Democrats and Republicans who were ready for the Story court to be gone, directed more attacks against the judge. They complained that he was lax in attention to procedure, that he approved fraudulent marshal's accounts, that he was incompetent[40] and used the court for political ends. They passed resolutions seeking his removal. In his 1874 testimony to the House Committee on Expenditures in the Department of Justice, Fort Smith attorney and Democrat Benjamin T. DuVal condemned the entire 1871 court reorganization. He proposed that Congress abolish the Western District branch at Fort Smith and restore Judge Caldwell's jurisdiction. That same year, attorney general of the United States, George Williams, appointed DuVal to conduct yet another investigation into expenditures of the marshal's office. In February of 1875 DuVal submitted the report, which was highly critical of the marshal's office and of Story.[41]

A May 1873 bribery charge against Story sealed his fate. The charge accused the judge of taking $2,500 to dismiss a June 1872 indictment against Frank J. Nash, a druggist from Fort Gibson, Indian Territory,[42] for illegally selling liquor to the Indians. United States attorney James H. Huckleberry was accused of taking $500.00 in the same case. According to later testimony by Newton Temple, who in 1874 was United States attorney for the district, Nash had used a go-between to deliver the bribes and had talked about it freely in Fort Gibson. After the bribe allegation circulated, Nash was arrested and brought to Fort Smith to show cause why he should not be punished for contempt for having made the charge. Story decided that he had no grounds to hold Nash but wanted Temple to indict Nash for perjury because Nash refused to testify to the grand jury about the bribery charge, claiming he would incriminate himself. Temple refused to press for an indictment arguing that there was no proof that Nash had ever said that the bribe actually reached Judge Story. The court clerk testified that at Story's direction he had written to the attorney general requesting that Nash be pardoned for any supposed bribery and be compelled to disclose who might have received a bribe from him. The letter continued that the judge believed that an effort was being made to prevent an investigation and to keep a cloud hanging over him. Fort Smith attorney James S. Robinson, a Clayton supporter and attorney for Nash, vigorously pushed the bribery charge against Story.[43]

Antagonism between Story and Robinson intensified in July of 1873, during proceedings in the Nash case when Story held Robinson in contempt and struck his name from the bar. According to the testimony, this occurred after the grand jury reported that several jurors had seen Robinson talking with a potential witness, for whom a subpoena had been issued in the case and who then could not be found to testify. Story and Robinson later exchanged words that led to the disbarment. Robinson acknowledged in later testimony during the investigation of Story, that by the time he was disbarred he had lost respect for Story and had declared that he could impeach the judge. Moreover, Robinson claimed that he could prove the charge against Story by producing an affidavit from Nash about the incident and the actual bribery notes that Nash had prepared. Robinson cast doubt on his own veracity, however, when he responded during the hearings that he had once called Nash "the most corrupt villain I ever knew" and speculated that Nash's original attorney in the matter may have received and kept the money and "put the job on" Story. Still disbarred in April of 1874 when he testified against Story, Robinson by then had brought action before the United States Supreme Court to restore his membership in the bar. In the meantime Benjamin T. DuVal had taken up Nash's case.[44]

Politics also worked in the Robinson-Story feud. The year before the bribery charge was lodged, Robinson had complained to Attorney General Williams about Story's appointment of jury commissioners whose job was to select individuals to act as grand and petit jurors at the November 1872 term of court. These jurors would be the men empowered to issue indictments and who would hear trials of election officials. Robinson claimed that politics drove Story's appointments. He believed that the men the judge appointed as commissioners would select jurors who would either indict registrars and election officials or deter them from doing their jobs in the 1872 elections. Robinson identified recently suspended Marshal Logan Roots as one of those who had been appointed and argued that Story and all three commissioners opposed Robinson's and Williams's wing of the Republican Party at every level. Robinson further asserted that one of the three commissioners was not even qualified to serve in that capacity. During later testimony in the hearings about Story, however, a witness cast some doubt on Robinson's knowledge of Story's political leanings when the witness stated that in 1872, Story had actually supported President Grant, who was also Robinson's candidate.[45]

As the campaign against Story grew, the charges played out in the papers. The official Republican paper, the *Little Rock Republican*, emphasized the bribery story.[46] The *Van Buren Press*, however, expressed skepticism about the charge arguing that "whatever Judge Story's shortcomings may be in other respects, he probably did not take a bribe."[47] Attorney General Williams said in later testimony to the investigating committee that he believed that the bribery charge that Robinson had made was a "fabrication" and, of course, Story firmly denied having been offered or having taken a bribe.[48] L. B. Whitney, an examiner from the secret-service division of the Department of Justice who had been sent to investigate the marshal's office in 1872 and 1873, commented on the ongoing Story-Robinson feud, saying he believed "Story the most honest man."[49] The *Van Buren Press* speculated that a ring had been formed to force

Story's resignation. Who might be leading the ring? Powell Clayton, the paper was certain, in order to make room for a "pliant tool."[50] Why bribery? As Erwin Surrency reminds readers in his *History of the Federal Courts*, impeachment is the only constitutional procedure provided to remove a United States district judge, who must then be convicted of treason, bribery, or other high crimes and misdemeanors. Poor management and political differences would not rise to the impeachment standard.[51] The hostile members of the Fort Smith bar, along with their allies, were surely well aware of these constitutional requirements for impeachment.[52] While Judge Story had defenders, his opponents had momentum.

By 1874, the Western District was coming unraveled. Three marshals had fallen and after a three-month period of hearings before both the United States House Committee on Expenditures in the Department of Justice, which was examining the Western District, and also before the United States House Judiciary Committee, which was examining numerous charges against him, Judge Story resigned on June 17[53] and stopped the impeachment process. In some minds, questions remained. Why, for example, could Frank J. Nash, who had been subpoenaed, not be found to testify about the bribery charge? Were allegations of bribery, corruption, and other charges simply ways to derail the judge or was he really guilty? Regardless, impeachment was over, Story was out, and many in Fort Smith remained convinced of the judge's guilt.

After Story left the bench he left the state and moved to Colorado, still a territory at the time. Story and his wife settled first in Denver with their young daughter Ada Belle. Their second child, William Olin, was born in Denver on October 31, 1874. In deciding on Colorado and eventually the town of Ouray in the southwestern Rockies, Story could have had contact with his former Milwaukee law associate, Frederick W. Pitkin. Pitkin, elected governor of Colorado in 1878, had moved to the southwestern Rockies for health reasons in 1874, the same year Story moved to Denver. Pitkin established a law practice, invested in mining, and claimed Ouray as his address when he was nominated for governor. Story and Pitkin probably crossed paths during those years and could have known of each other's Colorado plans before moving.[54]

When Story moved to Ouray in 1877 it was a young but growing mining town that quickly attracted population. Silver was being mined there and gold was discovered two years before Story arrived. For Story it was a place to make a fresh start. During periods of his first ten years there he was attorney for the city and county of Ouray and for a short time he was Ouray County judge. He thus reclaimed and retained the title of judge. Story built a large Ouray law practice, specializing in mining law, and partnered from 1883 to 1897 with Democrat, Judge Theron Stevens, in the firm of Story and Stevens. In 1897 he formed a partnership with his son, who styled himself William Jr. and was a recent Cornell University Law School graduate. They practiced in the Story and Story firm. Story also became a significant property owner in Ouray. Through an 1893 foreclosure he gained possession of a large building that became the anchor of his Story Block, composed of several lots he owned that fronted Main Street. He located his law firm and other businesses in this 1893 acquisition, and identified the building by a plaque titled Story Block. Two years later he bought four lots a block east of the Story Block where he and his wife built a $6,000 Queen Ann–style house for themselves and their two children. Part of the community fabric, Story sometimes made featured addresses at public events and offered guidance at times of public dispute. For example, in a 1902 crisis that involved Chinese laundry workers whom local labor organizations wanted to expel from Ouray, Story spoke forcefully about the importance of adhering to the rule of law rather than allowing mob rule to reign. The family attended the Episcopal Church and contributed to it. Story also maintained ties with the Republican Party, running successfully as the party's candidate for lieutenant governor in 1890 for a term that ran from 1891 to 1893.[55]

From the time of his arrival in Ouray, Story invested in corporations to build roads, water facilities, eventually railroads and more. In the 1880s he joined Lucien Lucius Nunn of nearby Telluride in mining, banking, and power production enterprises. Story served as the first president of Nunn's San Miguel Valley Bank in Telluride at about the time Butch Cassidy (Robert Leroy Parker) and three others robbed it in Cassidy's first bank robbery. When the bank later burned, Story continued as president of the successor bank, the First National Bank of Telluride, and was attorney for Nunn's Telluride Power Company. Story was a longtime stockholder and member of the board of directors of both the bank and the power company,[56] but in 1912 power company stockholders and Nunn broke, with Nunn removed from the power company presidency over differences in the direction of the company. These differences, which had been developing for several years, led to the sale of the company the same year Nunn lost the presidency. They contributed to the end of the Nunn/Story relationship, as well, a relationship that dated back well over two decades but that had had rocky times along the way. After Nunn left the company, power company headquarters moved to Salt Lake City where the Storys also relocated although they retained their Ouray residency and property. Story and another of the former Telluride Power Company directors who had also opposed Nunn formed a law practice along with Story's son William and retained the reorganized Salt Lake City–based power company as a client.[57]

While William Story recovered from his turbulent years as United States district judge in Arkansas and built a successful Colorado career as lawyer, businessman, and politician, themes from the stormy Arkansas past resurfaced on at least three occasions. Almost as soon as he arrived in Colorado, Story became involved in a headline-grabbing incident that led a Denver paper to report that he had been cowhided by a woman he insulted. The incident made news in the *Denver Democrat*, was forwarded to the *Arkansas Gazette*, picked up by the *Fort Smith Independent*, reprinted by the *Cherokee Advocate* in the Cherokee Nation, and no doubt received attention in other papers as well. The *Advocate* reported the full and humiliating account with an addendum from the *Independent* that pointedly reminded readers of Story's "carpet bagger" origins. The *Gazette* added its own editorial comment on the late "Judge of the United States Court of the Western District of Arkansas," reporting on similar treatment Story had received at the hands of a man while Story served as circuit judge in eastern Arkansas.[58]

Later in his 1890 run for lieutenant governor, baggage from those years rolled out in the press again. The *Denver News* opened its attack on Story with selections of testimony about the 1873 bribery charge against him. In a late October 1890 edition the *News* ran a scathing editorial on Story's conduct as US district judge and accompanied the editorial with excerpts from Benjamin T. DuVal's 1875 report to the Department of Justice on the Western District.[59] The *Colorado Graphic* defended Story, condemning the *News* as a partisan press and claiming satisfaction from an answer given by Story and a letter from Judge Henry Clay Caldwell that had been published on the matter.[60] Story was apparently concerned enough about the attack by the *News* or by other bad news that before the paper's second installment appeared he telegraphed the United States district clerk in Fort Smith requesting all papers from the 1873 contempt proceedings against James Robinson.[61] This episode must certainly have represented the most heated revival of those issues but a negative reference to Story's Arkansas judgeship surfaced again during the controversy that led to Nunn's ouster from the power company. Citing Story as an early opponent of Nunn in the struggle, an anonymous letter that was critical of Nunn's foes referred to Story's having "acquired the title of judge during the 'carpet bag' days in Arkansas from which he resigned under fire to escape impeachment."[62]

While Story's opponents found the Arkansas years ripe with ammunition to use against him, the 1899 *Colorado Portrait and Biographical Record* reported only that Story had resigned his Arkansas judgeship and moved to Colorado "in hope of recovering his health, which had been greatly shattered."[63] Poor health became the most common reason given for the resignation. That explanation was probably picked up from the biography and then made its way into later articles and into obituaries in several papers. Health problems did eventually cause Story's retirement from work in Salt Lake City. After retirement, he spent much time in Los Angeles where he died at the age of seventy-eight on June 20, 1921, survived by his wife of nearly fifty years, his daughter, son, several grandchildren, a sister, and a brother.[64]

Wisconsin native William Story moved rapidly through the ranks of the state and federal judiciary in his adopted Arkansas home. Yet his participation in the era of bitter Reconstruction rivalries and the firestorm that erupted over his judgeship brought on an equally swift fall, an end to his federal judicial career and to his stay in the state. Colorado offered fresh opportunity in law, business, and politics. While reminders of the Arkansas years periodically resurfaced in Colorado, Story survived the challenges and lived to see the Arkansas period largely recast in the Colorado record.

CHAPTER 11

ISAAC CHARLES PARKER

1875–96

Morton Gitelman

THE MOST famous district court judge in the history of federal courts in Arkansas is I. C. Parker, the so-called hanging judge. Because the 1871 Western District court's jurisdiction over Indian Territory continued for twenty-five years, almost co-incident with Parker's tenure, it was the most active criminal court in the federal system. More than 13,000 criminal cases were docketed in the twenty-one years that Parker presided, and a significant number of murder cases were tried in his court. Many books have been written about Judge Parker and his court,[1] but they all tend to focus on the "Wild West" aspect of the court and the notorious criminal characters that appeared in court and, often, on the gallows in Fort Smith.

Just before the death of Judge Parker in November 1896, Congress terminated all of the court's jurisdiction over the Indian Territory by establishing territorial courts within the remaining territory.[2] The Western District court then became indistinguishable, in the jurisdictional sense, from other federal district courts. The court of Judge Parker,

A portion of this article was published as "The Civil Side of Judge Parker" and appeared in *Oklahoma Law Review* 56 (2003): 129. It is reprinted here with permission of the *Oklahoma Law Review.*

Isaac C. Parker. *Courtesy United States District Court for the Western District of Arkansas.*

however, was unique in the history of the federal judiciary, and the remarkable activity of that court is justly deserving of study.[3]

The Background of Judge Parker

Most of the books and articles about Parker and the Western District court are in agreement about the details of the life of the judge prior to his taking the bench in 1875. He was born in Belmont County, Ohio, October 15, 1838. His early education was sporadic because of working on the family farm, but at age seventeen he decided to become a lawyer and began teaching school and attending Barnseville Academy to fulfill his ambition. In 1859 Parker was admitted to the Ohio bar.

About the same time he became a lawyer, Parker succumbed to the "go West" fever and traveled by boat to St. Joseph, Missouri, which was the gateway to the West at that time. He saw the need for legal practitioners in that bustling frontier town and settled there. He soon met his future wife, Mary O'Toole, a local girl and a Catholic. Religious differences delayed the marriage, as Parker was a Protestant, but they did marry.

Parker soon became city attorney in St. Joseph. He was an active Democrat and a supporter of Stephen A. Douglas. When Lincoln was elected and the South seceded, Parker switched parties and was very active in seeking to keep Missouri out of the Confederacy. He remained a staunch Republican for the rest of his life.

During the Civil War, Parker was an enlisted corporal in the state militia, but never left St. Joseph; he served as assistant provost marshal in the town. In 1864, he was a presidential elector for Lincoln's second term and was elected prosecuting attorney.

After the war, Parker was elected to a six-year term as circuit judge in 1868. He served but two years, running for Congress and getting elected in 1870. Even though the Democrats were increasing their power in Missouri, and gerrymandered his district, Parker was reelected to a second term in 1872. While in Congress he was a member of the Committees on Territories and Appropriations. Although Parker sponsored a bill in 1874 (which failed of passage) to open Indian Territory to white settlement, he was generally regarded as sympathetic to Indians and was referred to as the Indian's best friend in Congress.

In 1874, Parker did not stand for reelection, due to the sweeping resurgence of the Democratic Party in Missouri; all thirteen congressional seats went Democratic, and the Republicans were in disarray. In March 1875 Parker became one of a number of Republican ex-House members seeking appointments from President U. S. Grant. Parker's prospects for obtaining party favors were strong because of his membership on the powerful Appropriations Committee, and President Grant appointed him as chief justice of the Territory of Utah.

At the time of the appointment to Utah, Arkansas's Western District judgeship was open. William Story, who had been appointed in 1871, resigned in 1874 under threat of impeachment for corruption.[4] Judge Caldwell of the Eastern District was serving both districts.

The Arkansas Republican Party was in the throes of the Brooks-Baxter war in 1874–75, and Senator Powell Clayton asked President Grant to appoint an outsider to the vacant judgeship. Grant withdrew the nomination of Parker to the Utah post and appointed him to the Western District position.[5]

Isaac Parker, his wife, Mary, and their two children arrived at Fort Smith by boat on May 2, 1875. The town population at the time was between 2,000 and 2,500, and it was a much rougher place than St. Joseph. There were no sidewalks, paved streets, or public schools. The citizens of Fort Smith were expecting the arrival of another "carpetbagger" like Story. When Parker and his family alighted, the local population was somewhat impressed by his physical appearance: "They saw a broad-shouldered man over six feet tall, weighing two hundred pounds, with piercing blue eyes and tawny mustache and goatee."[6]

Judge Parker set out immediately to prove that he was not a corrupt carpetbagger. He began court on May 10, only eight days after his arrival in Fort Smith. The judge immediately attacked the backlog, commencing court at 8:30 each morning except Sunday, and going often into the night. In the first term, he had eighteen murder cases. Fifteen defendants were convicted, and eight were sentenced to hang on September 3. Of those first eight capital sentences, one defendant had his sentence commuted by President Grant due to extreme youth, and another was killed while trying to escape jail. The remaining six were hanged together before a crowd estimated at 5,000 that included many newspaper reporters.

After this first mass execution, Parker was ever after known as the hanging judge. The local citizenry, however, more cognizant of the heinous crimes committed by those executed, were generally appreciative of the law-and-order nature of the new federal judge and the appellation of carpetbagger was rarely heard again in Fort Smith in reference to Parker.[7]

Parker and his family became very much a part of the Fort Smith community, and as the years progressed the community accepted the Republican judge from Missouri. Parker was twice elected a member of the Fort Smith School Board and reportedly never missed a meeting. One anecdote illustrates that he was not an aloof figure nor did he play the magisterial judge when off the bench:

> Judge Parker loved children and served for years on the Fort Smith school board. During a secret session of the board to deal with a rather delicate case, a teacher declared furiously: "Judge Parker, I'll have you know you are not on your bench now. Here in this school building, you are just an ordinary man and if you try to run over me I'll pull every hair out of that beard of yours."[8]

The same source also recounts the judge's love of baseball and an amusing incident in that connection:

> He loved to take his big umbrella and a palm leaf fan and watch a baseball game. Earl Hardin played with the Fort Smith amateurs and his team had matched a game against Jim Hoey's famous Jenny Lind miners. The Fort Smith team lacked a good pitcher and a scout discovered that a man named White, serving a sentence in the U.S. jail for violating the liquor laws, was a wonderful pitcher.
>
> Earl visited the jail and found that "White" really was an alias for Cy Sizemore, one of the best pitchers of the southwest. Cy could win for Fort Smith but jailer Berry said he would lose his job if he let Cy out long enough to pitch a baseball game. Hardin appealed to the judge and the necessary leave of absence was secured. The judge attended the game and watched Sizemore strike out 19 Jenny Linders.[9]

Toward the end of his life, Parker told a reporter in an interview that he had not intended to stay in Fort Smith for very long: "I did not expect to stay here more than a year or two when I came. The President had said to me, 'Stay a year or so and get things started,' but I am still here, as you see."[10]

The Criminal Jurisdiction of the Court

When Parker took the bench in 1875, the Western District court had geographic jurisdiction over several counties in Arkansas and over Indian Territory—an area of more than 74,000 square miles reaching from Fort Smith to the borders of Colorado and New Mexico, encompassing what is now the state of Oklahoma. This area was the home of several Indian tribes or nations, in particular the Five Civilized Tribes (Creek, Cherokee, Choctaw, Chickasaw, and Seminole). Under the federal statutory scheme, the Indian nations had jurisdiction over their members, including criminal jurisdiction, and tribal courts were existent throughout the territory. However, Congress mandated that crimes involving non-Indians committed in the territory were without the jurisdiction of the tribal courts and were to be prosecuted in the federal court for the Western District.

The great difficulty in many of the cases brought in the Western District involved the definition of "Indian." From the time the Indian Territory was established in the 1830s the Indian nations were given the right by treaties to maintain their own laws and order of society insofar as they did not contradict the Constitution. Within the five nations, Indian law differed as to citizenship; while nativity was the common source of Indian citizenship, citizenship by adoption, naturalization, or through intermarriage was governed by tribal law. Moreover, after the Civil War, in the reconstruction treaties of 1866, the Indians agreed to free their slaves and grant them the rights, privileges, and immunities of Indian citizenship.[11] Thus, for jurisdictional purposes, an "Indian" could be a native American, a white person, a black person, or a foreigner. In criminal cases arising in Indian Territory, the indictment would have to specify, for example, "a white man and not an Indian," or "a Negro and not an Indian." If at trial, or afterward, proof was adduced that both parties to the crime were Indians, by blood, treaty, or adoption, the federal court at Fort Smith lost jurisdiction. Judge Parker had to learn, and he became well versed in, the laws of the various Indian nations that bestowed citizenship on non-natives.[12]

The aftermath of the Civil War upset the quiet and relatively peaceful conditions in Indian Territory. The Creek Nation had sided with the Union and freed its slaves, while the Choctaws sided with the Confederacy and raised soldiers for the South. The Cherokee chief, Ross, tried unsuccessfully to maintain neutrality but the Cherokee Nation was sharply divided. Factions existed in all the nations, but after the war Congress treated all the nations as Confederate sympathizers and the 1866 treaties of reconstruction diminished many of the prewar treaty rights of the nations.

After the Civil War, the non-Indian population of the Indian Territory increased substantially. Former slaves, rootless whites, and, most significantly, an assortment of lawbreakers who sought refuge from the authorities—there was no interstate extradition from Indian Territory—settled in the territory. The coming of the railroads also had a tremendous impact on the Indian Territory. Well before the end of Judge Parker's tenure, the Indians were a minority in their own territory.[13] Even after the geographic jurisdiction of the Western District court was reduced in 1883[14] the criminal caseload did not decrease. The constant pressure of non-Indian settlement, the increasing "Boomer" movement to open Indian land to whites, and the reputation of the territory as a haven for those evading law enforcement in the states, all played a role in keeping Parker's court an extremely active criminal court.

The Nature of Federal Criminal Law

Federal criminal law and procedure were, in large measure, responsible for Parker becoming known as the "hanging judge." On the substantive side, federal criminal law was a matter for Congress. By 1812, the Supreme Court had firmly established the principle that federal courts could not rely on the common law to define what activity constituted a crime and that federal crimes are only those codified by Congress.[15] On the procedural side, however, the Constitution and common law were the sources of law.

Criminal procedure in the federal courts in the early 1880s was rather primitive. In state courts, the movement toward fact pleading and court-promulgated rules, along with statutory guides, was fairly well advanced. However, both Congress and the Supreme Court had not moved much beyond the inherited common law confusion. Moreover, procedural due process, a staple of modern criminal procedure constitutionalism, was not well developed. The difficulties were described in US attorney general Benjamin Brewster's annual report for 1883:

> It is desirable that the attention of Congress should be directed to the want of proper legislation for criminal cases, in order that the pleadings may be simplified, a uniform system of challenges provided, and the trials shorn of the technical objections and numberless dilatory motions that can now be interposed to prevent a speedy trial upon the merits.
>
> In preparing indictments for offenses against the United States, it is found necessary to follow the common-law forms of the last century, with all the technicalities, verbosity of descriptions, repetitions, and precision of statements formerly required, whereby that which should be a simple and concise written accusation becomes a lengthy and painfully confused mass of descriptions and allegations, wholly unintelligible to the defendant who is called upon to answer, or to the jury selected to try the case.[16]

The report goes on for several pages to describe the problems of common-law criminal procedure, such as the necessity, in homicide cases, of describing the exact cause of death in the indictment, in larceny cases, the exact value of the property taken, and the necessity of correct spelling of names in the indictment. Any discrepancies between pleading and proof were fatal.

Many of the procedural problems had particular impact in Judge Parker's court; criminal cases from the Indian Territory, the vast bulk of the court's docket, ran the entire gamut of common-law crimes because jurisdiction was founded on the place of the crime (Indian Territory), the status of the victim and the alleged perpetrator (non-Indians involved) rather than the type of crime. For example, in one notorious case, an Arkansas doctor, William Cooper, and a married woman patient, Mrs. Elizabeth Alexander, went to Indian Territory and took up sexual cohabitation. They were arrested, taken to Fort Smith, and prosecuted in Parker's court—Dr. Cooper for adultery and Mrs. Alexander for fornication (her husband had obtained a divorce prior to the trial).[17]

Another problem mentioned by the attorney general was also an issue in the Western District: "Questions frequently arise as to the competency or credibility of witnesses who are entitled, in the event of the conviction of a defendant, to compensation or reward by reason of any loss or damage sustained, or for the arrest or apprehension of the defendant. A law should be passed making all such persons competent witnesses."[18] A substantial number of the criminal cases before Parker involved rewards for arrest or conviction and defense lawyers were constantly raising the argument that the arresting marshals and witnesses for the prosecution were seeking rewards rather than telling the truth.[19]

The attorney general in his 1883 annual report recommended to Congress the enactment of a number of statutory reforms in criminal procedure, but the plea did not engender any response.[20] Judge Parker had been a trial judge in Missouri prior to his congressional career and was somewhat familiar with state criminal procedure under the common-law forms, but after 1890, when appeals to the Supreme Court in capital cases became available, the high court was compelled to address more often the concept of a fair trial in appeals from Parker's court.

Appeals from the Western District Court

During most of the time Judge Parker presided over the Western District, no appeals could be taken from criminal convictions. The Western District was one of four in the nation that had been established as both a district and circuit court, so appeals to the Eighth Circuit were not possible. Also, no appeal to the Supreme Court was available. This state of affairs was not very significant for most of the country because relatively few criminal cases and even fewer capital cases were heard in federal courts. Parker's jurisdiction over the vast array of crimes committed in Indian Territory, however, meant that the ever-increasing number of criminal convictions could not be reviewed.

Throughout most of the nineteenth century, conventional wisdom held that the Constitution did not establish a right of appeal in criminal cases.[21] Congress legislated very little in this area; the most significant change came in 1879 when Congress enabled federal circuit courts to issue, as a matter of discretion, writs of error in all cases of imprisonment or fines exceeding $300.[22] This, of course, had no impact on the Western District court because Parker was also the circuit judge.

The notoriety ensuing from the number of executions in Fort Smith spurred a movement in Congress, led by John H. Rogers from Fort Smith (who would become Judge Parker's successor), to establish a right to appeal by the writ of error to the Supreme Court in capital cases. Rogers was on the House Judiciary Committee and shepherded a writ of error bill in 1888, along with a companion measure to establish independent circuit court jurisdiction for those district courts that also had circuit powers. On the floor, he spoke several times about the shocking situation and injustice of no appellate review of death sentences, at one point noting: "In one of these courts [referring to district courts with circuit powers], namely, that which refers to Arkansas, I can not state the exact number of cases, but in the last fifteen years approximately one hundred capital cases have been tried, and the parties have been sentenced to death without the right of revision by any other court."[23] Some opposition was raised by House members who were opposed to any increase in federal court jurisdiction, but the bill easily passed the House and Senate and became law without the president's signature in 1889.[24]

The availability of Supreme Court review in capital cases had an immediate impact in Parker's court. Convicted defendants who could afford counsel could now lodge an appeal to the Supreme Court and receive an automatic stay of execution. Between 1891 and Parker's death in 1896, the Supreme Court reviewed more than forty capital sentences imposed in the Western District. Thirty convictions were reversed; some defendants were convicted at second trials, and a few, after second appeals, at third trials. Several were retried and convicted of manslaughter.[25] By contrast, in the 1891–1896 period, sixteen capital convictions in Parker's court were not appealed to the Supreme Court.

Judge Parker became very critical of Supreme Court review, stating publicly that the court reversed him on the slimmest of technicalities and that the publicity surrounding appeals was responsible for the increased murder rate in the Indian Territory. Parker was also very critical of the performance of the appellate attorneys for the United States, accusing them of incompetence in arguing the appeals (in a few cases the solicitor general's office confessed error). He also criticized the justices of the Supreme Court for having no familiarity with criminal conditions in the territory or with criminal law generally.

By 1894 Judge Parker was engaged in a very public battle with the Justice Department and with the Supreme Court. In one case when Supreme Court justice White ordered a prisoner released on bond, Parker refused, arguing that Justice White did not have the power to grant bail after a conviction.[26] That ruling was appealed, and the court ruled against Parker, stating that he misunderstood the powers of the court and his own duty.[27]

Parker also unburdened himself to a reporter for the *St. Louis Globe Democrat*, and was quoted as saying that the Supreme Court was "knifing the trial judge in the back and allowing the criminal to go free."[28] Parker expressed the view that the Supreme Court should see the full transcript of capital trials, rather than summaries, in order to better understand the nature of the crimes committed.

Chief Justice Fuller, in several of his opinions reversing Parker, went out of his way to be critical of the way Parker behaved on the bench. On the converse, Justice Brewer—who was the circuit justice for the Eighth Circuit—often dissented, stating that Parker had acted appropriately. During all of this period, the Supreme Court was articulating a rudimentary concept of fair trial in what were mostly cases of first impression. Relying not on citations of authority or definitions of due process, the court, when reversing Parker, was most often disagreeing with Parker's jury instructions, especially in cases involving self-defense. In several of those cases, federal marshals had been killed in gun battles with wanted men, and Parker was always solicitous of the safety of the court's marshals.[29] Also, Parker was reversed three times for using a biblical quotation in explaining to the jury why flight or escape from law officers was evidence of consciousness of guilt. The expression Parker used was: "The wicked flee when no man pursueth, but the innocent are as bold as a lion."[30]

Parker's bitterness toward the Supreme Court and the Justice Department was fueled not so much by the trial judge's dislike of being reversed, but because he truly believed that the delays brought about by appeals, retrials, and further appeals was having a real and deleterious effect on crime in the Indian Territory. Probably the one incident that was most responsible for Parker's bitterness was the Cherokee Bill affair.

Cherokee Bill, whose real name was Crawford Goldsby, had a short but brutal criminal career during his eighteenth year. Early in 1895, Goldsby—while participating in a robbery at a small store in Lenapah, Indian Territory—noticed a man watching the robbery. Goldsby turned and deliberately shot and killed the bystander. Not long after, the killer was arrested (some say that his friends turned him in for the reward, but that has not been substantiated). He was brought to Fort Smith, tried, convicted, and sentenced to hang. Cherokee Bill engaged an attorney to file an appeal with the Supreme Court and received a stay. While he was in the Fort Smith federal jail awaiting the outcome of his appeal, someone smuggled two pistols into his cell. The guards found and confiscated one pistol, but Cherokee Bill successfully hid the other one. On July 26, 1895, he took out his pistol and sought to foment a general jail break. One of the two guards, Lawrence Keating, drew his gun and was shot and killed by the prisoner; the other guard managed to go for help. Cherokee Bill was holed up in his cell, periodically firing his pistol, letting out a ferocious and blood-curdling turkey gobble every time he fired.[31] He finally surrendered after another prisoner, with the jailer's permission, was allowed to go to the killer's cell.[32] The entire community was outraged by the killing, as Keating was a popular man and left a widow and four children. Harrington writes:

> Of all the killings in his district, this one angered Isaac Parker most. The Judge gave his views in a public interview. He lashed out at the sentimentalists who shed tears for such border outlaws as Cherokee Bill. He denounced the government for being miserly in appropriating money for guards. He said bitter words about the Supreme Court of the United States. The court's delay in acting on appeals gave murderers a "long breathing spell," said Parker. Which, in this case, had meant death for a citizen whose life was "worth more to the community and to society at large than the lives of one hundred murderers."[33]

Cherokee Bill was immediately indicted, tried, and convicted of Keating's murder, all within sixteen days after the killing. His was the only murder case in Parker's court that did not occur in Indian Territory; jurisdiction was founded on the fact that the jail was federal property. This conviction was also appealed to the Supreme Court. While Cherokee Bill was still waiting, in solitary confinement and irons, the Supreme Court affirmed his earlier capital conviction, and he was executed on March 17, 1896; the Supreme Court dismissed his pending appeal for killing Keating as moot.[34]

What Parker could not understand was how the Justice Department lawyers handling appeals in the Supreme Court constantly failed to argue and demonstrate the heinous nature of the crimes for which the appellants received the death penalty. Parker apparently felt that neither the court nor the Justice Department understood the unique role of the Western District court as the only symbol of justice and law and order in the vast Indian Territory.

Judge Parker and Capital Punishment

The hangings in Fort Smith drew widespread public attention to Parker and the court. Capital cases amounted to only a small percentage of the court's criminal work, however. Actually, many more capital indictments were brought in the Eastern District of Texas, at Paris, after that court gained jurisdiction over a portion of Indian Territory in 1889. However, Judge Bryant of the Texas court never received much attention because so few capital convictions were returned by the Texas juries.[35] It was the number of executions and the frequency of multiple hangings on the same day that attracted the national attention to Parker's court.

The local newspapers reported on most of the executions but never in the lurid manner that newspapers in the North and East utilized. Even the local *Fort Smith Elevator*, however, used colorful, if factual terminology in its reportage. For example, in reporting on the double execution of Henri Stewart and William Elliott Wiley (alias "Colorado Bill") the paper reported:

> On Friday morning last the day dawned bright and beautiful, the sun shed its lustrous rays through the prison bars of the U.S. Jail as if endeavoring to cheer the hearts of the two unfortunate beings whose names appear at the head of this article, and who were so soon to go into eternity.[36]

The two "unfortunate beings" had been convicted of separate murders. On the scaffold, the paper reported, Wiley reiterated his self-defense argument and Stewart had nothing to say about his crime, "but made a few remarks concerning his fate, saying he was thankful for the privilege of leaving this world by the speedy means by which he was to go, at the same time dangling the rope that was to end his existence." Stewart was not the usual bandit or desperado. He was thirty-one years old, had been born in Choctaw Nation, and had been educated at Yale and Harvard Medical School. At the time he killed his victim, Stewart was married, and left a wife and four children. (Actually, according to the evidence adduced at trial, Stewart shot at the victim but missed and his companion, a cousin named Wiley Stewart, who was drunk, fired the fatal shot in front of twenty-three witnesses; the cousin escaped and was never apprehended.) Before returning to Indian Territory, he had had a varied career as a ship's physician traveling to Cuba and the coast of South America.

Modern-day opponents of the death penalty have sometimes used Parker as a symbol of bloodthirstiness, tying him to the Supreme Court revival of the death penalty in recent years. For example, in one law review article the author states:

> Judge Isaac C. Parker of the federal court in Fort Smith, Arkansas, who between 1875 and 1896 sentenced 144 men to hang from the gallows on the front lawn of his courthouse, surely would have been pleased with this reemergence of traditional civilization and humanity orchestrated by his admirer, Chief Justice William Rehnquist, who recently quoted Judge Parker's parting words:
>
> I never hanged a man. It is the law. The good ladies who carry flowers and jellies to criminals mean well. There is no doubt of that; but what mistaken goodness! Back of the sentimentality are the motives of sincere pity and charity, sadly misdirected. They see the convict alone, perhaps chained in a cell; they forget the crime he perpetrated, and the family he made husbandless and fatherless by his assassin work.[37]

Assertions of this sort reflect an ignorance of the federal criminal law at the time of Judge Parker and are wide of the mark of his feelings regarding capital punishment.

When Parker said that he didn't hang men, the law did, he meant it literally. The statutes of the time made capital punishment the only available penalty for murder and rape, the two capital crimes that came into the Western District court. Neither the jury nor the judge had any discretion regarding a lesser sentence than hanging.[38]

The only means by which an execution could be avoided after a conviction for murder or rape was executive clemency. Lawyers for convicted murderers often petitioned the president for clemency or commutation. On at least one occasion Judge Parker himself sought clemency for three defendants he had sentenced to hang:

> [I]n March, 1883, three Creek teenagers—Luce Hammon, He-wah-muck, and one Wiley—fired between twenty and thirty rifle shots into the camp of a white traveler named Owens. One of the bullets struck Owens in the hip, and he died a week later. When the three came to trial in the summer of 1885, their own confessions, as well as the testimony of other witnesses established their guilt beyond a doubt. . . . Parker pronounced the sentence on July 2, 1885, then, recognizing the extenuating circumstances of the case, he began

preparing a brief requesting a presidential commutation for the three. Assisted by District Attorney W. H. Sandals, the Judge submitted a list of reasons for leniency: the defendants had been mere boys when they committed their crime, unable to comprehend fully its consequences; some question remained as to whether or not they actually intended to harm Owens; and the attack had occurred during a factional war among the Creeks, when traditional standards of law and order were relaxed. President Grover Cleveland accepted these arguments, and issued commutations for all three convicts on April 19, 1886, reducing their sentences to life imprisonment. Parker had successfully intervened to save the boys from the death penalty he had imposed.[39]

The federal criminal law, unlike that of the states, recognized no degrees of murder, a state of affairs that led to several pleas by the attorney general of the United States for Congress to amend the law. In 1889 Attorney General W. H. H. Miller said:

In most of the States a distinction is recognized between degrees of murder, and punishment graded accordingly. In the United States statutes no such distinction is recognized. The result is that convictions are had, and sentences of death imposed, in cases which, according to the practice in most of the States, would be murder in the second degree. As a natural consequence there immediately follows an application for executive clemency. The judge is constrained by the laws to impose a sentence against which his judgment protests, and the only remedy is to immediately importune the President to undo the action of the court by a commutation. I think this should be remedied by statute.[40]

The "flowers and jellies" quote is somewhat out of context. When Judge Parker made that statement he was expressing his concern about the delays that appeals introduced into the criminal process, as well as about the lack of experience with crime and criminals on the part of appellate judges whose exposure prior to taking the bench had been solely in civil matters. Indeed, in the same interview, Parker went on to say: "I favor abolition of the death penalty, provided there is a certainty of punishment, whatever the punishment might be, for in the uncertainty of punishment following crime lies the weakness of our halting justice."[41] He also expressed his belief that appeals in criminal cases are proper, but that the system ought to provide for special courts of criminal appeal, state and federal, and that appellate courts should see the whole record of the trial and reverse only if innocence is manifest on the record. Although the term was not then in vogue, Parker was referring to the concept of harmless error.

Parker also sought to put capital punishment in context. He told the interviewer that in the five-year period, 1890–95, 43,000 persons were murdered in the nation; there were 723 legal executions and 1,118 lynchings.[42] Parker laid the blame for the doubling of the murder rate on the courts: "The bench is not alive to its responsibilities. Courts of justice look to the shadow in the shape of technicalities instead of the substance in the form of crime."[43] Nor was Parker alone in the practice of multiple hangings. In the 1880s hangings were often public spectacles. In the same years that Parker would have several capital sentences carried out simultaneously, state courts were doing the same.[44]

Thus, rather than exhibiting a bloodthirsty preference for capital punishment, Parker shows a modern and enduring emphasis on victims' rights and a modern notion of certainty of punishment being more important than quantity, as well as a humane concern for imprisonment rather than execution in cases with extenuating circumstances.

More than one source supports the assertion that Parker disliked imposing the death penalty. A former court stenographer in a 1932 newspaper reminiscence states:

> The judge was known to his friends as kindhearted, loving and merciful. Miss Annie Hite, editor of the Fort Smith Saturday City Item, was an intimate friend of the Parker family.
>
> She said that whenever he passed the death sentence, the judge would come home in low spirits and would hardly touch food.[45]

The author also reports that in noncapital cases Judge Parker would often reduce a penitentiary sentence after a visit to his house by the convict's wife and children pleading for mercy.[46]

Considering that only a tiny percentage of the thousands of criminal cases in Parker's court involved capital crimes, one should look at the larger picture in assessing Parker's philosophy of criminal punishment. In this context, consider that Judge Parker took a keen interest in prison conditions and rehabilitation. In sentencing defendants to prison terms,

Parker most often directed incarceration in the federal prison at Detroit, although it was more distant, because of its superior reputation for education and rehabilitation programs.[47]

Parker also exhibited concern for the rights of those arrested. In one case, after a long and hard day in court, a half-dozen guilty pleas in liquor cases were taken up:

> It was past supper time when the judge reached the last man who had been arrested at Durant [Oklahoma]. This prisoner put up the usual stock plea that he had bought the six or eight quarts at Sherman [Texas] for his sick wife and some neighbors and was only pleading guilty to retail liquor dealing to get out of jail and back to his invalid wife.
>
> "You see, judge, they kept me in jail at Dallas for 28 days before that commissioner would examine me and send me on to you."
>
> It was very late and the judge was worn out after a fatiguing day, but when he caught the words, "28 days at Dallas," he jerked up his head and fairly shouted:
>
> "What's that? Did that commissioner make you lie in a Dallas jail 28 days? Mr. Hagin [deputy clerk], look up the papers and see if this man is telling the truth about that 28 days." Ed found the prisoner's statement correct and the judge exclaimed: "Perfectly outrageous to have subjected this prisoner to such unexcusable delay! We are compelled to appear dilatory here because we have at this moment 124 prisoners in our jail, but the Dallas commissioner has no excuse whatever. Mr. Clerk, figure this man's sentence so it will expire today. No, wait a minute: We don't want to put him outdoors tonight. Make his sentence expire tomorrow morning."[48]

Judge Parker was also tireless in seeking to improve conditions in the federal jail. In the early years of the Western District, the jail was in the basement of the fort building, under the courtroom. It was divided into two rooms, always overcrowded and dangerous to health. Parker and others lobbied the attorney general for funds to build a new jail. Attorneys general, in turn, lobbied Congress for an appropriation. Typical is the following:

> The jail consists of two rooms, partially under ground, with barred doors and windows, but with no cell arrangements whatever. The rough stone floors are damp, and the air is fetid in spite of the plentiful use of lime and whitewash, as indeed, it must be, where

> fifty or more prisoners are confined, the sick and the well together, in a small space almost utterly devoid of any of the modern sanitary appliances. It is not surprising, therefore, that the reports of the Detroit house of correction, in which United States prisoners sentenced from the western district of Arkansas are confined, are said to show that many of the deaths in that institution are among those convicts who were held in jail at Fort Smith previous to their trial and sentence.
>
> Not only is the health of these prisoners almost certain to be impaired or ruined by this mode of imprisonment, but it is manifestly unjust and cruel to confine detained witnesses and boys charged with minor and first offenses in the same room with murderers and outlaws.[49]

In 1886 Congress responded and a new three-story jail was begun. It was completed in 1889.[50]

Noncapital Criminal Cases

Of the 13,490 criminal cases docketed in Judge Parker's court between May 10, 1875, and September 1, 1896, only 344 were capital crimes. Also, some 4,000 petty cases were dealt with before the commissioners' courts. Naturally, the hangings attracted most of the public and media attention, but the noncapital cases reflect the Western District court's role as the center of criminal justice for most crimes in the Indian Territory—at least those involving non-Indians.

Because jurisdiction in the court was founded on location (Indian Territory) and status (either the victim or perpetrator being non-Indian), the whole range of common law crimes covering violence (e.g., assault, arson), crimes against property (e.g., larceny), and crimes against society (e.g., bigamy, adultery) came before the court. Also, a major portion of the court's docket was devoted to violations of federal criminal statutes, most notably the intercourse laws that restricted trade within the Indian Territory, especially the introduction of liquor. Another important federal statutory crime in Parker's jurisdiction was timber trespass—the illegal taking of trees from public lands.

The more than 13,000 noncapital prosecutions in the Western District resulted in a conviction rate of about 70 percent. Obviously, most of the convictions resulted from guilty pleas and as there was no appeal—

except in capital cases after 1889—the court was one of last resort. Post-conviction challenges to jurisdiction were possible and Parker, sitting as a circuit court, did rule in some cases of that sort, but these were rare. In such cases, habeas corpus writs were the vehicle for review, and many habeas cases were heard. Habeas corpus along with demurrer pleas were also frequently used to test jurisdiction prior to trial.

Some of the most interesting and difficult cases in the Western District involved the issue of jurisdiction, and Judge Parker wrote several published opinions dealing with jurisdiction. Many of these cases involved very fundamental issues of sovereignty, comity, citizenship, and interpretation of treaties, and Parker's opinions in these cases are noteworthy.

1. Jurisdiction

In 1878 and 1879 Parker decided two cases that analyzed the jurisdiction of Indian courts and the federal court in Fort Smith. In the first case, *Ex parte Kenyon*,[51] Kenyon filed a petition for habeas corpus in the Western District court after his conviction in a Cherokee court for larceny of a mare and his confinement in the Cherokee penitentiary at Tahlequah. The facts showed that the petitioner was a white man who lived in the Cherokee Nation with his wife, a Cherokee citizen. After his wife died, Kenyon moved to Kansas taking the mare; at the time he left the Cherokee Nation, no letters of administration had been taken out on the estate of his deceased wife. Parker first held that the federal court in Fort Smith had the authority to issue a writ of habeas corpus to run in the Indian Territory. Very forcefully, he stated that the writ "is the highest right possessed by an American citizen, and in a proper case his right to this writ follows him in the Indian country, as well as elsewhere."[52] Parker then ruled that the Indian court did not have jurisdiction because Kenyon was not an Indian. Despite the argument raised that, by marrying a Cherokee, Kenyon had become an Indian by adoption, Parker said: "[F]or the purposes of this case, it not necessary to decide whether the terms of the treaty and the intercourse law include Indians by adoption as well as by birth—that is, Indians belonging to the tribe as well as those belonging to the race—for the principle that is applicable in this case would apply with equal force to either."[53] He goes on to establish that the principle is that when Kenyon left his domicile in Indian country and gained a domicile in Kansas the offense, if any, was committed after he changed his domicile. "[H]ence the petitioner had clearly abandoned the Indian nation, and was then only subject to the laws of the place of his domicile. He was a citizen of the United States, and was subject to the laws of the state of Kansas. Therefore, the court which convicted him did not have jurisdiction over his person . . . [and] it could not try and sentence him to imprisonment."[54]

This case established some important ground rules that governed many future issues regarding the jurisdiction of Indian tribal courts. In 1978 Chief Justice Rehnquist cited Parker's opinion as a historic precedent for the principle that Indian tribal courts do not have jurisdiction over non-Indians living on an Indian reservation.[55]

A year after *Kenyon*, in *Ex parte Reynolds*,[56] Parker took up the other side of the coin, so to speak. The defendant in a murder case brought in the Western District sought discharge by habeas corpus on the ground that the court had no jurisdiction because both he and his victim were Indians. Both Reynolds and Puryear, the victim, were white men married to Indian wives and living in the Choctaw Nation. Parker wrote that no statute governed the definition of who was an Indian, contrasted with statutory definitions of the African race that dealt with the quantum of blood: "Does the quantum of Indian blood in the veins of the party determine the fact as to whether such party is of the white or Indian race? If so, how much Indian blood does it take to make an Indian, or how much white blood to make a person a member of the body politic known as American citizens?"[57] Parker disagreed with the one federal case precedent on the issue:

> In the case of *United States v. Sanders* [Case No. 16,220], the court held that the quantum of Indian blood in the veins did not determine the condition of the offspring of a union between a white person and an Indian; but further held that the condition of the mother did determine the question. And the court referred to the common law as authority for the position that the condition of the mother fixed the status of the offspring. The court is sustained in the first position by the common law, and also in the last position, if applied to the offspring of a connection between a freeman and a slave, upon the principle handed down from the Roman civil

> law, that the owner of a female animal is entitled to all her brood, according to the maxim partus sequitur ventrem. But by the common law this rule is reversed with regard to the offspring of free persons. Their offspring follows the condition of the father, and the rule partus sequitur patrem prevails in determining their status.[58]

Parker found that the evidence showed that Mrs. Puryear, the victim's wife, had a paternal grandfather who was a white man, living in Mississippi. Therefore, "Mr. Puryear was married to a woman who was legally a member of the white race, or of the body politic known as citizens of the United States. He did not, therefore, become a Choctaw by marriage, but was a citizen of the United States, and being killed in the territorial jurisdiction of this court, it has jurisdiction, and the writ must be dismissed and the defendant remanded to the custody of the marshal."[59]

This pair of cases was important in the allocation of jurisdiction between the federal court and the Indian courts for crimes committed in Indian Territory. However, the issues of status had to be assessed on a case-by-case basis.[60] The Indian press was critical of Parker in these matters—claiming diminution of tribal sovereignty—because the treaties of 1866 seemingly conferred criminal jurisdiction over adopted or intermarried citizens of the Indian nations. After Congress established federal courts within the territory as of September 1, 1896, this type of jurisdictional problem pretty much disappeared, because the Western District court no longer had territorial jurisdiction. However, the nations were even more critical after 1896 when the tribal courts became essentially obsolete, losing most of their remaining jurisdiction. Judge Parker was friendly toward Indian institutions and sympathetic to their development, but he felt obligated to follow the law even when that diminished jurisdiction in the Indian courts.

2. Extradition

Another setback to Indian jurisdiction came about in a case where Parker had to make a basic and important interpretation of the Constitution. In April 1883, Frank Morgan shot and killed Albert Johnson, sheriff of the Sequoyah District of the Cherokee Nation. Both Morgan and Johnson were Indians. Johnson had many friends high in the Cherokee government and Morgan, who felt he acted in self-defense, fled to Arkansas fearing for his safety. On July 13, 1883, the principal chief of the Cherokee Nation, Dennis W. Bushyhead, signed a requisition asking Governor James H. Berry of Arkansas to issue a warrant for Morgan's arrest and for his return to the Cherokee Nation. Berry issued the warrant and, on September 11, 1883, Morgan was arrested at Fort Smith. Morgan's attorney filed a petition for a writ of habeas corpus in Parker's court.

In *Ex parte Morgan*,[61] Parker ruled that under the interstate rendition clause of the Constitution, the Cherokee Nation was not a state or territory and, therefore, the prisoner could not be extradited to the Cherokee Nation. Parker began by stating:

> Interstate extradition is regulated by law. No such power can ever be exercised by the chief executive of a state on the ground of comity. . . . Nor has it ever been, in this country, properly and legally exercised on such ground. Comity may and does afford a strong reason for the enactment of laws providing for the extradition of criminals, that they may be brought to justice, and society be thus protected. But we must look to the law for the right to exercise this extraordinary power.[62]

Parker then took up the issue of whether the Cherokee Nation could meet the constitutional definition of state or territory:

> Both the word "state" and the word "territory" have attached to them, under the constitution and laws of the United States, a technical meaning. The Cherokee Nation does not come within this meaning, but it is a part of what is called "Indian country." Early in the life of the country a certain section of the domain of the nation was set apart as Indian country. By the advancing tide of white population and the formation of new territories first, and then states, much of what was then Indian country has ceased to be such, and has become states in the Union; but the Cherokee Nation maintains the same status today in its relations to the federal government as it did when first set apart by such government,—not as a state or territory, but as the home of the Indian. These Indians have, from the foundation of the government, been treated as being separate and apart from the states and territories of the Union, and this tribe as well as all others are contradistinguished by a name appropriate to themselves, and one differing from either

> a state or a territory. They belong to the republic, though they are neither a state or territory in it.[63]

Parker concluded that the governor of Arkansas could not legally issue a warrant for the arrest of Morgan, and he granted the writ. This decision not only diminished the authority of the Indian nations but it now established the other end of the strange situation that allowed Indian Territory to become a haven for criminals. Those who committed crimes in the states and were able to flee to Indian Territory could not be extradited and those Indians who committed crimes in the territory and were able to flee to the states could not be extradited.

3. Timber Trespass and Boomers

Subject matter jurisdiction also caused problems for the justice system in Indian Territory. This was presented most starkly in a timber trespass case, one in which Judge Parker expressed his frustration at having to rule the way he did.

The western progress of the railroads was the source of the denuding of vast forests for timber. Because much of the land containing mature trees was public land, public resources were being taken at an alarming rate:

> The rolling hills in eastern Oklahoma and western Arkansas were once home to magnificent old forests of white oak and southern pine. During the last quarter of the nineteenth century, the tall trees in these green reserves underwent an assault unmatched in America's forest history. Though defined as "iron roads" in most languages, railroads could have been more accurately designated as "wooden roads." Rail line construction consumed great quantities of mature timber; a mile of track took approximately 2,640 crossties, and it took an acre of forest to yield 200 ties (an average). . . . Railroad interests created and sustained a burgeoning timber market that ravaged the forests of the Parker court jurisdiction throughout the last quarter of the nineteenth century.[64]

In June of 1878 Congress finally responded to requests for action by passing the Timber Cutting Act.[65] The statute made it a crime to take timber from "lands of the United States which, in pursuance of law, may be reserved or purchased for military or other purposes."

Soon after passage of the act Parker had to decide if the act applied to lands of the Cherokee Nation. In *United States v. Reese*,[66] the defendant was charged by an information preferred by US attorney W. H. H. Clayton for "unlawfully cutting timber on lands situated and lying in the Cherokee Nation, in the Indian country, in the Western District of Arkansas, which said lands, in pursuance of law, may be reserved and purchased by the United States for military or other purposes." The defendant demurred on the grounds that the information did not state an offense and that the court lacked jurisdiction.

Parker stated that: "To determine the question whether these are lands of the United States, requires a consideration of the title by which they are held by the Cherokee Nation. To any one who has given any attention to this subject, it presents a question not free from doubt or intrinsic difficulty."[67] Parker had to interpret the treaty of May 6, 1828, wherein the United States "agrees to possess and guarantee to the Cherokees, forever, seven million acres of land" provided "that such lands shall revert to the United States if the Indians become extinct or abandon the same." The judge analyzed the treaty in terms of property law and concluded that what the Cherokee Nation enjoyed was a fee simple title with a possibility of reverter: "This Indian title being a base, qualified, or determinable fee, with only the possibility of a reversion, and not the right of reversion, in the United States, all the estate is in the Cherokee Nation of Indians. I cannot, therefore, see how these lands, which have been depredated upon, can be held to be 'lands of the United States,' in the sense of the language used in section 5388."[68]

Parker was unhappy that he had to hold the penal statute inapplicable, because the timber thieves regularly preyed upon the Indian lands:

> It is to be regretted that it cannot be held to be an offence, as the complaints of depredations upon the timber of the Indian lands are constantly being made to officers of this court. There is a class of men on the borders of Indian country who revel in the idea that they have an inherent, natural right to steal from the Indians. This right is not to be questioned. They think it a tyrannical use of authority if they are interfered with.
>
> There should be a law enacted, the penalty of which would teach persons that Indians have rights which should be respected as well as the rights of citizens. . . .
>
> If the law-making power will give us a law, we shall lay its

> mailed hand upon its violators in such a way that the timber in that Indian territory will be protected from the rapacity of those who are now stealing it.[69]

Parker seldom thundered so forcefully in his opinions, so we can assume he was really disgusted at the rampant timber thievery.

Parker clearly disliked timber thieves. He was even more opposed to the so-called boomers, a group of whites who hungered for settlement of Indian lands not occupied by Indians. This group, whose most prominent leader was David L. Payne, claimed that any lands not actually occupied by Indians were public lands open to homesteading, on the theory that the Indian nations had ceded those lands to the United States in the 1866 treaties. As the boomers grew in number they set up camps on the southern border of Kansas and began to plan their occupation of unassigned lands in the Indian Territory. On April 26, 1880, Payne led a small party of boomers across the Kansas line. They began staking claims and built a stockade on the Canadian River not far from present-day Oklahoma City. Federal troops arrested Payne and his group and escorted them to the Kansas border, where they were hailed as heroes. A second incursion in July resulted in the army taking the boomers into Fort Smith to appear before Judge Parker. District Attorney Clayton filed a civil complaint under the intercourse laws against Payne on August 13, 1880. Demurrers and motions to dismiss and counter motions delayed the decision in the case until May 1881. Parker ruled against the boomers holding that the unassigned lands were not open to homesteaders, and Payne was fined $1,000, the maximum under the intercourse law.[70] This ruling, however, did not end the continuing efforts of the boomers to colonize the unassigned lands. Finally, a case came up in 1884 that gave Parker another chance to remonstrate with the boomers.

Some of Payne's followers (Payne died suddenly in November of 1884) claimed access to the Cherokee Outlet or "strip," a narrow band of land running just south of the Kansas border west to the 100th meridian. (From the 100th meridian west to the Colorado border, the strip was known as "no man's land" because neither the federal courts nor the nations had jurisdiction; this strip, now known as the Oklahoma Panhandle, became a part of the Oklahoma Territory in 1890.) An incursion of boomers resulted in a situation where a Cherokee policeman, Connell Rogers, not only evicted some interlopers, but he burned a shack they had erected in the strip. The owner, a boomer, charged Rogers with arson in the federal court at Wichita, Kansas, and obtained a warrant for the arrest of Rogers. Rogers, learning of the warrant, went to Fort Smith where he surrendered on December 30, 1884, and petitioned for a writ of habeas corpus in Parker's court to avoid extradition to Kansas.

In *United States v. Rogers*,[71] Parker was faced with the argument that Congress in the Act of January 6, 1883[72]—that provided "all that part of the Indian Territory lying north of the Canadian river and east of Texas and the 100th meridian, not set apart and occupied by the Cherokee, Creek, and Seminole Indian tribes, shall . . . be annexed to and constitute a part of . . . the judicial district of Kansas"—meant Parker did not have jurisdiction because the shack was in the area assigned to the district of Kansas.

Judge Parker was not swayed by the argument. He held that the Cherokee Nation had, at all times since it obtained the Outlet, claimed it and exercised jurisdiction over it. Therefore, he reasoned, the Cherokees "occupied" the strip even though no Indians were settled there; consequently, the Kansas district court did not have jurisdiction over the strip. "Hence, when a nation or body of people have the title to land, and the same is subject to their will and control, it is occupied by them,—legally, it is in their possession."[73] In this habeas ruling, Parker established Cherokee title to and dominance over some 6,000,000 acres of land and helped, temporarily at least, stave off the boomers. This decision was hailed by the Cherokees because the nation derived considerable income from leasing grazing rights in the Outlet to the Cherokee Strip Live Stock Association. During 1889 the Cherokee Nation was negotiating a fifteen-year lease with the cattle grazers that was worth $6.6 million. In the unassigned lands, the Creek Nation also leased grazing rights, and in the Choctaw Nation, coal-mining leases brought considerable funds into the coffers.

In 1889, however, Congress opened the unassigned lands to white settlement and it created the Territory of Oklahoma in 1890. The Cherokee Outlet was not part of the new territory, but many white settlers appeared in the strip, and agitated for recognition.[74]

4. Liquor Cases

Another important Parker opinion, involving statutory interpretation, touched on the liquor issue. Parker and many others attributed much of the lawlessness in the territory and many other Indian problems to the introduction of liquor into the territory. The first massive bout of liquor running in Indian country came with the construction of the railroads beginning in 1866. The Missouri, Kansas & Texas Railway (MKT) was one of the first to push into Indian Territory under the provisions of the treaty of 1866, which had specified that railroads could be granted the right to enter the territory:

> In the summer of 1870, the tracks of the MKT were pushed southward from Chetopa across the Cherokee Nation. It drew into the Indian country a motley flotsam of laborers, suppliers, and assorted camp followers, with much disorder and a ready market for liquor. . . . Muskogee [terminus of the MKT] late in 1871, soon became noted as the scene of many episodes of violence.
>
> Attempts by the United States marshal to lessen the problems by confiscating the liquor that was their prime stimulus aroused the wrath of railroad executives. . . . Eventually the Attorney-General had to ask the marshal to restrain his deputies [from entering freight cars and searching for liquor].[75]

When Parker took the bench in 1875, the illicit liquor trade in the territory was well established, and prosecutions for liquor violations numbered in the thousands.[76] A grand jury report in 1887 remarked:

> Notwithstanding the stringency of the law in regard to introducing and selling intoxicants in the Indian country, we find that about ninety-five per cent of the criminal matter presented to us is directly or indirectly traceable to intoxicants as the cause. . . . We deplore the fact that white men and women are the principal offenders in both the introduction and sale of intoxicants, and we see no remedy that would be entirely effectual short of unarming the inhabitants of the Indian country, prohibiting the manufacture of intoxicants, or backing the sturdy and brave marshal and staff by U.S. troops.[77]

One liquor case from Fort Smith reached the Supreme Court. In *United States v. Ellis*,[78] the defendant was charged with introducing ten gallons of lager beer into the Indian country. Judge Parker instructed the jury in the case that the statutory language—"that no ardent spirits shall be introduced," and that "every person who . . . introduces or attempts to introduce any spirituous liquor or wine into the Indian country, shall be punishable"—included beer. The defendant, an agent of Anheuser-Busch in St. Louis, claimed that beer was not "ardent spirits." A similar case in the Northern District of Texas had been won by the brewery, but Parker had a different approach. He told the jury that when the Indians were being removed from their homes in the east to the frontier country, they asked that the government of the United States should pledge them security and protection in their new homes:

> Intoxicating liquor was one of the things that they recognized as the greatest evil to them and their people; that this court takes judicial notice of, because it is a part of public history; one of the greatest evils, I say, because it has swept whole tribes out of existence. There are few left of the Delaware tribe up in the Indian country. That tribe was at one time one of the most powerful people of that race upon the continent, and they have been swept out of existence to a great extent owing to the use of intoxicants brought to them and given to them in order to steal from them their rights by the white men. There is now left of that powerful tribe of people only about 400. The wise and good men who were leaders of these Indian people knew the baneful influence of this destructive power of drink, and they asked that the government of the United States should not only say in its treaties that they should be protected,—they and their young men, and their people generally,—but that laws should be enacted making it a penalty upon the part of the white man, or the Indian man, or any other man, to introduce into that country that which would destroy them.[79]

Parker went on to tell the jury that if beer could produce intoxication it should be viewed as "ardent spirits" and charged the jury that beer was covered by the statute.

The jury returned a guilty verdict. On appeal the Supreme Court reversed Parker. In *Sarlls v. United States*, Justice Shiras said:

> The Century Dictionary defines "spirituous liquors;" as "containing much alcohol; distilled, whether pure or compounded, as distinguished from fermented; ardent: applied to a liquor for

> drinking." "Malt liquor" is defined by the same authority as "a general term for an alcoholic beverage produced merely by the fermentation of malt, as opposed to those obtained by distillation of malt or mash."
>
> Webster defines the word "spirituous" as rum, whisky, brandy, and other distilled liquors, as distinguished from wine and malt liquors. Worcester says that "ardent spirits" is a term applied to liquors obtained by distillation, such as rum, whisky, brandy, and gin.
>
> So far, therefore, as popular usage goes, according to the leading authorities, "lager beer," as a malt liquor made by fermentation, is not included in the term "spirituous liquor," the result of distillation.[80]

The breweries won the battle but Congress amended the statute to include ale and beer along with ardent spirits as prohibited items in Indian country. That was a temporary setback, however, because when Indian Territory was dissolved and Oklahoma became a state, the intercourse act was no longer a factor.

5. Other Interesting Cases

In a pair of cases decided the same day, Judge Parker held that persons charged in the federal court at Muskogee in Indian Territory with "infamous" crimes must, under the Fifth Amendment, be charged by indictment or presentment of a grand jury, and cannot be legally charged by information.[81] Also, that same day, he held that the Indian Territory court at Muskogee did not have jurisdiction to hear a case of larceny based on a grand jury indictment, because the statute of March 1, 1889, establishing the court, did not authorize it to impanel a grand jury.[82] This trio of cases relegated the federal territorial courts to the role contemplated by Congress—handling minor crimes and civil suits in the territory. Congress specified that the criminal law of Arkansas should be the source of crimes for the Muskogee court.

One unusual habeas corpus case came up in 1886. Three leaders of the Cherokee Nation, Wolf, Ross, and Phillips, were indicted in the District of Columbia for conspiracy to defraud their people of some $22,500 by obtaining a sum of money from Principal Chief Bushyhead under false pretenses in connection with the sale of a portion of Cherokee land to the government to be used to settle some other Indian tribes; the acts in furtherance of the conspiracy were alleged to have occurred in Washington, DC. The petition alleged that as the defendants were all Cherokees and the fraud, if any, was against the Cherokee Nation, the federal court did not have jurisdiction. Parker ruled against the defendants holding that: "The indictment . . . is sufficient to show jurisdiction of place and person, the existence of, and jurisdiction over, the subject-matter by the supreme court of the District of Columbia."[83]

A very short and cogent opinion was filed by Judge Parker in *United States v. Howe*.[84] In a murder case, the prosecution called Dr. Bennett as an expert witness. Bennett refused to testify unless paid a reasonable compensation for his expertise, and the prosecutor moved to hold the witness in contempt. Parker, in a one paragraph opinion, held there was no contempt, noting a wide distinction between a witness called to give an opinion based on his skill in a particular profession or trade, and a witness called to testify as to facts that he observed.

Administration of Justice in the Western District

The unique characteristics of the jurisdiction of Judge Parker's court and the fact that it was the only court handling criminal cases arising in the Indian Territory made the administrative machinery of the court noteworthy. Also, the nature of the federal system at the time caused unusual problems for the court.

Enforcement of the criminal laws in Indian Territory being its primary concern, the Western District court had to have a force of deputy marshals to serve warrants and arrest and bring in for trial those accused of criminal acts. Soon after Parker began holding court in 1875, some two hundred deputy marshals were designated. Arresting desperados was a dangerous task, and during Parker's twenty-one years, some sixty-five deputies and posse men lost their lives in the line of duty. The marshals who rode out to make an arrest employed a posse, usually one or two individuals, to assist them if the situation appeared risky. The posse riders were often Indian policemen, known as "light-horse." The marshals not only had to arrest and return defendants to Fort Smith, but also to bring in witnesses.

The work of the deputy marshals was not only dangerous, but it was also ill paid. The federal system at that time was based on fees, not salaries. The deputies were paid mileage, expenses, and arrest or service fees. The pay was minimal, and if a deputy could not find his quarry or lost a prisoner due to escape, he lost his fees; if he had to shoot and kill an escaping desperado, the deputy not only wasn't paid his mileage, but he also had to bury the deceased at his own expense.

In 1894 a grand jury report from the Western District was sent to Attorney General Richard Olney, who published the entire statement in his annual report. In part, the grand jury stated:

> The fees and emoluments provided by the law for the arrest and transportation of criminals is doubtless sufficient in the execution of the law in the several States, where means of communication by mail, telegraph, railroads, etc., are ample, where law and order is the rule instead of the exception; where the officers of the law have and feel the need of aid which in cases of necessity they are entitled to from every citizen of the country through which he [*sic*] passes, and his duties rarely take him through a country not populous, but the conditions of the Indian country are exactly the reverse. . . .
>
> The conditions for the execution of legal process are so materially different in the Indian Territory to what they are in the States that it is practically useless to apply them to that jurisdiction. The law allows fees for specific purposes, but the payment of the fees depend upon the contingency that the officer accomplishes the object of the mission he is sent on. He is allowed $2 for making an arrest, 6 cents a mile for going to the place of arrest, and 10 cents a mile for himself and the same for the prisoner returning to court. One-fourth of these fees go to the chief marshal, and the other three-fourths to the deputy. Should he fail to make the arrest, no matter how long or how much he is out in time or money, he gets nothing. It is true there is a clause in the fee law allowing the officer his actual expenses, not to exceed $1 a day, for endeavoring to arrest when he fails to make the arrest, but this allowance is so restricted by the requirements of the Department at Washington that it is no practical benefit to the deputy in the Indian Territory.
>
> One of these requirements is a receipt or voucher for all his expenses. We imagine that a traveler would meet with less difficulties to obtain receipts or vouchers in the English language among the Hottentots and Eskimos than in the majority of route localities in the Indian Territory, and the receipt requirement in this instance

> really amounts to a strong inducement to the deputy to commit forgery. . . .
>
> If the deputy is killed or crippled in the attempt to arrest, although he loses his life or is crippled in the service of the Government, it pays no attention to him or his family. . . .
>
> If the Government offers a reward for the capture of a desperate criminal, by a rule of the Department the officer can not be paid this reward, because the officer is paid for making an arrest, and it is in the line of his duties.
>
> Now let us examine into the hardships of this rule. The Government offers $500 for the capture of a criminal. A deputy after months of work and much expense, locates his man. He now employs a citizen to assist in making the capture. They get him after a hard fight. The citizen gets $500 and the deputy gets $1.50 and three-fourths of the mileage account. In addition to all other drawbacks and disadvantages that affect his service is another which might be termed "the last straw." Congress, in its appropriation for fees and expenses of marshals, restricted the advance payment of actual expenses and payment for earnings to final payment upon settlement. The effect of this restriction is that the deputies can not obtain any money from the marshal on their accounts, but are forced to sell them to people who speculate in them, and by that means sacrifice 10 to 15 per cent of their accounts.[85]

No wonder that so much turnover occurred in the force of deputy marshals. Some, over the years, themselves turned to crime, most notably the Dalton brothers.[86]

Often deputy marshals would ride out into Indian country and return with several wanted men. In this manner they could maximize their mileage fees, collecting mileage for each prisoner. Of course, if dealing with violent offenders, this practice multiplied the dangers.

At any term of court in Fort Smith, significant numbers of criminal cases would be on the docket, and in most of them a large cohort of witnesses from Indian Territory had to be present and available to testify in court. After giving testimony, the witnesses were supposed to be paid their mileage and witness fees in cash. Sometimes, court had to close down because there was no money in the account for payments. The unpaid witnesses had to linger in Fort Smith waiting to be paid. The 1894 grand jury report also complained about this problem:

> Owing to the parsimonious action of Congress the court for more than half the time is without any money to operate with. Witnesses, and sometimes jurors, are compelled to go unpaid and often have to wait months to get what is due them. If the courts would stop when the money gave out they would not be running half of the time, and in that event the Indian Territory would be a pandemonium indeed. Owing to the rapid accumulation of business they are bound to run, notwithstanding all the difficulties, hindrances, and inconveniences mentioned. This court dispenses over 1,000 criminal cases annually besides the civil suits. The recent grand jury, in a three weeks' session, found 330 true bills of indictments, ranging from murder to the smaller crimes.[87]

Sometimes witnesses grew tired of waiting to be paid and, selling some of their belongings, returned home to the territory.

In October of 1889 the attorney general inquired of the marshal in the Western District about the amount of money requested for witnesses, close to $75,000 for the fiscal year. Marshal Yoes answered the inquiry in a letter dated October 25, 1889, stating that in the 1888–89 year thirty-three defendants were tried for murder, fourteen convicted, fourteen acquitted, and five convicted of manslaughter. "All these cases were contested with unusual vigor and in each of them there were more than the usual number of witnesses."[88] Marshal Yoes then addressed the reasons for so much expense for witnesses:

> I might give you the reason in a very few words by saying "want of funds to try the cases when ready." While that is the principal cause, there is another which contributed its share, viz, the passage of the act of Congress diminishing the territorial jurisdiction of the court. While the effect of diminishing the business of the court by this bill has only set in now, because of the large number of violations of law committed prior to the passage of the act, it did have the effect of postponing important trials because of the anticipation of a large decrease in the business of the court in the future, thereby allowing such cases more time and attention. This accounts for the presence of so many important cases upon the docket at the end of last February term. It was the term then coming on, the May term, at which all the business wound up. Both sides were ready and their witnesses were summoned. Then five days before the beginning of the term notice came up from the Attorney General's

> office the witness appropriation was exhausted. Steps were taken at once to stop witnesses from coming, but the time was too short in most instances and nearly a thousand witnesses came to court only to be discharged upon entering the court-house. As stated before, a large percentage of the important cases pending were old ones, witnesses coming long distances, many of them entitled to $30 and $40 mileage. The marshal having but a few dollars in his hands, these witnesses were not paid until they returned again at this term. The forced continuance of this mass of business entailed a loss upon the Government of not less than $25,000.[89]

These sorts of problems made the Western District court one of the most expensive in the United States. In some years, when the entire national budget for federal court operations was some $3 million, Judge Parker's court cost nearly $300,000. In most years, only the District of Columbia federal court expenses exceeded those of Fort Smith.

The business of the Western District court obviously was an important part of the economy of Fort Smith. Jurors, witnesses, deputies, and others had to stay in Fort Smith, eat and drink, and otherwise entertain themselves until the court business was dispatched. Hotels and boarding houses, saloons and brothels flourished; merchants looked for increased sales to jurors and witnesses from out-of-town. Some have noted that in hard economic times, the number of hung juries increased. At $3 a day, jurors were in no hurry to decide cases.[90]

Over the years the organization and methods of the Parker court drew criticism. All the jurors were drawn from Arkansas counties, mostly Sebastian, Crawford, and Washington. In the early years, Indian Territory newspapers complained about Indians having to go to court in Fort Smith as defendants or witnesses in cases to be heard by white strangers. Judge Parker took the position that the importance of having disinterested neutral jurors far outweighed any negatives. In the later years, the complaints came from white settlers in Indian country who wanted courts of their own, rather than having to go to Fort Smith. In 1896 the *Fort Smith Elevator* took umbrage at an editorial from a newspaper in Oklahoma Territory:

> Judge Parker and ex-Judge Stuart [from the territorial court in Muskogee] are in Washington lobbying in the interests of a continuance of the Hessian jurisdiction of the Fort Smith and Paris

> [Texas] courts. We are surprised that two such eminent jurists should so far forget their honor and dignity as to work against the best interests of the inhabitants of the Territory. Many think that their actions may be dominated by base motives. We hope not, but surely Congress will not yield to the importunities of the saloon-keepers, gamblers and various dens of iniquity of these border hell-holes, even if their claims are urged by gentlemen whose acts should be virtuous. Give us home jurisdiction! The constitution governing this glorious Union guarantees not only a speedy trial but that the prisoner be not carried a great distance from his home. —*Nowata Ranch and Range*[91]

Securing witnesses from Indian country was often difficult in cases of murder and other violent crimes. Witnesses were fearful that vengeance would be exacted by friends and relatives of convicted defendants.[92] Near the end of his tenure, Parker mentioned this problem in his charge to a grand jury:

> At the first term of court it was rather hard to get good, honest men to come out of that country and give testimony against these desperate characters. A reign of terror existed over there, and the peaceful, law-abiding citizens would rather put up with the annoyances they were subjected to than to come out and testify against the criminals and thus incur the enmity of these bad men and their friends and risk life by assassination at their hands.[93]

As might be expected, criticism of Parker's court was loud from the defendant class. The criminal defendants often complained about unfair treatment and bias and prejudice. The infamous Henry Starr who had been convicted of murder twice before Judge Parker and also of several robberies had this to say:

> Arkansas is noted for ignorance and Hill-Billyism, and fifty per cent of the jurymen were drawn from backwoods counties and were completely dominated by the powerful personality of Judge Parker, who was no doubt an able man, and of extensive legal learning. But he had fought evil-doers so long that it was claimed by even his most intimate friends that his mind was warped on that particular subject, and those closest to him admitted that he was a Monmoniac [*sic*] on the subject of crime. I can scarcely take so charitable a view of the Judge because he conspired to convict Alf Chaney when the densest mind in the court room could see that he

> was wholly innocent. And I have personal knowledge of two other cases where rewards were offered for conviction. I do not charge that he got any part of the rewards; on the contrary, I don't think he would have taken money under any condition, but he knew where the money went.[94]

Although some of the men who were executed stated from the gallows that they were innocent and were "railroaded" in Parker's court, many of those who protested most loudly about the judge's bias toward the prosecution also confessed their crimes while standing on the gallows.

Parker was unrelenting in his efforts to impress juries to return a guilty verdict where the evidence was strong, but he did not hesitate to suggest that the prosecutor reduce the charge to manslaughter where the case of murder was doubtful, and Parker was known to direct verdicts of acquittal. In one such case, a posse went to Checotah to search for a man wanted for train robbery in Texas. The posse invaded the suspect's home just before daylight without a warrant. The suspect, not knowing the invaders were lawmen, shot and killed one of the posse, a Cherokee policemen named Jim Nakedhead. Judge Parker instructed the jury to acquit the defendant of murder stating that he had a right to resist an attack by officers who had no warrant to arrest him or enter his home.[95]

Civil Cases

The books and articles about Judge Parker have touched only minimally on the civil cases that came into the Western District court. The more than 13,000 criminal cases over the twenty-one-year tenure of the judge have overshadowed some 1,400 civil cases that were docketed in that same period.[96] The geographic jurisdiction of the court covered a substantial part of western Arkansas in addition to the 74,000 square miles of Indian Territory. A number of civil cases—based on federal question jurisdiction—came from Indian country in addition to federal question and diversity of citizenship cases originating in Arkansas.

Parker filed about twenty-five written opinions in civil cases, approximately half of them as the circuit court. Those opinions demonstrate quite well that Judge Parker was a thoughtful, sometimes eloquent, jurist, who wrote clear, well-organized opinions. One striking aspect of Parker's written opinions is his technique of elucidating basic principles of law.

Bankruptcy

In his first civil case opinion Parker dealt with the issue of whether a state court suit to enforce a vendor's lien on land could be removed to federal court by the defendant who claimed that his deed to the land was from the borrower's assignee in bankruptcy. In *Connor v. Scott*,[97] Parker upheld the removal in an opinion that demonstrates his basic principle approach. He wrote:

> The field of jurisdiction is a wide one, and one in which there are frequently to be found many difficulties in the way of a correct solution of the question.
>
> The question involves the relative powers of the two systems of courts, which are a part of our duplex system of government. . . . Jurisdiction is given to the courts of the Union in two classes of cases. In the first, their jurisdiction depends on the character of the cause; in the second, the jurisdiction depends entirely on the character of the parties.
>
> The first class comprehends all cases in law and equity, arising under the constitution, the laws of the United States, and treaties . . . [T]he act of congress of the 3d of March 1875, which provides for the removal of a certain class of causes, dependent upon the subject matter of the same, is identical in meaning with the clause of the second section of the third article of the constitution.[98]

Parker then goes on to ask, rhetorically, "Does the correct decision of this case depend on the construction of a law of Congress? Or does the case involve any question arising under a law of the United States?" Parker answers by reciting a series of questions to show the construction of the federal bankruptcy law is involved, for example, "Is a vendor's lien preserved in bankruptcy?," "Can the holder of lien enforce it after discharge? If so, how? Can any one answer without placing a construction on the bankrupt act?" Parker overruled the motion to strike the case from the docket, of course, but made the following interesting statement:

> I cannot pass this case without making a remark as to the delicate position in which a judge of the federal court is placed when called on to settle a question of jurisdiction arising between his own court and the court of a state, especially when that question has been passed on by the judge of that court. Yet, with due deference to the judge of the state court, and with high regard for his opinions, I

> adopt the language of Chief Justice Marshall, in *Cohens v. Virginia*, while speaking with reference to the jurisdiction of the supreme court: "It is most true that this court will not take jurisdiction if it should not, but it is equally true that it must take jurisdiction if it should. The judiciary cannot, as the legislature may, avoid a measure because it approaches the confines of the constitution; we cannot pass it by because it is doubtful. With whatever doubts, with whatever difficulties a case may be attended, we must decide it if it be brought before us; we have no more right to decline the exercise of jurisdiction which is given, than to usurp that which is not given; the one or the other would be treason to the constitution. Questions may occur which we would gladly avoid, but we cannot avoid them. All we can do is to exercise our best judgment and conscientiously perform our duty."[99]

Judge Parker was basically a positivist in his legal philosophy. He followed the law strictly, even in cases where he disliked the result. The timber trespass case discussed earlier makes that clear. He did the same thing in a bankruptcy case in 1876 where the plaintiff, assignee in bankruptcy, sued the bankrupt to set aside the discharge and recover property that the bankrupt fraudulently omitted from the schedule—several pieces of diamond jewelry worth five thousand dollars. The defense was the statute of limitations. Parker held for the defendant, stating:

> The court has no hesitation in saying, if it be true, as alleged in the petition, that the defendant was guilty of the act charged against him, that it presents a most flagrant and outrageous case of fraud, and one which this court will, if it can, aid in uncovering. But, bad as this case may be, we must treat it legally, and if a remedy is wanting under the law, it is not with the court (which does not make laws, but construes and administers those already made), but with the lawmaking power. . . .
>
> From the language . . . and the general policy of the law of bankruptcy, I am inclined to the opinion that congress intended to limit the creditors, or any one representing them, to two years from the date of the discharge, as the time alone within which they might seek to set aside or annul the same. This is the interpretation . . . by all well-considered cases. I am aware that a different construction was placed upon the section by Judge Taft, of the superior court of Cincinnati . . . where he held that the discharge could be attacked

> at any time and in any court for fraudulent concealment by the bankrupt. But, with all due respect to that learned judge, I think this is not good law, that such a construction is not deducible from the language of the bankrupt law, or from its intent or spirit.[100]

This opinion by Judge Parker was widely circulated in the *Albany Law Journal*, the *Century Law Journal*, and the *New York Weekly Digest*. It is all the more interesting because the Cincinnati judge, Taft, later became President Taft and Chief Justice Taft.

Usury

Although Parker followed the law strictly, even when the result was distasteful, he sometimes was able in an opinion to suggest an alternative. This approach can be seen in *Kinsey v. Little River County*.[101] In this case the county desirous of building a courthouse borrowed $3,000 from a Little Rock bank and issued a note bearing 30 percent interest, with $5,000 worth of county warrants as collateral. The bank sold the warrants to the plaintiff for $1,900. The bank also sold the paper to the plaintiff, who brought suit against the county for $8,200. The county claimed that the warrants were ultra vires under Arkansas law and the interest rate was usurious under the National Bank Act. Parker found for the defendant stating, "The rule of law is, that these warrants issued by counties are unlike negotiable paper. They have not that quality of negotiable paper which prevents an inquiry into its fraudulent character or its consideration, when in the hands of an innocent holder for value before due. . . . I am therefore of the opinion that the plaintiff cannot recover. I am of the opinion, however, the county having received a sum of money from the bank, that this money, less the amount which has been paid, can be recovered back, with legal interest thereon, by an action of the proper kind, to wit, for money had and obtained."[102]

In *Dryfus v. Burnes*,[103] Parker held that a married couple who secured a mortgage loan for $8,000 at 10 percent interest could not claim usury based on an agreement with an agent for 2 percent for negotiating the loan. Parker said that the loan agency fee was not part of the sum paid for the loan, citing an Arkansas case.[104]

Judge Parker held in one case where the plaintiff alleged a usurious arrangement, that even though the contract as he saw it wasn't usurious, it was so unconscionable that the court would give some form of relief.

In *Tilley v. American Building & Loan Association*,[105] the plaintiff seeking to borrow $30,000 on his farm in Sebastian County, agreed to subscribe for six hundred shares of stock in the building and loan association, a Minnesota organization. The agreement provided that Tilley would pay $360 per month as dues on the stock for nine years, a total of $38,880. The association in turn loaned Tilley $30,000 on his stock with 6 percent interest, secured by a mortgage on the land. At the end of the nine years Tilley would surrender his stock. Judge Parker felt that he had to find the payments on the stock not to be interest because they were not made for the use of the money borrowed, but to acquire a partnership interest in the association. However, said the judge, even if the contract was not usurious as a matter of law, it could be viewed as one-sided, unjust, unconscionable, or otherwise inequitable. He did so view the contract, and in the end said the court "may refuse to enforce so much of the contract as is inequitable or harsh, or will work a hardship on the plaintiff . . . or, because the court may construe the sum named in the bond as a penalty, it may give such relief as may be responsive to the demands of equity and good conscience."[106]

County Indebtedness

Suits on Arkansas county warrants were common in the 1880s as counties often defaulted on their obligations. Some of these suits found their way into Parker's court. In two such cases, ten years apart, Parker filed opinions. In *National Bank of Western Arkansas v. Sebastian County*,[107] the bank having purchased the county warrants brought suit to collect. The county defense was an Arkansas statute passed in 1879 that repealed the statutes stating that a county could sue or be sued. The bank demurred and Parker sustained the demurrer: "It is a proposition not debatable that the legislature of the state cannot take away the right of the plaintiff to sue in a federal court, as such right is secured by a law of congress, which, with the constitution of the United States, is the supreme law of the land."[108] The same issue came up in 1889 in *Hoover v. Crawford County*.[109] Again, Parker ruled against the county, stating the proposition more forcefully:

> The purpose of the legislature evidently was to take away from the federal courts the right to entertain a suit against a county in the state. . . . Previous to that time [1879, when the Arkansas

> statute was passed] many suits had been brought in the federal courts in the state against counties upon evidences of indebtedness similar in character to these sued on in this suit. Judgments had been obtained, and payment compelled, by such courts. . . . This act seems to be but the exhibition of a foolish and futile purpose founded on an unwarrantable and unreasonable prejudice against federal courts, which are as much the courts of the whole people as the courts of the counties or of the circuits in a state.[110]

In another suit against a county, the court had to decide a motion to transfer the proceedings from the Western District to the Eastern District federal court on the ground that, after the case was filed in the Western District, Congress had changed the makeup of the federal districts and had put Woodruff County, the defendant, into the Eastern District. Parker held that once jurisdiction attaches, a subsequent realignment of districts does not deprive the court of jurisdiction. He based the holding on a Supreme Court decision holding that when Congress created the Western District of Arkansas in 1851, cases pending in the old district of Arkansas did not have to be transferred.[111]

Indian Territory Problems

Two of Judge Parker's opinions dealt with some major issues of Indian rights and federal court jurisdiction. In both cases Parker found he had to rule against the tribal interests. One involved the Creek Nation and the other the Cherokee Nation.

In the reconstructionist Indian treaties of 1866 the tribes agreed to cede their nonsettled lands to the federal government upon demand and payment. The idea behind this provision was either to purchase tribal lands for the purpose of settling other tribes in Indian country, or to have sufficient land to settle the Negro slaves the slaveholding tribes agreed to emancipate, and possibly, ex-slaves from the defeated South. This provision of the treaty proved to be troublesome in the 1880s when the boomers insisted that those lands were open to homesteading, and it also caused dissension within tribal councils. The provision also became the wedge by which the railroads invaded Indian Territory.[112]

In the case of *United States ex rel. McIntosh v. Crawford*,[113] Judge Parker was faced with an unusual claim. In 1889 the Interior Department began negotiations with the Creek Nation to purchase their unsettled lands for $2.28 million. Even though an international tribal council determined in 1888 to resist all attempts to purchase land from the nations, the Creeks and Seminoles decided to sell off lands they would never need just a year later. The Seminole deal was for about the same amount as the Creek sale. These lands would form the nucleus of the new territory of Oklahoma to be opened for settlement. The Creek Nation sent a three-man delegation to Washington—Pleasant Porter, David M. Hodge, and Espar Hecher. The delegation had previously retained, in 1885, Samuel J. Crawford and others as agents for the nation in negotiations with the government. The agreed fee was $270,283.71. The relators, disaffected Creeks, filed suit in Parker's court alleging that the contract for legal services was fraudulent and designed to cheat the Creek Nation out of their money, and asked for a judgment in that amount. Crawford, a former governor of Kansas, and a resident of that state, made a special appearance to contest jurisdiction over him. Judge Parker agreed that jurisdiction was lacking and dismissed the suit. The opinion relies on fundamental concepts of service of process and begins with the Judiciary Act of 1789. Parker states: "The rule that a person can be sued in any court of the United States, and required to leave his home, and travel thousands of miles, it may be, to defend the suit, is an extremely harsh and oppressive one, and one that may work a great hardship upon the party sued."[114] Parker also found a lack of subject matter jurisdiction. In this part of the opinion he analyzed the set of statutes passed to protect Indians from overreaching contracts by requiring all contracts with Indians or Indian tribes to be vetted by the government; a specific provision in those statutes provided that no money belonging to Indians arising from the sale of their lands should be paid to any agent or attorney without meeting certain stringent conditions.

However, said Parker, the Congressional Act of March 1, 1889, to consummate the sale of the Indian lands to the United States specifically authorized the secretary of the treasury to "pay out of the appropriation hereby made the sum of two hundred and eighty thousand eight hundred and fifty-seven dollars and ten cents to the national treasurer of the Muskogee (or Creek) Nation, or to such persons as shall be duly authorized to receive the same." Parker held that the intent of Congress was to bypass the older statutes, and he cited correspondence from the secretary of the interior to the chairman of the House Indian Affairs Committee recognizing the deal the tribe had made in 1885—a contingent fee arrangement with former governor Crawford.[115]

Although this case did not focus on the impending Oklahoma land rushes when sections of the new territory were subsequently opened for settlement, the Creek and Seminole land deals were immediately responsible for the white settlement of central Oklahoma; the population of Oklahoma City, Guthrie, and surrounding towns zoomed, for example, from a few dozens at Oklahoma Station (the earlier designation) to 10,000 in Oklahoma City almost overnight.[116] What the boomers tried to do in 1880 became reality ten years later.

An important civil case dealing with Indian rights came before Judge Parker in 1888. The Cherokee Nation filed for an injunction to stop a railroad from building a line south from the Kansas border across Cherokee lands. An act of Congress on July 4, 1884, granted the Southern Kansas Railway Company a right of way to build a line across the Cherokee lands.[117] The Cherokee national council passed an act on December 12, 1884, protesting the railway and filed its protest with the secretary of the interior; the council act also instructed the tribe's Washington delegates to resist any building or maintenance of a rail line. In 1886 the Southern Kansas filed a map with the Interior Department locating its proposed line, and in April of that year the Cherokee Nation renewed its protest and rejected any purported compensation provided for in the 1884 statute. The Interior Department ignored the protests, appointed three commissioners to assess compensation, and approved the construction of the line. The commissioners assessed compensation at a little over $7,300 for the right of way for the main line and branches.

The Cherokee Nation did not want the rail line, knowing that it would be a magnet for white would-be settlers. The Indian tribes were well aware of the troubles that came with the railroads, especially the introduction of intoxicating liquor, and the theft of timber for crossties. The Cherokees also felt that even if they could not stop the construction of the line, the compensation awarded by the commissioners was wholly inadequate; the nation thought the right of way was worth at least $500 per mile.

The suit filed in the Western District, *Cherokee Nation v. Southern Kansas Railway Co.*,[118] asked for an injunction to stop further construction, removal of the ten miles of track already built, and, in the alternative, an appeal from the monetary award of the commissioners as being inadequate. The railroad was represented by U. M. Rose and George B. Rose of Little Rock; they filed a demurrer on the grounds of lack of jurisdiction, want of equity, and improper joinder of legal and equitable causes of action.

In a lengthy opinion Judge Parker explored the nature and basic status of the Cherokee Nation. He concluded that the Cherokee Nation did own the land in fee simple, with a possibility of reverter in the national government (the condition being abandonment by the tribe or its extinction). However, the Cherokee Nation, politically, did not enjoy the status of a sovereign. It was not a state, nor an independent political entity but, rather, a dependent Indian tribe. Not being a sovereign, the right of eminent domain—an attribute of sovereignty—rested in the United States, not in the Cherokee Nation. Consequently, the United States could legislate to take Cherokee Nation lands for public purposes, that is, a railroad. Finally, as to the valuation of the land, Parker held that, as the bill for equitable relief failed, the alternative request for money damages could not be joined, and the relief sought by the plaintiff would have to be filed on the law side of the federal court. The demurrer was sustained and the bill dismissed without prejudice. The railroads, with all their promise and troubles, could not be kept out of Indian country. However, once the railroads criss-crossed Indian country, enterprising citizens of the nations found that profit and prosperity could follow through the opening of national markets for cattle, grain, and other products.

Judge Parker and Railroads

Even though the railroad won the right to continue its line across the Cherokee lands, and Parker's jurisdictional views meant that federal courts could not override congressional grants of right of way, Parker was no friend of the railroads. He wrote opinions in a number of cases where a railroad was one party, and those opinions show that the railroads could not expect favorable treatment in his court.

In personal injury cases Judge Parker would give jury instructions favorable to plaintiffs and uphold large damage awards. In *Shumacher v.*

St. Louis & San Francisco Railway Co.,[119] a railroad employee was on top of some gravel cars. In a switching operation the cars were run down an incline and the brakeman was unable to stop or slow down the cars. The cars slammed into the train throwing the plaintiff onto the tracks; his foot was run over and eventually he had his leg amputated. The plaintiff sued for $15,000 damages and the jury awarded $8,000. The railroad moved for a new trial based on the judge's refusal to give several defense instructions. Parker denied the motion and in his opinion pointed out that the conductor had a duty to "know that one brakeman managing one brake could not control that train of 10 loaded cars. . . . It seems to me from the testimony that there was an entire absence of that prudent and proper care which, when there is a failure to exercise it, shows that conscious indifference to consequences which make a state of case in which there is constructive or legal willfulness."[120] Parker also stated that in light of the evidence he was justified in giving the plaintiff's instruction on the injury being produced by an act that was in law willful. Finally he said that at one time he thought the damages were excessive, but that he would not interfere in the absence of a showing that the jury was swayed by prejudice, preference, partiality, passion, or corruption.

In the autumn of 1889 Parker was in a position to chastise the Southern Kansas Railway, whose invasion of Indian country he was forced to uphold less than a year earlier. In *Briscoe v. Southern Kansas Railway Company*,[121] the plaintiff brought a suit against the railroad for negligently killing his horses. The railroad challenged the verdict for the plaintiff in a post-trial motion on the grounds that the court did not have jurisdiction under the statute that had authorized the building of the railroad and that, in any event, the Southern Kansas could not be held liable because it had leased the operation of the railroad to the Atchison, Topeka & Santa Fe prior to the incident. Judge Parker overruled the motion for a new trial, held that the Western District court had jurisdiction under the statute, and found the lease unauthorized.

As to jurisdiction, the statute that authorized the railroad provided that the federal district courts for the Western District of Arkansas, the Northern District of Texas, and the District of Kansas should have concurrent jurisdiction, without regard as to the amount in controversy in suits between the Southern Kansas and the nations or tribes through whose territory the road runs, as well as "controversies arising between the inhabitants of said nations or tribes and said railway company . . . without distinction as to citizenship of the parties."[122] The railroad argued that the statutory provision only applied to controversies over the right of way and not to common-law torts. Parker disagreed:

> If this proposition is true, the nation or tribe, or the inhabitants thereof, were left by congress without any remedy for torts committed by the railroad company, for, as there is no remedy for torts such as was sued for in this case at the place where the same was committed, there could be no remedy anywhere. As the plaintiff could not sue in the Indian country, he could not sue anywhere.[123]

On the question of the lease, Parker found that the enabling statute said nothing about any right of the railroad to lease the operation of the line and even if the law of Kansas permitted such a lease, the express language of Congress prevailed: "The said Southern Kansas Railway Company shall accept this right of way upon the express condition, binding upon itself, its successors and assigns, that they will [not try to get more land from the tribes]." Parker said that the use of the words "assigns" and successors" did not imply that the corporation can transfer its property and franchise by lease.

In 1892 Judge Parker heard a wrongful death case brought by the widow and children of the yardmaster of the Frisco line in Fort Smith. The jury brought in a very large (for that time) verdict for the plaintiff of $17,820. Parker rejected the motion for a new trial, based on eleven grounds. The tenth ground—that the damages were excessive and rendered under the influence of prejudice or passion—generated a strong response from Parker. First, he noted that the deceased's age, physical strength, life expectancy, and training indicated the amount of damages was not shocking to the sense of justice. Then, Judge Parker, in addressing the rule that grief could not be the basis for damages in such a wrongful death action, said:

> When we have a statute so barbaric, and almost brutal, as to prohibit the consideration by the jury of that terrible agony, grief, and suffering of the faithful wife and little children for their loss by death of such a husband and father as Dwyer, we should award fairly compensatory damages. The award should be made with a reasonably liberal spirit. Under this statute, man is considered only

> as an animal, a beast of burden, like a horse or a mule, with nothing to be considered when he is killed by negligence but his earning capacity.[124]

Judge Parker went as far as he could possibly go to help plaintiffs who were the victims of railroad negligence.

However, sometimes the plaintiffs were overreaching and Parker would rule against them. For example, in *Stephens v. St. Louis & San Francisco Railway Co.*,[125] the plaintiff, an Arkansas resident, filed a suit against the Frisco in the Arkansas state courts in Washington County, for damages, alleging that he had been forcibly expelled and thrown off a train in Missouri in the middle of his journey from one point in Missouri to another, claiming damages of $4,999. The railroad filed for removal of the case to federal court. On the same day the plaintiff sought leave to amend his complaint, and was permitted to amend so as to pray for damages in the amount of $1,999. Then the plaintiff sought to have the case remanded back to state court on the ground that the amount in controversy was less than the requisite $2,000. Parker obtained a transcript of the Washington County Circuit Court proceedings and found that—contrary to plaintiff's assertions—the petition for removal was filed at 1:30 p.m. on May 15 and the amendment was not asked for by plaintiff until at least 5:00 p.m. on that day.

In that same case, and in another one that same year,[126] Parker had to decide the jurisdictional issue of whether the Frisco was a Missouri or Arkansas corporation, or both. In the *Stephens* case plaintiff argued that the federal court did not have jurisdiction because both the plaintiff and the defendant were Arkansas residents. In the *James* case, a few months earlier, Parker had overruled the Frisco's demurrer to jurisdiction in a wrongful death case brought in the Western District court by a Missouri widow based on negligence in Monett, Missouri. Parker found that the Frisco, a Missouri corporation, had become a domestic Arkansas corporation under the provisions of an 1889 Arkansas statute. The two cases, taken together, establish that the Frisco railroad was a citizen of both states for diversity jurisdiction purposes.

Another interesting railroad case, not involving personal injuries—but of great interest in Fort Smith—dealt with the construction of a bridge across the Arkansas River, connecting the city with Indian country. From the time the Western District court came to Fort Smith in

1871, the only way that those in Indian country could get to the city was by ferry or skiff. As the city grew and commerce with Indian country increased, construction of a bridge was sought by Fort Smith. A bridge was also in the mind's eye of railroad tycoon Jay Gould, who was seeking to control most of the railroads leading into the Indian Territory. His control of the Missouri Pacific line included the Kansas and Arkansas Valley Railroad, a line that ran to Fort Smith. On the other side of the river Gould's interests included the Kansas & Texas, a north-south line through Indian Territory. In 1891 the Kansas and Arkansas Valley began construction of a bridge over the river. A suit was brought in Judge Parker's court to enjoin the condemnation of land for construction of bridge approaches for use by wagons and persons on foot, on the theory that the railroad's right of way grant did not include the right to build a wagon or foot bridge on the right of way. The plaintiff was the operator of a ferry across the Arkansas River. Parker refused to dissolve the temporary injunction he had granted because the grant of right of way was for a railroad bridge and, in Parker's view, the construction of a wagon and foot approach amounted to the imposition of an additional servitude on the plaintiff's land.[127]

Parker expressed regret in his opinion:

> I have arrived at the conclusion that defendant has now no power to condemn the land of plaintiffs for use as an approach for a wagon and footway bridge; and to get the right, and use the same for such purpose, defendant must either go to congress for authority to exercise the right of eminent domain, or negotiate with plaintiffs for the use of the right of way as an approach to its wagon and footway bridge. It is in my judgment a matter of great regret that authority to condemn has not been given, as it works delay in the completion of a great thoroughfare, which will be an important agency in securing the development, progress, and prosperity of the country, and consequently of great and lasting benefit to the people.[128]

The wagon and footpath were important to Gould, because the bridge was to be a toll bridge. An appeal of Parker's decision was taken immediately by John H. Rogers to the newly created circuit court of appeals, and on January 5, 1892, the appellate court reversed and dissolved the injunction.[129] The formal dedication of the new bridge attracted some 25,000 people to Fort Smith, and a banquet for 200 distinguished guests was held in the Main Hotel on the evening of the dedication, lasting until 3:00 a.m. the next day.[130]

Miscellaneous Civil Cases

The opinions in civil cases may have been few over the years, but a wide variety of interesting cases came into Parker's court. There was one trademark infringement case where Judge Parker held that the similarity of defendant's plug tobacco to the product of the plaintiff would create confusion among members of the general buying public, thus warranting an injunction. Parker utilized the test of comparing with his own eyes the two products.[131]

In *United States v. Culver*,[132] Parker ordered the cancellation of two land patents on the ground that the defendants made false representations in making a cash entry for agricultural lands with full knowledge that the lands were mineral lands and thus not open to entry.

Judge Parker adhered to the majority rule in dismissing a cause of action for mental suffering against the telegraph company for failure to deliver a wire. In *Crawson v. Western Union Telegraph Co.*,[133] the plaintiff complained that a telegram—sent from Sallisaw to Van Buren beseeching him to come to Sallisaw on the evening train to see his mother-in-law who was dying and wanted all her family in attendance—was not delivered and he was prevented for a period of twenty-four hours from going to the bedside of his mother-in-law. The plaintiff claimed he suffered great anguish and uneasiness of mind. Parker stated the issue as whether the plaintiff could recover for mental suffering alone, unaccompanied with any other injury. Parker sustained the defendant's demurrer, recognizing that the supreme courts of Indiana, Alabama, Kentucky, Tennessee, and Texas had upheld causes of action for mental suffering alone due to negligent delay in delivering telegrams. However, Parker stated, these cases had no support in other states or English common law.

An unusual issue was presented in a habeas corpus proceeding brought by a Fort Smith police officer who had been jailed for contempt by the Fort Smith police court judge for refusing to return to jail a woman who had been jailed for nonpayment of a $5 fine and $1.50 court costs, and released by order of the mayor because of her health. In *In re Monroe & Marquandt*,[134] Parker granted the writ on behalf of both the police officer and the woman, finding that the Fort Smith ordinances authorized the mayor to release prisoners from the local jail for reasons of health. In the course of the opinion Judge Parker said:

> [D]oes the federal court have jurisdiction to issue a writ in behalf of the liberty of a citizen who is alleged to be illegally restrained? How far may the federal court go in its investigation of the legality of the process, which, as is alleged, is in restraint of the liberty of a citizen of the state, or of the United States? There seems to be a misconception in the public mind as to the power of the federal court in this regard, and it is a mystery in my mind how that misconception can exist in the face of the constitution and laws of the United States. There is no invasion of any prerogative or power of the state by the exercise of jurisdiction of this kind, because there is no prerogative that belongs to any state, nor is there any power or jurisdiction in a state to deprive any citizen of liberty without due process of law.[135]

Perhaps Parker should be remembered as a civil libertarian judge instead of a hanging judge.

Faults and Virtues

Assessing Judge Parker is quite difficult. His court was unique in the history of American jurisprudence, but looking solely at the court and not the man would not present a complete view. Therefore, looking at Parker's faults and his virtues will help to round out the picture.

Some of Judge Parker's faults grew out of his virtues. Most historians and biographers agree that Parker came to Fort Smith as what we would call a political hack. He sought the job because he was a Republican in a Democratic state and was one of a number of departing Republican congressmen in 1874 who needed an appointment.[136] That said, once he arrived and began holding court, Parker continually grew as a jurist dedicated to overseeing and improving the only real justice system for the vast Indian Territory. When he was in Congress in the early 1870s, he advocated and presented a bill that would have opened Indian Territory to white settlement. After he had been on the bench in Fort Smith for a few years his position had turned 180 degrees. He wanted to protect the Indians from the incursion of settlers and from the depredations of whites. By the 1890s the Indian nations saw Parker as one of their best friends, and opposed the reduction of his jurisdiction over Indian country.

As the years passed in Fort Smith Parker saw his judgeship in a special light, one that we do not usually associate with federal judges—a mission to deter crime in the territory. To that end he was stern on the bench, felt he had to make sure juries did the right thing, and used capital punishment to deter others. In his 1896 interview with a reporter, when Mrs. Parker noted that his twenty-one years in Fort Smith had made the judge an old man and that it might have been a mistake to stay, Parker stated: "No[,] Mary, not a mistake, for we have been enabled to arrest the floodtide of crime here, as we would not have had an opportunity to do elsewhere."[137]

This sense of mission is what led Judge Parker into his bitter dispute with the Supreme Court and the Justice Department. Because Parker believed that juries had to be "led," he went overboard in his jury instructions. In capital cases he would often take three hours to charge the jury. In doing so he created most of the errors that led to reversals by the Supreme Court after 1891. One of Parker's admirers put it thus:

> Candor compels the statement that Parker's charges to the jury were too long. He was prone to emphasize first the government's and then the defendant's theory of the case. His affirmances illustrate that he often used strong statements favorable to the prosecution which would have been error except for the fact that they were cured by equally vigorous statements favorable to the accused. It was difficult for Parker to frame his charges in colorless language.[138]

This is the most serious fault in Judge Parker's career—his strong commitment to aid the prosecution when he was convinced the defendant was guilty. And, Parker would praise or scold his juries for their verdicts. Shirley states: "These juries were praised for the way they upheld the law. They were usually composed of high-caliber men, and the judge was 'very solicitous of their welfare.' But it was more, perhaps, because Parker never hesitated to let them know when he wanted a conviction."[139] And Harrington writes:

> To hang his killers, Isaac Parker went beyond the functions of an ordinary judge. As was customary, he presided, checked court

> accounts, instructed grand and petit juries, and handed out the sentences. Had he stopped there he might have sent two dozen to their doom in his twenty-one years in Fort Smith.
>
> But to Parker that was not enough. There was pandemonium in the Indian country, there was need to terrify the border bandits, to shock the men of blood into dread of the law. The Hanging Judge therefore chose to aid the marshals who rounded up the bad men. He helped the district attorneys prosecute the murderers; he steered the jurors toward the death verdict.[140]

These views may be too strong. In the nineteenth century, trial judges in criminal cases did tend to "lead" juries, comment on the evidence, and signal their feelings about guilt or innocence.[141] When Parker was charging juries, very little Supreme Court development of the fair trial concept had been established.

Also, perhaps too much has been made of the fact that no appeals were possible from the capital convictions in Fort Smith until after 1889. Parker was too careful a judge not to follow the law as it existed; he did study the case law in other courts and his written opinions are replete with relevant citations. When the Supreme Court was deciding appeals from Parker's court it was usually writing on a clean slate.

However, it must be said, that when the Supreme Court did start defining fairness in criminal trials, Parker's reaction made him look anachronistic.[142] Moreover, Parker's view—that appellate courts should not reverse the trial courts unless a review of the full transcript of the trial showed manifest innocence—is exceptionally narrow and unrealistic.

One of Judge Parker's virtues was his willingness to work hard to keep up with the burgeoning docket of the court. The May and November terms merged into a full-time court that operated from early morning until dark, or even later, six days a week. No holidays were recognized except for Christmas and July 4. Once in a while court had to stop because of lack of funds to pay witnesses and jurors. And the judge did in the later years take a few short vacations; he also traveled to Washington a few times to testify in Congress on Indian matters and to lobby the Justice Department on behalf of his court, pleading for more money. Unfortunately, his docket kept increasing despite his efforts. The population of non-Indians in the territory kept increasing, as did crime.

Another virtue was Parker's liberal view on Indian policy. In his

1896 interview he said of Indians: "Twenty-one years of experience with them has taught me that they are a religiously inclined, law-abiding, authority-respecting people. The Indian race is not one of criminals. There have been sporadic cases of crime among them, it is true, but as a people they are good citizens."[143] Parker was convinced that gradual assimilation into the majority society would be the salvation of the Indians, and he opposed the opening of Oklahoma Territory to white settlement because the time was too soon. Realizing that white settlement was inevitable, Parker hoped that the federal government would not rush into immediate fulfillment of the demands to open the territory. He lost that battle, but not for want of trying.[144] Parker expressed the view that the Western District court had a duty to protect the Indians: "The territory was set apart for the Indians in 1828. The government at that time promised them protection. That promise has always been ignored. The only protection that has ever been afforded them is through the courts. To us who have located on this borderland has fallen the task of acting as protectors."[145]

Judge Parker believed in, and supported as much as he could, the force of deputy marshals who rode into the territory to make arrests and summon witnesses. His devotion to the marshals was such that despite the low pay and danger they were proud to refer to themselves as "Men who rode for Parker." He also sought to raise their pay and the pay of jurors, so as to attract good people to serve in those crucial roles.

Whether one agrees or disagrees with Parker's view that he had a special mission in regard to Indian Territory, almost everyone accepts the view that Judge Parker performed well in furthering that mission. Judge Bryant, who was the federal district judge in the Eastern District of Texas and took over part of the criminal jurisdiction of Indian Territory, said: "No court has ever wielded a more salutary influence over a semi-civilized country filled with the worst of criminals."[146]

Off the bench, Judge Parker was admired by the residents of Fort Smith. He was seen as a kind, benevolent man. Years after Parker's death, a Fort Smith lawyer who had appeared in Parker's court in his youth (Henry L. Fitzhugh) said: "He was the kindest and most considerate judge to the young lawyer whom I have ever seen upon the bench."[147] When Judge Parker died in November 1896,

> It was a state funeral, as nearly as the little city where he had lived knew how to make it. Notable personages came from far and near. Public and private business was suspended. Flags stood at half mast. The National Cemetery, where he was buried was too small for the thousands who accompanied his body to its last resting place. The most fitting and appropriate tribute of all came when Chief Pleasant Porter, of the Choctaws [*sic*], placed upon his grave a simple garland of wild flowers.[148]

Perhaps the best tribute to Judge Parker is found in a single footnote in a massive treatise. Professor John Henry Wigmore wrote the final revision of volume one of Greenleaf on Evidence, just prior to releasing his own treatise, Wigmore on Evidence. In the work, published in 1899, when the text discusses the issue of flight as evidence of guilt, Wigmore inserts a footnote containing an editorial comment:

> See the reasoning in the charges of Parker, J. (late the Federal District Judge for Western Arkansas and one of the greatest American trial judges), in *Starr v. U.S.*, 164 U.S. 627, and *Alberty v. U.S.*, 162 id. 499.[149]

CHAPTER 12

John Henry Rogers

1896–1911

Morton Gitelman

JOHN HENRY ROGERS was judge of the United States District Court for the Western District of Arkansas from 1896 to 1911. His fifteen years on the federal bench reflected the social and economic changes occurring throughout the nation; the Industrial Revolution was at its height and a number of bankruptcy cases and labor disputes found their way into the federal court. Judge Rogers was a prolific writer of opinions in a wide variety of civil cases falling under federal jurisdiction. The court itself underwent a drastic change as at the very beginning of Rogers's tenure, all remaining jurisdiction over the Indian Territory had been removed, and the court at Fort Smith, a monument to Judge Isaac Parker's twenty-one-year oversight over the Indian Territory, now would be indistinguishable from other district courts around the country.

Judge Rogers's Background

John Henry Rogers was born October 9, 1845, in Bertie County, North Carolina. His father, Absolom Rogers, was a successful planter and slaveholder, and his grandfather, a farmer and mechanic of Irish ancestry, reared a large family in the area near Greenville, North Carolina. When

John H. Rogers. *Courtesy United States District Court for the Western District of Arkansas.*

John was seven years old, the family relocated to Madison County, Mississippi, where Absolom Rogers either acquired or operated a cotton plantation. John attended local schools until the onset of the Civil War. In 1861 and 1862, when he was fifteen years old, he became the drill-master for a company of home guards, and on March 10, 1862, he was mustered into Company H, Ninth Regiment, Mississippi Volunteers, as a private soldier. He served in the same regiment throughout the war until it surrendered at Greensboro, North Carolina, on May 1, 1865.

The young soldier saw a considerable amount of action, participating in the battles of: Mumfordville (Green River), Kentucky (September 1862); Murfreesboro (Stone River), Tennessee (December 1862); Chickamauga (September 1863); Mission Ridge (November 1863); Reseca, New Hope Church, and Peach Tree Creek, Georgia, and the siege of Atlanta (Summer 1864); Jonesboro, Georgia (September 1864); and the battles of Franklin, Tennessee (November 1864), and Nashville (December 1864). Rogers was twice wounded, in Kentucky and in Tennessee. When the Confederate army was reorganized after the Tennessee debacle under Hood, General Joseph E. Johnston awarded Rogers a battlefield commission as first lieutenant for gallantry at Franklin. John Rogers was nineteen years old at the time; Johnston's special order also named Rogers as commander of Company F, Ninth Mississippi Regiment, Sharp's Brigade, Hill's Division, Lee's Corps.

At the end of the war, when Johnston's army surrendered at Greensboro, North Carolina, John Rogers walked some thousand miles back to his family's home in Mississippi, where he immediately set to work studying to enter college. There were no colleges open in the Confederacy, so, in 1865, John Rogers entered the sophomore class at Center College in Danville, Kentucky. He spent two unhappy years there, because the college was in political upheaval due to dissension in the Presbyterian Church that ran the school. In 1867, he transferred to the junior class of the now re-opened University of Mississippi, and graduated with the class of 1868. During the summer of 1867, and throughout his senior year, Rogers studied law on his own initiative, and in the summer of 1868 was admitted to the bar at Canton, Mississippi. He did not immediately practice law, taking a job as a schoolteacher, while continuing his private law studies. In January of 1869, John Rogers moved to Fort Smith, Arkansas, and began practicing law. No information is available on his reasons for going to Fort Smith, but soon after he arrived, Rogers was invited to occupy desk space in the law office of an eminent lawyer, Judge William Walker.

Within two years after joining Judge Walker's law office, Rogers entered into a partnership with Walker, which lasted until 1874, when the two amicably agreed to separate. Rogers then continued to practice alone in Fort Smith until 1877. In that year, the Twelfth Judicial Circuit was created. Rogers ran for and was elected circuit judge. He was once reelected to the circuit judgeship and served until 1882 when he resigned, citing health reasons.

Either Rogers's health dramatically improved upon his resignation, or the health reason was simply a "cover" for his new political plans, because Rogers immediately announced his intention to run for Congress. His law partner, Judge James F. Read, put it a little differently in his remarks at the memorial service for Rogers, where he stated: "As soon as he [Rogers] made up his mind to enter the race for Congress he at once tendered the Governor his resignation as judge. He did not deem it dignified to become a candidate for the office of congressman while he was upon the bench." John Rogers was elected to Congress in November 1882.

Rogers's Congressional Career

John Rogers was elected to the Forty-Eighth Congress, and reelected to the Forty-Ninth, Fiftieth, and Fifty-First Congresses, serving from 1883 until March 1891. After his second term, Rogers became a member of the Judiciary Committee and made that his primary focus. He was very active in writing and securing passage of an act reforming federal criminal procedure and claimed credit for a statutory reform granting the writ of error to persons convicted of federal felonies. The writ of error bill was especially interesting because for many years complaints were heard about the lack of a right of appeal from death sentences handed down by Judge Isaac Parker. After 1889, with the writ of error available, a number of Parker's death sentences were appealed to the Supreme Court and many reversed by the high court.

On the civil side, Rogers was very interested in what turned out to be the creation of the United States Circuit Court of Appeals. On

April 4, 1890, he introduced a measure, designed to alleviate the congested docket of the Supreme Court. Rogers's bill advocated the fusion of district and circuit courts and the creation of nine intermediate courts of appeal. These nine courts would have final decision in diversity cases and two circuit judges would be added for each circuit (making a total of three). Also, the Supreme Court justices would be relieved of all circuit duties. In August of 1890, Senator Evarts substituted a bill of his own for the House bill, which had been passed. Evarts's bill modified Rogers's plan considerably by providing for direct appeals to the Supreme Court in important cases, with all other cases going to the circuit courts of appeal for final decision, subject to review by the Supreme Court; also, the old circuit courts would be retained and the Supreme Court justices would be permitted to attend them. Only one judge would be added to each circuit (making a total of two). Evarts's bill prevailed and became law on March 3, 1891. Rogers was disappointed, feeling that the act was imperfect and unsatisfactory.[1] Rogers's reason for relieving Supreme Court justices from circuit duty was his belief that the Supreme Court should be a "great constitutional court" with limited supervisory control over the circuit courts of appeal. The act that was adopted did allow for three circuit judges, but retained the rule that Supreme Court justices could also sit as circuit judges, and that district judges could also sit by designation. After he left Congress, Rogers continued to advocate his scheme, which, of course, has never materialized.

In 1890, Congressman Rogers achieved national notoriety in connection with the crisis over seating southern democrats and the allegations surrounding the actions of the Speaker of the House in seeking to advance Republican reconstructionist views. Rogers was a leading opponent of the Speaker, Thomas B. Reed of Maine, and was constantly berating the Speaker. The Speaker was frequently referred to as "Czar Reed" and provoked the enmity of the Democrats by enacting the "Reed Rules," which, among other items, required all present representatives to vote and counted absent members for the quorum, thus ensuring that the power of the majority party was strengthened. Reed's Rules also initiated the power of the House Rules Committee.

Rogers's speeches on the floor and off were regularly reported by the press, and his background as a Confederate war hero, plus his imposing demeanor, cast him in the role of a leading spokesman for the southern point of view. Although the Republicans were able to advance a new "Force Bill" through the House, it was defeated in the Senate, thus ending the reconstructionist movement. In the 1892 elections the Democratic Party emerged victorious, and many of the Republican reconstructionists in the Congress were defeated.

In March of 1891, John Rogers announced that he would retire from Congress and resume his law practice in Fort Smith. Again, his public statement was somewhat misleading in that he indicated the reason for retirement was a need to devote himself to the education of his children and that public life was too demanding on family interests. However, Rogers clearly did not retire from politics and public life. The popularity he enjoyed in Arkansas during his battles for the South led him to the chairmanship of the Arkansas delegation to the Democratic National Convention, where he was a leading supporter of Grover Cleveland.

Also belying the claim that he relished the private life of law practice was the rash of press reports after Cleveland's election that John Rogers was on the "short list" for some major public appointments. The "spoils system," on the way out since Garfield's tenure as president, was not yet completely dead. On February 17, 1893, the *Arkansas Gazette* reported that Rogers was slated for the attorney-generalship, "as it has been known for some time that the President was considering favorably Judge Rogers's well-known fitness for the position." The article went on to indicate that Cleveland was also considering U. M. Rose for the same position. Again, on February 21, the *Gazette* reported that either Rogers or Rose would be named, although there was a possibility that a Texan, Judge Culberson, could be named. Cleveland, however, turned north and appointed Richard Olney of Massachusetts as attorney general.

In March, the *Gazette* reported, under the headline, "Rolling for Rogers," that "Judge Rogers left for home today [the dateline was Washington, March 9] and with the highest expectation that he will be the next Solicitor-General." Alas, that also was not to be, as the appointment went to Lawrence Maxwell Jr. of Ohio. Apparently, Rogers then set his sights a bit lower in terms of a federal appointive office, for just a few days after the report about the solicitor-general position, on March 16, 1893, the *Gazette* stated that there was "reason to believe" that John Rogers would be named first assistant secretary of the interior, in charge of appeals from the General Land Office, the Patent Office, and from the Indian Bureau. That appointment did not materialize either, and the next and last mention of a federal appointment was in a newspaper article on June 18, 1893:

> There is a well-defined rumor current here today that ex-Congressman Rogers, of Fort Smith, would be Minister Blount's successor at Honolulu, that gentleman having tendered his resignation. It is well known that the President has all along been desirous of giving Judge Rogers a position, and it is not unlikely that he is seriously contemplating his name in connection with the Hawaiian mission.

James H. Blount of Georgia was appointed minister on May 9, 1893, presented his credentials on May 23, and announced his resignation soon after, in early June. He actually left the post on August 8, 1893, and Albert S. Willis of Kentucky was appointed on September 13, 1893.

Even though Rogers received no federal spoils from Cleveland in 1893, Rogers continued, while practicing law, to commit himself to public life at a lower level. He became a member and president of the Fort Smith Board of Education and in December 1894 Rogers was elected permanent chairman of the Arkansas Convention of Mayors. In 1895, Center College in Danville, Kentucky, awarded Rogers an honorary degree.

John Rogers as US District Judge

After the death of Judge I. C. Parker in the autumn of 1896, Rogers was appointed to the district bench on November 27 of that year. As a practicing lawyer, Rogers enjoyed a reputation of honesty and integrity, and very aggressive advocacy. Even at his memorial service in 1911, Rogers's closest associates described him as being a diligent student and plodder, not given to great intellectual feats, but well prepared through studious effort, somewhat of a "bulldog" who would occasionally win cases through aggressive attack. When he was appointed to the federal bench these personal characteristics led some to question Rogers's judicial temperament. In retrospect, his former law partner, Judge Read, stated in the eulogy he delivered in the Western District courtroom: "Judge Rogers had the appearance of being brusque and severe at times upon the bench. He was; but at the bottom he was the tenderest hearted man I ever knew."

Even more telling was the eulogy delivered by Charles Warner:

> As a lawyer Judge Rogers possessed great force, though it may not be said that he was endowed with profound ability. He was diligent, painstaking and faithful, was aggressive and fought to win. . . . Being of an extremely impetuous and high spirited nature, it was supposed by some of his friends when he assumed judicial office as the Federal Judge that his temperament would detract from his ability as a judge.

The picture that emerges of John Rogers as a judge is one of stern demeanor, perhaps a little short of patience, and a person who did not suffer fools gladly. Yet, his integrity and passion for fairness were unquestioned. The record left by Judge Rogers's written opinions reinforces, to some extent, the descriptions of his character.

Judge Rogers decided a large number of cases with written opinions. In part this is due to the fact that in 1889 Congress created a circuit court in the Western District of Arkansas with appeals to the Supreme Court.[2] Representative Rogers apparently shepherded this act through Congress. From 1871 to 1889, the district court in Fort Smith, under Judges Story and Parker, was the final word in cases arising in the Indian Territory; a presidential pardon was the only recourse in criminal cases. Although the district and circuit courts were separate institutions, records of the two are frequently intermingled because there was only one judge and one clerk for both entities.

Rogers left a record of about sixty opinions, and these opinions range over a wide area of legal issues. The opinions are marked by a style that conforms to the descriptions of Rogers's character limned by his eulogizers. In particular, Rogers can be said to have given painstaking attention to accurate iteration of the facts in each case, followed by a review of case authority, leading to a swift opinion.

Two of Rogers's earliest opinions well illustrate his style. In *In re Christian*,[3] Judge Rogers had before him a habeas petition that alleged a sentence was invalid. The petitioner was convicted of perjury in the United States Court for the Central District, Indian Territory and sentenced to a fine of one dollar and a three-year term of imprisonment to be served at the Detroit House of Correction in Detroit, Michigan.[4] The allegation in the writ was that the sentence was illegal because the statutory provisions relating to imprisonment for perjury specified that imprisonment was to be at hard labor, and that the order of commitment for Christian specified a penitentiary in Michigan without any hard labor. The law in 1897 was quite clear that punishment for federal crimes had to strictly follow the statutory mandate. Rogers's opinion in this case contains a painstaking review of all the authority to be found, none of which was exactly on point. The opinion carefully extrapolates from existing case law to reach a conclusion that holds the sentence facially invalid but also allows the United States to have a chance to resentence the petitioner. In reaching that conclusion, Rogers states that "there is ground for belief that the court in sentencing Christian, sentenced him to imprisonment at hard labor, and that it was an inadvertence or misprision of the clerk that the judgment did not contain the sentence of hard labor." Remarkably, Rogers then goes on to say that this feature of the case was not raised in the pleadings, but only adverted to in the arguments. However, that "feature of the case" undergirds the holding that the "petitioner be discharged from . . . custody . . . but without prejudice to the right of the United States to take any lawful measures to have the petitioner sentenced in accordance with law upon the verdict . . . or to correct the judgment if the same was by misprision of the clerk erroneously entered." This opinion is evidence that Rogers's jurisprudential approach is one of positivism, strict interpretation of the law, but also a clever use of factual interpretation to reach a "just" result.

Unfortunately, however, Christian's attorney did not give up easily, and he filed another habeas petition alleging that Rogers had no authority or jurisdiction to order removal of Christian back to the court in Indian Territory for resentencing. Again, Rogers took up the pen in a lengthy and painstaking exploration of the authority of federal courts to act in such a situation.[5] The only analogy he could find concerned persons who were sentenced in one jurisdiction and fled to another where they were caught and extradition was sought. Rogers could not quite make the analogy work, because Christian's attorney persuasively argued that the statute in force at the time authorized federal courts to order removal of a prisoner to another district *for trial*, and as Christian had already been tried and convicted the removal statute was inapplicable. Rogers finally latched on to some attorneys-general opinions and worked his way out of the dilemma by holding that the district court in Indian Territory, having the power to issue writs, could issue a warrant addressed to the marshal of the Western District to arrest Christian, and that an officer could be sent to Fort Smith to take Christian back to Indian Territory for resentencing. Christian's attorney then asked for bail, which Rogers denied, and he ordered the prisoner held until the court in Indian Territory was notified and given a reasonable time to send someone to fetch the prisoner.

Another example of Rogers's technique is his opinion in one of the early civil cases, a complicated issue of comity and conflict of laws. *Hale v. Bugg*[6] is an interesting case that resonates with the modern day savings and loan crisis of the late 1980s. In this case, a Minnesota S & L became insolvent; it had property in several states, including Arkansas. Several Arkansas creditors, in February 1896, filed creditors' bills in state court in Fort Smith and attached the property. The defendant S & L made an appearance and removed the case to federal court; however, a motion to remand was filed and the case was remanded to state court. Subsequently, in November 1896, a receiver, appointed by a Minnesota state court in the insolvency proceeding, filed a bill in Rogers's court seeking appointment of an ancillary receiver in Arkansas to sell the property and remit the proceeds to the Minnesota court handling the insolvency matter. The receiver also alleged that the plaintiff creditors in the Arkansas state court suit were also stockholders of the S & L and were seeking a preferential stake in the assets.

Judge Rogers discusses, in his opinion, several Supreme Court cases on receivers, but none of them was exactly on point. However, he garners from them the rule that federal courts should not, on grounds of comity, interfere with property in the custody of state courts of coordinate jurisdiction. Although Rogers cannot find direct authority for his holding, he uses the technique of approaching the answer from the negative side:

> Counsel have not been able to cite any case which authorizes a federal court to interfere by injunction or by receiver, or by its marshal, with property in the custody of the law in a state court of co-ordinate jurisdiction, and I have been unable to find any modern decision of any state or federal court recognizing that doctrine.

Rogers goes on to say that "the state court, having first acquired jurisdiction of that question, must be left to determine it." And, on the equitable issue, he concludes:

> Authorities have been cited to enforce that doctrine [federal courts can enjoin defendants from prosecuting suits in state court], but

> all the cases upon that point rest upon the theory that some fraud or unjust advantage has been taken . . . ; but in this case, while the allegations in the bill allege that the plaintiffs in the state court are seeking to secure an unjust advantage, it is manifest that the question can be decided in the state court just as well as in this court . . . There is therefore no fraud in this case, nor is there any reason why the rights of the parties in that court cannot be adjudicated as fairly and justly there as if they were here.

Finally, Rogers does issue a decree appointing a receiver for all the S & L property in Arkansas that is not in the custody of any state officer, and authorizes the receiver to seek possession of the tract already in the jurisdiction of the state court, and retains jurisdiction. Again, we see Rogers taking a conservative and strict view of the law, but by retaining jurisdiction of the case, seeking to ensure that "justice" is done to the out-of-staters in the Arkansas state court.

These two cases typify Rogers's approach to the law—careful, meticulous, conservative, and steady, but modified with a sense of fairness and justice. In many cases where Rogers wrote opinions, the opinions are considerably overwritten, in the sense that too much quotation from authority and too much detail in the factual exposition are presented on what are, in essence, simple factual issues. For example, in *Monroe v. Williamson*[7] the only issue was whether the case had been properly removed from state court to federal court; the opponent to removal conceded that the facts showed the case was properly removable and argued only about the propriety of the surety bond. Rogers, in upholding removal, felt compelled to reproduce verbatim most of the pleadings, discuss every case extant, and the applicability of those cases, resulting in an opinion of some twelve pages (in a small typeface).

Not all of Rogers's opinions were verbose. Sometimes, in bankruptcy cases, or on procedural issues, he would decide in but a few paragraphs.[8]

Labor Disputes

Judge Rogers did not shy away from the controversial issues of the day. In the summer of 1899 he wrote opinions in a pair of cases arising out of the same events and firmly put himself in the camp of those opposing labor union strikers. The cases arose out of a violent coal miner strike at Huntington, Arkansas. In the first opinion, *United States v. Sweeney*,[9] Rogers faced a number of union strikers who had allegedly violated a restraining order issued by Rogers in April of that year. The United States was prosecuting the strikers for contempt, alleging that they had engaged in a series of violent acts against strikebreakers brought in by the coal company to keep the mines in operation. Rogers, in his opinion, thoroughly recounts all the acts charged against the defendants, including attempts by the white strikers to blow up a boardinghouse where black strikebreakers were housed. Relying heavily on the Supreme Court opinion in *In re Debs*,[10] Rogers, after quoting from the opinion, stated:

> That case was argued by as great lawyers as are in this country, and was decided by the greatest court in the world. Until it is overturned, it must be held to be the law of the land. These defendants must be made to know that the very rights they strive to take away from others—the right to work, the right to make their own contracts, the right to follow any lawful occupation at any place in this country, the right to life, liberty, and the pursuit of happiness—are all preserved for them and all others by public law, administered always by courts organized for that purpose.

Rogers concluded by sentencing all the defendants for contempt, imposing eight-month jail sentences.

The other case, arising out of the same strike, was a suit brought by a state prosecutor against the railroad and the coal company to enjoin them from bringing into Arkansas a bunch of hooligan strikebreakers. In *State of Arkansas v. Kansas & Texas Coal Co.*,[11] Rogers held that the state was interfering with interstate commerce in seeking to restrain entry of the strikebreakers. The complaint, brought by the Sebastian County prosecuting attorney in the state court, alleged that the coal company and railroad were about to import "a large number of armed men of the low and lawless type of humanity, to wit, about two hundred, to the great danger of the public peace, morals, and good health of said county." The companies sought to remove the case to federal court and the prosecutor argued that there was no federal jurisdiction and no basis for removal. Rogers denied the motion for remand to the state court, in a rather unusual opinion.

First, Rogers found that the motion to remand was insufficient in that the words "lawless" and "armed" were not sufficiently specific and that the allegation that there would be mayhem caused by the strike-breakers was pure speculation. Second, he analogized the situation to a series of cases where states had tried to prevent aliens from landing, specifically, *In re Ah Fong*,[12] where California tried to deny entry to a Chinese woman who had been labeled by a state official as a lewd and debauched woman, and *Chy Lung v. Freeman*,[13] where the Supreme Court held the California statute void under the commerce clause. In the end, Rogers denied the motion to remand and dissolved the injunction, but also denied the coal company's motion to restrain the prosecution of the suit in state court, saying: "If the state sees fit to continue the prosecution of this case in the state court, it will be permitted to do so, so long as in its prosecution it does not interfere with the relief granted the defendants in this suit in this court." The case was appealed to the Supreme Court where Justice Fuller, in a brief opinion, reversed Judge Rogers and directed him to remand the case to state court.[14] The Supreme Court held that the state of Arkansas could not be subject to removal and that raising the issue of interference with interstate commerce did not make the case removable.

Bankruptcy Cases

A substantial number of the opinions Rogers wrote were in bankruptcy cases. One of the more interesting cases was *In re Matthews*.[15] That case dealt with the issue of whether the holder of a mechanic's lien would have preference over a mortgagee. Rogers interpreted the Arkansas Mechanic's Lien Law proviso giving mechanic's liens preference over any prior liens or encumbrance or mortgage on the land "provided, however, that in all cases where said prior lien or encumbrance or mortgage was given or executed for the purpose of raising money or funds with which to make such erections improvements or buildings, then said lien shall be prior to the lien given by this act." Rogers held that the mortgagee could prevail over the mechanic's lien only to the extent that proceeds from the mortgage were actually used in making buildings or improvements on the land.[16]

In another case, *In re Virginia Hardwood Manufacturing Co.*,[17] Rogers had to deal with the issue of whether a mortgage of the bankrupt's property could be voided as a preference on the ground that the mortgagee believed or had reason to believe at the time of the mortgage that the debtor was insolvent. Rogers engages in a considerably detailed probing of the business affairs of the bankrupt since it first arrived in Fort Smith early in 1904, and concludes that the mortgagee must have known at the time of the mortgage (within four months of the bankruptcy) that he was receiving a preference. Rogers declared that the mortgagee was to be treated as an unsecured creditor.

Liquor

Sometimes, Rogers's personal views show through his opinions. In a quartet of cases, all different factually and legally, we can see the judge's attitudes toward "Demon Rum" expressed in the opinions, sometimes in a frustrating way, as Rogers finds his duty to the law and precedents leads him to a result he is reluctant to reach.

In *In re Wilson,*[18] Rogers had before him a bankrupt cotton merchant whose receiver complained that the bankrupt was withholding assets and books and accounts. Wilson also was charged with failure to appear in response to a court order. Rogers painstakingly reviews the facts in the case, and concludes:

> Taking the most charitable view of this evidence which can justly and fairly be done, and making every possible allowance for the bankrupt's drunkenness and dissipation, I reach the conclusion, and so find, that he has wholly failed to account for, and now has in his possession and under his control, the sum of $3,817.61, which he has failed to schedule or turn over to the trustee in bankruptcy. It is therefore ordered that the said bankrupt turn over and deliver to the trustee within 10 days the said sum of $3,817.61, in default of which he stand committed to the marshal of this district, to be incarcerated until he obeys the order of this court.

The second case involving liquor was *In re Lamberton,*[19] a very interesting case where Lamberton, who was a federal deputy internal revenue collector, filed a habeas petition alleging he was being unlawfully held by the sheriff of Boone County. The hapless "revenuer" had refused to answer questions before a Boone County grand jury about the names and addresses of establishments having federal revenue liquor licenses, claiming that the information sought by the grand jury was confidential.

Rogers granted the writ and ordered Lamberton discharged from the custody of the sheriff, stating:

> If the principle involved presented an original question, I should feel constrained to remand the prisoner to the custody of the sheriff. Reluctantly, I have reached the conclusion that he must be discharged. The information which the state seeks in this case is to enable it to punish its own citizens for the violation of its own laws. The information is within the knowledge of the petitioner . . . and was acquired by him while in the discharge of his official duties.

Rogers goes on to find that federal revenue statutes authorized the commissioner of internal revenue to promulgate regulations regarding official records and a regulation provided that disclosure of any records regarding federal liquor licenses was contrary to public policy. Although he could find no cases in point, Rogers did find a close analogy in a Supreme Court case and "reluctantly" concluded that he had to extend it to the facts before him. Of course, in 1903, no freedom of information or sunshine laws were on the books, and though Rogers would have liked to help the authorities in "dry" Boone County catch liquor sellers who had paid their federal license fees, he could not in good conscience do so.

In *Mellwood Distilling Co. v. Harper*,[20] Judge Rogers dealt with an unfair competition case. Mellwood Distillery in Kentucky marketed a high-grade whiskey under the trademark "Mellwood." Defendant, a Fort Smith liquor distributor and dealer, sold a cheap whiskey with a label designating it as "Mill Wood." The Mill Wood label claimed the contents to be a celebrated handmade sour mash whiskey aged in the barrel for eight years, none of those claims being true. There was no Mill Wood Distillery and the evidence showed that the defendant merely had the labels printed up to put on its bottles of cheap whiskey. Judge Rogers said:

> This is unfair competition, and an infringement of complainant's rights, such as a court of equity will protect, without regard to the purposes defendants had in mind in adopting the label. . . . In determining whether packages are so dressed up as to be calculated to deceive purchasers, equity regards the consumer, as well as the middleman, for it is to him more than the jobber or wholesale purchaser that the various indicia of origin appeal; and the courts will not tolerate a deception devised to delude the consuming

> purchaser by simulating some well-known and popular style of package.

Rogers, of course, granted the injunction, and referred the case to a master to ascertain damages and costs. The opinion does not indicate whether "Mellwood" and "Mill Wood" were put to the taste test by Judge Rogers.[21]

A completely different liquor problem was presented to Rogers in the case of *United States ex rel. Friedman v. United States Express Co.*[22] Here, the sellers of liquor complained that the express company refused to transport their shipments into the former Indian Territory, now the state of Oklahoma. The complaint was based on the Interstate Commerce Act of 1887, which made it unlawful for any common carrier to give an undue preference or prejudice. The defendants relied on the fact that the Intercourse Act of 1897 forbade the introduction of intoxicating liquor into the Indian Territory and that the enabling act admitting Oklahoma into the Union in 1906 provided that furnishing intoxicating liquor in those parts of the state known as Indian Territory and the Osage Reservation and any other Indian reservations "is prohibited for a period of twenty-one years from the date of admission . . . and thereafter until the people of said state shall otherwise provide." Rogers granted the mandamus against the express company, reasoning that when Oklahoma was admitted as a state it became sovereign and on an "equal footing" with the other states: "Congress cannot exact of a state—even a state coming into the Union—the surrender or waiver of any of the constitutionally inherent powers of sovereignty under the Constitution or such as belong to the original states." Therefore, he continued, "Congress knew that the moment Oklahoma was admitted into the Union as a state that the laws regulating interstate commerce must apply to Oklahoma as to all the other states." Rogers also indicates, rhetorically, that if Congress really intended to protect Indians from the evils of liquor, would Congress have admitted Oklahoma with all the powers of statehood? Toward the end of the long opinion in this case, Rogers reflects on the correctness of his own reasoning by stating:

> It is to be hoped this case will be carried to the appellate court, and a controlling decision had. If the decision is sound, the common carriers should not be harassed by vexatious litigation so long as their shipments remain interstate commerce, nor should carriers

> be subjected to indictment in the United States courts for discharging their duties under the interstate commerce laws. On the other hand, if the decision is erroneous, the Indians are entitled to the protection contemplated by the act of January 30, 1897 [the Intercourse Act], and that statute should be enforced by the United States courts.

Judge Rogers's invitation to appeal was acted upon, and in *United States Express Co. v. Friedman*,[23] the Circuit Court of Appeals for the Eighth Circuit reversed Rogers. The appellate court reasoned that Congress did not relinquish its power to control shipment of liquor from other states into Indian Territory by admitting Oklahoma into the Union. Since 1802, the federal government had restricted liquor trade with Indians and every statute since enacted was more rigorous. One paragraph at the beginning of the opinion summarizes federal power in this area:

> The national power over the subject of the suppression of the liquor traffic with the Indians is derived from various sources: First, the treaty-making power. Second the power to regulate interstate commerce. Third, the power to regulate commerce with the Indian tribes. Fourth, the ownership, as sovereign, of lands to which the Indian title has not been extinguished. Fifth, the plenary authority arising out of its guardianship of the Indians as an alien but dependent people.

The court concludes that Rogers's "equal footing" theory, giving Oklahoma its own police powers, in no way contradicted federal power to control commerce into the Indian lands within the state. The opinion also points out that the section of the enabling act committing Oklahoma to restrict liquor dealing for twenty-one years, would make no sense if Congress was thereby disabled from regulating shipment of liquor from outside of Oklahoma into the Indian lands. The United States Supreme Court adopted the reasoning of the Eighth Circuit in two subsequent cases.[24]

Other Civil Cases

In 1899 Rogers had before him a case involving the validity of a Fort Smith ordinance licensing and heavily taxing the business of providing trading stamps to retail buyers, redeemable for gifts. The plaintiff, a

Missouri trading stamp provider, hired the Rose Law Firm of Little Rock to represent him in the challenge to the $75 per month license tax imposed by the ordinance. The complaint in *Humes v. City of Fort Smith*[25] alleged that the ordinance was adopted at the behest of merchants in competition with those who had signed up for the trading stamp operation, and they were bent on destroying Humes's business. The legal theories offered by George B. Rose were the Arkansas constitutional provision requiring equality of taxation and the Fourteenth Amendment. The City first argued that federal jurisdiction was improper as the amount in controversy did not exceed $2,000. Rogers quickly disposed of that argument, stating that federal jurisdiction is not measured by the amount the complainant would have to pay for his license, but is determined by the value of the right to be protected or the extent of the injury to be prevented by the injunction. This succinct and correct statement was recognized subsequently and the *Humes* case has been cited frequently by other federal district and circuit courts facing the same issue. Rogers then waved aside the state constitutional issue and the Fourteenth Amendment issue. A state statute authorized regulation of gift enterprises and Rogers stated that the police power and taxing power are different. As for the Fourteenth Amendment, Rogers cited the *Slaughterhouse Cases* and said, "the supreme court of the United States excepts from the operation of the fourteenth amendment pursuits 'injurious to the community.' It recognizes the principle that such occupations or pursuits as fall within the police powers of the states are not affected by the fourteenth amendment." From that point Rogers had no difficulty in finding the business of trading stamps to be nuisance-like: "Manifestly, the legislature of the state regarded this gift enterprise business as detrimental to the community. I do myself. I do not regard it as a legitimate business." U. M. Rose filed an appeal in the Supreme Court, but it was dismissed with costs.[26]

One unusual civil case dealt with the rule against perpetuities. Although the report of the case is unclear as to the jurisdictional basis of a federal court action, presumably diversity jurisdiction was present. In *Hanley v. Kansas & Texas Coal Co.*,[27] the plaintiffs were the descendants of a black woman who was the former slave of the testator, and the defendant was a coal company that allegedly had appropriated the land for coal mining. The will, probated in 1870, left 320 acres of land in

Sebastian County to the testator's wife, if living at the time of the testator's death; after her death (which occurred shortly after the testator's), then the real estate was to go to Mariah, former slave "and the heirs and children of her body then surviving, share and share alike." A trustee was to be appointed for the use and benefit of Mariah and her children and their descendants for a period of two hundred years, then to the county for the benefit of paupers. The bill in equity alleged that the named trustee never acted, and that there was no record of how the coal company came into possession of the 320-acre farm. The prayer for relief asked for an accounting and a trustee and ouster of the coal company. Rogers's opinion in the case clearly interprets the testator's intent, but stumbles somewhat in the legal construction of the will. He construes the devise as creating an equitable fee simple in Mariah and the children of her body, with a contingent remainder in the county; because the contingent remainder was construed as vesting in interest only when it vested in possession, Rogers held it violated the rule against perpetuities. Most observers would find that Mariah's interest was an equitable estate for two hundred years with a vested remainder in the county (indefeasible), and no violation of the rule against perpetuities. Even if Rogers's construction is correct, the interest over to the county would be an executory limitation and not a contingent remainder. Because he grants the defendant's demurrer to the bill, Rogers avoids the issue of how the coal company "got" the land; also, curiously, the county does not appear in the action.

Criminal Cases

Judge Isaac Parker, Rogers's predecessor, had an unusually large criminal case docket. As is well known, seventy-nine defendants were executed during his tenure. However, that record must be seen in the context of the court's jurisdiction over the Indian Territory, the lack of any appeal from the court (until after 1889), and the lawless conditions in Indian country. Over a twenty-one-year period more than 13,000 criminal cases per year were docketed in Judge Parker's court. Even after 1889, when most of the jurisdiction over Indian Territory had been transferred[28] and when the writ of error brought about, in part, by the efforts of Congressman Rogers, allowed appeals from the Western District to the

Supreme Court, Judge Parker's criminal docket stayed close to 2,000 cases per year.[29]

When Rogers took the bench in November of 1896, criminal cases from Indian Territory were heard in the new federal courts for the territory, and a steady decline in the number of criminal cases in the Western District was immediately apparent. In the first full year of Rogers's tenure, the number of criminal cases declined by nearly two-thirds, to 548. In 1898 the number was up slightly to 682, but in 1898 it was way down to 398. In 1900, the total was 233 and in 1901, 116. In 1902, the last year for which summaries are available from the National Archives, only 20 criminal cases are recorded for Judge Rogers's court. Also, as far as can be determined, Rogers was not a "hanging" judge. The only federal crimes calling for capital punishment were murder and rape, and apparently no cases involving those crimes appeared in Rogers's court.

By far the greatest number of criminal cases in the Western District involved violations of the liquor laws. The only other offenses appearing with any sort of frequency were assaults, timber act violations, and counterfeiting. There is no way of supporting the conclusion, but one could reasonably assume that Rogers left most of the criminal cases to the US commissioner. Judge Parker had disliked the use of commissioners and had appointed only two in the first fifteen years of his tenure.[30]

Judge Rogers and the "Lost Cause"

Rogers's background as a Confederate veteran and his political and judicial career resulted in many occasions to speak to groups about the Civil War. Perhaps the highlight of this aspect of Rogers's life was his keynote address delivered in New Orleans in May 1903 to the convention of United Confederate Veterans.

Rogers's speech was so well received by the Confederate veterans that the organization had it printed in pamphlet form, under the title, "The South Vindicated." The pamphlet was some forty pages and included a portrait of Judge Rogers, along with a sketch of his life. Several thousand copies of the speech were printed, and, at first, given away; the pamphlet version was later sold for five cents by the organization.

The thrust of Rogers's oration, which must have taken two hours to deliver, was that the secession of the Confederate states was perfectly lawful under the Constitution and that no "treasonous" blame should be attached to the southern states. Rogers also spoke, however, of the result of the war being beyond question and the South as fully reconciled to the Union. Finally, he spoke of the Reconstruction era in terms of the real "lawless" period in the history of the war.

Rogers was always available to talk about the Civil War, and his last public appearance, a few weeks before his death, was to deliver a speech at the campfire of the blue and gray state reunion held in Fort Smith.

Death of Judge Rogers

On April 5, 1911, Judge Rogers traveled to Little Rock to hear cases for Judge Jacob Trieber, who was overburdened with a complex case involving railroad rate regulation. Just before going to Little Rock, Rogers had been on a hunting trip with friends in McCurtain County, Oklahoma; the weather was nasty and the judge came down with a bad cold. He could not get rid of the cold, but continued to hear Trieber's cases in Little Rock. On the morning of Monday, April 17, 1911, Judge Rogers was due in court at 9:30 to sentence two defendants who had been found guilty the previous Friday; when he did not appear, Judge Trieber and others went to Rogers's hotel room and found him dead. He died in his sleep, apparently of a heart attack. His death was sudden and, from all accounts, he had not been ill, except for the bad cold, before his demise.[31] He was buried in Fort Smith. Rogers's wife, Mary Gray Rogers, and four children survived the judge (the couple's first child, a daughter, died in childhood). A memorial record was made in the district court in July 1911 under the auspices of Rogers's successor, Frank A. Youmans.

CHAPTER 13

FRANK ABIJAH YOUMANS

1911–32

Morton Gitelman

WHEN JOHN H. Rogers died on April 17, 1911, while in Little Rock to hear cases for Judge Jacob Trieber, the newspapers began to speculate on his successor even before the funeral. The *Arkansas Democrat*, on the very day of Rogers's death, put in its front-page article, a statement that a movement had already begun to support the appointment of Joseph Hill to replace Rogers.[1] That early political gesture, perhaps in questionable taste, blossomed.[2] Joseph Hill, son of a distinguished Confederate general, Daniel Hill, practiced law in Eureka Springs from 1883 to 1887 and then in Fort Smith. He served as chief justice of the Arkansas Supreme Court from 1904 to 1909, when he resigned to act as chief counsel for the state in a group of railroad rate cases, which he won before the Supreme Court.

The only problem that apparently made Hill's appointment questionable was his heavy involvement in Democratic Party politics. Nevertheless, a strong effort was made on Hill's behalf. Only two days after Rogers's demise, the *Democrat* reported the passage of a resolution by the Arkansas Senate, concurred in by the House, urging President Taft to appoint Hill.[3] At the same time a movement to support W. H. Arnold of Texarkana for the position emerged.[4]

Frank Abijah Youmans. *Courtesy United States District Court for the Western District of Arkansas.*

A hint that the Arkansas General Assembly resolution and the resolutions supporting W. H. Arnold might bear no fruit came in the Fort Smith newspaper report on April 20:

> It is known in Fort Smith that an important conference of Republican leaders is to be held at the Planters hotel, St. Louis, tomorrow night for a sort of general discussion of Arkansas politics. There is also strong intimation that a successor to the late Judge Rogers is to be one of the matters brought up for consideration and probably action.
>
> In certain directions there are rumors that Judge [*sic*] Frank A. Youmans will be a candidate for the vacant federal judgeship. When importuned last night to affirm or deny these he positively declined to make any statement whatsoever.[5]

The newspaper in Fort Smith obviously saw a good story in the St. Louis meeting and had a reporter there. On April 22, a front-page story told that Frank Youmans had met the day before in St. Louis with General Powell Clayton, Republican national committeeman and state committeeman of Arkansas. The article went on to state that Youmans was considered the strongest candidate for the appointment, and quoted Powell as saying: "The consensus of opinion as far as I have been able to gather it, among Republicans, is that Mr. Youmans is the most available candidate . . . . He is spoken of well, even by his opponents and is a man of unquestioned integrity and singular professional ability."[6] Two days after the news report, Judge Hill made public a letter of appreciation he had sent to the legislature, in which he stated: "While I shall not personally seek this position, or apply to the president for it, . . . I would not decline it should the president in this instance, as he has in others, pass his party lines and select me for it."[7]

Clearly the Arkansas Republican Party felt they had a strong candidate in Frank Youmans, and despite the solid Democratic delegation in the Congress and the endorsement of the state legislature, an active Democratic stalwart like Judge Hill stood little chance of appointment. Also, the slight boom for W. H. Arnold seemed confined to the region of southwest Arkansas and did not spread beyond that corner of the state.

The president acted expeditiously; the state of the Western District docket dictated a quick appointment, especially because Judge Trieber of the Eastern District was trying to fill in while at the same time handling his own docket.[8] Within two or three weeks after the Republican meeting in St. Louis, Frank Youmans had been selected. On May 19, 1911, Youmans was summoned to Washington to meet with President Taft, and the Fort Smith newspaper reported that trip as tantamount to selection.[9] Ten days later, just after his fifty-first birthday, Frank Youmans was nominated by the president.[10] The confirmation process took nearly a month, but by the end of June 1911, Youmans had been confirmed as the Western District judge.

Background of Judge Youmans

Frank A. Youmans was born in Missouri near Jefferson City, in 1860. His paternal ancestors went back to the American Revolution and were residents of New York. Frank Youmans's father was a medical steward all through the Civil War, and afterward hung out a shingle as a country doctor. His mother was an immigrant from Germany. After the war, the family moved to Hannibal, Missouri; in 1873, the Youmans family moved to Arkansas, residing in Columbia and Union counties for five years, and then settling in Lewisville, in 1878. Frank Youmans left Lewisville in 1880 to attend college at the University of Missouri, where he received a BL degree in 1884. He then taught school for a short period of time.

After completing his college education, Youmans moved to Little Rock where he read law in the office of Burrill B. Battle (later a justice on the Arkansas Supreme Court). Youmans was admitted to the bar in 1885, and in 1886 he established a solo practice in Fort Smith. After a year as a solo practitioner, he joined the firm of Clendening and Read. In 1891, Judge Read left the firm and it became Clendening, Meachem & Youmans.

Youmans engaged in a general practice until 1897, when he was appointed assistant US attorney under Thomas H. Barnes; Barnes died in 1898, but the post of US attorney did not go to Youmans but went to James K. Barnes, brother of the deceased. Prosecuting attorneys in that era were allowed private practice, and Frank Youmans formed a partnership with his brother, George, listed as Youmans & Youmans. Frank Youmans continued as an assistant US attorney until 1905, when he resigned and commenced full-time general practice with his brother. Frank was still active in public life, as a member of the Fort Smith School

Board (since 1899),[11] and as a candidate for district attorney in 1909. He was unsuccessful in that race, losing to John Washington. He also ran unsuccessfully for Congress twice and for Arkansas attorney general.

In 1888, soon after establishing his law practice at Fort Smith, Frank Youmans married Delia Enroughty of Springfield, Missouri, daughter of a Presbyterian clergyman. The couple had six children.[12]

By all accounts, Youmans was a very plain and unassuming man. He never owned a carriage or an automobile, preferring to walk or use either a streetcar or, occasionally, a livery stable. He loved to ride the train, always taking books along to read. The story is told that when he received the summons to come to Washington and meet with President Taft, Mrs. Youmans suggested that her husband have a new suit to wear. Frank Youmans dutifully went to a local haberdashery and purchased a suit that his wife carefully packed in tissue paper in his valise so that it would not get wrinkled. Upon returning from the presidential visit, she found the suit still in the valise, undisturbed, and asked the soon-to-be judge if he had worn it. His reply was that he forgot.[13] His plain habits are also illustrated by the time a client gave Youmans a frock tailcoat as a gesture of thanks, and the recipient did not know what to do with it, except perhaps to wear it to church. Youmans was a regular church-goer and taught a Sunday School class in the Methodist Church. His family knew him as a scholar who kept an extensive library at home including every issue of the National Geographic, which was his favorite. He also had many books in German as he was a fluent reader in that language.[14]

The Judicial Career

Judge Youmans had a lengthy tenure on the federal bench, from 1911 to 1932, nearly twenty-one years. Yet, in that period of time, only thirty-two published district court opinions appear in the reporters. Of those thirty-two opinions, nineteen were filed in the years from 1911 through 1914. After 1914, the record of opinions is quite sparse. There was one in 1919, one in 1923, two in 1926, one in 1927, one in 1928, one in 1929, three in 1930, and one each in 1931 and 1932. These few district court opinions do not indicate any aversion to writing, for Judge Youmans authored about fifty opinions while sitting on three-judge panels at the Eighth Circuit level. Panel opinions, of course, are often restrained by the input of two other judges, so the paucity of written district-level opinions makes assessment of Youmans's judicial philosophy and performance difficult.

In looking at the personality and temperament of Judge Youmans, one finds that he was highly regarded for integrity and fairness and that, although he occasionally showed temper when a lawyer "tried to put something over on him on the bench," he was usually pleasant to everyone and spoke kindly to all. Youmans's fairness is illustrated by an anecdote told in a short article, "Justice and the Law" by Will Luce in the *Arkansas Gazette* Sunday Magazine:

> Although the judge was a consistent Methodist he had a close friend and admirer in Father Horan, priest of the Catholic church at Fort Smith, and the priest was a firm believer in Judge Youmans' strict fidelity to justice. As is the case with most priests and preachers, Father Horan was besought frequently to intercede with the judge and get justice tempered with mercy. He would be asked to see Judge Youmans and plead in behalf of some fellow who was clearly guilty and, to quote the priest's own words: "I had promised to say something, but, knowing the judge as I did, and knowing that in his wonderful mind and heart justice always was tempered with mercy, and that no human could or should alter his wise decisions, I would call at his chambers and respond to the cheery greeting he always gave. Then I would say, 'Judge, John Doe asked to say something to you in hi[s] behalf. I have said something and I bid you good day,' and I could hear him chuckle as I walked out of his office."[15]

Family members remember Frank Youmans as quiet and reserved, studious and religious. One of his favorite pastimes was reading the Bible in German and comparing the German and English passages side by side.[16] After Judge Youmans's death, Joe Helm the janitor at the federal building who had been there throughout the tenure of Judge Youmans said that the judge was always quiet and that he "spoke to everyone in a kindly manner, and always stopped his work to aid Joe whenever he went to him for advice."[17]

The Early Years

One can only lament at the small number of Youmans's district-level opinions, because Judge Youmans wrote well, and, on occasion, elegantly. In his first written opinion, filed August 12, 1911, Youmans demonstrates his felicitous style. The case, *In re Greer*,[18] was an appeal from a bankruptcy referee's order directing the bankrupt to turn over $7,000 in assets to the trustee. Judge Youmans reversed and remanded the case because the referee had erroneously overruled the bankrupt's motion to make the trustees' demand more definite and certain; the trustee had charged that Greer fraudulently concealed assets. In response to the motion to make the petition more definite, the trustee alleged that it was physically impossible to do so. Youmans wrote:

> Just what is meant by the words "physical impossibility" is not clear. Physical impediments do not excuse indefiniteness in pleading. There is no logical connection between the two. Besides, the difficulty seems to have been psychical rather than physical. It was certainly physically possible to compare the statement of August 5, 1910, with the schedules filed by the bankrupt in October following, and thus see what articles in the statement were absent in the schedules if any such were absent. It was physically possible to introduce the schedules in testimony, so that the referee could make the comparison himself. But that was not done. . . . If it is physically possible now, by means of the testimony of the bankrupt, to designate the property still held by him, it was certainly possible then.[19]

This witty passage indicates that Youmans possessed a sense of humor attuned to the ironic, and this first opinion presaged a career of judicial opinion writing that would be appreciated by the bar.

The next two opinions, both in 1911, dealt with the subject of removal of state court filings to federal court. In *Symonds v. St. Louis & S.E. Ry. Co.*,[20] a railroad employee sued for injuries sustained while working. The railroad removed the case to federal court and the employee filed a motion to remand, based on the language in the Federal Employers Liability Act providing that "no case arising under this act and brought in any state court of competent jurisdiction shall be removed to any court of the United States." Judge Youmans wrote a very clear opinion showing that Congress's intent was to allow injured railroad workers a choice of state or federal forum. He utilized historical references, legislative debates, and an Arkansas Supreme Court opinion to support the conclusion that the worker was entitled to have the case remanded to state court.

Just a month after the *Symonds* case, Youmans extended his reasoning to a similar case in which a passenger injured in a train wreck sued the railroad in state court; the railroad engineer was joined as a codefendant and the railroad argued that any negligence on its part was based solely on the doctrine of respondeat superior and that the engineer was joined fraudulently solely to prevent removal to federal court. Youmans's opinion in *Armstrong v. Kansas City Southern Ry. Co.*[21] is a solid and thorough examination and analysis of the authorities on the issue of joinder of parties as affecting removal to federal courts. His conclusion that the burden of showing fraudulent joinder to prevent removal rests on the party seeking removal and that the railroad failed to sustain that burden illustrates that Youmans possessed a very good analytical legal mind.

In 1912, Judge Youmans issued opinions in several interesting cases. Two, in the bankruptcy area, posed unusual problems. The first, *In re Fayetteville Wagon-Wood and Lumber Co.*,[22] presented the issue of whether a bond holder of the bankrupt, whose bonds were secured by a mortgage on the real estate and machinery and who was seeking foreclosure of the mortgage, could restrain the trustee from selling the bankrupt's entire business as a whole. The trustee claimed that selling the stock and materials separately from the real estate and machinery would bring less than selling the entire business. The bondholder argued that a sale of the entirety would not bring enough to discharge the bonded indebtedness and that it should be allowed to pursue its foreclosure action. Youmans sided with the bond holder, citing cases holding that encumbered property should not be sold in a bankruptcy sale unless the trustee can show that the proceeds reasonably will bring enough to discharge the lien. In the second case, *In re Eureka Anthracite Coal Co.*,[23] Youmans ruled that stockholders of the bankrupt corporation were not entitled to intervene and defend against an involuntary bankruptcy petition. The opinion points out that while stockholders cannot appear as parties in suits against the corporation in law, in certain equity cases stockholders are allowed to intervene. Although bankruptcy proceedings are regarded as equitable, Youmans did not find enough facts to support the proposed intervention and upheld the motion to strike the stockholders.

Perhaps the most important opinion in the early years of Judge Youmans's tenure was *St. Louis Southwestern Rwy. Co. v. Miller Levee Dist. No. 2*,[24] a case seeking to enjoin the construction of a levee, but in reality, an inverse condemnation case involving the takings clause of the Fifth Amendment. The essence of the railroad's claim was that construction of the levee would raise the high-water mark so as to require the railroad, at its own expense, to raise its bridge across the Red River. As stated by Judge Youmans:

> The effect of the contention of the railway company is that having legally constructed its bridge and approaches under conditions then existing, at a height and in a manner warranted by the best engineering skill and foresight, it cannot now, by a change of conditions authorized and directed by the state, be put to the expense of raising and reconstructing its bridge and approaches. In other words, it having some years ago at great expense adjusted itself to conditions as they then existed, those conditions must remain unchanged unless it is compensated for the expense which a contemplated change will necessitate.[25]

Youmans very effectively analyzed the Supreme Court and Eighth Circuit cases,[26] concluding: "The injury to the railway company by the construction of the levee is not a taking of property in violation of the Constitution of the United States; nor is it a taking, appropriating, or damaging of property in violation of the Constitution of the state of Arkansas."[27]

In *MacKay Telegraph & Cable Co. v. City of Texarkana*,[28] Judge Youmans was asked to grant a temporary restraining order to halt the city from imposing allegedly invalid conditions on the plaintiff's franchise to install a telegraph line and to enjoin the city from interfering with the company's activities. The dispute arose because the city ordered the company to install a significant portion of its proposed line underground; the company agreed to some underground installation but claimed the city's demand was excessive. Youmans denied the TRO, stating that to grant it would in fact resolve the whole case prior to trial and that a trial was necessary to establish whether the city's conditions were indeed overreaching.

In December of 1912, an interesting bankruptcy question was presented.[29] The bankrupt was an ice company in Siloam Springs. The ice plant defaulted on a mortgage on its real and personal property and the assignee of the mortgagee claimed the entire property. The intervenor claimed the machinery that it had sold to the ice company was subject to a contract retaining title to the machinery until the full payment of the purchase price. The bankruptcy referee ordered the ice company sold free of all liens and that a portion of the receipts be retained to meet the pending claim of the intervenor. The assignee of the mortgagee disputed the intervention claiming that title to the machinery passed to the mortgagee and became part of the real estate. Judge Youmans explored the law of fixtures, including several Arkansas cases, and concluded that the machinery did meet the definition of a fixture. He denied the intervenor's claim. Today, of course, an issue like this would be decided under the Uniform Commercial Code.[30]

Judge Youmans issued what was probably a very unpopular opinion on New Year's Eve of 1912. The City of Fort Smith had enacted an ordinance limiting the price of natural gas to 25 cents per thousand feet. The gas company had, earlier in the year, raised its price to 40 cents. In *Fort Smith Light & Traction Co. v. City of Fort Smith*,[31] Youmans issued a restraining order against enforcement of the ordinance. The judge found that, under existing Arkansas law, the city was entitled to regulate rates, but that the enabling authority specified the city was authorized, "when complaint is filed . . . that any . . . gas . . . plant, is charging an exorbitant rate . . . to summon [the company] together with their books and make such examination as will be necessary to determine whether or not the prices charged" are exorbitant, and if so to fix a reasonable charge. Youmans held that the city did not make the requisite examination of the gas company's books; thus the 25-cent rate was arbitrary. The city's action was precipitated by the company's recent dramatic price increases and the fact that nearby Oklahoma towns were paying considerably less for natural gas. The company justified its rate hike on the ground that its sources were becoming depleted, but company officials acknowledged that depletion was speculative. The shivering citizens of Fort Smith were probably not too happy with Youmans's action.

In *Lee v. Kansas City Southern Ry. Co.*,[32] Youmans granted the defendant's motion for a new trial in a personal injury case. He held that the plaintiff's expert medical witness should not have been allowed to testify about what the plaintiff had told him in regard to the accident. Youmans relied on a number of state court decisions holding such statements to be inadmissible hearsay. The modern rule is quite different, as the Federal Rules of Evidence recognize, in Rules 803 (3) and (4), hearsay exceptions for statements made in connection with medical diagnosis and treatment. The Eighth Circuit reversed and remanded for a new trial, without discussing the hearsay issue, going off on the problems with the record in the case.

Four additional opinions were filed in the year 1913 and 1914. Two cases were run-of-the-mill bankruptcy disputes,[33] and one was a complicated contract dispute involving the City of Fort Smith and the municipal waterworks.[34] The final case of the early period was *United States v. Colo*,[35] which was a contempt proceeding against a number of union miners for violating a strike injunction. The case arose out of a very violent coal mine strike at Midland, in Sebastian County. Two company employees were killed and a mine was blown up. Judge Youmans's opinion painstakingly recounts all the evidence that associated the defendants with violent acts against nonunion scabs and the company, including threats with baseball bats on a train carrying workers to the mine, shipment of arms from a union official in Oklahoma to the strikers in Arkansas, and the display of guns and knives. Youmans found abundant evidence of defendants' guilt and sentenced most of them to serve in the Sebastian County jail for terms up to four months for criminal contempt. The judge indicated his feelings about the defendants when he ended the opinion with the trenchant observation: "It is proper to say, in this connection, that a conviction upon a charge of contempt for an offense which is also a crime does not bar prosecution for the crime."[36]

The Later Years

In the nine-year period between September 1914 and September 1923, only one district court opinion of Judge Youmans's appears in the reports. That case, in 1919, was an ordinary negligence case brought by a railroad passenger against the Missouri Pacific Railroad Company and the Director General of Railroads.[37] The Missouri Pacific filed a demurrer to the cause of action on the ground that when the federal government took over all the railroads as part of the war effort, the employees of the railroad were no longer the servants of the Missouri Pacific. The opinion by Youmans sustained the demurrer, holding in accord with other federal case authority, that the presidential proclamation nationalizing the railroads and vesting control of the lines in a director general meant suits could only be brought against the director general. In legal terms, Youmans held, there could be no respondeat superior doctrine where no master-servant relationship existed. In the opinion, Youmans says nothing about the continued viability of the lawsuit against the director general, also a named defendant.

Nothing accounts for the dearth of published opinions during those nine years. Judge Youmans did begin to sit on Eighth Circuit panels in the fall of 1914 and several times in 1915. He authored thirteen opinions in that term,[38] plus, of course, sitting on several panels where another judge wrote the opinion. He sat again in 1918 and 1919 (ten opinions),[39] the fall of 1921 (eight opinions),[40] the fall of 1922 (five opinions),[41] the winter and spring of 1926 (five opinions),[42] and finally in the fall of 1931 (three opinions).[43] Judge Youmans's district docket was quite full during those years as well, as illustrated by the number of appeals taken to the Eighth Circuit from the Western District court.

The one opinion published in 1923 stood alone until 1926, when the pace of opinion publication picked up; from 1926 until Judge Youmans's death in 1932, ten district court opinions appear in the reports. The 1923 opinion, *Southwestern Bell Telephone Co. v. City of Fort Smith*,[44] was a rate case where the telephone company sought to enjoin the city from putting ordinance rates into effect. The issue in the case dealt with competing valuations and depreciation schedules in arriving at a fair return on investment. Youmans sided with the telephone company, concluding:

> By allowing a valuation of $685,605, which includes a going value of 10 per cent., and by reducing the annual depreciation to 4 per cent., the city shows a return of 6.29 per cent. Its engineer admits that a fair return would be 8 per cent. The attempt to impose ordinance rates which admittedly will not produce a fair return on the value of the property devoted to public use is the taking of property without due process of law under the Fourteenth Amendment.[45]

In re Johnson[46] was an unusual bankruptcy case. The bankrupt, a merchant, was indebted to the Bank of Lockesburg and several other creditors. His store was destroyed by fire in December 1924. In January 1925, Johnson assigned his insurance policy for $8,000 to the bank to secure his loans. The insurance company denied liability on the policies and the bank hired Collins to bring suit for itself and Johnson. Subsequently, the other creditors of Johnson brought suit against the bank and garnished the bank and insurance company. The $8,000 policy, if paid, would have been enough to satisfy all creditors, but the insurance company continued to deny liability. Finally, Collins made a settlement with the insurance company for 75 percent of the policy on condition that all the garnishments were released. The bank agreed to accept 75 percent of its claim against Johnson and allow the rest of the insurance proceeds to be applied pro rata to satisfy the other creditors. With this agreement in hand Collins was able to get releases and the insurance company cut a check for $6,125 payable to the bank and Collins. Collins sent the check to the bank with instructions to deposit it to his credit. On January 2, 1926, with full knowledge of the bankruptcy proceedings the bank charged Collins the full amount of Johnson's indebtedness to the bank, $2,917.93. The bankruptcy trustee ordered the bank to repay 25 percent of that sum for the benefit of the other creditors, and the bank appealed, claiming that the trustee did not have jurisdiction over that money, and arguing that it had agreed to the insurance settlement only on the condition that Johnson, the bankrupt, would secure the full amount of the bank's claim against him. Youmans held that the bank was estopped because it knew of Collins's settlement agreement and of the bankruptcy proceedings: "Its possession [of the money] was the direct result of such agreement. It cannot now ignore that agreement on which the money was obtained, and stand on the original assignment of the policy by which it obtained nothing."[47]

Judge Youmans wrote an opinion denying a pro se petition seeking probation, stating that the petition presented an important question under the recently adopted federal probation act.[48] The petitioner, in a lengthy petition accompanied by a pro se brief, had been convicted with another person of mail fraud in a stock scheme. In his petition, Davis claimed poverty, hungry children, good faith restitution efforts, and he apologized for "an act unbecoming to a gentleman while confined in the Miller County jail, namely, the leaving of said jail without the permission of the United States marshal, though this act was committed in good faith and with no intent to defeat the ends of justice."[49] The government responded to the petition by claiming that once a defendant is sentenced, and the term of court ends, the trial court loses jurisdiction to grant probation. Youmans found three recent district court opinions discussing that issue, two of them agreeing that after the court term ends, the judge cannot award probation, and one decision going the other way. Youmans sided with the government and denied the petition. This decision, along with another the following year, and one in 1929, show Judge Youmans as a very strict constructionist on jurisdictional issues. The 1927 decision came in a bankruptcy case.[50] After the bankruptcy referee had made his order setting aside certain property of the bankrupt as exempt under Arkansas law, a judgment creditor who had won a tort case against Watson petitioned to have the exemption order amended so as to render the property subject to the judgment. In a brief opinion, Youmans held that the state-exempted property remains with the bankrupt, and title to it never passes to the trustee in bankruptcy. Therefore, the bankruptcy referee has no jurisdiction to deal with such property. The 1929 case, *Fidler v. Western Coal & Mining Co.*,[51] presented a removal issue. The plaintiff had sued Western Coal, a Missouri corporation, and two Arkansas coal companies for negligence. The defendant, Western, removed the case, plaintiff moved to remand, and Western claimed fraudulent joinder to prevent removal, on the ground that Mama Coal, one of the other defendants, had been dissolved and was hopelessly bankrupt. Youmans held that the burden of showing fraudulent joinder was on Western and that the burden had not been met. Mama Coal had been dissolved, but under Arkansas corporation law, corporations continue to have existence for three years after dissolution for the purpose of lawsuits. Furthermore, the plaintiff denied Mama's bankruptcy, and the sheriff had effected service on an agent of Mama.

In the case of *Hill v. Firemen's Insurance Co.*,[52] Youmans took the side of a beleaguered businessman against the collector of internal revenue. The Magnolia Window Glass Co. of Fort Smith had suffered a fire and brought claims against the insurers. The insurance companies had been served with a distraint order by the internal revenue office, claiming that Magnolia was responsible for back taxes owed by Model Window Glass Co., whose business had been purchased by Magnolia; the insurance companies sought and received the intervention of the revenue collector as a party defendant. Magnolia claimed that $12,000 of their fire loss was hand-blown glass that had nothing to do with Model and that the tax collector was improperly refusing to release the tax lien on at least that portion of the insurance. The evidence in the case, correspondence with the collector's office in Little Rock, indicated that the tax collector refused to release that portion of the distraint until Magnolia either paid the taxes due or proved to the collector's satisfaction that Model never had an interest in that glass. Youmans held that the undisputed evidence showed that Model never had an interest in the glass destroyed by fire and that the government could never have had a lien on it, or the insurance money for its loss by fire.

However, a few years later, Youmans took the government's side in a case seeking forfeiture of an automobile used by a bootlegger.[53] Joe Herring, a bootlegger allegedly selling the best whiskey in Fort Smith, was set up by prohibition agents who made more than three buys from Herring. Herring's modus operandi was to take orders over the telephone, tell the buyers where to meet him, drive to the location, and make the delivery. At the forfeiture trial, Herring claimed that when he was arrested, the bottle of gin was in his pocket; therefore, the car was not used to transport the booze. Naturally, Youmans upheld the forfeiture, quaintly stating:

> Herring carried on his business by means of the telephone and the automobile. The latter was as necessary as the former. To say that the liquor was transported on the person of Herring and was not transported in the automobile is to disregard the obvious facts. The automobile was more necessary to Herring in the transportation of the liquor that he sold than the pocket in his coat.[54]

An indication of Judge Youmans's facility at analytical interpretation is evidenced by his opinion in *In re Stroebel.*[55] This was a bankruptcy case where the bankrupt partner in a mercantile business allegedly purchased his copartner's interest in the goods several months prior to the bankruptcy; the copartner filed bankruptcy claims based on the three notes given by the bankrupt in payment. The other creditors alleged that the "sale" to Thompson, the copartner, was void because of failure to comply with the Arkansas Bulk Sales Law. The referee ruled for the creditors and refused to allow the claim. On appeal, Judge Youmans stated:

> The contention of counsel for Thompson is that the Bulk Sales Law of Arkansas is not applicable to a sale of an undivided interest in a stock of merchandise by one partner to another. It is conceded that the Supreme Court of Arkansas has not passed upon that identical

> question. It is also conceded that the authorities in other states are divided on that point.[56]

Youmans then proceeded to analyze a leading Kansas case, the subject of an ALR annotation, that supported the position urged by Thompson for nonapplicability of the Bulk Sales Law. He found that the case could be distinguished because in the Kansas case the facts indicated that creditors of the partnership were not prejudiced by the sale of the stock by one partner, while in the case at bar, the facts indicated something of a "scam" to undercut the creditors. Youmans also looked at and discussed other Arkansas cases interpreting the Bulk Sales Law in order to discern the attitude expressed by the Arkansas courts on the intent and purpose of the law. Finally, in a broad holding, Youmans concludes:

> I think the rule of liberal construction to correct the evil aimed at by the Bulk Sales Law of Arkansas required that the law shall be held to apply to a sale of his interest in a stock of goods by one partner to his copartner.[57]

In another bankruptcy case a year later, *Dealers' Finance Co. v. Coulter*,[58] Youmans upheld a bankruptcy trustee's rejection of the finance company claims of secured protection as invalid preferences within the four-month period preceding bankruptcy filing. The case was a classic "Music Man" situation; the bankrupt was a musical instrument dealer, and the factory representative selling him instruments on credit was also a manager of the finance company holding the notes. When the bankrupt fell behind, the instrument man put on his finance company hat and secured pledges of future accounts from the bankrupt. Both the trustee and Judge Youmans found that even though those pledges were timely under the bankruptcy act, transfer of possession was not until after the four-month window opened, and Youmans held that only those accounts where possession was transferred prior to the four-month period could stand as valid claims.

In *Ex parte Nash*,[59] Youmans wrote an opinion on a constitutional issue raised in a habeas proceeding. The prisoner was held in El Dorado for extradition to Louisiana on a felony charge. In the habeas petition the prisoner alleged that the order of extradition was defective in that he had been charged in Louisiana by information rather than indictment. Youmans's opinion rejecting the claim analyzed the issue of whether the constitutional language, "person charged,"[60] could include a prosecutorial information. Youmans noted that language in some Supreme Court cases used the term "indictment" in connection with extradition and also the term "affidavit before a magistrate of the state."[61] He also concluded that the manner of charging crimes for purposes of applying the extradition clause must be decided by reference to the law of state seeking extradition. Using this approach, Youmans found that Louisiana law clearly provided for charging by information, and that Nash was extraditable.

The last opinion filed by Judge Youmans was in February 1932. A group of cases was decided together as *Harp v. United States*.[62] All of the cases were suits challenging the denial of veteran's disability benefits under World War I war risk insurance policies. The veterans who were plaintiffs all claimed total disability due to war-related service, and all claimed that their insurance claims had been wrongly denied by the federal bureau of veterans' affairs (a predecessor to the Veteran's Administration). The defense was essentially failure to exhaust administrative remedies, and the government moved to dismiss for lack of jurisdiction. Youmans upheld the government and dismissed all the suits. The plaintiffs introduced a great deal of correspondence with the agency, including one letter signed by the director of insurance for the VA, stating:

> . . . the evidence is not sufficient to establish as a fact that the former insured was totally and permanently disabled at a time when the contract of insurance was in force and therefore the claim has been denied.[63]

The plaintiff replied with a letter stating that he accepted the denial of the claim as final "for the purpose of instituting suit." Youmans found that prior to the filing of the suit Congress had, in 1930, amended the statute to provide that "disagreement" over a claim "means a denial of the claim by the director or some one acting in his name on an appeal to the director." Youmans then found that an appeal to the director of the veterans' bureau was a jurisdictional prerequisite to a lawsuit, and he upheld the demurrers in each of the complaints.

The Judicial Record

Assessing Judge Youmans as a district judge requires more than reading his few opinions. One must look at jury trials, bench trials, evidentiary rulings, and the like to determine how well he performed. Large numbers of Youmans's cases were appealed, nearly two hundred. His rulings were reversed, in whole or in part in approximately 48 percent of the cases appealed. This reversal rate is probably about average for district judges in that era. However, by looking at the reversals in particular and in some of the affirmances, one can make a few characterizations about Judge Youmans. He was apparently a bit stingy when it came to awarding attorneys' fees, because he was reversed in two or three cases solely on the basis of inadequacy of fees awarded.[64]

In the early years, Judge Youmans ruled often for defendants in personal injury cases, especially those brought against railroads. In *Lee v. Kansas City Southern Ry. Co.*,[65] for example, the Eighth Circuit reversed in a case where Youmans had directed a verdict for the defendant railroad. In that case, the passenger train had gone through an open switch and jolted the passengers severely. Lee sued for injuries and the railroad countered that the plaintiff's medical condition was due to his suffering from Bright's Disease. In reversing, the appellate court held that even though the evidence conclusively established the plaintiff's disease, that did not mean that a jury could not find some injury resulting from the railroad's negligence.

In the later years, Judge Youmans was reversed in several personal injury cases that had resulted in plaintiffs' verdicts. In *Lion Oil Co. v. Lawrence*,[66] Youmans refused to direct a verdict for the employer in a case where an employee was injured while riding in an open trailer behind a truck. The trailer overturned when the truck made a turn, and several workers on the way to work in an oil field were thrown out of the trailer. Lion Oil, the employer, claimed that the negligence, if any, was attributable to the livery company who had been hired by Lion to transport workers. The Eighth Circuit held that the livery company was an independent contractor and Lion should have received a directed verdict. And in *Standard Oil v. Martin*,[67] the appellate court reversed a judgment for an employee of the oil company who was injured while riding in the back of an open truck when one end of a wooden board projecting outside the truck sides, on which some employees were sitting, struck a tree. The injured worker's leg was crushed when the other end of the board swung in toward the back of the truck cab. The court said: "The proximate cause of the injury was the projecting end of the board. There being no negligence in the placing of the board upon the truck, and no evidence that the position of the board was changed after it was placed thereon, and there being room for the truck itself to pass between the two trees, and no knowledge shown on the part of the company that the board did project beyond the side of the truck, there is an utter lack of any facts that would impute negligence to the company."[68]

Some of the reversals of Judge Youmans can probably be explained by confusion in the Eighth Circuit. Two cases involving injuries due to electric shocks will serve to illustrate this. In the first case, *Kaemmerling v. Athletic Mining & Smelting Co.*,[69] Youmans dismissed a personal injury case brought by a worker against the employer resulting from a severe electric shock received when the plaintiff threw a metal switch. The dismissal was based on the plaintiff's failure to allege specific acts of negligence. In reversing, the Eighth Circuit discussed the application of the res ipsa loquitur doctrine in master-servant cases and the issue of allegations of negligence based upon reasonable inferences in the pleadings. Judge Youmans heeded the lesson of this case three years later.

In *Dierks Lumber & Coal Co. v. Brown*,[70] another personal injury case, the Eighth Circuit reversed a plaintiff's verdict, holding that Youmans should have given a directed verdict. The claim was that the injury occurred when the plaintiff received an electric shock as she turned on a sewing machine, and that the defendant power company was responsible for excess current in the wires. The facts showed that there was a broken electrical wire outside the building. However, the defendant claimed that their system was properly grounded and that the fuses at the building were not blown. Youmans had instructed the jury on res ipsa loquitur, and a $2,500 verdict was returned. The appellate court held that the res ipsa doctrine did not relieve plaintiff from the burden of proving negligence, that even though the wire was broken, the power company was entitled to a reasonable time to discover the break, and that the defendant's medical evidence characterizing the plaintiff as "a neurotic" who probably fantasized or made up her claim, required a directed verdict for the defendant.

Another example can be found in a pair of cases involving the efforts of the United Mine Workers of America and its efforts to stop shipments of nonunion coal from western Arkansas. In *Dowd v. United Mine Workers of America*,[71] Youmans granted the union's motion to dismiss a case filed by the nonunion company against the union under the antitrust act.

Youmans concluded that the union, as an unincorporated association, could not be sued in its own name under the Sherman Act. The Eighth Circuit reversed and ordered reinstatement of the complaint. After this decision the case was tried in Fort Smith and a $200,000 verdict against the union was trebled by Youmans. That decision was affirmed by the Eighth Circuit but the Supreme Court reversed the judgment.[72] In 1924 Youmans was reversed by the Eighth Circuit in a companion case to the *Coronado* case that had first been filed in 1915. In *United Mine Workers of America v. Pennsylvania Mining Co.*,[73] Youmans held against the international union on antitrust counts of conspiracy to interfere with interstate commerce arising out of a violent strike at a Johnson County mine not far from the Coronado mine. In this case the Eighth Circuit found that there was insufficient evidence to attribute the acts of violence to the international union, and the case was remanded for a new trial.

In one interesting case, Judge Youmans was reversed by the Eighth Circuit but was vindicated by the Supreme Court. In *Harding Glass Co. v. Twin City Pipeline Co.*,[74] the glass factory, largest consumer of natural gas in the Fort Smith area, had a dispute with the gas supplier for insufficient supply. In settling a 1926 lawsuit between the gas supplier and several industrial customers, the gas company agreed to construct additional pipeline facilities. In return a contract was signed providing that, so long as the supplies were sufficient, the glass factory would purchase all of its gas from Twin City Pipeline at the published rate. A few years later, Harding Glass formed a subsidiary corporation to build a pipeline from the gas fields to its factory and began to purchase gas from its subsidiary. Twin City Pipeline sued to enforce the contract, and Judge Youmans entered a decree for specific performance. The Eighth Circuit reversed, holding that the contract was against public policy as a restraint of trade. The Supreme Court reversed, in an opinion by Justice Butler, based on liberty of contract, and rejecting the public policy rationale used by the Eighth Circuit.

Judge Youmans's Death

In 1930, Judge Youmans became eligible for retirement; also in that year he underwent serious surgery in St. Louis.[75] However, he recovered from the surgery and announced that he would continue to serve as long as he remained able. Considering that he published several opinions in 1930, Youmans's health was not impaired, and he apparently had no difficulty in keeping up with the docket.[76]

Early in April 1932, Youmans traveled to Harrison to hold the spring term of court in that division. After the first three days of the term, Judge Youmans became quite ill with what was thought to be influenza, and he took to his bed at the Hotel Seville in Harrison. By Saturday, April 8, he was semiconscious and his Fort Smith physician flew to attend him at the hotel, there being no hospital at the time in Harrison; the doctor stated that the judge's condition was not critical, and he flew back to Fort Smith the same day. Also, on that Saturday, Youmans's family began converging on Harrison. By Monday night, April 10, Youmans was declared to be in critical condition, and on the morning of April 11, 1932, he died.

The exact cause of Judge Youmans's death was never clear. The *Arkansas Gazette* reported that:

> Death was attributed to a complication of troubles, including possibly, a blood clot on the brain, but the immediate cause was given by the attending physician as peritonitis which developed last [week] as a result of toxic poisoning.[77]

The *Arkansas Democrat* reported only that "the cause of his death was given as a complication of diseases brought on by a general physical breakdown."[78] The Fort Smith newspaper, in a lengthy article, said nothing about the cause of death. At the time of his death, Frank A. Youmans was a month shy of his seventy-second birthday.

The obituaries of Judge Youmans reported the respect and praise of his judicial career from other judges and politicians. The most interesting comment, however, came from Sid R. Redding, a Fort Smith resident who was the federal district court clerk. Redding said that Judge Youmans was always noted for his courtesy and fairness to all.

CHAPTER 14

HEARTSILL RAGON

1933–40

Heartsill Ragon III

HEARTSILL RAGON was the son of Alfred Jackson Ragon, a captain in the Confederate army, and Anna Eliza Heartsill Ragon. He was born on a farm in Logan County near Dublin, Arkansas, on March 20, 1884, and was one of the family's five sons. His parents were early settlers in Arkansas and were natives of Tennessee and Georgia, respectively.

Ragon attended local schools, graduating from the Clarksville, Arkansas, high school. He then attended the College of the Ozarks in Clarksville (now the University of the Ozarks) and the University of Arkansas at Fayetteville. He received a law degree from Washington and Lee University in Lexington, Virginia, in 1908 and was also admitted to the bar that year. He and Mattie Smith of Star City, Arkansas, married on August 20, 1916. The couple had one child, Heartsill Ragon Jr., born on June 14, 1917.[1]

Heartsill Ragon began his law career following graduation from law school in 1908, practicing law in Clarksville, Arkansas, with George O. Patterson. His natural aggressiveness and his ability to think fast were said to have clearly identified him as a young lawyer with a promising future. Ragon's political career began with election to the state House of Representatives where he served consecutive terms, 1911 and 1913.

Heartsill Ragon. *Courtesy United States District Court for the Western District of Arkansas.*

He served as prosecuting attorney for the Fifth Judicial District for two terms, from 1916 to 1920 and was a delegate to the Democratic National Convention at San Francisco. In 1928 he served as chairman of the Arkansas Democratic Campaign Committee. In civic work he was especially interested in addressing the unique problems of underprivileged boys in Fort Smith and successfully led fundraising and development efforts for the city's first boys club, located on Wheeler Avenue.

In 1922, Ragon was elected to Congress from the Fifth District, which ceased to exist in 1963, where he served for ten years and became the ranking member on the House Ways and Means Committee. When home from Washington, DC, the Ragons lived at the Goldman Hotel in Fort Smith, Arkansas. The latter part of his tenure in Congress coincided with the Great Depression that swept the nation from 1929 to 1933, and his position within the leadership of the Congress rose substantially with the election of fellow Democrat Franklin Roosevelt to the presidency. Ragon was a lifelong Democrat and was closely associated with Arkansas senators Joe T. Robinson, Thaddeus H. Caraway, and Hattie W. Caraway.

During his service in Congress, the Democratic Party courted Ragon in 1932, to run for the United States Senate to succeed Hattie Caraway, the nation's first elected female United States senator, should she not run for reelection. While considered a potential front-runner, he chose not to run in order to devote attention to his responsibilities before the House Ways and Means Committee.

In May of 1933, Ragon resigned from Congress to accept appointment by President Roosevelt as United States district judge for the Western District of Arkansas, the district once presided over by the famed jurist Judge Isaac C. Parker. Nominated by the president and confirmed by the Senate on May 12, 1933, Ragon received his commission on May 17.[2] He succeeded Judge Frank Youmans. Following Ragon's resignation from Congress, David D. Terry was elected to the Fifth District seat in a race that opponent Brooks Hayes unsuccessfully contested.[3] At the time of Judge Ragon's appointment, the district bench had been vacant for an extended period because of Judge Youmans's death over a year before. Upon his investiture, Judge Ragon faced a seriously overcrowded docket but after establishing demanding trial schedules his docket slowly cleared. He eventually received citations that recognized him for presiding over the United States district court with the lowest backlog of cases.

One of Judge Ragon's published decisions, *U.S. v. Miller*,[4] has often been cited in connection with the nation's ongoing debate regarding the government's ability to regulate gun ownership. In that case, the defendants were charged with transporting sawed-off shotguns in interstate commerce in violation of the new National Firearms Act. Judge Ragon was required to determine the enforceability of this federal statute that mandated payment of a federal tax and required obtaining a proof-of-payment stamp. In a three-paragraph decision Judge Ragon ruled the statute unconstitutional because the Second Amendment provided that "a well regulated militia, being necessary to the security of the free state, the right of the people to keep and bear arms, shall not be infringed." Despite the literal reading of the Constitution, the United States Supreme Court overturned Judge Ragon's decision.

Judge Ragon heard a wide variety of cases that included issues involving statutes of limitations, utilities, personal injury, bankruptcy, and more. In *Futrall v. Bartee*[5] Judge Ragon had to determine if a three- or a five-year statute of limitations applied to efforts by a receiver of a national bank to enforce an assessment on bank stock from the failed bank's shareholders. Congress had established no time limitation on the commencement of actions. In an analogous Arkansas case, however, a court had held that a suit to enforce liability upon a bank stock assessment must be brought within three years. In a similar case heard by the United States Supreme Court, the court established no definitive statute of limitations and remanded the case to the lower court to determine if a contract existed to which any statute of limitations would apply. In that case, the court held that without a definitive precedent from the United States Supreme Court and without a federal statute to the contrary, it was bound to follow definitive state law that set a three-year statute of limitations. Following precedent, Judge Ragon held that the three-year state statute applied.

In the 1936 case of *Arkansas Louisiana Gas Company v. City of Texarkana, Arkansas*,[6] the utility company that supplied natural gas to Texarkana had petitioned the city council for a rate increase. Objections to the rate increase and challenges to the various components of the proposal touched on numerous issues, including maintenance practices, depreciation reserve, set asides, state and federal taxation reserves, managerial services, and compensation. To resolve the dispute, Judge Ragon analyzed virtually all of the utility company's expense items and depreciation entries that were associated with its provision of gas to Texarkana. He held that reasonable expenses were allowed so that rate-making would not be deemed confiscatory in nature. The court found that rate-making was solely an obligation of the city and any evidentiary tribunal it might be authorized to implement. It found that the court could not establish gas rates, but rather that it could merely determine whether the city's rate regulating body had fixed a rate so low that it amounted to confiscation. It recognized that rates set by city councils were not subject to being disturbed unless they were so low that they resulted in a taking of private property for public use without just compensation. The court found that costs of management services would not be allowed as legitimate operating expenses for rate purposes in the absence of evidence of the costs of such service and its value to the company. It further found that certain maintenance practices should be considered in determining the rate of depreciation to be allowed for rate-making purposes, that depreciation reserves should be considered, and that the utility should distribute depreciation losses evenly over the estimated service life of the property. Finally, it found that payments of state and federal income taxes were proper expenses to be considered for rate-making purposes.

The 1937 case, *U.S. Fidelity & Guaranty Co. v. Pierson*,[7] arose because the defendant's wife was injured as a result of the operation of an automobile belonging to Guy Shrigley, who was insured by the plaintiff. Pierson's wife, who was driving the car, sued for and recovered damages. Her husband, L. H. Pierson, sued Shrigley in the Johnson County Circuit Court for damages Pierson sustained for the loss of her services, society, and for sums expended for medical attention as a result of the injuries to his wife. US Fidelity & Guaranty Co. sued Pierson, making Shrigley a party, and asked for a declaratory judgment and an injunction against the proceedings in the circuit court pending trial of the issues in the US district court. The defendant moved to dismiss. Pierson contended that no controversy of a justiciable nature existed, arguing that before there was any controversy between Pierson and the insurance company, Pierson would first have to secure a judgment against Shrigley, and there must be an unsuccessful return on an execution on such judgment. Reviewing the policy, the judge found that sections of the insurance policy provided that no recovery against the insurance company shall occur until the amounts of loss shall have been determined either by final judgment against the insured or by written agreement. Therefore, if the plain provisions of the policy place the company under no obligation to indemnify Shrigley until Pierson had recovered a final judgment, then certainly Pierson or Shrigley could not have an actual controversy of a justiciable nature with the company until that time. In other words, there was no matured claim that either Pierson or Shrigley could presently maintain. The Declaratory Judgment Act authorized the court to exercise discretion in accepting jurisdiction. The court found that where Pierson's damages suit continued in state court, the federal court would refuse to take jurisdiction and exert declaratory judgment powers. The court sustained the defendant's motion to dismiss.

U.S. Fidelity & Guaranty Co. v. Shrigley,[8] decided in 1939, grew out of the same set of facts referenced in the previous case. In 1931, the plaintiff issued Guy Shrigley a policy of insurance that carried a provision "to pay all sums which the assured shall become liable to pay as damages imposed upon him by law for bodily injury." On June 23, 1937, the plaintiff filed a petition for declaratory judgment. It alleged that Mr. L. H. Pierson, whose wife, Arch Pierson, had been injured in the accident that involved Shrigley's automobile and who was covered by the policy issued to Shrigley, had filed suit in the Johnson County Court for damages arising out of the bodily injuries Mrs. Pierson had received as a result of the accident. The question before the court was whether Pierson could recover damages for the loss of services of his wife because of her injuries from the automobile accident. Following similar cases that involved similar language in other jurisdictions, the court found that the Shrigley policy restricted recovery to actual bodily injuries and did not include Pierson's claim for the loss of his wife's services. It further found that because there was no liability under the policy for the Pierson claim, the company was under no obligation to defend the suit against Shrigley.

In another personal injury case, *King v. Shepherd*,[9] the plaintiff sought damages stemming from an automobile accident. The defendant filed a third-party complaint against the insurance company alleging that the third-party defendant carried an insurance policy that indemnified the defendant against loss. The third party moved to dismiss the action, arguing that the Western District court had no jurisdiction in the case. The motion to dismiss noted that the third-party plaintiff resided in Missouri and the third-party defendant resided in Oklahoma. Neither party resided in Arkansas. The court held that jurisdiction was inappropriate in the Western District of Arkansas and sustained the third-party defendant's motion to dismiss.

In *McCallum v. General American Oil Co. of Texas*,[10] also a personal injury case, the plaintiffs sought damages from the defendant as a result of injuries from an automobile accident. The matter originated in state court where a motion was made to remove the action to federal court. The issue was whether the petition and bond for removal from state to federal court were filed within the required time. Judge Ragon found that the plaintiff had complied with the state statutes on giving notice of litigation and that the defendant had not answered within the specified time period. According to federal statutes, because the defendant had not answered within the time required by the state statute, the matter could not be removed to federal jurisdiction.

Central United National Bank v. Fort Smith and W. RY. Company[11] grew out of a railroad bankruptcy. The railroad had solicited land and capital donations from Fort Smith residents as a condition for constructing a railroad terminus in Fort Smith. The agreement provided that when the railroad terminated services the citizens who had contributed would be repaid. The railroad had since failed. The issue involved whether the repayment obligation constituted a covenant that ran with the land and rendered the railroad's receiver in bankruptcy liable to make the repayments. The court held that the repayment agreement did not constitute a covenant that ran with the land and that the railroad's usage had become obsolete as its revenue loss led to its financial failure. The court found no basis in the principles of bankruptcy law that obligated the receiver and it dismissed the citizens' request for payment.

In the case of *Wood v. U.S.*,[12] Margaret E. Wood had established a trust for her nephew, Henry Clay Wood. The terms stipulated that he would receive the body of the trust when he reached age twenty-nine, but if he died before that time his interest in the trust would pass to the Van Buren, Arkansas, public school system to construct a school. Margaret Wood died when her nephew was seventeen. The executor of her estate, in filing the federal estate tax return, deducted an amount equal to the value of the contingent interest in the estate that was vested in the Van Buren school system. The United States government filed a demurrer, contending that the school district's interest under the estate was insufficient to justify the deduction. The issue before the court was whether the contingent interest of the school district allowed the estate a credit deduction. The court found that because the beneficiary would vest at age twenty-nine and that he was likely to reach that age, it would be impossible and unreasonable to place any value on the school district's contingent interest in the estate. It held that the credit taken by the executor was not deductible from the estate because its valuation was merely speculation.

U.S. v. Giger[13] grew out of S. A. Smith's federal crop mortgage loan. Smith died, and Roy Giger was appointed administrator of Smith's estate. A. M. Smith and Jessie Giger were sureties on the administrator's bond. The indebtedness was not paid and the government sought to hold the administrator personally liable and to hold the sureties personally liable on the bond of Roy Giger as administrator. The court held that the statutes to which the government referred in its case had nothing to do with the personal liability of sureties on bonds; that the estate's administrator had yet to prioritize asset dispositions; and that the plaintiff's actions were premature since until the estate was liquidated it was uncertain if the plaintiff's indebtedness would be paid. Further, action on the administrator's bond was not sustainable until the probate court had adjusted the accounts of the administrator and had ordered him to pay over amounts found to be in his hands and that administrator had failed to so fund. Only at that point could an action against the administrator's bond be asserted.

The volume of bankruptcy cases Judge Ragon heard hints at the difficult economic times of the 1930s. In *In re Harris Bros.*,[14] Harris Brothers, a copartnership, filed an involuntary petition in bankruptcy on August 3, 1931. The law required that proofs of claim be filed within six months of the date of filing. No proof of claim was filed by Fordyce Bank and Trust Company within that time, although Fordyce petitioned that it be permitted to file its claim as of one month after the date of bankrupt adjudication. The trustee objected to the timeliness of the proof of claim by Fordyce. Fordyce had mailed its proof to the referee in bankruptcy, assumed it had been received, but had failed to inquire. The proof was first discovered eighteen months after the date of the bankrupt's adjudication. Judge Ragon noted that the trend in bankruptcy was to expedite cases, giving other creditors a right to have their claims reasonably passed on and payments made. To permit a creditor to mail a claim and make no inquiry to see if it had been properly filed for eighteen months would constitute an indulgence, not promoting the expeditious settlement of a bankrupt estate. Judge Ragon held that Fordyce did not comply with the terms of the bankruptcy statute.

In *In re Magness Bros.*,[15] Magness Brothers, a mercantile business, was the subject of an involuntary bankruptcy petition filed against the business, individuals, and partnerships associated with it. The case centered on whether the debtors should be discharged from the debts. Those who protested against discharge argued that, in contradiction to the bankruptcy statutes, the bankrupts did not keep accurate records and they relied on false statements in obtaining extensions of credit. While the court found that the business used loose accounting methods, they were not seen to be inconsistent with businesses in rural communities. Judge Ragon noted, however, that Troy Magness, a brother and partner in the business, had submitted false financial statements on several occasions, which painted a more solvent picture than the business enjoyed. Moreover, the other brothers had given Troy their power-of-attorney to execute any and all documents on their behalf in connection with business and borrowing activities. The court found that the partners were obligated to prevent the wrongdoing and, however innocent of wrongdoing themselves, they should not be permitted to enjoy the fruits of the false financial statements without bearing the burden of their own agent's wrongdoing. The judge, therefore, refused the request to discharge all brothers except Troy, finding that they had negligently established a means by which fraud could occur in the delivery of the erroneous and fraudulent financial statements and calling the actions reckless and incorrect.

In *In re Jackson*,[16] creditors of a bankrupt debtor filed a petition for review of a referee's order holding that certain mortgages granted to creditors should be set aside given the preferential nature of such transactions. The issue involved whether sufficient evidence existed to allow the bankruptcy referee to set aside mortgages as preferential transactions. The court concluded that evidence supported the referee's finding that the mortgagee had knowledge of the insolvent condition of the bankrupt grantor and had reasonable cause to believe that deeds of trust executed in their favor would affect preferences in their favor over other creditors. Judge Ragon sustained and approved the referee's order.

At issue in *In re Cherokee Public Service Company*[17] was whether plaintiff Orr could continue to levy upon and perfect a judgment that had been obtained more than four months before the filing date of

Cherokee's bankruptcy petition, but which was secured through prejudgment attachment prior to all preference periods. Judge Ragon found that if the effect of a judgment rendered within four months of the bankruptcy petition filing had been to create a lien, the judgment would be void under federal bankruptcy statutes. If the effect of the judgment, however, was merely to enforce a preexisting lien perfected through prejudgment attachment that was valid and existing at the time of the petition, the judgment was not affected by the bankruptcy statute. Orr's judgment in *In re Cherokee* represented the mere enforcement of a valid and preexisting lien and was not voided by the bankruptcy act.

Harrod v. Missouri Pac. Co.,[18] filed in the Texarkana Division of the Western District, arose out of an accident at a railroad crossing in Little Rock in December of 1939. Harrod alleged that as he drove his truck across the company's tracks on East Second Street, the defendants, through their joint and concurrent carelessness and negligence, backed a switch engine on to the crossing, striking Harrod's truck, demolishing it, and injuring Harrod. Further, the switch engine was being operated by the defendant Strack as engineer. The plaintiff filed suit in Nevada County Circuit Court against Missouri Pacific and Thompson. The plaintiff later amended the complaint to include Missouri Pacific engineer Strack of Pulaski County as a defendant. The defendant contended that J. J. Strack was fraudulently joined to the litigation to deprive the US court of jurisdiction. The issue before the court was whether Strack was a lawful and legitimate codefendant to the litigation. Following its review of the law, the court concluded that it must be guided by what the pleadings show at the time the petition is filed and that a cause of action of negligence is obviously stated in the complaint against the subject codefendant. The court found that the codefendant was proper and remanded the case to the Nevada County Circuit Court.

Yoes v. Continental Oil Company[19] involved injury to the plaintiff in an automobile accident in which Mead was driving a truck for the defendant. The issue was whether a motion to remand the case to a lower court should be granted based upon the allegation of fraudulent joinder of Mead and the defendant. The court found that the fraudulent joinder of a "sham" defendant was an issue of state law. It further held that the case should be remanded to the state court to determine the nature of the business relationship between Mead and Continental Oil according to the written contract between them. The test of liability as laid down in this case rested not upon whether the company directed the manner of Mead's delivery activities, but whether the company had the right to control all aspects of the delivery.

Judge Ragon's abilities as a jurist were recognized when a bill was introduced in Congress to create an additional judgeship on the Eighth Circuit Court of Appeals. All senators of the states comprising the Eighth Circuit agreed that Judge Ragon would be recommended for the position. While he had served by special appointment on the Eighth Circuit on several occasions, Judge Ragon did not live to see his investiture on that court.

He died suddenly on September 15, 1940, just a day after he appeared to be in excellent health and had driven to Fayetteville to watch the University of Arkansas football team practice. A physician diagnosed the cause of his death as acute coronary thrombosis and indicated that this condition was brought on by emotions associated with a lengthy and highly publicized liquor conspiracy trial over which the judge had presided. The case involved the state's revenue commissioner. Certain individuals had been charged with conspiring to transport liquor into the dry states of Oklahoma and Kansas. The state officials were acquitted, another of the defendants was convicted, and a mistrial was declared in the case of the fourth defendant. Judge Ragon's recent involvement in over fifteen trials and the sentencing of over two hundred defendants on a single day several months before his death had also taxed his energy.

The judge was reported to have exhibited immense patience while sitting on the bench, pronouncing sentences in criminal matters only after a careful investigation and study of the personal history and personality of each criminal defendant. It was common for persons whom he had sentenced to express their appreciation of his fairness in person and to give assurances that they would avoid future troubles. At his funeral, the federal prisoners whom Judge Ragon had sentenced and who were in the Fort Smith county jail sent one of the most poignant floral tributes.

Judge Ragon was buried in Fort Smith and was survived by his wife and son. According to newspaper reports, he "was known for the wit he displayed on the bench and for the way he cut through red tape and attorneys' eloquence to get to the heart of a case in a hurry."

CHAPTER 15

John Elvis Miller

1941–67

Susan Scafidi, Susie Margaret Ross, and Bradley J. Nicholson

JOHN ELVIS MILLER, one of eight children of John and Mary Harper Miller, was born near Aid, Missouri, on May 15, 1888, and grew up on a 160-acre farm. He attended rural schools and helped the family raise corn and cotton. After finishing the ninth grade, he taught grade school while attending high school. He later taught school in southeastern Oklahoma then served as principal of a three-room school in Aid. Miller began studying law at Valparaiso University in Indiana and in 1912 received a law degree from the University of Kentucky College of Law.[1]

The day after he finished at Kentucky, Miller left by train for Searcy, Arkansas. On the advice of an Arkansas lawyer he met on the train, Miller entered law practice in Searcy and partnered with J. N. Rachel at a salary of $50.00 per month. He also began a successful political career serving first as city attorney in 1913. In 1918, Miller opened his own law practice in Searcy, and from 1919 until 1922, he served as prosecuting attorney for the First Judicial Circuit of Arkansas. In 1928, he joined the Little Rock firm of Mehaffy and Mehaffy and two years later was elected Arkansas's Second District congressman. Miller served in Congress until 1937, when he resigned and successfully challenged Governor Carl E.

John Elvis Miller. *Courtesy United States District Court for the Western District of Arkansas.*

Bailey in a special election to fill the Senate seat of the late majority leader Joseph T. Robinson. On January 31, 1941, President Franklin Roosevelt nominated him to succeed Heartsill Ragon as United States district judge for the Western District of Arkansas, based in Fort Smith. Judge Miller received his commission on March 12 of that year. He served as chief judge from 1958 to 1967.[2]

Miller considered President Roosevelt a good friend and often dined with the president at the White House during his years in Congress. He disagreed with Roosevelt, however, on issues he felt represented federal encroachment "on matters which should be controlled by various states." He credited this grassroots philosophy of government, in part, to his experience as a prosecutor in a district where some counties considered certain behaviors as crimes that other counties did not. In 1920, for example, Miller asked a Phillips County grand jury to investigate cockfighting and horse racing. The jury foreman replied that some offenses did not require rigid law enforcement and "since this is our way of life, we should determine what offenses should be prosecuted and what ones should not." Later, as a judge, he was also critical of the courts' handling of school desegregation cases, believing that judges substituted their own judgment for that of school board members across the country. This, he believed, overloaded the courts with civil rights cases. In 1973, Judge Miller received the Hatton W. Sumners Award from the Southwestern Legal Foundation of Dallas for "outstanding service in the improvement of the administration of justice." In his remarks he emphasized his concerns about the role of the courts, saying that: "There have always got to be changes made in the laws to meet the growing needs of the people. But in my opinion, the Supreme Court has over-extended its development of the law to follow the sound judgment of the people."[3]

Known for his wit and sense of humor, Judge Miller often displayed them from the bench. In a nine-day trial in 1972, a lawyer instructed a witness to take his time in recalling an event. "We've got lots of time," the lawyer said, to which the eighty-four-year-old judge retorted, "speak for yourself, sonny." Occasionally the judge's comments met with criticism. In a 1969 hearing, for example, a preacher insisted that a church should be first to collect its deposit from a bankrupt institution. Judge Miller emphasized that no depositor would receive preferential treatment. "But your honor, this is God's money," the preacher insisted, to which the judge replied, "well then, God should have taken better care of it." Several editorialists criticized the remark.[4]

Of selected opinions of Judge Miller, Susan Scafidi noted that he "included extensive findings of fact and lengthy quotations from both binding and non-binding case law. He rarely offers personal opinions or rhetorical flourishes." Many of his opinions from the late 1940s and early 1950s dealt "with wartime rent control and other price restrictions, veterans returning to the work force, veterans' and survivors' benefits, fair wages and hours, and rights of eminent domain."[5]

In the 1945 case of *Kempe v. United States*,[6] the defendant was convicted of violating wartime regulations relating to price control and rationing. In this case the commodity was gasoline. He admitted having delivered gasoline, and the issues at trial were whether the price exceeded the maximum and whether he had received the appropriate ration coupons. In an opinion written by Judge Miller, the Eighth Circuit held that evidence of previous illegal gasoline sales was inadmissible to identify the defendant or to prove intent. The court also held that, because violations of war regulations were misdemeanors, proof of specific criminal intent was unnecessary, despite the statutory requirement that the offenses be "wilful." The case was remanded for a new trial, and the defendant was again convicted.[7] Most of the other federal circuits and several state courts cited Judge Miller's opinion.

The case of *King v. Sweatt*[8] required Judge Miller to examine definitions of urban and rural property and of city, town, and village at a time when those distinctions were becoming blurred by the extension of highways and by increased automobile traffic. The plaintiff sought the sale of the defendant's property in order to collect a judgment. Judge Miller held that the defendant's real property was a rural homestead of less than eighty acres and was thus exempt from judgment under Arkansas law. The real property consisted of less than one acre where the defendant's residence, an eight-unit "tourist court" and a building rented to a commercial tenant were located. This opinion was cited in later Eighth Circuit and Arkansas decisions.

Over the decades that Judge Miller served on the bench, he heard cases with similar issues that arose in different contexts. The following cases involved individuals who claimed religious exemptions from military service, the first during World War II and the others during the

Vietnam era. In *Gibson v. Reynolds*[9] the plaintiff was convicted of violating the Selective Training and Service Act of 1940, following denial of his application for exemption from service as a minister. This conviction was overturned and the plaintiff then sued members of the local draft board and others for allegedly violating his civil rights. Judge Miller dismissed the complaint on the grounds that the defendants were acting within the scope of their governmental authority and were therefore immune to suit. The judge added that "When the conditions and circumstances surrounding the Selective Service system are considered: the national emergency; the need for drastic and effective action in mobilizing our manpower; the broad powers granted the agencies charged with carrying out the purposes of the Act; the uncompensated services rendered by these conscientious citizens (members of the Local Boards and Appeal Boards); and the obvious need for free and unrestrained action on the part of the men responsible for the accomplishment of the desired results, it becomes apparent that public policy demands that men in the position of these defendants be accorded the protection of the rule of immunity from civil liability for acts performed by them within the scope of their authority."[10]

In the 1969 case of *United States v. Owen*,[11] the defendant was convicted of refusing induction into the armed services after his requests to be classified as either a conscientious objector or a ministerial student were denied. The Eighth Circuit reversed this conviction. It held that the local draft board denied the defendant due process when it solicited and included in the defendant's file the adverse comments of a local minister who was not connected to the board and who was unknown to the defendant and then offered the defendant no opportunity to challenge the minister's opinion. Judge Miller, sitting as a visiting member of the Eighth Circuit Court of Appeals, also noted that the classifications sought by the defendant were not contradictory and that to deny the opportunity to apply for either one would "undermine the principles of individual conscience. It is enough that registrants are confronted with a complex administrative process which is nonetheless deliberately nonadversary [*sic*], and in which the right to be represented by counsel is expressly denied."[12] The year before in *United States v. Bryant*,[13] Judge Miller had decided a case in which the draft board had denied conscientious objector status to the defendant who then refused to report for induction. The court found the defendant not guilty, since objection was based on religious beliefs rather than a personal moral code, and it held that the board should have granted conscientious objector status.

Judge Miller's tenure on the bench also coincided with the rise of school desegregation cases. Eastern District judge Thomas Trimble had taken senior status in January of 1957 and both he and Eastern and Western District judge Harry Lemley were ill so Judge Miller heard the initial cases filed in the Little Rock desegregation controversy. They "featured several prominent lawyers including Thurgood Marshall, Wiley Branton and Herschel Friday."[14] In the first of these cases, *Aaron v. Cooper*,[15] Judge Miller reviewed the requirements of *Brown v. Board of Education*,[16] and concluded that the plan of integration for the Little Rock School District was adequate. Although the plaintiffs requested an injunction to compel the defendants to admit them to all free public schools without discrimination, the judge denied the request because the defendants "have made a prompt and reasonable start toward full compliance with the requirements of the law." He continued that:

> This court is of the opinion that it should not substitute its own judgment for that of the defendants. The plan which has been adopted after thorough and conscientious consideration of the many questions involved is a plan that will lead to an effective and gradual adjustment of the problem, and ultimately bring about a school system not based on color distinctions.[17]

Judge Miller concluded that it would be an abuse of discretion to fail to approve the plan or to interfere as long as the defendants moved in good faith. Judge Ronald N. Davies from North Dakota, who was on temporary assignment to Arkansas's Eastern District in August of 1957, enjoined the attempt by Governor Orval Faubus to impede the desegregation plan by using the Arkansas National Guard and ordered the Guard removed.[18] The next year, 1958, the school board requested that the integration plan be suspended until January 1961. Judge Harry J. Lemley granted the petition, which the Eighth Circuit reversed.[19]

In September 1958, recently passed Act 4 closed the Little Rock high schools and set a special election to determine whether to integrate the schools. The majority of votes cast at the election favored segregation, and the high schools remained closed. The school board and superintendent then requested a ruling on whether they could transfer the title, possession, and operation of the school district to the "Little Rock Private School Corporation." Black students brought suit asking for an order restraining such a transfer, or alternatively, that the defendants be required to operate the private school under the integration plan. Judge Miller responded that the court would not issue an advisory opinion to the defendants and denied additional injunctive relief to the plaintiffs. The plaintiffs appealed to the Eighth Circuit, which affirmed as to the advisory opinion, but reversed as to the plaintiffs' request.[20] Judge Miller then permanently enjoined the school board from transferring the school district's property and ordered that the board move forward with the integration plan.[21]

In *Aaron v. McKinley*,[22] the plaintiffs attacked the constitutionality of state Acts 4 and 5. Act 4, as noted, closed the high schools and provided for an election on the issue of integration. Act 5 withheld state funds from any district in which a school had been closed, and made those funds available on a per-capita basis to any other public school or nonprofit private school that might be attended by students of a closed school. A three-judge panel consisting of Judge Miller, Eighth Circuit judge John B. Sanborn, and Judge Axel Beck of the District of South Dakota ruled that Arkansas Acts 4 and 5 were unconstitutional.

Aaron v. Tucker[23] represented Judge Miller's final appearance in the Little Rock desegregation controversy. In it he found that the student assignment procedure was acceptable and that the constitutional rights of several black students were not violated when the school board denied their applications for reassignment within the school system. He concluded "that the action of the defendants herein complained of by plaintiffs was performed in the utmost good faith without bias or prejudice and with a desire and intention to protect and to enforce the constitutional rights of all concerned."[24] Judge Miller also observed that:

> Aside from the strictly constitutional or legal point of view, dedicated school officials must be and are concerned with a transition in the sense of making the change in a manner to reach the desired end result without destroying children and the system in the process, and to arrive at a state of operation of a constitutional school system wherein all children can get at least as good an education,

> and preferably better, as was available under the former school system.[25]

He continued:

> It is not necessary for the court to refer again to the chaotic conditions that existed in the Little Rock high schools during the school year of 1957–58. However, those conditions cannot be forgotten by a law-abiding people. The defendants, through their dedication to their duties under the law and in a conscientious effort to do justice to all under the law, have brought order out of chaos. They deserve the support of every person who has an interest in the maintenance of a free school system operated in accordance with constitutional principles, to which we so often glibly give lip service.[26]

Judge Miller dismissed the case, seeing no further need to retain jurisdiction because the enforcement of any of the rights adjudicated were personal to the individuals who could assert their rights separately. The court of appeals reversed, concluding that (1) the initial student assignments were racially discriminatory and (2) the reassignment "standards and criteria were applied by defendants for the purpose of impeding, thwarting and frustrating integration."[27] The Eighth Circuit Court of Appeals ordered the district court to retain jurisdiction in order to carry out integration.

During Judge Miller's career on the bench, many lawyers had an opportunity to observe his handling of court-related matters. While he was a practicing attorney, the late United States district judge, subsequently circuit judge, J. Smith Henley had much of his trial experience in Judge Miller's court. Judge Henley learned techniques from Judge Miller that proved invaluable when Judge Henley took the bench in the 1950s. These included "what to do with motions, which ones to pay some attention to and give time to, how to impanel a jury without wasting time, how to keep a case moving along and get it closed." Judge Henley went on to say that "John stayed current and when you filed a lawsuit in his court you better be ready for trial in about 90 days." He remembered Judge Miller as one who "insisted that his rules be followed . . . he didn't fool around; he had a lot of work to do and he wanted it done and you did it and that's all there was to it."[28]

Judge Miller served full time on the bench from 1941 until 1967 when he took senior status, a form of semiretirement. He continued hearing jury trials until late 1976 and according to his obituary wrote opinions in civil cases until he retired in 1979, although the Federal Judicial Center indicates that his service ended with his death in 1981. Judge Miller was first married to Ethel Lindsey of Searcy and the couple had two children, Mary Louise Miller Goodloe and John E. Miller Jr. After Ethel Lindsey Miller's death in 1956, Judge Miller married Ethel Skinner of Fort Smith later that year. Following a long life and a distinguished career as attorney, elected official, and judge, John E. Miller died at the age of ninety-two on January 30, 1981, in Fort Smith, Arkansas. He is buried there in Forest Park Cemetery.[29]

PART V

EASTERN AND WESTERN DISTRICTS OF ARKANSAS 1939–1975

CHAPTER 16

Harry Jacob Lemley

1939–58

Susan Webber Wright

HARRY JACOB LEMLEY, commissioned to new seats in the Eastern and Western Districts of Arkansas, was known for his great ability to express his thoughts clearly and incisively. Although Judge Lemley apparently discouraged his friends from putting on a campaign endorsing him for the new judgeship, several prominent Arkansans wrote to Washington, DC, officials in support of his appointment.[1] Nominated by President Franklin Roosevelt in April of 1939, Lemley received his commission on May 11 of that year and served until he assumed senior status on September 5, 1958. From 1948 to 1958 he served as chief judge of the Western District.[2]

As a United States district judge, Judge Lemley held court at every federal courthouse in Arkansas at one time or another. He had a reputation for treating every matter with precision. The Eighth Circuit Court of Appeals affirmed his rulings in the vast majority of cases in which his decisions were appealed. One friend commented that it was difficult for Judge Lemley to stop concerning himself with a criminal case after he had imposed sentence.[3]

His disposition of one criminal case revealed his strong sense of patriotism and his personal belief that the law should not be lenient

Harry Jacob Lemley. *Courtesy United States District Court for the Eastern District of Arkansas.*

on a cattle thief. The defendant, a young Arkansas tenant farmer, had pleaded guilty to participating in the interstate transportation of a stolen cow and had received about $50 for this criminal activity. But this defendant had served in the military and had won the Bronze Star with clusters for heroic action in combat. The judge remarked as follows in imposing sentence:

> I am going to make an exception here (of never placing a cattle thief on probation) but I am not in any way establishing a precedent. Solely because of your excellent war record, and in spite of what I admit is perhaps a prejudiced view on my part toward cattle thieving, I am going to place you on probation for two years; but let me warn you here and now, if you violate in any way the terms of your probation or are ever back in this court, I have now paid back the debt the country owes to you, and I will then give you exactly the treatment which should be given to all cattle thieves.[4]

In a 1952 article Judge Lemley was quoted as stating that in his opinion, the most important case he had decided was *Barksdale v. Ford, Bacon & Davis*,[5] in which he held that the Fair Labor Standards Act's wage and hour provisions were inapplicable to ordnance plant employees because production of munitions of war was not "production of goods for commerce." The Eighth Circuit Court of Appeals upheld this ruling in a similar case, *Aaron v. Ford, Bacon & Davis, Inc.*,[6] but a divided Supreme Court of the United States reversed it in *Powell v. United States Cartridge Co.*[7]

One precedent-setting case, which originated in Judge Lemley's court, was *United States of America v. Miller*.[8] In this case, the United States Supreme Court held that an indigent defendant was entitled to have his counsel prepare a bill of exceptions, or a formally prepared, written statement providing a factual context for the defendant's objections to the trial judge's rulings so those rulings could be reviewed on appeal. Another famous case to come before Judge Lemley was the first in the protracted school desegregation litigation in Little Rock. This case, *Aaron v. Cooper*,[9] was initially on the docket of Judge Thomas Trimble of the Eastern District. Because both Judges Trimble and Lemley were ill, the case was initially assigned to Judge John Miller of the Western District of Arkansas, who approved a plan of desegregation for Little

Rock schools that was to be implemented in the fall of 1957. After the now-infamous events of that fall when nine African American students enrolled in Central High School, the Little Rock School Board, in 1958, asked the court's permission to suspend operation of the plan. By that time Judge Trimble had taken senior status and Chief Judge Archibald K. Gardner of the Eighth Circuit Court of Appeals assigned the case to Judge Lemley. After a hearing, Judge Lemley ruled that operation of the plan be suspended until the 1960–61 school year.[10] The Eighth Circuit reversed this ruling, and the Supreme Court of the United States affirmed the Eighth Circuit.[11] The United States Supreme Court action in reversing Judge Lemley did not solve desegregation problems in central Arkansas. Shortly after the Supreme Court's decision Judge Lemley assumed senior status, a form of semiretirement that allows a judge to take a limited caseload.

Judge Lemley had several landownership cases that arose as a result of rivers that changed course. Philip G. Alston, a longtime law clerk to Judge Lemley, wrote that Judge Lemley enjoyed these "accretion" cases. In a case he called the "Boggy Bayou Case," *Bryant v. Chicago Mill & Lumber Co.*,[12] before considering the facts and contentions particular to that case, Judge Lemley carefully and succinctly summarized the great body of Arkansas property law that had developed as a result of the changing courses of the Mississippi, Arkansas, Red, and other rivers. In *Ussery v. Anderson-Tully Co.*,[13] he explained the process of accretion and the types of evidence (such as the pattern of forestation of the area) helpful and admissible in determining, for example, which of two former riverbanks was the source of origin of the area in controversy.

Judge Lemley was born on August 6, 1883, in Upperville, Fauquier County, Virginia. His maternal grandfather served in the Mexican War, and his paternal grandfather was a Confederate veteran. He received his education at Randolph-Macon Academy and the University of Virginia, and he received his law degree from Washington and Lee University in 1910. In 1912 he entered private practice with his brother, Judge W. Kendall Lemley in Hope, Arkansas, and also operated a large plantation. He remained in private practice until 1939. He married Miss Caroline McRae in 1912, and this union produced two sons, Major General Harry J. Lemley Jr. and Colonel Kenneth McRae Lemley.

Judge Lemley was active in civic affairs and public service. He was on the first Arkansas Highway Audit Commission in 1932–33, served as president of the Board of Trustees of the State A&M College at Magnolia, now Southern Arkansas University, and was a founder and the vice president of First National Bank of Hope. Many Arkansans remember him for his scholarly articles on the Civil War and for extensive knowledge of Indian archeology. Lemley was an outstanding authority on the history of the Civil War and on the various Indian tribes in the United States and was an active and devout member of the First Presbyterian Church of Hope.

After Judge Lemley died on March 5, 1965, Philip Alston wrote as follows:

> He was well-born, yet he understood the lowly. He was well educated but did not lose the common touch. He firmly believed in justice to all but not to the exclusion of mercy. He never forsook his fundamental beliefs. Not only did he have an extremely fine sense of justice which he applied conscientiously in every ruling, but he possessed unusual capacity for written expression. He wrote with a clarity that was unmistakable. . . . While his rulings were definite and incisive, they had no sting or brusqueness to counsel, litigant or witness.[14]

CHAPTER 17

Jesse Smith Henley

1959–75

Susan Webber Wright

When Jesse Smith Henley moved his family to Little Rock in the fall of 1958 to begin what would become thirty-nine years of federal judicial service, he did so not knowing whether he would be a federal district judge there very long. President Dwight D. Eisenhower appointed Judge Henley to the United States District Court for the Eastern District of Arkansas by recess appointment; in other words, he was not confirmed by the Senate and thus did not have a permanent job. Judge Henley was finally confirmed to the United States District Courts for the Eastern and Western Districts of Arkansas on September 2, 1959, and received his commission six days later. He served as chief judge of the Eastern District until his elevation to the United States Court of Appeals for the Eighth Circuit. Nominated by President Gerald Ford to the Eighth Circuit on January 28, 1975, Judge Henley's confirmation hearing quickly resolved itself into a torrent of praise coming from both sides of the aisle, and Judge Henley was promptly confirmed by the Senate on March 13, 1975, and received his commission the next day. He assumed senior status on May 31, 1982, but remained an active member of that court until his death on October 18, 1997.[1]

Jesse Smith Henley. *Courtesy United States District Court for the Eastern District of Arkansas.*

A product of north Arkansas and the Ozarks, Judge Henley was born in St. Joe, Arkansas, on May 18, 1917, in a hotel his parents, Benjamin Harrison Henley and Jessie Smith, built during the railroad, mining, and war boom years. His family owned most of the town, including the town mercantile. Judge Henley was an avid reader as a child, often covering two grades in one year as a result of being present in a classroom where one teacher would instruct two grades at a time. He did not, however, officially graduate from high school, but rather, having obtained enough credits through summer school to do so, simply entered the University of Arkansas. After taking a three-year hiatus in the midst of his legal studies, during which time he taught in St. Joe and in 1938 met and married Dorothy Ingram, Judge Henley graduated with honors from the University of Arkansas School of Law in 1941. He was, in fact, the first graduate of the University of Arkansas School of Law ever to serve on the Eighth Circuit Court of Appeals.[2]

Prior to his appointment to the federal district court, Judge Henley practiced law in Fayetteville, Arkansas, from 1941 to 1954, including a stint as a city attorney. His involvement with the federal courts did not begin at the time of his appointment to the federal bench, however, as Judge Henley served as a referee in bankruptcy (the forerunner of present-day bankruptcy judges) in the Western District of Arkansas from 1943 to 1945, and was often retained by area attorneys for his expertise with the newly adopted rules of federal civil procedure. During the four years preceding his appointment to the federal bench, Judge Henley served first as associate general counsel for the Federal Communications Commission under the Eisenhower administration (primarily performing appellate work in the District of Columbia), and then as director of the Office of Administrative Procedure in the Justice Department.[3]

Although Judge Henley is known to have remarked that he tried more condemnation cases than anything else, he is best remembered for his impact on the course and conduct of prisoner litigation in Arkansas and the country as a whole. Senior district judge Garnett Thomas Eisele of the Eastern District of Arkansas described Judge Henley as "tolerant of human frailties, but . . . not tolerant of any abuse of official power."[4] Judge Henley was among the first district judges to hold an entire state penal system unconstitutional, remarking in 1970 in the now-legendary case *Holt v. Sarver*:

> For the ordinary convict a sentence to the Arkansas Penitentiary today amounts to a banishment from civilized society to a dark and evil world completely alien to the free world, a world that is administered by criminals under unwritten rules and customs completely foreign to free world culture.[5]

With bribery and extortion rampant in the prisons, medical attention virtually nonexistent, serious sanitary violations, and abuse of power by armed trustys, Judge Henley successfully effected institutional reform not by issuing direct orders engendering resentment from the State, but rather by involving the State in the solution by saying: "[L]ook, this is wrong. You've got to stop it and fix it. Now tell me how you want to fix it."[6] This "collaborative" approach to institutional reform was also apparent in his involvement in the many local school desegregation cases.[7] As Judge Eisele noted:

> It was [Judge Henley's] objective to bring the citizenry along as he moved to enforce the Constitution and insure the equal rights of all of the inhabitants of this land. He was very successful in this regard. Consent decrees became common as the local citizens and school patrons accepted their responsibilities.[8]

Particularly as to the school desegregation litigation, however, Judge Henley confessed his frustration at the lack of discernable guidelines from the Eighth Circuit as to what the court, school board, and patrons needed to do in order to satisfy the goal of desegregation. As Judge Henley stated, "I complained in one opinion . . . that all I could get was the answer 'do more, do more,' that this situation reminded me to some extent of Poe's raven sitting high on a judicial tree crying—rather than 'evermore'—'do more, do more.'"[9]

Judge Henley was known not only as a fair, intelligent jurist with the ability to project an appropriately stern judicial demeanor when circumstances so required—he was also legendary for his dry sense of humor. In perhaps the most famous anecdote demonstrating his wit, Judge Henley presided over a case involving moonshine whiskey, where the government (which was seeking to forfeit the vehicle transporting the moonshine) neglected to obtain an expert witness to testify that the substance offered into evidence was in fact moonshine. Judge Henley, based on his past moonshine-tasting experiences in north Arkansas, smelled the contents, took a swig, and promptly informed the jury he believed it to be moonshine, albeit raw and rotten moonshine.[10]

Despite achieving prominence and success on the bench, Judge Henley remained, simply, "the Judge from St. Joe." After his elevation to the Court of Appeals, Judge Henley moved his chambers from Little Rock to Harrison, where he and Mrs. Henley had maintained a home all along. He later served diligently as a senior judge for the Eighth Circuit, reaching out to a fellow judge on court business late in the evening a mere three days before his death.[11] Judge Henley's lasting contributions, both professional and personal, are aptly described by his colleague on the Eighth Circuit, the late Judge Gerald Heaney:

> A husband and father is judged by love, support and concern he gives to his family. A man is judged by the respect he enjoys from those that know him well. A judge is evaluated by his scholarship, his integrity and his compassion. By all these measures, Judge Smith Henley has set a standard that the rest of us can only hope to achieve.[12]

NOTES

1. Introduction: The Structure of the United States District Courts in Arkansas

1. Act of June 15, 1836, c. 100, 5 Stat. 50.

2. Act of March 6, 1820, c. 22, 3 Stat. 545.

3. Act of June 15, 1836, c. 100, § 4, 5 Stat. 50.

4. Act of September 24, 1789, c. 20, 1 Stat. 73 (setting forth the powers of the United States courts in Kentucky, which were the same powers conferred on the United States courts in Arkansas in 1836). See Act of June 15, 1836, ch. 100, § 4, 5 Stat. 50 (referencing the grant of power to Kentucky courts). The circuit courts of that time, though they had some appellate jurisdiction, were not the same as the courts of appeals for the circuits that exist today. Originally, "[t]he circuit courts were to have jurisdiction over major diversity and criminal cases, copyright and bankruptcy cases, as well as limited appellate jurisdiction over appeals from decisions of district courts." Eduardo C. Robreno, "Learning to Do Justice: An Essay on the Development of the Lower Federal Courts in the Early Years of the Republic," *Rutgers Law Journal* 29 (1998): 555, 561.

5. Act of March 3, 1837, c. 34, § 1, 5 Stat. 176–77.

6. Act of March 3, 1837, c. 34, § 3, 5 Stat. 177.

7. Act of March 3, 1837, c. 34, 5 Stat. 177.

8. Petition of John McKinley, S. Doc. No. 27-99, 396 Serial Set 99 (2d Sess. 1842).

9. Act of June 17, 1844, c. 103, 5 Stat. 680. In 1834, Congress defined the Indian Territory as "that part of the United States west of the Mississippi, and not within the states of Missouri and Louisiana, or the territory of Arkansas." Act of June 30, 1834, c. 161, § 1, 4 Stat. 729. This broad grant of jurisdiction raises interesting possibilities. At the time the Indian Territory was defined, all of the West was owned by Mexico. Glenn Shirley, *Law West of Fort Smith: A History of Frontier Justice in the Indian Territory* (1957), 9–10. As a result of the Mexican-American War (1846–48), a huge swath of land came into the United States possession. Richard Hofstadter et al., *The American Republic* (1959), 487–91. In theory, the Western District of Arkansas's jurisdiction could have extended all the way to the Pacific Ocean during the interval between when these lands were handed over to the United States and California became a state in 1850. See Act of June 30, 1834, c. 161, § 1, 4 Stat. 729. As a practical matter, the cases that reached Fort Smith were from events that occurred in today's eastern Oklahoma. See 212 F.R.D. 611, 633 (2003).

10. 212 F.R.D. 632–33 (2003).

11. Ibid., 633.

12. Act of March 3, 1851, c. 24, 9 Stat. 594.

13. Act of March 3, 1851, c. 24, § 1, 9 Stat. 594. See map, Arkansas in 1851. See also Report of the Judiciary Committee to the Senate, S. Doc. No. 29-372, 476 Serial

Set 372 (1st Sess. 1846) (accompanying S. 200 and explaining the need to divide Arkansas into two districts). Sebastian County did not exist until 1851 and thus was not part of this list. See *Pruitt v. Sebastian County Coal & Mining Co.*, 215 Ark. 673, 678–79, 222 S.W. 2d 50, 52, 54–55 (1949). This held that the 1851 act that created Sebastian County was constitutional. It was created from Scott, Polk, and Crawford Counties. Ibid. at 676, 222 S. W. 2d at 52.

14. Act of March 3, 1851, c. 24, § 2, 9 Stat. 594.

15. Ibid.

16. Act of March 3, 1851, c. 24, § 4, 9 Stat. 594.

17. Compare Act of March 3, 1851, c. 24, § 2, 9 Stat. 594 (lacking a requirement that the district judge reside in the district in which he served), with S. 172, 36th Cong. (1st Sess. 1860) (specifically requiring the district judge to reside in the district in which he served), available at http://lcweb2.loc.gov/ammem/ amlaw/lwhbsb.html (last visited October 2, 2003).

18. Letter from the Secretary of the Interior relative to Holding a Term of Court for the Western District of Arkansas at Okmulgee Once in Each Year. This relates to the difficulties in transporting prisoners. H.R. Exec. Doc. No. 42-153, 1513 Serial Set 153 (2d Sess. 1872).

19. Ibid.

20. Memorial of the Citizens of Arkansas Remonstrating Against the Establishment of a United States Court in the Indian Territory, S. Misc. Doc. No. 44-42, 1665 Serial Set 42 (1st Sess. 1876).

21. Ibid.

22. Act of January 6, 1883, c. 13, § 2–4, 22 Stat. 400.

23. Act of January 6, 1883, c. 13, § 2, 22 Stat. 400.

24. Act of March 1, 1895, c. 145, § 1, 28 Stat. 693.

25. See Thomas A. DeBlack, "Between the Hawk Buzzard: The Civil War in Arkansas," *Arkansas: A Narrative History* (2002), 166, 167.

26. Act of July 15, 1862, c. 178, § 1, 12 Stat. 576.

27. H.R. 641, 38th Cong. (2d Sess. 1865), available at http://lcweb2.loc.gov/ http://lcweb2.loc.gov/ammem/amlaw/lwhbsb.html (last visited October 2, 2003).

28. Act of July 23, 1866, c. 210, § 2, 14 Stat. 209.

29. S. Rep. No. 95-117, at 45 (1978), reprinted in 1978 U.S.C.C.A.N. 3569, 3607–8.

30. S. Rep. No. 95-117, at 46 (1978), reprinted in 1978 U.S.C.C.A.N. 3569, 3608–9.

31. Act of March 8, 1871, c. 106, § 5, 16 Stat. 471. See map, Arkansas in 1871. Lee County was not established until 1873, out of Phillips, Monroe, Crittenden, and Saint Francis Counties. Clay County was established the same year out of Randolph and Green Counties. Dallas T. Herndon, ed., *Annals of Arkansas* (1947), 668.

32. Act of March 3, 1871, c. 106, § 5, 16 Stat. 471.

33. Act of March 3, 1871, c. 106, §§ 1–2, 16 Stat. 471.

34. See Act of July 15, 1870, c. 298, § 1, 16 Stat. 363 (setting compensation for grand and petit jurors at three dollars per day [including travel days] plus five cents per mile traveled between a juror's residence and the court).

35. See, e.g., H.R. Rep. No. 61-1166, 5593 Serial Set 1166 (1910) (justifying the creation of the Jonesboro division on the "great savings to the [g]overnment"); see also note 102 and accompanying text.

36. Act of March 3, 1871, c. 106, § 5, 16 Stat. 471.

37. *Cong. Globe*, 41st Cong., 3d Sess. 1460–61 (1871).

38. Four days after the bill's defeat in the Senate, with Arkansas's other senator—Senator McDonald—present, the Senate agreed to rehear the bill and passed it 25 to 20. *Cong. Globe*, 41st Cong., 3rd Sess. 1460-61, (1871).

39. Ibid. Arkansas could have had Western, Eastern, and Middle Districts.

40. H.R. 3445, 42nd Cong. (3d Sess. 1873), available at http://memory.loc.gov/cgi-bin/ampage?collId=llhb&fileName=042/llhb042.db&recNum=0 (last visited October 2, 2003).

41. 212 F.R.D. 611, 634 (2003). This may have been unconstitutional. See note 141.

42. S. 278, 35th Cong. (1st Sess. 1858), available at http://memory.loc.gov//cgi-bin/ampage?collId=llsb&fileName=035/llsb035.db&recNum=0 (last visited October 2, 2003).

43. Act of January 31, 1877, c. 41, 19 Stat. 230.

44. Ibid. See map, Arkansas in 1877.

45. Ibid.

46. Ibid.

47. Ibid.

48. "[I]n Arkansas the district court sits in three places, and the circuit court but one. If circuit courts were required to be held simultaneously with the district courts, it would therefore be a very great convenience to litigants." Report from the Committee on the Judiciary concerning the Reorganization of the Judiciary of the United States, H.R. Rep. No. 44-45 at 4 (1876).

49. 212 F.R.D. at 632.

50. Act of February 28, 1887, c. 273, § 1, 24 Stat. 428.

51. Ibid. See map, Arkansas in 1887.

52. See notes 43–44.

53. S. Rep. No. 49-1748, 2456 Serial Set 1748 (1887).

54. Ibid.

55. Ibid.

56. Ibid.

57. See note 50 above and accompanying text.

58. See notes 12, 48–49 and accompanying text.

59. Act of February 6, 1889, c. 113, 25 Stat. 655.

60. Act of February 6, 1889, c. 113, § 2, 25 Stat. 655.

61. Act of April 10, 1869, c. 22, § 2, 16 Stat. 44.

62. Act of March 3, 1891, c. 517, 26 Stat. 826 (establishing the regional courts of appeal).

63. See Shirley, *Law West of Fort Smith*, 139.

64. 212 F.R.D. 611, 631 (2003).

65. See Shirley, *Law West of Fort Smith*, 139.

66. Act of February 6, 1889, c. 113, § 6, 25 Stat. 655, 656. By way of comparison, since 1802 the United States Supreme Court had possessed appellate jurisdiction over cases, where immediate imprisonment was not at stake, in which there was a dispute among circuit judges on the same panel. Act of April 29, 1802, c. 31, § 6, 2 Stat. 159, 159–61.

67. Jeffrey Morris, *Establishing Justice in Middle America: A History of the United*

States Court of Appeals for the Eighth Circuit (Minneapolis: University of Minnesota Press, 2007), 36. At the time this article was originally published, the article authors had an unpublished copy of the book manuscript on file. The epithet "hanging judge" is perhaps unfair. Death was the customary penalty in all capital cases, and it is said that as many deputy United States marshals were killed by outlaws in the Western District of Arkansas of that day and age as convicted murderers were hanged. Ibid. at 21–22; National Park Service—Fort Smith History, available at http://www.nps.gov/fosm/history/court/usdmrisks.htm (last visited October 2, 2003) (noting that sixty-five deputy marshals were killed in the line of duty during Judge Parker's time on the bench).

68. Act of February 20, 1897, c. 269, 29 Stat. 590, 590–91. This article is concerned exclusively with the history of the structure of the United States district courts in Arkansas (with some allusions to the old circuit courts). It needs to be noted that, in 1891, Congress passed the Evarts Act, which finally abolished circuit-riding by Supreme Court justices and, for the first time, established a uniform, regularized, three-tiered system, with regional circuit courts of appeals corresponding to each of the numbered circuits. Act of March 3, 1891, c. 517, 26 Stat. 826. Henry Clay Caldwell, who had been United States district judge for the Eastern District of Arkansas since 1864, became the first chief judge of the Circuit Court of Appeals for the Eighth Circuit, since 1948 called the United States Court of Appeals for the Eighth Circuit. 212 F.R.D. at 636; see Erwin C. Surrency, *History of the Federal Courts* (2d ed. 2002), 97. The old circuit court system was formally abolished in 1911. Act of March 3, 1911, c. 231, § 289, 36 Stat. 1167.

69. Report from the Committee on the Judiciary concerning the Reorganizing of the Judicial District of Arkansas, H.R. Rep. No. 54-2842, 3556 Serial Set 2842 (1897) (accompanying H.R. 10278).

70. Ibid.

71. See note 41 above and accompanying text; see also Act of February 20, 1897, c. 269, 29 Stat. 590.

72. Act of February 20, 1897, c. 269, §§ 2–5, 29 Stat. 590–91.

73. Act of February 20, 1897, c. 269, § 1, 29 Stat. 590.

74. Act of February 20, 1897, c. 269, § 5, 29 Stat. 590–91. See map, Arkansas in 1897.

75. Act of February 20, 1897, c. 269, §§ 1–5, 29 Stat. 590–91. The Fort Smith Division consisted of Benton, Carroll, Boone, Newton, Madison, Washington, Crawford, Franklin, Johnson, Sebastian, Logan, Scott, Yell, and Polk Counties. See map, Arkansas in 1897.

76. Act of February 20, 1897, c. 269, § 2, 29 Stat. 590–91.

77. Ibid.

78. Act of February 20, 1897, c. 269, § 2–3, 29 Stat. 590–91.

79. Act of February 20, 1897, c. 269, § 2, 29 Stat. 590–91. See map, Arkansas in 1897.

80. Act of February 20, 1897, c. 269, § 3, 29 Stat. 590–91.

81. Those counties were, from north to south: Van Buren, Pope, Conway, Faulkner, White, Woodruff, Prairie, Lonoke, Pulaski, Perry, Montgomery, Garland, Saline, Hot Spring, Grant, Jefferson, Arkansas, Clark, Dallas, Cleveland, Lincoln, Desha, Drew, Bradley, Ashley, and Chicot. William Thorndale and William

Dollarhide, *Map Guide to U.S. Federal Censuses 1700–1920* (1987) 40–41. See map, Arkansas in 1897.

82. 28 U.S.C. § 83 (1961).

83. Act of March 18, 1902, c. 222, § 2, 32 Stat. 72.

84. Report from the Committee on the Judiciary concerning the Western District of Arkansas, H.R. Rep. No. 57-788, 4402 Serial Set 788 (1902) (accompanying H.R. 7458).

85. Ibid.

86. Ibid. See map, Arkansas in 1902.

87. H.R. Rep. No. 59-3795, 4907 Serial Set 3795 (1906).

88. Ibid.

89. Ibid. In 1944, Federal Rule of Criminal Procedure 20 was adopted. Fed. R. Crim. P. 20 advisory committee's note.

90. H.R. Rep. 61-1166, 5593 Serial Set 1166 (1910).

91. See note 78 and accompanying text.

92. Act of June 23, 1910, c. 371, 36 Stat. 603.

93. Report from the Committee on the Judiciary concerning the United States Courts at Jonesboro, Arkansas, H.R. Rep. No. 61-1166, 5593 Serial Set 1166 (1910) (accompanying S. 6719).

94. Act of June 23, 1910, c. 371, § 2, 36 Stat. 603.

95. Act of March 4, 1915, c. 170, 38 Stat. 1193.

96. Act of March 4, 1915, c. 170, § 1, 38 Stat. 1193.

97. However, a check on MapQuest.com reveals that it is only one mile farther from Dermott, Arkansas, to Little Rock (115 miles) than from Dermott to Helena (114 miles). Of course, one must assume that the roads to Little Rock were not as developed as they are now, and going to either city was likely to be equally rough going. Nevertheless, traveling by direct line, a litigant from Lake Village would shave only about 20 miles off his journey by going to Helena instead of Little Rock. Most likely, these counties were shifted because their residents could get to Helena via the Mississippi River. Available at http://www.mapquest.com/directions/ (last visited September 18, 2003.)

98. Act of March 4, 1915, c. 170, § 2, 38 Stat. 1193.

99. Act of April 12, 1924, c. 87, § 71, 43 Stat. 90.

100. Ibid.

101. See note 92 and accompanying text.

102. H.R. Rep. No. 61-1166, 5593 Serial Set 1166.

103. Act of April 12, 1924, c. 87, § 71(e), 43 Stat. 90. See map, Arkansas in 1924.

104. Ibid.

105. Act of April 12, 1924, c. 87, § 71(f), 43 Stat. 90. See also H.R. Rep. No. 61-1166, 5593 Serial Set 1166.

106. See notes 72–82, 92, 99–101 and accompanying text.

107. See note 83 and accompanying text. See map, Arkansas in 1924.

108. Jeanie M. Whayne, "Darker Forces on the Horizon: Natural Disasters and Great Depression," *Arkansas: A Narrative History* (2002), 303, 307.

109. Act of April 16, 1926, c. 147, 44 Stat. 297. Ashley and Bradley Counties were taken from the Western Division of the Eastern District and thus changed districts

as well as divisions. Act of April 16, 1926, c. 147, § 71(b), 44 Stat. 297. The idea of a district court sitting in south-central Arkansas was not a new one. As early as 1870, attempts were being made to have the Eastern District sit twice a year in Camden, Arkansas. S. 1138, 41st Cong. (1870), available at http://lcweb2.loc.gov/ammem/amlaw/ lwhbsb.html (last visited August 20, 2003).

110. Alan C. Paulson, *Roadside History of Arkansas* (1998), 152.

111. Act of April 16, 1926, c. 147, § 71(b), 44 Stat. 297. See map, Arkansas in 1926.

112. After this change, the Texarkana Division consisted of Sevier, Howard, Pike, Little River, Hempstead, Nevada, Miller, and Lafayette Counties. Ibid.

113. Act of April 16, 1926, c. 147, § 71(e), 44 Stat. 297.

114. IEA State Census Data Center, available at http://www.aiea.ualr.edu/census/other/history.html (last visited October 2, 2003).

115. See note 41 and accompanying text.

116. H.R. Rep. No. 75-2034, at 3 (1938).

117. Ibid.

118. Act of May 31, 1938, c. 290, 52 Stat. 585.

119. Act of May 31, 1938, c. 290, § 4(f), 52 Stat. 585 (appointing one judge for the combination of Eastern and Western Districts of Arkansas).

120. Ibid.

121. After these alterations, Arkansas had ten divisions; by way of comparison, consider that California only had half as many. Act of June 25, 1948, c. 646, § 83, 62 Stat. 869.

122. Act of June 11, 1940, c. 321, § 71, 54 Stat. 302.

123. Act of June 11, 1940, c. 321, § 71(b), 54 Stat. 302. See map, Arkansas in 1940.

124. Report from the Committee on the Judiciary Providing for Terms of the United States District Court for the Western District of Arkansas at Fayetteville, H.R. Rep. No. 76-1746, at 2, 10441 Serial Set 1746 (1940) (accompanying H.R. 7421).

125. Act of June 11, 1940, c. 321, § 71(b), 54 Stat. 302. See map, Arkansas in 1940.

126. Report from the Committee on the Judiciary Establishing the Hot Springs Division of the Western Judicial District of Arkansas, H.R. Rep. No. 76-1961, at 2–3, 10441, Serial Set 1961 (1940) (accompanying H.R. 7811).

127. Ibid.

128. Act of June 11, 1940, c. 321, § 71(f), 54 Stat. 303. See map, Arkansas in 1940.

129. Report from the Committee on the Judiciary Holding Court for the Eastern Division of the Eastern District of Arkansas at Forrest City, H.R. Rep. No. 76-2360, at 103, 10442 Serial Set 2360 (1941) (accompanying H.R. 9531).

130. Act of May 20, 1961, Pub. L. No. 87-36, 75 Stat. 81.

131. Act of May 20, 1961, Pub. L. No. 87-36, 75 Stat. 84.

132. Ibid. See map, Arkansas in 1961.

133. Ibid.

134. Ibid.

135. Act of May 20, 1961, Pub. L. No. 87-36, 75 Stat. 80.

136. Act of October 20, 1978, Pub. L. No. 95-486, 92 Stat. 1629.

137. Act of July 10, 1984, Pub. L. No. 98-353, 98 Stat. 333.

138. Federal Judgeship Act of 1990, Pub. L. No. 101-650, 104 Stat. 5101.

139. Federal Judgeship Act of December 1, 1990, Pub. L. No. 101-650, 104 Stat. 5098.

140. Ibid.

141. *Quaere*: Can Congress constitutionally reduce the geographic jurisdiction of a judge who has been nominated by the president, and, by and with the advice and consent of the Senate, appointed by the president to serve a certain area? If the judge's commission reads "United States District Judge for the Eastern and Western Districts of Arkansas," as did the commission of the two judges who were "rovers" in 1990 (Judge Elsijane Trimble Roy and Judge George Howard Jr.), do their commissions retroactively shrink? We doubt it. In fact, when the first-named author was chief judge of the United States Court of Appeals for the Eighth Circuit, he declined to give these "rovers" special designations to sit in the Western District, believing that their original commissions already conferred that power.

142. Federal Judgeship Act of 1990, Pub. L. No. 101-650, 104 Stat. 5102.

143. 28 U.S.C. § 105 (1994).

144. 28 U.S.C. § 98 (1994).

145. 28 U.S.C. § 123 (1994).

146. Available at http://quickfacts.census.gov/gfd/ (last visited January 19, 2004).

2. Benjamin Johnson (1836–49)

1. See generally Leland Winfield Meyer, *The Life and Times of Colonel Richard M. Johnson of Kentucky* (New York: Columbia University Press, 1932), 20–41, and Thomas A. DeBlack, *A Garden in the Wilderness: The Johnsons and the Making of Lakeport Plantation, 1831–1876* (unpublished PhD thesis, University of Arkansas at Fayetteville, 1995). A little-known fact about Richard Mentor Johnson is his marriage to the family slave Julia Chinn, whom he regarded as his wife and who bore him two daughters. Remarkably for the time, both daughters married white men. United States Senate, "Richard Mentor Johnson, 9th Vice President" (1837–1841), http://www.senate.gov/artandhistory/history/common/generic/VP_Richard_M_Johnson.htm.

2. Marriage and admission to the bar, Meyer, *Life and Times*, 20. "Considerations of a private nature," William Littell to President Monroe, September 14, 1820, in Clarence E. Carter and John P. Bloom, eds., *Territorial Papers of the United States* (Washington, DC: United States GPO, 1934–75), 19:216. Yellowstone expedition, Annlies Corbin, *The Life and Times of the Steamboat Red Cloud; or, How Merchants, Mounties and the Missouri Transformed the West* (College Station: Texas A&M University Press, 2006), 13–14; United States Senate, "Richard Mentor Johnson." US House of Representatives, *Documents in Relation to the Claim of James Johnson for Transportation on the Missouri and Mississippi Rivers* (Washington, DC: Gales & Seaton, 1821), 28.

3. Establishing the District of Arkansas, *Statutes at Large of the United States of America* 2 (1856): 743 (enacted June 4, 1812). Establishing the Territory of Arkansas, ibid., 3 (1856): 493 (enacted March 2, 1819). Fixing the western boundary of Arkansas, ibid., 4 (1856): 305 (enacted May 24, 1828, Sec. 8). Western District of Arkansas,

Larry D. Ball, "Before the Hanging Judge: The Origins of the United States District Court for the Western District of Arkansas," *Arkansas Historical Quarterly* 49 (Autumn 1990): 199–213, 201. For an account of the beginnings of the courts in territorial Arkansas, see Lynn Foster, "The First Years of American Justice: Courts and Lawyers on the Arkansas Frontier," in Patrick G. Williams, S. Charles Bolton, and Jeannie M. Whayne, eds., *A Whole Country in Commotion: The Louisiana Purchase and the American Southwest* (Fayetteville: University of Arkansas Press, 2005), 121–45.

4. Circuit courts moved around multicounty "circuits"; courts of common pleas met in one place only, usually the county seat, and sometimes had more limited jurisdiction. At this point Arkansas had only five counties: Arkansas and Lawrence comprised the first circuit, and Clark, Hempstead, and Pulaski Counties, the second circuit. Establishing the judicial circuits, *Laws of the Territory of Arkansas* (Little Rock: 1821), 70–82 (enacted August 3, 1819). Crittenden's appointments, Executive Register for the Arkansas Territory, Carter and Bloom, *Territorial Papers*, 19:789, 791–95, 801.

5. First judicial session, Petition to the President by the Territorial Assembly, February 11, 1820, Carter and Bloom, *Territorial Papers*, 19:144–45. Complaint about prisoner, Recommendation to the President by the Territorial Assembly, April 1820, ibid., 19:170–71. "Virtually shut," Memorial to Congress by the Territorial Assembly, October 1820, ibid., 19: 234. Appointment of Selden, James Monroe, Commission of Joseph Selden as Judge, May 13, 1820, ibid., 19:182–83. Resignation of Jouett, *Arkansas Gazette*, November 18, 1820. Appointment of Thompson, John Thompson to John Quincy Adams, August 30, 1820, ibid., 19: 213–14. Thompson's change of mind, *Little Rock Arkansas Gazette*, November 18, 1820. Indeed, John Quincy Adams, the secretary of state, wrote: "[t]hey have accepted the appointments, and received the salaries to the last hour that they could, and never went to the Territory." John Quincy Adams, *Memoirs*, 5:212 (quoted in Carter and Bloom, *Territorial Papers*, 19:249).

6. Johnson's appointment, James Monroe, Commission of Benjamin Johnson as Judge, January 23, 1821, Carter and Bloom, *Territorial Papers*, 19:258. Support for Johnson, Richard M. Johnson to the Secretary of State (September 26, 1820), ibid., 19:219. Also see generally ibid., 19:203–4, 207–8, 241. Benjamin Johnson did not, however, have the support of Governor Miller, Secretary Crittenden, or Judge Scott, who all wrote the president urging the appointment of Judge Neil McLane. Governor Miller, Judge Scott, and Secretary Crittenden to the President (no date), ibid., 19:253.

7. *Statutes at Large*, 3 (1856): 493 (enacted March 2, 1819), Sec. 7.

8. The scope of the original criminal jurisdiction of the court was well described by Judge Selden in a charge he made to the grand jury, published in full in the *Little Rock Arkansas Gazette* of November 3, 1821. Major federal crimes consisted of treason, trading with Indians without a license, and counterfeiting. Arkansas had adopted those Missouri territorial laws in force in 1819, such as murder, manslaughter, robbery, and assault. They were available to the bench and bar in *Geyer's Digest*, supplemented by the printed acts of the Arkansas territorial legislature.

9. Samuel H. Hempstead, *Reports of Cases Argued and Determined in the United States Superior Court for the Territory of Arkansas, from 1820 to 1836; and in the United States District Court for the District of Arkansas, from 1836 to 1849; and in the United States Circuit Court for the District of Arkansas, in the Ninth Circuit, from 1839 to 1856* (Boston: Little, Brown and Company 1856), vii–viii.

10. For an incisive account of the latter years of the Family, see Michael B.

Dougan, "A Look at the 'Family' in Arkansas Politics, 1858–1865," *Arkansas Historical Quarterly* 29 (Summer 1970): 99–111.

11. For accounts of the legal system, and life in general, in Arkansas under the French and Spanish, see generally Morris S. Arnold, *Unequal Laws unto a Savage Race: European Legal Traditions in Arkansas, 1686–1836* (Fayetteville: University of Arkansas Press, 1985) and *Colonial Arkansas 1686–1804: A Social and Cultural History* (Fayetteville: University of Arkansas Press, 1991). When the territory of Arkansas was established, large tracts of land were reserved to the Quapaws, the Caddos, the Cherokees, and shortly thereafter, the Choctaws. The last of these lands were not ceded to the United States until 1835, less than a year before Arkansas became a state. See generally S. Charles Bolton, *Arkansas, 1800–1860: Remote and Restless* (Fayetteville: University of Arkansas Press, 1998), 67–87, for a history of the Indian frontier as it moved westward through Arkansas. Military Tract set-aside, *Statutes at Large* 2 (1856): 728 (enacted May 6, 1812). New Madrid certificates, ibid., 3 (1856): 211 (enacted February 17, 1815). See generally Paul W. Gates, *History of Public Land Law Development* (Washington, DC: Government Printing Office, 1968) for a definitive treatment of federal laws and policy regarding public land.

12. "A Crafty Land Speculator," Chilo Moultier to Josiah Meigs (April 10, 1822), Carter and Bloom, *Territorial Papers*, 19:420, 422.

13. See *Lytle v. Arkansas*, 50 U.S. (9 How.) 314 (January 1850 Term); *Rector v. Ashley*, 73 U.S. (6 Wall.) 142 (December 1867 Term), Hot Springs Cases, 92 U.S. 698 (October 1875 Term); *Muse v. Arlington Hotel*, 168 U.S. 430 (1897), as well as other cases discussed below.

14. *Russell v. Wheeler*, Hempstead, p. 3, 21 F. Cas. 66 (1821) (No. 12,164a). Persons buying land from New Madrid claimants at one time or another, before the final settlement, included Governor Miller and attorney Chester Ashley. Persons buying land from preemption claimants during 1819 included Secretary Crittenden, Speaker of the House Joseph Hardin, attorney Robert C. Oden, territorial judge Andrew Scott, receiver Henry Conway, William Trimble, and Thomas Eskridge (these latter two would later sit on the territorial superior court). See Lonnie J. White, *Politics on the Southwestern Frontier: Arkansas Territory 1829–1836* (Memphis: Memphis State University Press, 1964), 30–32.

15. None of this background is explained in *Russell v. Wheeler*. Accounts of the early controversy over Little Rock land can be found in White, *Politics*, 30–32; Bolton, *Arkansas 1800–1860*, 36–38; and Margaret Ross, *Arkansas Gazette: The Early Years 1819–1866* (Little Rock: Arkansas Gazette Foundation, 1969), 35–39. Since Judge Scott owned some of the disputed land, he recused himself and Johnson wrote the opinion. Ross, *Arkansas Gazette*, 36. Russell, Hempstead at 7, 21 F. Cas. at 15. Thomas James, "A scene of True Western Life," *Three Years Among the Indians and Mexicans*, ed. Milo Milton Quaife (1846; rpt., New York: Citadel Press, 1966), 108–9. The compromise, A Bill of Assureances [*sic*], and Samuel Anderson to Josiah Meigs, November 21, 1821, Carter and Bloom, *Territorial Papers*, 19:357, 364–65. Until 1818, the land in dispute belonged to the Quapaw Indians, which fact would have weakened the claims of both sides had either faction taken the other to court.

16. The Baptist Meeting-House, Fay Hempstead, *A Pictorial History of Arkansas from Earliest Times to the Year 1890* (St. Louis: N. D. Thompson Pub. Co., 1890), 192. Conway's house, *Little Rock Arkansas Gazette*, October 11, 1825. "On one

occasion," William F. Pope, *Early Days in Arkansas; Being for the Most Part the Personal Recollections of an Old Settler* (Little Rock: Frederick W. Allsopp, 1895), 143. Pope arrived in Arkansas in 1832 to serve as a secretary to his uncle, Governor Pope, replacing a prior secretary, also a nephew named William, who had been killed in a duel.

17. Two court terms, *Laws of the Territory of Arkansas* (Little Rock: 1821), 70, 76 (enacted August 3, 1819), Sec. 11. Act creating circuits, *Laws of the Territory of Arkansas* (Little Rock: 1821), 118 (enacted October 25, 1820). Postponement of circuits, ibid., 123.

18. The original Sulpicius was a jurist who wrote more than one hundred treatises on Roman law. *The New Encyclopaedia Britannica* 379 (15th ed. 1984), 11:379. "Judicial camels," *Little Rock Arkansas Gazette*, August 18, 1821. Abolition of circuits, *Acts Passed by the General Assembly of the Territory of Arkansas* (Little Rock: 1822), 3–6, 11 (enacted October 24, 1821).

19. Pope, *Early Days*, 36. Pope takes pains to state that this account is verbatim what was told him by Scott's son, perhaps because even then it sounded farfetched.

20. *Little Rock Arkansas Gazette*, June 15, 1824, April 13, 1824. Territorial representative William Allen had been killed in a duel by attorney Robert C. Oden in 1820. The territorial legislature had penalized dueling the following fall, and forbidden territorial officials to duel. *Laws of the Territory of Arkansas* (Little Rock: 1821), 110–13 (enacted October 23, 1820).

21. No prosecution, *Little Rock Arkansas Gazette*, June 8, 1824, at 3. Conway's letter, Henry Conway to John Quincy Adams, June 23, 1824, Carter and Bloom, *Territorial Papers*, 19:679. Appointment of Trimble, James Monroe, Commission of William Trimble as Judge, June 26, 1824, Carter and Bloom, *Territorial Papers*, 19:681. Duel reason for nonrenewal of appointment, Martin Van Buren to the Secretary of State, January 12, 1827, Carter and Bloom, *Territorial Papers*, 20:366. Appointment of Eskridge, John Quincy Adams, Commission of Thomas P. Eskridge as Judge, March 3, 1827, Carter and Bloom, *Territorial Papers*, 20:412.

22. "A very impressive manner," *Little Rock Arkansas Gazette*, October 26, 1824. Reported execution, *United States v. Cha-to-kah-na-pe-sha*, Hempstead 27, 28, 25 F. Cas. 414, 414 (1824) (No. 14,789a). Postponements, pardon, and release, *Little Rock Arkansas Gazette*, October 19 and 26, 1824, December 21 and 28, 1824, January 24, 1825, February 22, 1825, April 5 and 19, 1825, May 3, 1825, and June 7, 1825.

23. *Little Rock Arkansas Gazette*, July 5, 1824.

24. *Acts Passed at the Fifth Session of the General Assembly of the Territory of Arkansas* (1828), 34–38 (enacted October 23 and 24, 1827).

25. Legislative amendments, *Statutes at Large*, 4 (1856): 261–62 (enacted April 17, 1828). G. W. Featherstonhaugh, *Excursions Through the Slave States* (London: John Murray, 1844), 2:93–95.

26. Yell accident, Albert Pike, "The Superior Court," in John Hallum, *Biographical and Pictorial History of Arkansas* (Albany, NY: Weed, Parsons and Company, 1887), 77. Limit on appellate jurisdiction, *Acts Passed at the Fifth Session of the General Assembly of the Territory of Arkansas* (Little Rock: 1828), 34 (enacted October 23, 1827).

27. *United States v. Crittenden*, Hempstead 61, 25 F. Cas. 694 (1828) (No. 14,890a).

28. *Statutes at Large*, 4 (1856): 52–56 (enacted May 26, 1824). Prior to that, a commission had decided such claims. The 1824 act called for land claims to be handled as equity cases, in a special one-time session of the court.

29. An arpen, or arpent, is 63.75 yards; a square arpent is .85 of an acre. Gates, *Public Land Law*, 89. Background and confirmation of claims, *United States v. Samperyac*, Hempstead, 118, 119–23, 27 F. Cas. 932, 932–34 (1831) (no. 16, 216a), *aff'd*, *Sampeyreac v. United States*, 32 U.S. (7 Pet.) 222 (January 1833 Term).

30. Roane and Wirt, William Wirt to Samuel C. Roane, October 31, 1828, Carter and Bloom, *Territorial Papers*, 20:761. See generally their correspondence at ibid., 20:288–89, 344–45, 565–66, 596, 673–74, 759–68. See also House Document No. 45 (21st Cong. 1st Sess.).

31. John J. Bowie was the brother of the Bowie of Bowie knife fame. "Bowie" is misspelled as "Borrie" in the first portion of *Samperyac*, which can be confusing to the first-time reader. Court permission to withdraw documents, Isaac T. Preston to George Graham, October 10, 1829, Carter and Bloom, *Territorial Papers*, 21:72, 73. Graham's suspicions, George Graham to Samuel C. Roane, April 30, 1829, ibid., 21:24. "Most persons here," William S. Fulton to Andrew Jackson, September 7, 1829, ibid., 21:67. Postponement of patents, George Graham to William S. Fulton, October 13, 1829, ibid., 21:81. Request for annulment, George Graham to Samuel C. Roane, November 27, 1829, ibid., 21:119.

32. "The toute ensemble," Isaac T. Preston to George Graham, ibid., 21:72, 77, 78.

33. *Little Rock Arkansas Gazette*, February 9, 1830, July 28, 1830.

34. Roane and rehearing, George Graham to Samuel C. Roane, November 10, 1829, Carter and Bloom, *Territorial Papers*, 21:96. "The more I searched," Richard Searcy to George Graham, November 16, 1829, Carter and Bloom, *Territorial Papers*, 21:160.

35. Delegate Ambrose H. Sevier, Conway's successor, was accused of having "caused" Trimble to be removed. White, *Politics*, 120; *Arkansas Advocate*, June 22, 1831. Congress's reversal of land decrees, *Statutes at Large* 4 (1856): 399–401 (enacted May 8, 1830). Pope's comment, *Little Rock Arkansas Gazette*, August 4, 1830.

36. Regarding Trimble's arguing a cause he had ruled on, today's Model Rules of Professional Conduct prohibit an attorney from participating in a case where he or she served as a judge, unless "all parties to the proceeding consent after consultation." Model Rule of Professional Conduct 1.12(a). The nineteenth century did have conflict-of-interest statutes, but they were much more limited than today's rules. *Sampeyreac v. United States*, 32 U.S. (7 Pet.) 222 (1833).

37. Josiah H. Shinn, *Pioneers and Makers of Arkansas* (Baltimore: Genealogical Pub. Co., 1908), 91.

38. "So well executed," Samuel C. Roane to George Graham, July 20, 1829, in Carter and Bloom, *Territorial Papers*, 21:155. Preston's scorn of forgery, Isaac T. Preston to George Graham, October 10, 1829, in Carter and Bloom, ibid., 21:74. Trimble as a friend of Crittenden, White, *Politics*, 127. Sevier and Congress, Carter and Bloom, *Territorial Papers*, 21:150, n. 50. "The only Lawyer of reputation," Samuel C. Roane to George Graham, November 8, 1829, Carter and Bloom, *Territorial Papers*, 21:158, 160. "Men of the deepest thought," Isaac T. Preston to George Graham, October 10, 1829, Carter and Bloom, *Territorial Papers*, 21:74, 78. Jaw-Bone letters, *Little Rock Arkansas Gazette*, August 11, 1830, at 2, September 1, 1830, at 2. Ashley as Jaw-Bone, Ross, *Arkansas Gazette*, 93. Innocent purchasers, Memorial from the Territorial Assembly to Congress, November 5, 1831, Carter and Bloom, *Territorial Papers*, 21:421–22. William Trimble, by then Speaker of the House, signed the memorial.

39. "The most skillful persons," Samuel C. Roane to George Graham (July 20, 1829), Carter and Bloom, *Territorial Papers*, 21:157. The case Roane referred to was appealed to the US Supreme Court and decided in 1836 as *Soulard's Heirs v. United States*, 35 U.S. (10 Pet.) 100 (January 1836 Term). See also Gates, *Public Land Law*, 101–8, for a discussion of Missouri land claims.

40. Shinn, *Pioneers and Makers*, 202.

41. *Little Rock Arkansas Gazette*, April 6, 1831.

42. Quoted poem, "To a Bank Note," *Little Rock Arkansas Gazette*, November 13, 1839.

43. See generally Stephen A. Smith, "Arkansas Advocacy: The Territorial Period," *Arkansas Law Review* 31 (Fall 1977): 467–68. "Constitutional Judges," *Little Rock Arkansas Gazette*, December 29, 1830.

44. *Little Rock Arkansas Gazette*, April 28, 1835.

45. Egbert Harris to the Speaker of the House of Representatives (January 9, 1833), Carter and Bloom, *Territorial Papers*, 21:593.

46. William Cummins to Benjamin Johnson, *Little Rock Arkansas Advocate*, October 24, 1832, reprinted in Carter and Bloom, *Territorial Papers*, 21:632, 636. For more allegations regarding this charge, see generally Statements of Orson V. Howell, December 2, 1832, and James H. Caldwell, November 13, 1832, Carter and Bloom, *Territorial Papers*, 21:614, 618–19.

47. "Violent reprimand," Statement of Orson V. Howell (December 2, 1832), Carter and Bloom, *Territorial Papers*, 21:614, 615. For other accounts of this incident, see Statements of Dr. John H. Cocke (December 8, 1832), James H. Caldwell (November 13, 1832), Absalom Fowler (November 17, 1832), ibid., 21:612–13, 619, and 628–29; and William Cummins to Benjamin Johnson, *Arkansas Advocate*, October 24, 1832, reprinted in Carter and Bloom, *Territorial Papers*, 21:636. Sevier's rebuttal, *Little Rock Arkansas Gazette*, February 27, 1833.

48. The third charge, Statements of John Saylor, December 3, 1832, and Washington Smith, November 10, 1832, Carter and Bloom, *Territorial Papers*, 21:623–24, 625; and William Cummins to Benjamin Johnson, *Arkansas Advocate*, October 24, 1832, reprinted in Carter and Bloom, *Territorial Papers*, 21:636. Moss's refutation, Smith C. Moss to Ambrose Sevier, November 28, 1832, Carter and Bloom, *Territorial Papers*, 21:659–60.

49. "Wholly unfit to perform," Statement of Orson V. Howell, December 2, 1832, Carter and Bloom, *Territorial Papers*, 21:615–16. Other accusations, see Statements of Dr. John H. Cocke, December 8, 1832, and John Caldwell, November 13, 1832, Gilbert Marshall to William Cummins, November 10, 1832, and Statements of Thomas W. Johnston, December 1, 1832, and Absalom Fowler, November 17, 1832, ibid., at 613, 619–20, 620, 621–22, and 629. Too drunk to sit on the bench, William Cummins to Benjamin Johnson, *Little Rock Arkansas Advocate*, October 24, 1832, reprinted in Carter and Bloom, *Territorial Papers*, 21:637.

50. "Peevish, irritable," William Cummins to Benjamin Johnson, *Little Rock Arkansas Advocate*, October 24, 1832, reprinted in Carter and Bloom, *Territorial Papers*, 21:637. "No Lawyer would make such a motion," Statement of Orson V. Howell, December 2, 1832, ibid., 21:616. Also see Statements of Andrew Scott, December 12, 1832, and Absalom Fowler, November 17, 1832, ibid., 21:617, 629.

51. Statements of Orson V. Howell, December 2, 1832, and Absalom Fowler, November 17, 1832, ibid., 21:616, 629; and William Cummins to Benjamin Johnson, *Little Rock Arkansas Advocate*, October 24, 1832, reprinted in ibid., 21:638.

52. Statement of James Lemon, November 2, 1832, ibid., 21:626; and William Cummins to Benjamin Johnson, *Arkansas Advocate*, October 24, 1832, reprinted in ibid., 21:638.

53. William Cummins to the House of Representatives, December 8, 1832, Statement of Absalom Fowler, November 17, 1832, ibid., 21:597–98 and 630; and William Cummins to Benjamin Johnson, *Little Rock Arkansas Advocate*, October 24, 1832, reprinted in Carter and Bloom, *Territorial Papers*, 21:638.

54. White, *Politics*, 145–46.

55. Sevier's defense, *Little Rock Arkansas Gazette*, February 27, 1833. The prominent Arkansans defending Johnson included the governor, other superior court judges, prominent attorneys, and several clerks of court, among others. See generally Carter and Bloom, *Territorial Papers*, 21:641–68. For the House report, see House Report 88, 22d Cong. 2d Sess. (1833).

56. Pope, *Early Days*, 165–66.

57. George B. Rose, "Bench and Bar of Arkansas," in *Historical Review of Arkansas; Its Commerce, Industry and Modern Affairs*, ed. Fay Hempstead (Chicago: Lewis Pub. Co., 1911), 1:433–34.

58. *Statutes at Large* 5 (1856): 176–77 (enacted March 3, 1837).

59. Pope, *Early Days*, 151.

60. *United States v. Ta-wan-ga-ca*, Hempstead 304, 28 F. Cas. 18 (1836) (No. 16,435). "Crimes, offences, or misdemeanors," *Statutes at Large* 5 (1856):147 (enacted March 1, 1827). See generally Larry D. Ball, "Hanging Judge," 199, 201, discussing Johnson's opinions concerning the Indian Territory.

61. *United States v. Terrel*, Hempstead 411, 28 F. Cas. 40 (1840) (No. 16,452) and *United States v. Terrel*, Hempstead 422, 28 F. Cas. 41 (1840) (No. 16,453).

62. *United States v. Alberty*, Hempstead 444, 24 F. Cas. 765 (1844) (No. 14,426). Annexation statute, Act of June 17, 1844, 5 Stat. 680.

63. *United States v. Rogers*, 45 U.S. (4 How.) 567 (January 1846 Term). For a discussion of this case, see John P. Frank, *Justice Daniel Dissenting: A Biography of Peter V. Daniel 1784–1860* (Cambridge, MA: Harvard University Press, 1964).

64. *United States v. Ramsay*, Hempstead 481, 27 F. Cas. 694 (1847) (No. 16,115). *United States v. Sanders*, Hempstead 483, 27 F. Cas. 950 (1847) (No. 16,220).

65. *Little Rock Arkansas Gazette*, April 24, 1844. Frank, *Justice Daniel*, 282–83.

66. Act of July 17, 1844, 5 Stat. 676. *Putnam v. United States*, Hempstead 332, 20 F. Cas. 90 (1846) (No. 11,484). *Callendar v. United States*, Hempstead 334, 4 F. Cas. 1074 (1846) (No. 2321).

67. *Valliere v. United States*, Hempstead 335, 28 F. Cas. 929 (1847) (No. 16,822).

68. *Law v. United States*, Hempstead 338, 15 F. Cas. 17 (1848) (No. 8131). For a popular account of Law's career, see Jack Weatherford, *The History of Money* (Three Rivers Press, 1997), 129–32.

69. See *Winter v. United States*, Hempstead 344, 30 F. Cas. 350 (1848) (No. 17,895). See Joshua G. Clarke to President Monroe, Carter and Bloom, *Territorial Papers*, 19:114–15.

70. Memorial to Congress by the Territorial Assembly, referred November 20, 1820, Carter and Bloom, *Territorial Papers*, 19:233. John Miller to Josiah Meigs, February 4, 1822, ibid., 19:401.

71. *Winter*, Hempstead at 378, 30 F. Cas. at 363.

72. Ibid. at 379–80, 30 F. Cas. 364.

73. *De Villemont v. United States*, Hempstead at 389, 7 F. Cas. 560, *aff'd as Heirs of De Vilemont v. United States*, 54 U.S. (13 How.) 261 (December 1851 Term).

74. *Glenn v. United States*, Hempstead 394, 10 F. Cas. 472 (1849) (No. 5481), *aff'd*, 54 U.S. (13 How.) 250 (December 1851 Term).

75. "A man of excellent ability," Pike, in Hallum, *Biographical and Pictorial History of Arkansas*, 72. "But little influence," Rose, "Bench and Bar of Arkansas," 428.

76. Tribute of Respect to the Memory of the Honorable Benjamin Johnson, 10 Ark. [iv] (1850).

3. Daniel Ringo (1850–61)

1. John Hallum, *Biographical and Pictorial History of Arkansas* (Albany, NY: Weed, Parsons and Co., 1887), 146–48; Fay Hempstead, *Historical Review of Arkansas* (Chicago: Lewis Publishing Co., 1911), 443–44; Arkansas Secretary of State, *Historical Report of the Secretary of State* (n.p., 1986), 551; Margaret Smith Ross, "Daniel Ringo Pulaski County Pioneer," *Pulaski County Historical Review* 2 (1954): 10; "Death of Hon. Daniel Ringo," *Arkansas Gazette*, September 4, 1873.

2. Act of June 15, 1836, *U.S. Statutes at Large* 5 (1846): 51.

3. Ark. Const. of 1836, Art. VI, § 7.

4. Dallas T. Herndon, ed., *Annals of Arkansas*, vol. 1 (Hopkinsville, KY: Historical Record Association, 1947), 129–30.

5. Hempstead, *Historical Review of Arkansas*, 443–44.

6. Hallum, *Biographical and Pictorial History of Arkansas*, 146; Hempstead, *Historical Review of Arkansas*, 457.

7. Uriah M. Rose, *Addresses of U. M. Rose* (Chicago: G. I. Jones, 1914), 17.

8. Michael B. Dougan, *Arkansas Odyssey* (Little Rock: Rose Publishing Co., 1994), 123. See also, *Proceedings of the Eighteenth Annual Session of the Bar Association of Arkansas* (n.p., 1915), 152, comparing the system devised by Ringo to that prevailing in England prior to the nineteenth century. Code pleading abolished the old style of pleading and simplified the provisions for plaintiffs to sue and defendants to answer.

9. The vote was 51 to 39, indicating that Ringo still had some support in the legislature. *Journal of the House of Representatives for the Fifth Session of the General Assembly of the State of Arkansas* (Little Rock, AR: S. Borland & Co., 1845), 39.

10. Sol F. Clark, who delivered a eulogy to ex-chief justice Ringo at the May 1878 term of the Arkansas Supreme Court, alluded to the fact that: "In a State which was highly democratic, the political opinions of Judge Ringo were continually adverse to his promotion to office or station."

11. 4 Ark. 302 (1842).

12. Yell's role in the Real Estate Bank controversy is described in greater detail in Melinda Meek, "The Life of Archibald Yell," *Arkansas Historical Quarterly* 26 (1967): 232–39.

13. *Valliere v. U.S.*, 28 F.Cas. 929 (D. Ark. 1847); *Winter v. U.S.*, 30 F.Cas. 350 (D. Ark. 1848).

14. *De Villemont v. U.S.*, 7 F.Cas. 560 (D.C. Ark. 1848), *aff'd* 54 U.S. 261 (18[?]).

15. *Federal Rules Decisions* 40 (1967): 169. Ringo was confirmed on June 10, 1850, History of the Federal Judiciary, www.fjc.gov (Accessed July 29, 2015.)

16. Act of March 3, 1851, *U.S. Statutes at Large* 9 (1851): 594. The political battles that led to the creation of the Western District are described in Larry D. Ball, "Before the Hanging Judge: The Origins of the United States District Court for the Western District of Arkansas," *Arkansas Historical Quarterly* 49 (1990): 199–213.

17. Although several reported cases were issued by circuit court panels on which Ringo served, the opinions were written by another panel member. *Sneed v. Hanly*, 22 F.Cas. 712 (Cir.Ct. Ark. 1853). (Statute of limitations does not begin to run against an attorney who holds money belonging to a client until the client demands the money from the attorney); *Tunstall v. Worthington*, 24 F.Cas. 324 (1853) (Garnishment action dismissed for lack of complete diversity where plaintiff was citizen of Arkansas and one of garnishees was citizen of Arkansas); *Greenwood v. Rector*, 10 F.Cas. 1183 (Cir.Ct. Ark. 1855) (Suit for debt in federal court is not arrested by subsequent issuance of writ of garnishment on same debt by state court); *Read v. Haynie*, 20 F.Cas. 354 (Cir.Ct. Ark. 1855) (Continuance denied when based on affidavit of attorney attesting to what client told attorney); *Trigg v. Conway*, 24 F.Cas. 196 (Cir.Ct. Ark. 1855) (Federal court does not lose jurisdiction in a diversity of citizenship action when plaintiff dies and is replaced by an administrator who is a citizen of the same state as the defendant).

18. 20 F.Cas. 905 (Cir.Ct. Ark. 1851).

19. 20 F.Cas. at 908.

20. 54 U.S. at 476.

21. 18 F.Cas. 916 (Cir.Ct. Ark. 1854).

22. The reporter's head notes indicate that the case was heard by Judge Ringo with associate Supreme Court justice Daniel absent.

23. 18 F.Cas. at 917.

24. Sec. 30, Act of September 24, 1790, *U.S. Statutes at Large* 1 (1845): 89.

25. 16 F.Cas. 856 (Cir.Ct. Ark. 1854).

26. 20 F.Cas. 187 (Cir.Ct. Ark. 1854).

27. 25 F.Cas. 788 (1853).

28. Act of March 3, 1851 (9 Stat. 594).

29. 25 F.Cas. at 790.

30. 21 F.Cas. 1089 (Cir.Ct. 9th Cir. 1854).

31. Robert B. Walz, "Arkansas Slaveholdings and Slaveowners in 1850," *Arkansas Historical Quarterly* 12 (1953): 38.

32. Stephen E. Wood, "The Development of Arkansas Railroads," *Arkansas Historical Quarterly* 7 (1948): 114.

33. According to one scholar, Ringo resigned from the federal bench at the same time that Arkansas seceded. William M. Robinson Jr., *Justice in Grey* (New York: Russell & Russell, 1941), 18. A comprehensive list of departures from the federal bench, however, states that Ringo was removed. Emily Field Van Tassel, "Resignations and Removals: A History of Federal Judicial Service—And Disservice—1789–1992," *University of Pennsylvania Law Review* 142 (1993): 333, 408.

34. Chapt. 61, 1st sess., Provisional Cong. of the Confederate States (May 16,

1861), *Statutes at Large of the Provisional Government of the Confederate States of America*, ed. James M. Matthews (Richmond: R. M. Smith, 1864), 75.

35. Chapt. 54, § 3, 1st sess., Provisional Cong. of the Confederate States (May 21, 1861), *Statutes at Large of the Provisional Government of the Confederate States of America*, ed. James M. Matthews (Richmond: R. M. Smith, 1864), 152. Congress later created a separate Confederate court for the Indian Territory portion of the Western District. *True Democrat*, February 6, 1862.

36. Ringo was nominated and confirmed on May 21, 1861. *Journal of the Congress of the Confederate States of America 1861–1865* (58th Cong., 2d sess, 1904, S. Doc. 234): 1:268. After the permanent Congress of the Confederate States convened in 1862 Ringo was again appointed and confirmed. Ibid. 2:108, 2:156. Ringo's commission, dated April 15, 1862, which was four days after his second confirmation, is on file at the Arkansas History Commission.

37. H. M. Rector to Jefferson Davis, November 28, 1861, Official Records, Series I, Volume 8, 699.

38. *True Democrat*, December 19, 1861.

39. *True Democrat*, January 23 and February 27, 1862. The Peace Society movement is discussed at length in Ted R. Worley, "The Arkansas Peace Society of 1861: A Study in Mountain Unionism," *Journal of Southern History* 24 (1958): 445–56.

40. Herndon, *Annals of Arkansas*, vol. 2, 634. A copy of an 1864 application to lease the plantation confiscated from Ringo is on file with the Arkansas History Commission (Kie Oldham papers).

41. Hempstead, *Historical Review of Arkansas*, 443.

42. "Death of Hon. Daniel Ringo," *Arkansas Gazette*, September 4, 1873.

43. "A Marker for the First Chief Justice," *Arkansas Gazette*, May 6, 1963.

4. Henry Clay Caldwell (1864–90)

1. As George B. Rose stated of Caldwell, "It is safe to say that no man ever did more for Arkansas than Judge Caldwell; indeed, I have heard my father say that no one had ever done so much." George B. Rose, *In Memoriam—Henry Clay Caldwell*, 117 Ark. 645, 647 (1915).

2. Fay Hempstead, *Historical Review of Arkansas* (Chicago: Lewis Pub. Co., 1911), 314.

3. Larry W. Roeder Jr., "Henry Clay Caldwell: The Early Years," *Historical Society News* 6 (1997): 1.

4. Larry W. Roeder, the great-great-grand-nephew of Henry Clay Caldwell, states that economic hardship as well as a feud between Van Caldwell and the Tomlinson family of Moundsville over Van's inability to make payments on an inn caused the Caldwells to leave Virginia. See ibid. The feud turned into a legal suit that continued until just before Van Caldwell's death in 1856. See ibid., 3. Roeder postulates that this feud with the Tomlinson family was probably what "influenced Clay to use the bench to fight unregulated loans and a predatory system in Arkansas he called the 'Anaconda Mortgage.'" Ibid., 1.

5. See ibid., 2.

6. See Captain Addison A. Stuart, *Iowa Colonels and Regiments* (Des Moines: Mills & Co., 1865), 591–92.

7. Many sources differ on the year Caldwell was admitted to the bar: 1851 or 1852. I have chosen 1851 because Judge Caldwell seems to have used that date. See "City Honors Man Who Captured It During Civil War," *Arkansas Democrat*, March 19, 1914, 1. Moreover, the historians in Iowa, who would have access to the bar record, use that date. See *Journal of the House of the Thirty-Sixth General Assembly of the State of Iowa*, Annals of Iowa, 3d Ser., 154,2147 (July 1915); and Edward H. Stiles, *Recollections and Sketches of Notable Lawyers and Public Men of Early Iowa* (Des Moines: Homestead Publishing Co., 1916), 235.

8. See note 6 above.

9. See Stiles, *Recollections and Sketches of Notable Lawyers*, 593.

10. See "Notes: Hon. Henry Clay Caldwell," *American Law Review* 30 (1896): 282, 284.

11. See *Journal of the House*, 2147.

12. See Brig. Gen. Guy E. Logan, Iowa General Assembly, *Roster and Record of Iowa Soldiers in the War of the Rebellion, 1861–1866*, vol. 4 (1910), 419.

13. See note 7 above.

14. See Logan, *Roster and Record of Iowa Soldiers in the War*, 432.

15. See Stiles, *Recollections and Sketches of Notable Lawyers*, 218; and Stuart, *Iowa Colonels and Regiments*, 432.

16. See Theodore Fetter, *A History of the United States Court of Appeals for the Eighth Circuit* (n.p.: Judicial Conference of the United States Bicentennial Committee, 1977), 3; see also records of Eastern District of Arkansas.

17. See note 2 above.

18. John Hallum, *Biographical and Pictorial History of Arkansas*, vol. 1 (1887), 482–83.

19. Ringo would later appear before Judge Caldwell in circuit court under indictment for treason, but was dismissed and discharged from the indictment because he received a Special Charter of Pardon from President Andrew Johnson on April 16, 1866. See Docket Book of the Eighth Circuit Court of Appeals, April 20, 1867.

20. See United States District Court for the Eastern District of Arkansas, Memorial: Henry Clay Caldwell, 1915, p. 6–7, "Henry Clay Caldwell," Arkansas History Commission.

21. See Hallum, *Biographical and Pictorial History*, 484.

22. An interesting note is that the famous case invalidating the loyalty requirement for admission to the federal bar came up out of Judge Caldwell's court. In 1862, Congress passed an act prescribing that every person holding or taking an office in the government of the United States take a loyalty oath affirming that he had taken no part in the rebellion. See Act of July 2, 1862, ch. 128, 12 Stat. 502. Three years later, Congress extended the provisions of the oath to embrace attorneys and counselors of the courts of the United States. See Act of January 24, 1865, ch. 20, 13 Stat. 424. The amendment also provided that no persons would be admitted to the respective bars of any of the federal courts without taking this oath. See Act of January 24, 1865, ch. 20, 13 Stat. 424. Petitioner Augustus H. Garland had been admitted to the bar of the United States Supreme Court in 1860 and had followed his state into the Confederacy. See *Exparte Garland*, 71 U.S. (4 Wall.) 344, 375 (1866). In fact, he had represented his state in both houses of the Confederate Congress. In July 1865, Mr. Garland received a Special Charter of Pardon from President Johnson. In October, the United States

brought Mr. Garland before Judge Caldwell on an indictment of treason, which the judge dismissed on the basis of the pardon (340). Shortly thereafter, Mr. Garland traveled to Washington and moved to be admitted to the bar of the United States Supreme Court on the grounds that the act was unconstitutional, or that his pardon released him from compliance (375–76). The Court, in an opinion written by Justice Field, held that the act was in essence punishing Mr. Garland for his conduct in joining the Confederacy. Since the act was enacted in 1865, several years after the violation took place, the act was an ex post facto law and therefore violated the United States Constitution, Article I, Section 9 (377–78).

23. See American Council of Learned Societies, *Dictionary of American Biography*, ed. Allen Johnson, vol. 2 (New York: Scribner, 1929), 408.

24. See Powell Clayton, *The Aftermath of the Civil War in Arkansas* (New York: Neale Pub. Co., 1915), 207.

25. Rose, *In Memoriam—Henry Clay Caldwell*, 648.

26. This position was filled by David J. Brewer.

27. See Stiles, *Recollections and Sketches of Notable Lawyers*, 220–21.

28. 18 F.Cas. 846 (C.C.E.D. Ark. 1870) (No. 10,595), *rev'd*, 80 U.S. (13 Wall.) 654 (1871).

29. The 1868 Arkansas Constitution declared "all contracts for the sale and purchase of slaves are null and void." Arkansas Const. (1868), Art. XV, § 14.

30. See *Osborn*, 18 F.Cas. at 849–50.

31. 60 U.S. (19 How.) 393 (1857).

32. See *Osborn*, 18 F.Cas. at 853.

33. See *Osborn v. Nicholson*, 80 U.S. (13 Wall.) 654 (1871).

34. Act of March 2, 1867, ch. 390, 8 Stat. 168. The act was repealed by the Act of June 7, 1878, ch. 160, 20 Stat. 99.

35. Act of April 10, 1869, ch. 22, 16 Stat. 44.

36. See Fetter, *A History of the United States Court of Appeals*, 4–5.

37. McCrary was appointed from Congress where he was a principal sponsor of an act in 1875 that expanded federal courts' jurisdiction. He also was an organizer of the Electoral Commission that decided the presidential election of 1876.

38. See generally, Felix Frankfurter and James M. Landis, *The Business of the Supreme Court: A Study in the Federal Judicial System* (1928; rpt., New York: Johnson Reprint Corp., 1928); see note 24 above.

39. See Rose, *In Memoriam—Henry Clay Caldwell*, 648. In 1872, Republican Elisha Baxter, a loyalist slaveholder and Union veteran, won a contested gubernatorial election over Joseph Brooks, a carpetbagger backed by Democrats and native Unionists, who felt betrayed by the Republican northerners. Baxter may have been a Republican when elected, but he did not act like one in office; he pushed through a constitutional amendment re-enfranchising former rebels. The Republicans soon disowned their governor and took to supporting Brooks. Thus, the Brooks-Baxter war began with each camp having its own legislature and militia. Eventually President Grant recognized Baxter as governor and ordered Brooks's forces to surrender. This is generally recognized as the end of Reconstruction in Arkansas.

40. See Rose, *In Memoriam—Henry Clay Caldwell*, 649.

41. See Judge George D. Reynolds et al., *In Memoriam in United States Court of Appeals for the Eighth Circuit*, March 6, 1915, 3, "Henry Clay Caldwell," Arkansas History Commission.

42. See Hempstead, *Historical Review of Arkansas*, 315.

43. See Hallum, *Biographical and Pictorial History*, 484; "Judge Caldwell Has Retired," *Arkansas Gazette*, June 7, 1903, 1.

44. See Arkansas Const. (1868), Art. XII, § 6; Arkansas Const. (1874), Art. IX, § 7; Rose, *In Memoriam-Henry Clay Caldwell*, 650; *Portrait Biographical Album of Van Buren and Jefferson Counties, Iowa* (1890), 617.

45. See Rose, *In Memoriam—Henry Clay Caldwell*, 650.

46. See Arkansas Const. (1868), Art. XII, §§ 1–5; Arkansas Const. (1874), Art. IX, §§ 1–5.

47. At the time this article was originally published, Article 19, section 13, of the Arkansas Constitution provided:

> (a) General Loans:
>
> (i) The maximum lawful rate of interest on any contract entered into after the effective date hereof shall not exceed five percent (5%) per annum above the Federal Reserve Discount Rate at the time of the contract.
>
> (ii) All such contracts having a rate of interest in excess of the maximum lawful rate shall be void as to the unpaid interest. A person who has paid interest in excess of the maximum lawful rate may recover, within the time provided by law, twice the amount of interest paid. It is unlawful for any person to knowingly charge a rate of interest in excess of the maximum lawful rate in effect at the time of the contract, and any person who does so shall be subject to such punishment as may be provided by law.
>
> (b) Consumer Loans and Credit Sales: All contracts for consumer loans and credit sales having a greater rate of interest than seventeen percent (17%) per annum shall be void as to principal and interest and the General Assembly shall prohibit the same by law. Arkansas Const. (1874), Art. 19, § 13.

48. See ibid.

49. See Henry Clay Caldwell, "The Relation of Debtor and Creditor, 'Address before the Arkansas State Bar Association (Jan. 7, 1886),'" *Coin's Financial Series 2* (1895): 9–140.

50. See ibid., 5.

51. See ibid.

52. See note 20 above, Memorial: Henry Clay Caldwell, 6.

53. See Rose, *In Memoriam—Henry Clay Caldwell*, 651.

54. See "Judge Caldwell Has Retired," note 43; Rose, *In Memoriam—Henry Clay Caldwell*, 651.

55. See *National Cyclopedia of American Biography*, vol. 9 (Clifton, NJ: J. T. White, 1967), 478; "Judge Caldwell Has Retired," note 43.

56. See *In re Van Vliet*, 43 F. 761 (C.C.E.D. Ark. 1890).

57. See *Leisy v. Harden*, 135 U.S. 100 (1890).

58. *In re Van Vliet*, 766.

59. *A Digest of the Statutes of Arkansas* (Little Rock: Little Rock Printing & Pub. Co., 1874).

60. Reynolds et al., *In Memoriam in United States Court of Appeals for the Eighth Circuit*, March 6, 1915, p. 3, "Henry Clay Caldwell."

61. Rose, *In Memoriam—Henry Clay Caldwell*, 652.

62. Henry Clay Caldwell, "Trial by Judge and Jury," *American Law Review* 33 (1899): 321, 346. In this address given before the Missouri State Bar Association, Caldwell commended and advocated jury trials. Caldwell argued that justice is better served by juries than by courts, and he stated that complaints being voiced against the jury were groundless. See ibid., 334–36, 343. He maintained that "the consequences of an erroneous verdict by a jury are immeasurably less than an erroneous verdict by the judge; for one jury is not bound by the error of a former jury, but the law of precedent will compel the judge to adhere to his error, for it is a rule of fixed tribunals that consistency in error is to be preferred to a right decision." Ibid., 338–39. Caldwell noted the ability of a jury to take note of both moral and legal justification, whereas the law looks only to legal justification. See ibid., 334. He praised John Peter Zenger's jury as being "twelve patriots" whose names "should go down in history with those of the foremost patriots of the Revolution," and he then listed the names of these jurors. Ibid., 325. Caldwell inquired, "Suppose whenever the judge errs in deciding the law he was summarily ordered to step down off the bench. What would be the result? Not one single bench would be occupied next Monday; it is certain that this bench would be vacant, for the judges who sit here have been convicted of repeated errors by the Supreme Court." Ibid., 343.

63. See Rose, *In Memoriam—Henry Clay Caldwell*, 652.

64. See Hallum, *Biographical and Pictorial History of Arkansas*, 486.

65. See Reynolds et al., *In Memoriam in United States Court of Appeals for the Eighth Circuit*, March 6, 1915, p. 4, "Henry Clay Caldwell."

66. See Hallum, *Biographical and Pictorial History of Arkansas*, 484; *Kimberling v. Hartly*, 1 F. 571 (C.C.D. Kan. 1880); "Mr. Circuit Judge Caldwell," *American Law Review* 24 (1890): 299, 300.

67. See Henry Clay Caldwell, "Coon-skin Cap Law," *American Law Review* 37 (1903): 677.

68. Ibid., 678.

69. See note 67 above.

70. 20 F. 260 (C.C.E.D. Ark. J. 1884).

71. Caldwell claimed that the practice began when a Kentucky chancellor put in a receiver appointment order with the condition that the receiver agree to pay all wages accrued within the thirty days prior to that appointment. See Henry Clay Caldwell, "Railroad Receiverships in the Federal Courts" (remarks at the Green Leaf Law Club, St. Louis, Mo., February 24, 1896).

72. 99 U.S. 235 (1878).

73. 136 U.S. 89 (1890).

74. See note 10, "Notes: Hon. Henry Clay Caldwell," 283 n. 1.

75. See *Kneeland*, 136 U.S. 97.

76. See *Dow*, 20 F. 260. Caldwell would later cite the author of Dow (himself) as being the originator of the practice in a speech he gave on railroad receiverships. See note 71 above.

77. *Dow*, 267–68.

78. Act of March 3, 1887, ch. 373, § 3, 24 Stat. 552, 554.

79. Stiles, *Recollections and Sketches of Notable Lawyers*, 226–27 (quoting Seymour D. Thompson, "The Court Management of Railroads," *American Law Review* 27 [1893]: 481).

80. See Fetter, *A History of the United States Court of Appeals*, 15.

81. See ibid.; see also "Mr. Circuit Judge Caldwell," 300.

82. See "Mr. Circuit Judge Caldwell," 300.

83. See ibid.

84. See Fetter, *A History of the United States Court of Appeals*, 13.

85. Frankfurter and Landis, *The Business of the Supreme Court*, 87 (quoting Walter B. Hill, "The Federal Judicial System," 12 A.B.A. Rep. 289, 307).

86. In fact, the court's jurisdiction over criminal matters was enlarged by this act to include all cases of "infamous crimes." See Frankfurter and Landis, *The Business of the Supreme Court*, 109–11.

87. See Fetter, *A History of the United States Court of Appeals*, 14. The Eighth Circuit was the largest circuit in the country, spanning the heartland of the country from the Mississippi to beyond the Rockies, and from Canada to Texas and Louisiana. It included ten states: Arkansas, Colorado, Iowa, Kansas, Minnesota, Missouri, Nebraska, North Dakota, South Dakota, and Wyoming. It would later also include New Mexico, Oklahoma, and Utah, as they were admitted to the Union.

88. Remember, the circuit court at this time was a court of first instance only, so the number of reported cases is no indicator of volume.

89. Fetter, *A History of the United States Court of Appeals*, 14.

90. 99 F. 856 (1899).

91. See *McMaster v. New York Life lns. Co.*, 183 U.S. 25 (1901).

92. *McMaster*, 872 (Caldwell, J., dissenting).

93. Ibid.

94. Ibid., 880–81.

95. 83 F. 912 (8th Cir. 1897).

96. Judge Caldwell scorned injunctions. In a speech he gave before the Missouri State Bar Association approximately two years after the *Hopkins* decision, Caldwell stated that the use of the injunction worked to "undermine the constitutional right of trial by jury" and in fact "disregarded the constitution." He advocated the "customary and constitutional method of accusation, arrest, examination, indictment, and trial by jury." Caldwell, "Trial by Judge and Jury," 330. This speech directed the audience to his dissent in *Hopkins* and presented some of the arguments presented therein.

97. Ibid., 923–24.

98. Ibid., 924.

99. Ibid., 926.

100. Ibid., 930–40.

101. See Hempstead, *Historical Review of Arkansas*, 315; "Noted Jurist Dies in California City," *Arkansas Gazette*, February 16, 1915, 14.

102. See Fetter, *A History of the United States Court of Appeals*, 16; American Council of Learned Societies, *Dictionary of American Biography*, 408; Stiles, *Recollections and Sketches of Notable Lawyers*, 232–33.

103. "Notes: Hon. Henry Clay Caldwell," 285.

104. See Stiles, *Recollections and Sketches of Notable Lawyers*, 285–86.

105. Ibid., 286.

106. "Notes: Hon. Henry Clay Caldwell," 285.

107. See Stiles, *Recollections and Sketches of Notable Lawyers*, 232.

108. See Fetter, *A History of the United States Court of Appeals*, 16; American Council of Learned Societies, *Dictionary of American Biography*, 408.

109. See Stiles, *Recollections and Sketches of Notable Lawyers*, 233.

110. See Fetter, *A History of the United States Court of Appeals*, 16.

111. "Judge Henry Clay Caldwell—Thirty-nine Years on Federal Bench," *Case and Commentary* 22 (1915): 87.

112. Ibid., 88.

113. See Stiles, *Recollections and Sketches of Notable Lawyers*, 236–37.

114. Ibid., 237.

115. Judge Willis Van Devanter of Wyoming joined the Court on March 13, 1903. He was later appointed to the United States Supreme Court by President Taft in 1910. Judge Caldwell's successor was William C. Hook of Kansas. Also, at that time there was no senior status for federal judges. A judge could only do his full-time workload or retire.

116. See "Retires Next Year," *Arkansas Gazette*, September 27, 1901, 8.

117. See "Judge Caldwell Has Retired," 1.

118. See "Judge Henry Clay Caldwell—Thirty-nine Years," 88.

119. See ibid., 87.

120. See "City Honors Man Who Captured It During Civil War," *Arkansas Democrat*, March 18, 1914.

5. John Apps Williams (1890–1900)

1. *Arkansas Gazette*, July 8, 1890; *History of the Federal Judiciary*. http://www.fjc.gov. Website of the Federal Judicial Center, Washington, DC (Accessed April 1, 2015).

2. *Arkansas Gazette*, July 8, 1890.

3. Ibid.

4. Ibid.

5. *Muse v. Arlington Hotel Co.*, 68 Fed. 637 (C.C.E.D. Ark. 1895).

6. *C. F. Simmons Medicine Co. v. Simmons*, 81 Fed. 163 (C.C.E.D. Ark. 1897).

7. *In re Massey*, 45 Fed. 629 (E.D. Ark., W.D. 1890).

8. *Humes v. City of Little Rock*, 138 Fed. 929 (C.C.E.D. Ark. 1898).

9. *In re Rozelle*, 57 Fed. 155 (C.C.E.D. Ark. 1893).

10. *U.S. v. Niemeyer*, 94 Fed. 147 (E.D. Ark. 1899).

11. *Gordon v. Jackson*, 72 Fed. 86 (C.C.E.D. Ark. 1896).

12. *Farmers' Loan & Trust Co. v. Stuttgart & A.R.R. CO.*, 92 Fed. 246 (C.C.E.D. Ark. 1899).

13. *Allen v. Jones*, 79 Fed. 698 (C.C.E.D. Ark. 1897).

14. *Cockrill v. Butler*, 78 Fed. 679 (C.C.E.D. Ark. 1897).

15. *Rosenberg v. Jett*, 72 Fed. 90 (C.C.E.D. Ark. 1896).

16. *Hill v. Hite*, 79 Fed. 826 (C.C.E.D. Ark. 1897).

17. *Franz v. Wahl*, 81 Fed. 9 (E.D. Ark. 1897).

18. *Little Rock & M.R. Co., v. St. Louis, I.M. & S.Ry. Co.*, 59 Fed. 400 (C.C.E.D. Ark. 1894).

19. *Arkansas Gazette*, July 8, 1900.

20. *Pine Bluff Graphic*, July 8, 1900.

6. *Jacob Trieber (1901–27)*

1. Conrad, a student at the University of Frankfurt, remained as a professor of Latin dialects at that institution until his death. Johanna subsequently immigrated to St. Louis, Missouri, and married Charles Punch. She resided there until her death.

2. See I. Elbogen, *A Century of Jewish Life* (1944), 3–17; H. Sachar, *The Course of Modern Jewish History* (1958), 107–16.

3. The realm of Prussia was greatly increased by the war of 1866, which extended the Prussian constitution over the regions of Schleswig-Holstein, Hanover, and Hesse-Kessel. Elbogen, *A Century of Jewish Life*, 16. By 1870, Bismarck had created the German Empire "out of the blood and iron of the Franco-Prussian War" by uniting Germany's principalities against "the bogey of a common French enemy." Sachar, *The Course of Modern Jewish History*, 221.

4. David Trieber died in 1886, Blume in 1895, and Morris in 1898.

5. The Beth El Congregation of Helena was founded in 1870. By 1900, it had twelve pew owners and fourteen contributing members. *American Jewish Yearbook*, (C. Adler ed., 1899), 5660 at 108. Jacob and Ida Trieber were members of this congregation until they moved to Little Rock in 1897, at which time they joined the B'nai Israel Congregation. This latter congregation was founded in 1867, and in 1900 had a membership of 170. Ibid., 109.

6. Jacob Trieber married Ida Schradski on January 10, 1882, in Peoria, Illinois. They had two children, Harry and Bess. Harry became a lawyer and practiced in Little Rock, and Bess married Charles H. Newton and resided in Scarsdale, New York.

7. *Helena World*, July 8, 1896. The newspaper clippings furnished to the author did not always reveal information necessary for a full citation. All clippings, however, are on file with the Arkansas History Commission as part of its "Trieber Collection" and will henceforth be cited as AHC, Trieber Collection.

8. *Helena World.* AHC, Trieber Collection.

9. Powell Clayton (1833–1914) was born in Pennsylvania. He moved to Kansas in 1855, volunteered for the Union army in 1861, and eventually achieved the rank of general. He served in Missouri and Arkansas and was assigned the command of Pine Bluff after the capture of Little Rock in 1863. Remaining in Arkansas after the war, he became active in Republican Reconstruction politics. When the new Arkansas constitution was drawn up under the Congressional Plan of Reconstruction (1868), he campaigned for its adoption and was elected governor of Arkansas. He subsequently became Republican boss of Arkansas, a position he held for the remainder of his active life. He was a member of the Republican National Committee nearly every year from 1872 until his death. In 1871, he was elected US senator. He was appointed ambassador to Mexico in 1899, and served in that position until 1905. H. A. Johnson and P. Malone, *Dictionary of American Biography* (1958), pt. 2, 187.

10. Official Proceedings of the Republican National Convention (1880), 161–62.

11. Ibid., 162–63.

12. On December 28, 1926, the *Arkansas Gazette* (AHC Trieber Collection) reported an interview with then Judge Trieber, noting that the only two pictures in his chambers were those of Grant and Theodore Roosevelt. It quoted an earlier story about Grant and his supporters:

> Meanwhile, sat the grim old soldier in his home about whose head the political storm raged—stern, unperturbed, the man who had molded

> Lincoln's broken armies into a thunderbolt to launch against the South and with whose flags the eagles finally rode to victory. His Old Guard at Chicago like the Old Guard at Waterloo, was prepared to die, but not to surrender.

13. Congress ended the coinage of silver and put the country on the gold standard in 1873. This demonetization of silver became known as the "Crime of 1873." Liberal inflationists, those who wanted the value of money to decrease, took up the cry to restore free coinage of silver at the ratio of sixteen to one (sixteen times as much silver in a silver dollar as gold in a gold dollar). They saw the coinage of silver as a means of getting cheaper money, raising crop prices, and securing debtor relief. Those of the conservative, gold standard persuasion wanted to preserve the gold standard in the hopes of maintaining the value of the dollar. J. Blum, E. Morgan, W. Rose, A. Schlesinger Jr., K. Stampp, and C. Vann Woodward, *The National Experience: A History of the United States,* 3rd ed. (1973), 468–70.

14. The Force Bill, sponsored by Senator Lodge of Massachusetts, would have kept federal troops in the southern states to ensure the fairness of the ballot and to make sure that blacks were permitted to vote. The Osceola paper of October 27, 1892, in discussing the debate in that city, reported that McCulloch:

> With gifted eloquence . . . showed up the iniquity of the tariff, and with sledge hammer blows . . . struck the force bill. His tribute to the soldiers who wore the blue and the gray brought a ringing response from the audience, and many an old soldier's eye was dimmed with tears over the picture presented.

15. *Forrest City Times*, November 6, 1892. AHC, Trieber Collection.
16. *Helena World*, March 11, 1896. AHC, Trieber Collection.
17. *Helena World*, June 12, 1895. AHC, Trieber Collection.
18. Unidentified newspaper article. AHC, Trieber Collection.
19. *Helena World*, April 17, 1897, 1. AHC, Trieber Collection.
20. Unidentified newspaper article. AHC, Trieber Collection.
21. *Helena World*, March 23, 1898. AHC, Trieber Collection.
22. It was not uncommon, at that time, for United States district attorneys to take an active role in party affairs.
23. Jacob Trieber wrote to Clayton on a regular basis. On November 1, 1899, he wrote:

> Now as to the state of affairs here, I shall write more fully, than I did before, so that you may understand the situation fully. Ever since you went to Mexico, I have considered it the solemn duty of every man, who claims to be a friend of yours, to see to it that your interests are as fully protected, as if you were here in person, and that you had a right to expect from your friends, that the harmony which prevailed when you left, should be fully maintained.

Letter from Jacob Trieber to Powell Clayton, November 1, 1899.

In another letter, he wrote that "[Republicans] must pursue a more aggressive policy in state politics. This policy of apology for [the Democrats'] charges of abuse keeps us on the defensive continually and that is not good politics." Letter from Jacob

Trieber to Powell Clayton, October 7, 1898. (Copies of all letters are on file with the Arkansas History Commission.)

24. *Arkansas Gazette*, August 24, 1898. AHC, Trieber Collection.

25. Unidentified newspaper article. AHC, Trieber Collection.

26. *Arkansas Gazette*, August 29, 1898. AHC, Trieber Collection.

27. Ibid.

28. Ibid.

29. Ibid.

30. Ibid.

31. Ibid.

32. Ibid.

33. Letter from Jacob Trieber to Major Charles Gordon Newman, Pine Bluff, Arkansas, November 2, 1898.

34. Speech given at Memorial Day Exercises at National Cemetery, Little Rock (quoted in unidentified newspaper article). AHC, Trieber Collection.

35. *Arkansas Gazette*, July 8, 1900. AHC, Trieber Collection.

36. On July 10, 1900, Jacob Trieber wrote to Powell Clayton stating that he would abide by Clayton's desires in the matter of the appointment. Nevertheless, he gently prodded Clayton: "The unanimity of the sentiment in my favor, among the Republicans, and the members of the bar I cannot help but appreciate. Your friendship for me in the past and my fidelity to you, makes me confident of your support." Letter from Jacob Trieber to Powell Clayton, July 10, 1900.

In 1890, Jacob Trieber had made an unsuccessful attempt to secure an appointment as the federal judge for the Eastern District of Arkansas when H. C. Caldwell was elevated from that position to the United States Court of Appeals for the Eighth Circuit. Prior to his appointment as district judge, Caldwell had served as a general in the Union army and was regarded by many Democrats as a carpetbagger. Many of Trieber's supporters wrote endorsement letters to President Benjamin Harrison, including Judge M. C. Sanders, J. H. Carr, L. P. Featherstone, J. Donohoo, and the Helena Bar Association.

37. Letter from Jacob Trieber to Hon. Charles F. Amider, United States District Judge, Fargo, North Dakota, July 11, 1900.

38. The Democrats included Governor Dan W. Jones and United States senators James K. Jones and William H. Berry. On July 9, he received the following telegram from J. C. Cage Rembert: "If your democratic friends of Phillips County who have known you since boyhood can be of any service to you call on us without hesitation." Telegram from J. C. Cage Rembert to Jacob Trieber, July 9, 1900.

39. *Arkansas Gazette*, July 14, 1900. AHC, Trieber Collection.

40. Letter from H. L. Remmel to Jacob Trieber, July 21, 1900.

41. Jacob Trieber resigned from the Republican State Committee on August 2, 1900. His correspondence, however, indicates that he continued to advise the Republican leadership for the next few years.

42. Letter from Remmel to Trieber, February 23, 1903.

43. *Helena World*, July 19, 1900 (quoting *Arkansas Gazette*, July 17, 1900). AHC, Trieber Collection.

44. Letter from L. C. Stephenson to Jacob Trieber, August 2, 1900.

45. Jacob Trieber made three unsuccessful efforts to secure appointment to that

court. The first came in 1905 when Judge Amos M. Thayer died. Within two weeks, the Arkansas Bar, the "colored" Republicans of Arkansas, and the press, Democratic and Republican alike, recommended to President Roosevelt that Jacob Trieber be appointed. On April 28, the Democrat-controlled state senate unanimously adopted a resolution: "We recognize in Jacob Trieber one of the foremost citizens of our state, an honest, upright, fearless and capable judge, an eminent and learned lawyer and a judge well qualified to fill the vacancy." *Helena World*, April 29, 1905. AHC, Trieber Collection. The Arkansas General Assembly followed suit. The press reported the endorsement "is a compliment few republicans have ever received in the south." *Arkansas Gazette*, May 5, 1905. AHC, Trieber Collection.

The "colored" Republicans of Arkansas met and adopted a resolution recommending Trieber for:

> his soundness and patriotism in enforcing the amendments to one Constitution of the United States designed to protect all American citizens as illustrated by his able and comprehensive decisions, and charges respecting white-capping and peonage by means of which those crying evils are already well-suppressed in the State of Arkansas.

Resolution of the "colored Republicans of Arkansas" (May 1, 1905). They also wrote to Booker T. Washington, requesting him to use his influence on Roosevelt.

Judge Trieber's second effort to obtain an appointment to the court of appeals was made in 1910, when Judge Willis Van Devanter of the Eighth Circuit was elevated to the United States Supreme Court, and the third attempt occurred in 1912, when Eighth Circuit judge William C. Hook of Kansas died. The results were the same: political and geographical considerations combined to deny the appointment to Judge Trieber. In 1910, Judge Trieber also sought an appointment to the newly created court of commerce.

46. Through his work on the Eighth Circuit, Trieber won widespread respect within the court. Judge Kimbrough Stone referred to Trieber as "one of the very ablest, fairest and most learned judges I have ever known." Letter from Kimbrough Stone to Mrs. Jacob Trieber, September 19, 1927. Judge Walter H. Sanborn "esteem[ed] him very highly." Letter from Walter H. Sanborn to Ida Trieber, September 8, 1927. Judge William Kenyon wrote to Trieber, stating that the most pleasing experience of his brief judicial life had been the acquaintance he formed with Trieber. Letter from William Kenyon to Jacob Trieber, July 24, 1923. Judge Charles B. Faris, a district court judge for the Eastern District of Missouri, commented that "[t]here was not among all the judges of the 8th Circuit any man who was his par in legal knowledge and ability." Letter from Charles B. Faris to Ida Trieber, September 19, 1927.

47. See, e.g., Trieber, "Injunctions and the Judiciary," *New York Independent*; Trieber, "The Jurisdiction of Federal Courts in Actions in Which Corporations are Parties," *Report of the Proceedings of the Bar Association, Arkansas* 8 (1905) 35; Trieber, "Legal Status of Negroes in Arkansas Before the Civil War," *Arkansas Historical Association* 3 (1911): 175; Trieber, "The New Judicial Code," *Report of the Proceedings of the Bar Association, Arkansas* 15 (1912): 103; "The Relationship of the State and National Courts," *Proceedings of the Bar Association, Arkansas* 11 (1908): 86; Trieber, "A Review of the Act of Congress of February 13, 1925, Defining the Jurisdiction of the Circuit Courts of Appeals and of the Supreme Court," *Report of the Proceedings of the Bar Association, Arkansas* 28 (1925): 101; Trieber, "The Rights and Liabilities of Banks

at Law," *Arkansas Banker* 11 (1927): pt. 1, 5, *Arkansas Banker* 11 (1927): pt. 2, 21; Trieber, "Shall Statutes in Derogation of the Common Law Be Strictly Construed?," *Arkansas State Bar Association* (1889): 13.

48. On February 22, 1912, Judge Trieber wrote to Theodore Roosevelt, who was then governor of New York, and commented on Roosevelt's idea that when the Supreme Court of the United States declared an act unconstitutional, the people should have a right to vote on the issue. He gave his suggestions on implementations:

> But in order to obtain such a result now, if the decision holds that a statute is in conflict with the Constitution of the United States, the most important change to be made in that instrument is to simplify the manner of amending it, which, at the present time, is practically impossible. In my opinion, the Constitution ought to be amended by providing that a majority of all members elected to each house of Congress be sufficient for the submission thereof to the people; it should then be submitted to the vote of the people in each state at the time Presidential electors are chosen, and if at such election a number of states constituting a majority of the electoral colleges votes in favor of such an amendment it should be declared adopted, or, if it is feared that such a vote might lead to too many changes in the Constitution, and result in hasty or ill considered action, there might be added a provision requiring in addition to a majority of the electoral college a majority of the states.
>
> If such an amendment is adopted then the people will have an opportunity to make such changes in the Constitution as the changed conditions of our vast country and the great progress of our times may require.

Letter from Jacob Trieber to Theodore Roosevelt, February 22, 1912.

49. See, e.g., *Jenkinson v. First National Bank of Sheldon*, 295 F. 778 (8th Cir. 1924); *In re Weedman Stave Co.*, 199 F. 948 (E.D. Ark. 1912) (federal bankruptcy law supercedes state insolvency law); *Gould v. New York Life Ins. Co.*, 132 F. 927 (E.D. Ark. 1904); *In re Stone*, 116 F. 35 (E.D. Ark. 1902), *aff'd*, 120 F. 733 (8th Cir. 1903); *In re Meriwether*, 107 F. 102 (W. D. Ark. 1901).

50. See, e.g., *Vezina v. United States*, 284 F. 695 (8th Cir. 1922); *Chase v. United States*, 272 F. 684 (8th Cir. 1921); *United States v. Whitmire*, 236 F. 474 (8th Cir. 1916); *Taylor v. United States*, 230 F. 580 (8th Cir. 1916); *Conway v. United States*, 149 F. 261 (D. Neb. 1907).

51. See, e.g., *Murray v. United States*, 284 F. 573 (8th Cir. 1922); *Feeley v. United States*, 236 F. 903 (8th Cir. 1916); *Ammerman v. United States*, 216 F. 326 (8th Cir. 1914).

52. See, e.g., *McCourtney v. United States*, 291 F. 497 (8th Cir. 1923), *cert. denied*, 263 U.S. 714 (1923) (court can hold defendant guilty of contempt for violating injunction even if defendant was not a striker, if defendant aided strikers to violate injunction with full knowledge of injunction); *Silverstein v. Local No. 280*, 284 F. 833 (8th Cir. 1923) (garment workers' strike not an intentional interference with interstate commerce); *United Mine Workers of America v. Coronado Coal Co.*, 258 F. 829 (8th Cir. 1919), *rev'd*, 259 U.S. 344 (1922) (Trieber, writing for the Eighth Circuit, held that defendant miners' organization and its members had violated the Sherman Act by destroying mining companies' property. The Supreme Court reversed, holding that there is no violation of the Sherman Act where intent to injure, obstruct, or restrain interstate commerce did not appear as an obvious consequence of what was done);

Kroger Grocery & Baking Co. v. Retail Clerks' International Protective Ass'n., 250 F. 890 (E.D. Mo. 1918) (strike which would result in the closing of retail grocery stores and loss of perishable foodstuffs, and which involved threatening and insulting customers, held violation of Clayton Act § 20 and Food Conservation Act); *Huttig Sash & Door Co. v. Fuelle*, 143 F. 363 (E.D. Mo. 1906) (violation of injunction forbidding secondary boycott subjected both parties to the injunction and non-party aiders and assistors to punishment for contempt).

53. The Ku Klux Klan was officially disbanded in 1869, and was not officially reorganized until 1915. W. Randel, *The Ku Klux Klan: A Century of Infamy* (1974), i–x. Shortly after the Civil War, Governor Powell Clayton instituted martial law and hired black militia at a cost of over $330,000 to hunt down the Klan. Johnson and Malone, *Dictionary of American Biography*, vol. 2, pt. 2, 187. Although Clayton claimed to have eradicated the Klan, it continued to thrive under the name "whitecappers."

54. *Arkansas Gazette*, October 21, 1892. AHC, Trieber Collection.

55. *Helena World*, February 23, 1898. AHC, Trieber Collection.

56. *Arkansas Gazette*, October 7, 1903. AHC, Trieber Collection.

57. Letter from Jacob Trieber to Colonel H. L. Remmel, by then President of the Board of Trade of Arkansas (1901).

58. *Memphis Commercial Appeal*, September 19, 1901. AHC, Trieber Collection.

59. Letter from Jacob Trieber to W. A. Webber (June 12, 1901).

60. *Helena World*, April 6, 1897. AHC, Trieber Collection.

61. *Osceola Press*, October 27, 1892. AHC, Trieber Collection.

62. *Arkansas Democrat*, September 20, 1925. AHC, Trieber Collection.

63. Ibid.

64. *Arkansas Gazette*, March 17, 1904. AHC, Trieber Collection.

65. The whitecappers were indicted under Rev. Stat. § 5508, *reprinted* in 3 *U.S. Comp. St.* § 5508 (1901) (currently codified as revised at 18 *U.S.C.* § 241 (1985)) for conspiring to prevent blacks from exercising the right to contract, a right secured by 42 *U.S.C.* § 1981 (formerly Revised Statutes § 1977, derived from section 1 of the Civil Rights Act of 1866). For a detailed history of 18 *U.S.C.* § 241, *see United States v. Williams*, 341 U.S. 70, 72–82 (1951).

66. Enforcement Act of May 31, 1870, ch. 114, 16 Stat. 140 (codified as revised at 18 *U.S.C.* § 241 (1985)).

67. *United States v. Morris* 125 F. 322 (E.D. Ark. 1903).

68. The only published district court decision of *Hodges* and *Morris* is reported at *United States v. Morris* 125 F. 322 (E.D. Ark. 1903), which is Judge Trieber's denial of demurrers to the indictments in both *Hodges* and *Morris*.

69. *Helena World*, February 23, 1898. AHC, Trieber Collection.

70. *Arkansas Gazette*, March 18, 1904. AHC, Trieber Collection.

71. See Heaney, "Busing, Timetables, Goals and Ratios: Touchstones of Equal Opportunity," *Minnesota Law Review* 69 (1985): 735, 753 n. 116.

72. Civil Rights Cases, 109 U.S. 3, 19 (1883); *United States v. Cruikshank*, 92 U.S. 542 (1875).

73. Civil Rights Cases, 109 U.S. at 20–23.

74. *Arkansas Gazette*, October 7, 1903. AHC, Trieber Collection.

75. 125 F. 322 (E.D. Ark. 1903).

76. Ibid. at 330–31.

77. *Arkansas Gazette*, May 29, 1906. AHC, Trieber Collection. Four white men were ultimately convicted before the federal district court at Texarkana under the same law as the *Hodges* defendants. Judge John H. Rogers sentenced the men to one year's imprisonment in Fort Leavenworth. Because these convictions were based on the civil rights law declared unconstitutional in *Hodges*, the convictions were likely vacated after the Supreme Court's *Hodges* decision was announced.

78. *Arkansas Gazette*, March 18, 1904. AHC, Trieber Collection.

79. Ibid.

80. Ibid.

81. *Helena World*, March 21, 1904. AHC, Trieber Collection.

82. *Helena World*, March 18, 1904. AHC, Trieber Collection. Interestingly, on the same page of this paper is a short editorial: "The race question would be as well left alone. It has been settled a number of years in the South where the negroes are and it doesn't seem that it would be of much concern to people in other sections."

83. Judge Trieber's letter apparently refers to Judge Jones's jury charge in *Ex parte Riggins*, 134 F. 404 (N.D. Ala. 1904) *rev'd*, 199 U.S. 547 (1905). In *Riggins*, a gang of armed whites had taken a black man from a county jail "and murdered [him] by hanging him from the neck until he was dead." 134 F. at 405. Riggins and his codefendant brought a petition for a writ of habeas corpus, alleging that the black victim had no right, under federal constitutional or statutory law, to be free from "lawless violence at the hands of white men." 134 F. at 406. Judge Jones, relying in part on Judge Trieber's opinion in the *Morris* case, held that:

> as the purpose of the [reconstruction era–civil rights] legislation . . . was to secure and protect the former slave race from the aggressions of the master race, it is quite clear that the right to be free from attacks by members of one race, designed and intended to prevent the other race from enjoying the civil rights which go to make up that freedom, is a right, privilege or immunity "accorded by, or arising under, or dependent upon the Constitution," and that such right may be protected by Congress.

134 F. at 408.

The Supreme Court vacated this opinion and ordered the writ quashed on procedural grounds. *Riggins v. United States*, 199 U.S. 547 (1905). During the same term, the Supreme Court decided *Hodges*. See notes 78–81 and accompanying text. Riggins and his codefendant, Powell, then sought to quash the indictment on the authority of *Hodges*. Judge Jones reluctantly agreed. He stated: "Since [*Ex parte Riggins* was decided], the Supreme Court has decided the *Hodges* case . . . which held, in effect, contrary [to substantial precedent], that the rights and immunities claimed here under the Thirteenth Amendment were not secured under the Constitution or laws." *United States v. Powell*, 151 F. 650 (N.D. Ala. 1907), *aff'd*, 212 U.S. 564 (1909). The question presented in *Powell* was whether *Hodges* similarly barred the United States from prosecuting Riggins and Powell under authority of the Fourteenth Amendment. Judge Jones, in a lengthy and well-reasoned opinion, stated that, in his view, it should not:

> [I]t is urged that the fourteenth amendment could not have intended to permit Congress to deal with lawless private individuals. . . . [P]rior to the great War, . . . in that era of our constitutional history, which the Supreme Court itself describes as "historical and of another age," . . . the general

> government had no concern in the execution of our state laws, however necessary their enforcement to enjoyment of the fundamental rights of the citizen to life, liberty, or property. . . .
>
> The conditions brought about by war, demanded additional safeguards for these rights. . . . Race and sectional feeling, state action, and private lawlessness, operating alike in some form in every part of the Union, might hamper or prevent the enjoyment of these rights, and it was not deemed wise to leave their safeguarding wholly to the states. . . .
>
> The framers of the [fourteenth] amendment, and the people who adopted it, were not building upon the old system, but laying on new foundations a different system for the enjoyment of due process. . . . The [fourteenth] amendment conferred a new power for a benevolent purpose. We ought not to shrivel the power by treating it as a mere penal enactment against faithless state officers.

151 F. at 661.

In spite of his personal view, he held that, in light of the Supreme Court's *Hodges* opinion, the defendant must be released:

> A deep sense of the judicial subordination which all inferior tribunals owe to the Supreme Court compels this court, in view of the circumstances of this case, not to run counter to these last utterances of the Supreme Court, though, strictly speaking, they "went beyond the case . . . It must therefore take the Hodges Case as a binding authority that no right, privilege, or immunity in respect of due process, at any stage in the duty of affording it, arises under the fourteenth amendment, unless there be denial of the right by the state or its officers, and that no immunity whatever is secured under the Constitution or laws, in a case like this, against lawlessness of private individuals which frustrates the state's efforts to perform its constitutional duty, although thereby all enjoyment of the benefits of due process be prevented.
>
> Let an order be entered sustaining the demurrer to the indictment and each count thereof, and that the defendant go hence without [his] day [in court].

151 F. at 663–64.

The Supreme Court affirmed on the authority of *Hodges. Powell v. United States*, 212 U.S. 564 (1909).

84. Letter from Jacob Trieber to Thomas G. Jones, 1904.

85. *Hodges v. United States*, 203 U.S. 1 (1906), overruled, *Jones v. Alfred H. Mayer Co.*, 392 U.S. 409, 443 n. 78 (1968).

86. Ark. Stat. Ann. §§ 578–93 (1904).

87. See Heaney, "Busing, Timetables, Goals and Ratios: Touchstones of Equal Opportunity," *Minnesota Law Review* 69 (1985): 760.

88. Mary Frances Berry, *Black Resistance, White Law: A History of Constitutional Racism in America,* (1971), 128–55, see also Penguin Books, revised edition (February 1, 1995).

89. See A. Goldberg, *The Ku Klux Klan in Colorado* (1981), vii; W. Randel, *The Ku Klux Klan,* x.

90. Berry, *Black Resistance, White Law,* 128.

91. *Jones v. Alfred H. Mayer Co.*, 392 U.S. 409 (1968) (Title 42 U.S.C. § 1982, analogous to section 1 of the Civil Rights Act of 1866, barred all racial discrimination, private and public, in the sale or rental of property, and Congress had the authority under the Thirteenth Amendment to enforce the statute).

92. *United States v. Morris,* 125 F. 322 (E.D. Ark. 1903).

93. See Heaney, "Busing, Timetables, Goals and Ratios: Touchstones of Equal Opportunity," *Minnesota Law Review* 69 (1985): 757 nn. 123–24.

94. See note 14 above.

95. *Helena World,* October 9, 1892. AHC, Trieber Collection.

96. Sidney Crawford, "Arkansas Suffrage Qualifications," *Arkansas Historical Quarterly* 2 (1943): 331, 336–37.

97. Ibid.

98. *Knight v. Shelton,* 134 F. 423 (E.D. Ark. 1905) (reprinted in full in *Arkansas Gazette,* January 8, 1905). AHC, Trieber Collection.

99. Two prior opinions suggest that there is no federal jurisdiction in such a case. *See Luther v. Borden,* 48 U.S. I, 54 (1849) (Woodbury, J., concurring in part, dissenting in part); *Smith v. Goode,* 34 F. 204, 208 (D.R.I. 1888).

100. *Knight,* 134 F. at 425–26, 440–41.

101. Ibid. at 438.

102. Crawford, "Arkansas Suffrage Qualifications," *Arkansas Historical Quarterly* 2 (1943): 336–37.

103. The Twenty-Fourth Amendment to the United States Constitution, adopted in 1964, outlawed the poll tax as a requirement for eligibility to vote in any election for president, vice president, or United States senator or representative. See *Harper v. Virginia Board of Elections,* 383 U.S. 663 (1966); *Harman v. Forssenius,* 380 U.S. 528 (1965).

104. *Peonage Cases,* 136 F. 707 (E.D. Ark. 1905).

105. Ibid. at 707. Although the peonage system was widespread throughout the South, there was little attempt to use the federal anti-peonage laws to end this system, in part because it was well accepted and because convictions on peonage charges were hard to obtain. P. Daniel, *The Shadow of Slavery: Peonage in the South* (1972), 19–20. When a Florida jury found a defendant not guilty of peonage, Judge William B. Sheppard of the United States District Court for the Northern District of Florida stated that he believed the defendant was guilty despite the jury's verdict. Daniel, *The Shadow of Slavery,* 33–34. Even when the rare guilty verdict was secured, the Supreme Court reversed on procedural grounds. See *Clyatt v. United States,* 197 U.S. 207 (1905).

106. Unidentified newspaper article on "Elaine Riots." AHC, Trieber Collection.

107. *Peonage Cases,* 136 F. at 709.

108. Ibid.

109. 197 U.S. 207 (1905).

110. Ibid. at 218–22.

111. See, e.g., Rogers, "The Elaine Race Riots of 1919," *Arkansas Historical Quarterly* 19 (1960): 142; Waterman and Overton, "The Aftermath of *Moore v. Dempsey,*" *Arkansas Law Review* 6 (Winter 1951–52): 1; Wise, "The Elaine Massacre," *Southern Exposure* 1, no. 3–4 (Winter 1974): 9.

112. *Arkansas Gazette,* October 2, 1919. AHC, Trieber Collection.

113. Rogers, "The Elaine Race Riots of 1919," 143.

114. Waterman and Overton, "The Aftermath of *Moore v. Dempsey*," *Arkansas Law Review* 6 (Winter 1951–52): 1–2.

115. Ibid., 2–4.

116. Waterman and Overton, "The Aftermath of *Moore v. Dempsey*," *Arkansas Law Review* 6 (Winter 1951–52): 4.

117. 261 U.S. 86 (1923).

118. Ibid. at 91.

119. During this period of time, Judge Trieber also authored an article on the "Legal Status of Negroes in Arkansas Before the Civil War," *Arkansas Historical Association* 3 (1911): 175–83.

120. *Arkansas Gazette*, September 17, 1919. AHC, Trieber Collection.

121. Ibid.

122. *Arkansas Gazette*, September 2, 1919. AHC, Trieber Collection.

123. *Arkansas Gazette*, July 17, 1900. AHC, Trieber Collection.

124. *Helena World*. AHC, Trieber Collection.

125. Act of March 4, 1913, ch. 145, 37 Stat. 828, 847.

126. *Times*, May 29, 1914. AHC, Trieber Collection. It is interesting to note that the passenger pigeon, a migratory bird, became extinct in about 1914 because of wholesale slaughter. *Webster's New World Dictionary*, 2nd College ed. (1972), 1038.

127. *United States v. Shauver*, 214 F. 154, 160 (E.D. Ark. 1914).

128. For other cases in which federal district court judges held federal statutes unconstitutional, see *Howard v. Illinois Cen. R. Co.*, 148 F. 997 (W.D. Tenn. 1907) (Judge John E. McCall held the Federal Employers' Liability Act unconstitutional); *Brooks v. Southern Pac. Co.*, 148 F. 986 (W.D. Ky. 1906) (Judge Walter Evans held the Federal Employers' Liability Act unconstitutional). The Supreme Court upheld these two cases in the Employers Liability Cases, 207 U.S. 463 (1908).

129. *Shauver*, 214 F. at 156.

130. Ibid. at 157–59.

131. Ibid. at 156–57.

132. Ibid. at 160.

133. Ibid. at 160–61.

134. Ibid. at 161.

135. Ibid. at 160.

136. Kansas City Star, June 8, 1914. AHC, Trieber Collection.

137. Ibid.

138. *Republican* (Springfield, Missouri). AHC, Trieber Collection.

139. Unidentified newspaper article. AHC, Trieber Collection.

140. Convention between the United States of America and the United Kingdom of Great Britain and Ireland for the protection of migratory birds in the United States and Canada, August 16, 1916, United States–Great Britain, 39 Stat. 1702.

141. Act of August 16, 1916, ch. 128, 40 Stat. 755, *U.S. Comp. St.* 1918, at 1795.

142. *United States v. Shauver*, 248 U.S. 594–95 (1919).

143. *United States v. Thompson*, 258 F. 257–58 (E.D. Ark. 1919).

144. Ibid. at 268.

145. Ibid.

146. Later, both Judge A. S. Van Valkenburgh, in the Western District of

Missouri, and Judge J. C. Hutcheson Jr., of the Southern District of Texas, also sustained this second migratory bird act. See Bulletin of the American Game Protection Association (July 1919).

147. See, e.g., *United States v. United Shoe Machinery Co.*, 247 U.S. 32, 61–63 (1918).

148. Kramer, "The Supreme Court and Tying Arrangements: Antitrust as History," *Minnesota Law Review* 69 (1985): 1013, 1022; see *United States v. United Shoe Machinery Co.*, 222 F. 349 (D. Mass. 1915) *aff'd*, 247 U.S. 32 (1918).

149. Sherman Act, ch. 647, § 1, 26 Stat. 209 (1890) (current version at 15 U.S.C. § 1 (1982). This act provided that: "[e]very contract, combination in the form of trust or otherwise, or conspiracy, in restraint of trade or commerce among the several States, or with foreign nations is [hereby] declared to be illegal." (Language omitted from the United States Code appears in brackets.)

150. 224 U.S. 1 (1912), *overruled, Motion Picture Patent Co. v. Universal Film Manufacturing Co.*, 243 U.S. 502 (1917).

151. Kramer, "The Supreme Court and Tying Arrangements: Antitrust as History," *Minnesota Law Review* 69 (1985): 1019. "The 1912 National Platform of the Democratic Party stated: 'We regret that the Sherman Anti-Trust Law has received a judicial construction depriving it of much of its efficiency, and we favor the enactment of legislation which will restore to the statute the strength of which it has been deprived by such interpretations.'"

152. Clayton Act, ch. 323. § 3, 38 Stat. 731 (1914) (current version at 15 U.S.C. § 14 (1982)). This section states:

> It shall be unlawful for any person engaged in commerce, in the course of such commerce, to lease or make a sale or contract for sale of goods, wares, merchandise, machinery, supplies or other commodities, whether patented or unpatented, for use, consumption or resale within the United States . . . or fix a price charged therefore, or discount from or rebate upon, such price, on the condition agreement or understanding that the lessee or purchaser thereof shall not use or deal in the goods, wares, merchandise, machinery, supplies, or other commodities of a competitor or competitors of the lessor or seller, where the effect of such lease, sale, or contract for sale or such condition, agreement, or understanding may be to substantially lessen competition or tend to create a monopoly in any line of commerce.

153. Kramer, "The Supreme Court and Tying Arrangements: Antitrust as History," *Minnesota Law Review* 69 (1985): 1021.

154. *United States v. United Shoe Machinery Co.*, 222 F. 349 (D. Mass. 1915), *aff'd*, 247 U.S. 32 (1918).

155. *United States v. United Shoe Machinery Co.*, 247 U.S. 32 (1918). Justices Brandeis and McReynolds disqualified themselves. "Justice Brandeis not only had been counsel for the defendant, he subsequently had opposed the defendant's practices and worked toward the passage of the Clayton Act." Kramer, "The Supreme Court and Tying Arrangements: Antitrust as History," *Minnesota Law Review* 69 (1985): 1027 n. 70 and accompanying text. Justice McReynolds had served as President Wilson's attorney general during part of the case's pendency. Ibid. Justice Day, one of the three

dissenting justices, wrote for the majority when, four years later, the Supreme Court found the tying clauses violative of the Clayton Act. See notes 170–71, and accompanying text.

156. *United States v. United Shoe Machinery Co.*, 227 F. 507 (E.D. Mo. 1915), *rev'd*, 232 F. 1023 (8th Cir. 1916), *appeal dismissed*, 254 U.S. 666 (1921).

157. 227 F. at 511.

158. *United States v. United Shoe Machinery Co.*, 232 F. 1023 (8th Cir. 1916), *appeal dismissed*, 254 U.S. 666 (1921).

159. United Shoe filed an affidavit of prejudice against Judge Dyer, who subsequently disqualified himself.

160. Additionally, the law in this area was unsettled and in need of attention. Although the Supreme Court had held in 1912 that, under the Sherman Act, a tying arrangement could be incorporated as a condition of sale of a patented article, *Henry v. A. B. Dick Co.*, 224 U.S. 1, in 1917 it overruled this decision. *Motion Picture Patent Co. v. Universal Film Manufacturing Co.*, 243 U.S. 502 (1917). One year later, the Court held that the Sherman Act did not apply to United Shoe's tying arrangements because they involved leases rather than sales. *United States v. United Shoe Machinery Co.*, 247 U.S. 32 (1918). Thus, tying arrangements were enforceable under the Sherman Act when they were incorporated into a lease, but not when they were a condition of sale.

The efficacy of the Clayton Act was also still unsettled. In *Motion Picture Patent Co.*, the district court and the United States Court of Appeals for the Second Circuit found violations of the Clayton Act, but the Supreme Court did not reach that issue in affirming the decision.

161. *United States v. United Shoe Machinery Co.*, 234 F. 127, 143 (E.D. Mo. 1916) (on motion to dismiss).

162. Ibid. at 143–44.

163. Although Chief Justice Marshall suggested in 1824 that Congress's powers under the commerce clause were very broad, see *Gibbons v. Ogden*, 22 U.S. (9 Wheat) 1, 86–87 (1824), the Supreme Court in Trieber's day generally took a more restrictive approach to Congress's commerce power. See, e.g., *Hammer v. Dagenhart*, 247 U.S. 251 (1918); *United States v. E. C. Knight Co.*, 156 U.S. 1 (1895); L. Tribe, *American Constitutional Law*, 234–35 (1978). In 1937, the Supreme Court initiated its more liberal view in *N.L.R.B. v. Jones & Laughlin Steel Corp.*, 301 U.S. 1 (1937).

164. *United Shoe*, 234 F. at 145.

165. *United States v. United Shoe Machinery Co.*, 264 F. 138, 148 (E.D. Mo. 1920) (trial on merits) *aff'd*, 258 U.S. 451 (1922).

166. Ibid. at 154.

167. *United Shoe*, 234 F. at 148–49.

168. *United Shoe*, 264 F. at 175.

169. Ibid at 170.

170. *United States v. United Shoe Machinery Co.*, 258 U.S. 451, 465 (1923).

171. Ibid at 454–55.

172. *Arkansas Gazette*, August 29, 1898. AHC, Trieber Collection.

173. Ibid.

174. Ibid.

175. Ibid.

176. *Chicago R.I. & P. Ry Co. v. Ludwig*, 156 F. 152 (E.D. Ark. 1907), *aff'd*, 216 U.S. 146 (1910).

177. *In re Arkansas Railroad Rates*, 163 F. 141 (E.D. Ark. 1908).

178. *In re Arkansas Railroad Rates*, 168 F. 720, 722 (E.D. Ark. 1909).

179. Ibid. at 725, 733.

180. Ibid. at 735–37.

181. *In re Arkansas Rate Cases*, 187 F. 290 (E.D. Ark. 1911), *rev'd*, 230 U.S. 553 (1913).

182. *Allen v. St. Louis, Iron Mountain & S. Ry. Co.*, 230 U.S. 553 (1913). Ironically, Judge Trieber had requested the parties to agree to the appointment of a special master to supplement the data and make further calculation, but the parties would not agree. 187 F. at 294.

183. *Boyle v. St. Louis & S.F.R. Co.*, 222 F. 539 (E.D. Ark. 1915), *aff'd*, 244 U.S. 106 (1917). Perhaps the most significant thing about these cases was that Judge Trieber was willing to set the rates himself rather than to remand to the state rate-making board to establish a new rate. Perhaps he felt that the question of rail rates in Arkansas was so political that no fair rate could be set.

184. *Rowland v. Boyle*, 244 U.S. 106, 108 (1917).

185. 222 F. 562 (E.D. Ark. 1915), *rev'd*, 233 F. 235 (8th Cir. 1916).

186. 222 F. 569. The Eighth Circuit reversed on the grounds that although the double assessment was unlawful, the suit had to be brought before an Arkansas Commission set up to adjust property evaluations in the state to a common standard. See *Boyle v. St. Louis & S.F.R. Co.*, 222 F. 539 (E.D. Ark. 1915), *aff'd*, 244 U.S. 106 (1917).

187. 264 F. 127 (E.D. Ark. 1919).

188. Ibid. at 133.

189. *Great Northern Ry. v. Minnesota*, 238 U.S. 340, 345 (1915).

190. *Hines*, 264 F. at 134.

191. *St. Louis Post Dispatch*, June 12, 1912. AHC, Trieber Collection.

192. *New York Times*, March 8, 1923. AHC, Trieber Collection.

193. 151 F. 522 (E.D. Ark. 1907).

194. Trieber, "The National Employers' Liability Act," *Report of the Proceedings of the Bar Association, Arkansas* 18 (1915): 51, 54. Similarly, Judge Trieber, in a letter to Edward H. Hibbard, wrote:

> The Employers' Liability Act passed by Congress is quite a step in advance, still it is only the first step towards protection of the workingman and those dependent upon him. . . . Still, we are marching onward, and many beneficient statutes have been enacted within the last decade which could not have been passed before, and as experience adds to our wisdom, more reform measures are enacted.

Letter from Jacob Trieber to Edward H. Hibbard, September 25, 1908.

195. Employers Liability Cases, 207 U.S. 463 (1908).

196. *Watson v. St. Louis, Iron Mountain & S. Ry. Co.*, 169 F. 942 (E.D. Ark. 1909), *aff'd*, 223 U.S. 745 (1912).

197. *St. Louis, Iron Mountain & S. Ry. Co. v. Watson*, 223 U.S. 745 (1912) (mem.) *aff'd* 169 F. 942 (E.D. Ark. 1909).

198. 189 F. 471 (E.D. Ark. 1911).

199. Ibid. at 479–80.

200. 232 F. 349 (8th Cir. 1916).

201. Ibid. at 352.

202. One article stated:

> He was a great force among the bankers for the enactment of a state banking law. He . . . worked long and patiently on the provisions of a banking law for Arkansas that would be fair and helpful to the state banks of just that period in the state's development—a law that would fit the needs of that time and yet not retard wise and conservative state progress. . . . It is also recalled that Judge Trieber wrote and had passed by the Arkansas Legislature in 1901 or 1902, that part of the present banking law known as the law governing trust companies.

Arkansas Banker 11 (1927): 22.

203. See, e.g., Trieber, "The Rights and Liabilities of Banks at Law," *Arkansas Banker* 11 (1927): pt. 1, 5, *Arkansas Banker* 11 (1927): pt. 2, 21. (Based on a speech given by Trieber at the Eighth Annual Convention of the Arkansas Bankers Association, Little Rock, Arkansas, on April 21, 1898); Trieber, "The Jurisdiction of Federal Courts in Actions in which Corporations are Parties," *Report of the Proceedings of the Bar Association, Arkansas* 8 (1905): 35.

204. *United States v. Schlierholz*, 137 F. 616, 617 (E.D. Ark. 1905).

205. Letter from J. Marshall Trieber to the author, January 2, 1986.

206. See, e.g., *Vernon v. United States*, 146 F. 121, 123 (8th Cir. 1906) ("No matter how reprehensible the conduct of the defendant might have been, under the indictments there could be no conviction unless there was substantial evidence justifying a finding by the jury that he had offered, given or promised to [the federal officer] money for the purposes in the indictment set out. There is nothing in the statute under which he was indicted forbidding [the defendant] from persuading [the officer] to select the sites he recommended to the end that [the defendant] may receive a fee from the owners of the sites."); *United States v. Sandefuhr*, 145 F. 49 (E.D. Ark. 1906) (where statute prohibited the transportation of liquor in falsely labeled containers, no violation where defendant transported liquor in unlabeled containers); *United States v. Schlierholz*, 137 F. 616 (E.D. Ark. 1905) (defendant, although he was a special agent of the Land Department of the United States, was not an "officer of the United States" within the meaning of the statute in question, and, therefore, could not have violated the statute); *United States v. Ryan*, 123 F. 634, 636 (E.D. Ark. 1903) (where statute provided for punishment for using the mails to defraud, no violation where defendants wrote to one another "for the purpose of concocting schemes to defraud, but not for the purpose of carrying them into effect, nor were they written to be used as a part of the fraudulent scheme").

207. Unidentified newspaper article. AHC, Trieber Collection.

208. *Arkansas Democrat*, September 20, 1925. AHC, Trieber Collection.

209. Ibid.

210. Letter from Jacob Trieber to F. F. Kitchens, May 19, 1902.

211. Letter from Jacob Trieber to Marshall Ford, October 23, 1902.

212. Letter from Jacob Trieber to H. M. Jacoway, January 3, 1912.

213. *Arkansas Democrat*, September 27, 1925. AHC, Trieber Collection.

214. Ibid.

215. Trieber, Letter to the Editor, *Arkansas Bar Association Journal* 12 (1926): 424.

216. In a letter to his wife, Judge Trieber said, "We did a lot of work yesterday, but there is lots more. . . . There are 6 more whiskey cases, in which the parties demand a trial. . . . It is possible we may not finish tomorrow, but I'll try very

hard. . . . In court everything moves smoothly, and the lawyers don't waste time any more than I do." Undated letter from Jacob Trieber to Ida Trieber.

217. *Arkansas Democrat*, October 1926. AHC, Trieber Collection.

218. *Jonesboro Daily Tribune*, 1924. AHC, Trieber Collection.

219. Letter from J. Marshall Trieber to the author, July 9, 1985.

220. *Arkansas Democrat*, September 20, 1925. AHC, Trieber Collection.

221. *Jonesboro Daily Tribune*, September 9, 1925 (quoting *New York Times* editorial). AHC, Trieber Collection.

222. Letter from Augustus N. Hand to Jacob Trieber, September 19, 1925.

223. Letter from Emory R. Buckner to Jacob Trieber, September 16, 1925.

224. Letter from W. H. Taft to Jacob Trieber, November 20, 1925.

225. Letter from Augustus N. Hand to Jacob Trieber, April 29, 1927.

226. Unidentified newspaper article, September 19, 1927. AHC, Trieber Collection.

227. Unidentified newspaper article. AHC, Trieber Collection.

228. Unidentified newspaper article. AHC, Trieber Collection.

7. John Ellis Martineau (1928–37)

1. Fay Williams, *Arkansans of the Years*, 4 vol. (Little Rock: C. C Allard & Associates, 1951–), II: 213–16. Joseph Taylor Robinson later served as congressman, governor, and United States senator.

2. Ibid., 216.

3. Ibid., 209–10.

4. Ibid., 210.

5. Charles L. Steel, "Renaissance of a River: Part II," *Arkansas: Colony and State,* ed. Leland DuVall (Little Rock, 1973), 239.

6. Williams, *Arkansans of the Years*, II: 218, 210–11; I, 342.

7. *St. Louis-San Francisco Ry. Co., Missouri Pacific R. Co. and Chicago, R.I. and R. Ry, v. Board of Directors of St. Francis Levee District*, 2F. Supp. 38 (E.D. Ark. 1932), *rev'd*, 74 F. 2d 183 (8th Cir. 1934).

8. *Missouri Pacific R. Co. v. Norwood*, 13 F. Supp. 24 (W.D. Ark. 1932). Hal L. Norwood was attorney general of Arkansas.

9. *Williamson v. Chicago Mill and Lumber Co., et al.*, 51 F. 2d 918 (E.D. Ark. 1931), *modified* 59 F. 2d 918 (8th Cir. 1932).

10. *Okla.-Ark. Telephone Co. v. Southwestern Bell Telephone Co.*, 33 F.2d 770 (W.D. Ark. 1929), *aff'd*, 45 F. 2d 995 (8th Cir. 1930), *cert. denied*, 283 U.S. 822 (1931).

11. Williams, *Arkansans of the Years*, II: 219, 209; Leon C. Miller and Carl H. Moneyhon, "John Ellis Martineau (1873–1937)," the *Encyclopedia of Arkansas History and Culture,* www.encyclopediaofarkansas.net (Accessed August 29, 2015).

8. Thomas Clark Trimble III (1937–57)

1. *History of the Federal Judiciary*. http://www.fjc.gov. Website of the Federal Judicial Center, Washington, DC (Accessed April 1, 2015).

2. Fay Williams, comp., *Arkansans of the Years* (Little Rock: C. C. Allard & Associates, 1951), I: 387.

3. Ibid.

4. The firm consisted of Thomas Clark Trimble Sr., who had a distinguished legal career, and Joe T. Robinson, who later served as congressman, governor, and United States senator.

5. *Dixie Greyhound Lines v. McCarroll*, 22 F. Supp. 985 (E. D. Ark. 1938).

6. *Dixie Greyhound Lines v. McCarroll*, 101 F. 2nd 572 (8th Cir. 1939).

7. *McCarroll v. Dixie Greyhound Lines*, 309 U.S. 176 (1940).

8. *Hoxie School District No. 46 v. Brewer*, 135 F. Supp. 296 (E.D. Ark. 1955).

9. See *Brown v. Board of Education of Topeka*, 349 U.S. 294 *Brewer v. Hoxie School District* (1955).

10. 238 F. 2nd 91 (8th Cir. 1956).

11. *United States v. Baker*, Docket Number 13062 (E.D. Ark. 1939).

12. Williams, *Arkansans*, 390.

13. *Baker v. United States*, 115 F. 2nd 533 (8th Cir. 1940).

14. Williams, *Arkansans*, 390.

15. Ibid.

16. *United States v. Wakelin*, no docket number (E.D. Ark.); the trial took place in October 1938.

17. Williams, *Arkansans*, 392.

18. Ibid.

19. Ibid., 391–92.

20. Ibid., 391.

21. *Arkansas Democrat*, July 8, 1965.

9. Gordon Elmo Young (1959–69)

1. *Brown v. Board of Education*, 347 U.S. 483 (1954).

2. *History of the Federal Judiciary*. http://www.fjc.gov. Website of the Federal Judicial Center, Washington, DC (Accessed April 1, 2015). *Arkansas Gazette*, September 26, 1959.

3. *Gideon v. Wainwright*, 372 U.S. 335, 83 S. Ct. 792, 9 L.Ed. 2nd 799 (1963).

4. *Winters v. Beck*, 281 F. Supp. 793 (E.D. Ark. 1968).

5. *Rogers v. Board of Education*, 281 F. Supp. 39 (E.D. Ark. 1968).

6. Ibid., 40. Article I, Section II, Arkansas Athletic Association Bylaws.

7. *Jackson v. Bishop*, 268 F. Supp. 804 (E.D. Ark. 1967).

8. *Park v. Faubus*, 238 F. Supp. 62 (E.D. Ark. 1965).

9. The legislature divided the state into four districts with population as follows:

District 1	360,183
District 2	517,860
District 3	332,844
District 4	575,385
Total Population	1,786, 272

10. *Yancy v. Faubus*, 238 F. Supp. 290 (E.D Ark. 1965).

11. *Newsweek*, July 25, 1960.

10. William Story (1871–74)

1. Family Births and Marriages S Waukesha County Wisconsin Genealogy http://linkstothepast.com/waukesha/marS.html (Accessed March 28, 2007); William Story, letter, August 21, 1871, Western District Folder 2, Source-Chronological Files, 1871–84, General Records, Letters Received, 1849–1903, General Records of the Department of Justice, Record Group 60, National Archives Building, Washington, DC. Citations of records from the National Archives will hereafter conclude by giving branch, record group number, and institution such as Justice/RG60/NAB. Source-Chronological Files will be cited as Source-Chron. Justice/RG60/NAB.

2. Roster of Wisconsin Volunteers, War of the Rebellion, 1861–1865, http://www.wisconsinhistory.org/roster/search.asp (Accessed March 28, 2007); Union-Wisconsin Infantry (Part 3) http://www.civilwararchive.com/unreghst/unwiinf3.htm#39thinf (Accessed March 28, 2007).

3. *Waukesha Weekly Freeman*, July 21, 1921, in *Wisconsin Necrology*, vol. 19, p. 69, State Historical Society of Wisconsin, 816 State Street, Madison, WI 53706; *30 Federal Cases Circuit and District Courts 1789–1880*, Biographical Notes, "William Story," 1395–96, hereafter cited as *30 Federal Cases* with page numbers; *Portrait and Biographical Record of the State of Colorado. Containing Portraits and Biographies of many well known Citizens of the Past and Present* (Chicago: Chapman Publishing Co., 1899), 141, Colorado Historical Society, hereafter cited as *Portrait and Biographical Record* with page number.

4. *Portrait and Biographical Record*, 141; William Story, letter, August 21, 1871, Folder 2, Source-Chron. Justice/RG60/NAB; *Little Rock Weekly Arkansas Gazette*, April 30, 1867; *30 Federal Cases*, 1395–96.

5. *Louisville Ledger* as reported in *Little Rock Arkansas Gazette*, April 22, 1871.

6. *Little Rock Morning Republican*, April 14, 1869.

7. *Portrait and Biographical Record*, 141; Story, August 21, 1871, W. D. Folder 2, Source-Chron. Justice/RG 60/NAB; 30 *Federal Cases*, 1395–96; *Little Rock Weekly Arkansas Gazette*, January 1, April 30, 1867; *Little Rock Daily Arkansas Gazette*, July 29, 1868; William Story, Judge, to Logan H. Roots, December 23, 1868, Gen. m/f File: Roots, Letters of Logan Roots, 1840–1887, Arkansas History Commission, Little Rock, Arkansas; William B. Jones, Arkansas Judiciary—Arkansas Courts Historical Background, http://courts.state.ar.us/courts/history2.html (Accessed March 28, 2007).

8. *Forrest City Free Press*, October 22, 1870; *Little Rock Morning Republican*, September 12, 19, 1870, and October 13, 1870.

9. 1870 Arkansas Congressional Map, see Kenneth C. Martis, *The Historical Atlas of United States Congressional Districts 1789–1983* (New York: Free Press, 1982), 103, for boundaries of the Arkansas districts for the Forty-First Congress.

10. *Little Rock Arkansas Gazette*, October 25, 1870.

11. Erwin Surrency, *History of the Federal Courts* (New York: Oceana 1987), 287.

12. U.S. *House Journal*, 1869–1871, 41st Cong., 3rd Sess., February 28, 1871, p. 433; *Cong. Globe*, 41st Cong., 3rd Sess., p. 1135 (1871); U.S. Congress, *Senate Exec. Journal*, 41st Cong., 3rd Sess., March 3, 1871, p. 683; Application of William Story for U.S. District Judge Western District of Arkansas endorsed by B. F. Rice, A. McDonald, Logan H. Roots, "To the President of the United States," March 3, 1871, Arkansas 1873–1877 Story W., Appointment Files of Judicial Districts 1853–1905, Records Relating to Appointments and Other Actions for Positions in Federal Courts

and Judicial Districts, General Records Justice/RG60/NAB; John H. Decherd to Col. E. T. Golladay, May 3, 1872, H. R. 42A-F14.10–F14.13, Legislative House/RG 233/NAB; *Fort Smith Herald*, March 11, 1871; Story, August 21, 1871, Western District Folder 2, Source-Chron. Justice/RG/NAB; "Oath of William Story, April 4, 1871," Western District Folder 1 Source-Chron. Justice/RG60/NAB; *30 Federal Cases*, 1395–96.

13. *Little Rock Arkansas Gazette*, May 19, 1871, first reported in the *Fort Smith Herald*, May 11, 1871; U.S. House 1875, "Western Judicial District of Arkansas," February 23, 1875, 43rd Cong., 2nd Session, Executive Document No. 175, p. 20.

14. 1851 Map, 9 Stat. 594 (1851).

15. In 1871 the US Army abandoned facilities at Fort Smith, which the court moved into the next year after a fire in the court's rented building. Fort Smith National Historic Site—Federal Court History, http://www.nps.gov/archive/fosm/history/court/ (Accessed March 27, 2007); House, "WDA," Report 626, p. 145.

16. 1871 Map, 16 Stat. 471 (1871).

17. William Gillette, *Retreat from Reconstruction, 1869–1879* (Baton Rouge: Louisiana State University Press, 1979), 16–22 and ch. 2; 16 Stat. 140 (1870); 16 Stat. 433 (1871); for more on the use of the Enforcement Acts in Arkansas, see Everette Swinney, "*United States v. Powell Clayton*: Use of the Federal Enforcement Acts in Arkansas," *Arkansas Historical Quarterly* 26, no. 2 (Summer 1967): 143–54.

18. Henry C. Caldwell, Judge, to Attorney General George H. Williams, July 3, 1873, Folder 5, Source-Chron. Justice/RG60/NAB; House "WJDA" No. 175, p. 20.

19. *Little Rock Morning Republican*, January 1, 1872.

20. Logan H. Roots, US Marshal, to Lyman Trumbull, Chairman Judiciary Committee, May 13, 1872, and May 16, 1872, Papers re. Nominations, Britton, William A., Sen. 42 B-A6, 42nd Cong., General Records, Senate/RG46/NAB.

21. *Little Rock Arkansas Gazette*, October 29, 1871; *Van Buren Press*, November 7, 1871, as reported in *Little Rock Arkansas Gazette*, November 12, 1871.

22. Roots to Trumbull, May 13, 1872, Nominations Britton, Sen 42B-A6, Senate/RG46/NAB.

23. Stanley Kutler, *Judicial Power and Reconstruction Politics* (Chicago: University of Chicago Press, 1968), 61, 62, 149.

24. William Story, Judge, to George H. Williams, Attorney General, March 9, 1872, Folder 3, Source-Chron. Justice/RG60/NAB; William Story, May 16, 1872, Papers re. Nominations, Britton, William A., Sen. 42B-A6, 42nd Cong., General Records, Senate/RG46/NAB.

25. Map for Western Judiciary District of Arkansas: Existing and Proposed 1872, associated with HR 2204, A Bill Establishing a United States District Court in the Papers of the House Judiciary Committee (HR39A-F 13.12); 39th Congress: Records of the U.S. House of Representatives, Record Group 233, National Archives; Roots to Trumbull, May 13, 1872, Nominations, Britton, William A., Sen. 42B-A6, Senate/RG46/NAB; Story, May 16, 1872, Nominations, Britton, William A., Sen., 42B-A6, Senate/RG46/NAB.

26. *Little Rock Arkansas Gazette*, June 25, 1872; *St. Louis Republican* as reported in the *Little Rock Arkansas Gazette*, July 26, 1872; U.S. House 1874, "Western District of Arkansas, Report," June 1, 1874, 43rd Cong., 1st Sess., Report No. 626, pp. 1, 251, hereafter cited as House, "WDA," Report No. 626 with page number.

27. House, "WDA," Report No. 626, p. 1.

28. William A. Britton to George H. Williams, Attorney General, November 25, 1872, Folder 5, Source-Chron. Justice/RG60/NAB.

29. U.S. House 1874 "Affairs in Arkansas, Report," May 30, 1874, 43rd Cong., 1st Sess., Report 771; U.S. House 1874 "Affairs in Arkansas, Report by Mr. Poland," December 8, 1874, 43rd Cong., 2nd Sess., Report 2.

30. N. J. Temple, U.S. Attorney to George H. Williams, U.S. Attorney General, May (no day) 1873, Folder 3, Source-Chron. Justice/RG60/NAB.

31. House, "WJDA," No. 175, p. 3.

32. *Little Rock Arkansas Gazette*, May 17, 1871, as first reported in *Fort Smith Herald*, May 11, 1871.

33. *Little Rock Arkansas Gazette*, May 19, 1871.

34. Family Births and Marriages O Waukesha County Wisconsin Genealogy, http://www.linkstothepast.com/waukesha/marO.html (Accessed March 27, 2007).

35. House, "WDA," Report No. 626, pp. 157, 229, 232, 237; U.S. House, 1874, "Investigation of Charges Against Judge Story," House Judiciary Committee, April 6, 1874–June 4, 1874, 43rd Cong., 1st Sess., p. 200, Heiskell Collection, University of Arkansas at Little Rock Center for Arkansas History and Culture, Arkansas Studies Institute, hereafter referred to as "Investigation of Charges against Judge Story" with page number.

36. See, for example, *Fort Smith Western Independent*, May 22, 1873, for the death sentence of John Childers.

37. Logan H. Roots, U.S. Marshal, to George H. Williams, Attorney General, May 22, 1872, Western District Folder 5, Source-Chron. Justice/RG60/NAB.

38. House, "WDA," Report No. 626, pp. 250, 255.

39. "Investigation of Charges Against Judge Story," 89, 91, 106; House, "WDA," Report No. 626, pp. v, vi, vii, 114–17, 223, 241.

40. House, "WDA," Report No. 626, pp. 43, 46.

41. House, "WDA," Report No. 626, pp. 256–57; House, "WJDA," No. 175, pp. 3, 4.

42. *Tahlequah Cherokee Advocate*, October 14, 1871.

43. "Investigation of Charges Against Judge Story," 65, 199; James S. Robinson and Newton J. Temple, United States District Attorney, to George H. Williams, Attorney General of the United States, June 5, 1873, Folder 3, Source-Chron. Justice/RG60/NAB.

44. "Investigations of Charges Against Judge Story," 10, 11, 35, 50, 51, 55, 112; House, "WDA," Report No. 626, pp. 10–11, 39, 113–14.

45. "Investigation of Charges Against Judge Story," 27, 28, 196.

46. *Little Rock Republican* as reported in *Little Rock Arkansas Gazette*, July 29, 1873.

47. *Van Buren Press* as reported in *Little Rock Arkansas Gazette*, August 1, 1873, and May 8, 1874.

48. House, "WDA," Report No. 626, pp. 228, 254.

49. L. B. Whitney to Hon. A. J. Falls, December 10, 1872, Folder 1, Source-Chron. Justice/RG60/NAB; L. B. Whitney to Mr. A. J. Falls, August 10, 1873, and August 30, 1873, Folder 5, Source-Chron. Justice/RG60/NAB.

50. *Van Buren Press* as reported in *Little Rock Arkansas Gazette*, August 1, 1873, and May 8, 1874.

51. Surrency, *History of the Federal Courts*, 293–94.

52. Committee of the Bar, W. M. Fishback, Granville Wilcox, Ben T. Duval, Jesse Turner, to U.S. Attorney General, August 8, 1873, accompanied by request for investigation from the Bar of the Western District of Arkansas, August 5, 1873, Folder 5, Source-Chron. Justice/RG60/NAB.

53. Benjamin T. DuVal, Special Assistant U.S. Attorney Western District of Arkansas to Hon. George H. Williams, U.S. Attorney General, Report on Investigation of the Western District, January 15, 1875, Folder 1, Source-Chron. Justice/RG60/NAB.

54. Goddard-Reagan Family, descendants of John Roofe MacArthur, 5.6 Florence ("Flossie") Blanche MacArthur, http://www.bigballoonmusic.com/goddard reagan/MacArthurGenealogy.htm (Accessed March 27, 2007); for more on the Story court, see Jeffrey Burton, *Indian Territory and the United States, 1866–1906* (Norman: University of Oklahoma Press, 1995); Jason Brockman, "Biography of Frederick W. Pitkin," The Governor Frederick W. Pitkin Collection at the Colorado Archives, http://colorado.gov/dpa/doit/archives/govs/pitkin.html (Accessed March 27, 2007); *Durango Democrat,* July 20, 1901; "Judge William Story—'His Story'" Marvin Gregory, *Ouray County Plaindealer and Herald*, March 11, 1976, p. 7, courtesy Ouray County Historical Society. This source will hereafter be cited as "Judge William Story—'His Story.'"

55. Doris Gregory, *History of Ouray* (Ouray, CO: Cascade Publishing, 1995), I: 55, 56, 100, 342, 343, and II: 158, courtesy Ouray County Historical Society. This source will hereafter be cited as *History of Ouray* with volume and page numbers. "Judge William Story—'His Story'"; Colorado State Archives, Lieutenant Governors, http://www.colorado.gov/dpa/doit/archives/offic/ltgov.html#Story (Accessed March 27, 2007); *30 Federal Cases*, 1395–96.

56. See, for example, Letter, "Dear Sir," signed Wm, January 22, 1890, Box 1 Folder 1 and Letter, "Dear Sir," William Story to Cooper Anderson, November 3, 1902, Box 22 Folder 28 Western Colorado Power Company Collection M002, Series 2.1 Center of Southwest Studies—Fort Lewis College, Durango, Colorado, http://swcenter.fortlewis.edu/inventory/WCPC.htm#WPCPRG2 (Accessed March 27, 2007); www.loc.gov/rr/news/topics/cassidy.html (Accessed July 27, 2015).

57. Gregory, *History of Ouray,* 1: 16, 38; "Hon. Wm. Story Died Los Angeles Monday," June 23, 1921, *Ouray Herald*, courtesy Ouray County Historical Society.

58. *Tahlequah Cherokee Advocate*, October 17, 1874, as first published in the *Denver Democrat*, September 26, 1874.

59. *Denver News*, October 26, 1890, Special Collections, Mullins Library, University of Arkansas Fayetteville; *Denver Rocky Mountain News*, October 26, 1890, Stephen H. Hart Library, Colorado Historical Society.

60. *Denver Colorado Graphic*, Saturday, November 1, 1890, Stephen H. Hart Library, Colorado Historical Society.

61. Telegram, William Story to Clerk U.S. District Court, October 4, 1890, "Investigation of Charges Against Judge Story," np.

62. Letter, anonymous, undated, Lucien Nunn Papers, #37-04-1770, Series III, Telluride Power Company and the Power Industry TPC: Correspondence and Related

Documents; Story, William, Box 4 Folder 13, Division of Rare and Manuscript Collections, Cornell University Library.

63. *Portrait and Biographical Record*, 141.

64. *Fort Smith Times Record*, June 21, 1921; *Waukesha Weekly Freeman*, July 21, 1921, in *Wisconsin Necrology*, vol. 19, p. 69; "Hon. Wm. Story Died Los Angeles Monday," June 23, 1921, *Ouray Herald*, courtesy Ouray County Historical Society. Story and his wife are buried in San Gabriel Cemetery, Los Angeles County. William Story Sr. (1843–1921) www.findagrave.com (Accessed November 28, 2009).

11. Isaac Charles Parker (1875–96)

1. The first book to appear, S. W. Harman, *Hell on the Border: He Hanged Eighty-Eight Men* (Fort Smith, AR: Phoenix Publ. Co., 1898), was published two years after Judge Parker died. Harman was a frequent juror in Parker's court and the owner of a hotel. The financial backing for the book was provided by J. Warren Reed, a prominent defense attorney in Fort Smith who took many of the appeals from the Western District to the Supreme Court in the early 1890s. The book also lists C. P. Sterns as "compiler." The book, well over 400 pages, contains biographical sketches of court personnel and some attorneys, lists of capital defendants with further dispositions of their cases, and a considerable number of chapters that are devoted to the crimes and criminals that made up the capital case prosecutions. Although the book contains many inaccuracies, all the subsequent biographies rely on it to a great extent. The books by Fred Harvey Harrington and Glenn Shirley, both of which are cited below, clear up many of the inaccuracies, but they also concentrate entirely on the criminal episodes in Indian Territory.

2. Act, March 1, 1895, 28 *Statutes at Large* 693. Section 9 of the act specified that the court at Fort Smith would lose its jurisdiction over Indian Territory on September 1, 1896. For a thorough examination of the history of this act, see J. Burton, *Indian Territory and the United States, 1866–1906* (Norman: University of Oklahoma Press, 1995), 202–36.

3. See J. O. Murphy, "The Work of Judge Parker in the United States District Court for the Western District of Arkansas—1875 to 1896" (unpublished master's thesis, University of Oklahoma, 1939).

4. See Burton, *Indian Territory and the United States*, 52–61, for the details of the investigations into Story's behavior.

5. Joseph Burnham Kinsman of Maine was Grant's first choice for the Fort Smith vacancy, and the president nominated him on March 10, 1875. 20 *Journal of the Executive Proceedings of the Senate*, 20: 19. Kinsman's nomination was referred to the Judiciary Committee, which reported back favorably on March 16, the same day Parker was nominated to be chief justice of the supreme court of the Territory of Utah, to replace J. B. McKean. Ibid., at 31, 32. On March 18, the president withdrew Kinsman's nomination and nominated Parker for the Western District judgeship; at the same time, Parker's nomination to the Utah post was withdrawn and David P. Lowe (who had been nominated the previous day to be commissioner of pensions) was nominated for Utah. Ibid., at 40. On the next day, March 19, the Judiciary Committee reported favorably on Parker and the Senate immediately confirmed him. Ibid., at 45. What possibly transpired is the following:

> Before the appointment [to Utah] could be confirmed, however, Parker wrote the President a letter. Utah was all right with him, but it was far away. Furthermore, the job would be only temporary. As soon as Utah became a state, territorial officers would cease to function. On the other hand, there was a vacancy at Fort Smith, closer to Parker's home. He had lived and served as judge in a region not unlike Arkansas, and he knew better the needs of the Indian country. He had done much for the Indians; look at his record in Congress in handling Indian affairs.

G. Shirley, *Law West of Fort Smith* (New York: Henry Holt & Co., 1957), 29.

6. Shirley, *Law West of Fort Smith*, 30.

7. Ibid., 35–40. Also see F. H. Harrington, *Hanging Judge* (Caldwell, ID: Caxton Printers, Ltd., 1951), 30–47; M. M. Stolberg, "Politician, Populist, Reformer: A Reexamination of 'Hanging Judge' Isaac C. Parker," *Arkansas Historical Quarterly* 47 (1988): 3, 10–13.

8. W. Luce, "'Hanging Judge' a Soft-hearted Man," *Tulsa World*, October 16, 1932 (Sunday Magazine, 5).

9. Ibid. The article goes on to say that the next day Hardin called on the judge to argue that Sizemore should not be in jail exposed to the evil influences of men like Henry Starr and Cherokee Bill, and would be better off associating with the high-class boys composing the Fort Smith baseball club. Sizemore was released. This event would have been around 1895.

10. *Fort Smith Elevator*, September 18, 1896, 1.

11. 14 *Statutes at Large* 769. If an ex-slave took citizenship in the tribe he was due an allotment of land; not all freedmen took advantage of this offer. The freedman could elect to take a $100 government payment in lieu of tribal citizenship. Also, some free blacks had resided in the territory prior to the Civil War. The Choctaw Nation did not adopt its former slaves until nearly twenty years after the treaty.

12. At that time motion practice was virtually nonexistent in federal criminal procedure, and so the question of the court's jurisdiction was, at least in Parker's time, a jury question. See *United States v. Boyd*, 45 Fed. 851 (C.C. W.D. Ark. 1890). Parker charged the jury:

> The defendants are charged with the crime of murder, for having . . . taken the life of John Dansby, a negro, and not an Indian . . .

Dansby was living in the Choctaw Nation, and Parker instructed the jury that in order to be considered an Indian by adoption the evidence would have to show that "Dansby was registered as a citizen of that country; that he elected to become a citizen, and registered as such." Some of the evidence in the case indicated that Dansby had moved to Choctaw country after the Civil War and had done so after registering for a $100 payment under a statute providing for such payment to ex-slaves who elected to leave the country. Under those circumstances, said Parker, he would continue to be a citizen of the United States for purposes of jurisdiction in the Fort Smith court. Parker told the jury: "Now, you are to look into that question first, because that is a preliminary step to be taken by every jury in a case; to ascertain and pass upon the question as to whether or not the court has a right to try." Ibid., at 853.

13. By 1889, according to the *Report of Union Agencies*, 35, the Indian population of the territory was 65,800 and the non-Indian population 112,600.

14. Act, January 6, 1883, 22 *Statutes at Large* 400. That portion of the territory "north of the Canadian River and east of Texas and the one hundredth meridian not set apart and occupied by the Cherokee, Creek, and Seminole Indian tribes" was assigned to the District of Kansas (§ 2) and the remainder of the Indian Territory outside the Five Nations was assigned to the Northern District of Texas (§ 3). This geographical reduction did not matter too much in Fort Smith due to the fact that the court had dealt with very few cases from the territory beyond the boundaries of the five nations. The distances were just too great for the Western District court to deal with crime among the Plains Indians and other tribes settled in the territory after the Civil War. In 1889 Congress transferred some of the jurisdiction from the Northern District of Texas, at Graham, to the Eastern District of Texas, with a courthouse at Paris. The federal court at Paris also received some of Judge Parker's jurisdiction.

15. *United States v. Hudson and Goodwin*, 11 U.S. (7 Cranch) 32 (1812). The issue of whether the federal courts could try common law crimes was first raised in *United States v. Worrall*, 2 U.S. (2 Dall.) 384, 28 F.Cas. 774 (1798). There a federal grand jury indicted Worrall for attempting to bribe Tench Coxe, the federal commissioner of revenue, who had been authorized by Congress to build a lighthouse at Cape Hatteras. Worrall sought, by letter, to bribe Coxe to award Worrall the contract. Supreme Court justices Chase and Peters, sitting as a circuit court in Pennsylvania, divided on the issue, thus affirming the lower court conviction; that case did not reach the Supreme Court. In *Hudson and Goodwin*, the Court, in a brief opinion, held that the federal courts could not entertain a common law criminal jurisdiction in a libel case (the defendants were charged with publishing a libel in a Connecticut newspaper that the president and Congress had secretly voted a two-million-dollar payment to Napoleon Bonaparte in order to make a treaty with Spain).

16. *Report of the Attorney General of the United States*, 1883, 23. Attorney General Benjamin Harris Brewster repeated this request for reform in subsequent annual reports and his successor, Augustus H. Garland, also asked for the same reforms. One author says of the system of federal criminal law at the time: "Both the federal system of law and its administration in the Indian Territory were rotten at their roots." Burton, *Indian Territory and the United States*, 47.

17. Harrington, *Hanging Judge*, 115–16.

18. *Report of the Attorney General of the United States*, 1883, 27.

19. "The government of the United States sometimes put up rewards for criminals, as in cases of mail robbery and the murder of Federal employees. Deputies, however, could not share in these rewards, since they were already being paid by the United States to catch lawbreakers. There was much grumbling at this rule, and little wonder, for the rewards often totaled five hundred dollars, as against a ten- to fifty-dollar fee-and-mileage deal. (Deputy marshals could and did receive rewards offered by state and local governments, by railroad and express companies, and by private individuals.)" Harrington, *Hanging Judge*, 68.

20. After proposing a number of improvements, the attorney general noted: "In England and in most of the States, laws similar to the ones above suggested have been adopted, and after being in force for more than a quarter of a century are commended by the bench and the bar as valuable aids in securing a fair and impartial administration of justice."

21. See, generally, E. Surrency, *History of the Federal Courts* (New York:

Oceana Publications, 1987), 215, et seq.; M. M. Arkin, "Rethinking the Constitutional Right to a Criminal Appeal," *UCLA Law Review* 39 (1992): 503.

22. Act, March 3, 1879, 20 *Statutes at Large* 374. Earlier attempts to establish review of criminal convictions came to naught in 1854 and 1863. See *Report of the Attorney General of the United States*, 1885, p. 41.

23. Cong. Rec. H. 7636, August 16, 1888. In the Senate, George Vest (D. Missouri) was a vociferous and implacable foe of the court at Fort Smith and Judge Parker personally.

24. Act February 6, 1889, 25 *Statutes at Large* 655. Also see, Act, March 3, 1891, 26 *Statutes at Large* 826.

25. If one counts second and third appeals, a total of fifty death sentences were appealed from Parker's court between 1891 and 1896. Thirteen sentences were affirmed and thirty-seven reversed. Of the thirty-seven reversals, six were acquitted on retrial, four were quashed or nolle pros, ten were convicted or pleaded guilty to manslaughter, four were re-convicted and had their sentences commuted, two were executed after re-conviction, and eleven were either unrecorded or continued. Murphy, "The Work of Judge Parker in the United States District Court for the Western District of Arkansas—1875 to 1896" (unpublished master's thesis, University of Oklahoma, 1939), 55.

26. *United States v. Hudson*, 65 Fed. 68 (W.D. Ark. 1894). Parker filed a lengthy opinion to the effect that Justice White could not order bail because he was not, under the rules of the Supreme Court, a circuit or district judge, nor a justice allotted to the circuit.

27. *Hudson v. Parker*, 156 U.S. 277 (1895).

28. See Shirley, *Law West of Fort Smith*, 156.

29. For a close analysis of the Supreme Court decisions, see G. B. Dobbs, "Murder in the Supreme Court: Appeals from the Hanging Judge," *Arkansas Law Review* 29 (1975): 47. Also see W. H. Rehnquist, "Isaac Parker, Bill Sikes and the Rule of Law," *UALR Law Journal* 6 (1983): 485.

Self-defense was usually raised in cases where the accused was charged with murder for killing a deputy marshal or posse rider, the argument being that the law enforcement officers did not identify themselves and the defendant thought his life was in danger from armed strangers. Juries in Fort Smith would sometimes accept the argument and acquit, despite Judge Parker's instruction that a wanted criminal was in no position to invoke self-defense for shooting at those coming to arrest him.

One of Parker's cases spawned the famous Allen charge—sometimes called the dynamite charge—which urges jurors to reach a verdict in a case where the deliberations are stalled. *Allen v. United States*, 164 U.S. 492 (1896). This decision has been cited more than 1,700 times. See R. T. Dawson, "Judge Parker and the Allen Rule," *Fort Smith Historical Society Journal* 21 (1997): 5.

30. *Hickory v. United States*, 160 U.S 480 (1896); *Alberty v. United States*, 162 U.S. 499 (1896); *Starr v. United States*, 164 U.S. 627 (1897). An interesting recent case thoroughly exploring the use of biblical references at trial is *Carruthers v. State*, 2000 WL 257773 (Supreme Court of Georgia, March 6, 2000).

31. After the episode Judge Parker reportedly inquired about the gobbling and learned that it was an old Cherokee warrior custom.

32. The other prisoner was the colorful Henry Starr, a distant relation of Belle

Starr. Starr was a bright young man who had been convicted of killing Floyd Wilson, who was riding posse to a deputy marshal seeking to arrest Starr for jumping bond after an express office robbery. Starr's conviction was reversed by the Supreme Court; the Court held that Parker's jury instruction—that Starr's claim of self-defense required the jury assess whether the danger to Starr's life was brought about by his own wrongdoing—was erroneous. *Starr v. United States*, 153 U.S. 614 (1894). Starr was retried and again convicted and his conviction was reversed a second time, based on Parker's instruction that flight was evidence of guilt. *Starr v. United States*, 164 U.S. 627 (1897). His third trial, after Parker's death, netted him a fifteen-year sentence for robbery. Starr had a long string of bank robberies, including the bank in Bentonville, Arkansas, in 1893. While serving time after his third trial in the Western District he was pardoned by President Roosevelt, ostensibly for his bravery in getting Cherokee Bill to surrender (Starr later named his son Roosevelt). After his pardon, Starr was out of trouble until 1908; when Oklahoma achieved statehood, Starr was afraid that Arkansas would seek his extradition for the Bentonville bank robbery. He fled to Colorado and robbed a bank there. He was caught and incarcerated in Colorado. After his early release, Starr could still not resist banks—his stock remark upon entering a bank with guns drawn was "Hands up, and hands steady." He bragged that he had robbed more banks than any man in the United States and that he never shot anyone in the course of a bank holdup. He was again imprisoned in Oklahoma for an attempted double bank robbery in Stroud (two banks on the same day). Starr was foiled when he was shot by a young boy after the holdup. After serving a sentence, again shortened by early release and promises of leading a lawful life, Starr sold real estate in Tulsa, Oklahoma, and served as a consultant on a movie made about the Stroud robberies. Starr met his end in 1921 while attempting to hold up a bank in Harrison, Arkansas. The former bank president, W. J. Myers, had constructed the vault with a "bandit trap," a back door, and a loaded rifle stored therein. Myers happened to be in the bank when Starr and two companions entered with guns drawn and herded the people into the vault. Myers grabbed the gun and shot Starr, severing the bandit's spinal cord. Starr lingered three days before dying. *Arkansas Democrat*, February 19, 1921, 1 and 9. Also see C. W. Breihan and C. A. Rosamund, *The Bandit Belle* (Seattle: Superior Publ. Co., 1970), 95–100.

33. Harrington, *Hanging Judge*, 145.

34. Cherokee Bill's hanging was front-page news in Fort Smith and elsewhere. The *Fort Smith Elevator* published an extra edition, *Fort Smith Elevator Extra*, March 17, 1896, and a full, page-one account on March 20, 1896. In the very full news account the paper mentioned that Cherokee Bill spent his last days while awaiting the outcome of his appeals disposing of personal effects, most going to Henry Starr; Cherokee Bill accumulated some assets by hanging a blanket across the front of his cell, refusing to meet with visitors unless they made a cash payment. *Fort Smith Elevator*, March 20, 1896, 1.

35. Burton, *Indian Territory and the United States*, 230.

36. *Fort Smith Elevator*, September 5, 1879, 3.

37. M. D. Dubber, "Regulating the Tender Heart When the Axe Is Ready to Strike," *Buffalo Law Review* 41 (1993): 85, 154.

38. Not until 1897, after Judge Parker's death, did Congress provide for life imprisonment as an alternative in cases of murder or rape. Act, January 15, 1897,

29 *Statutes at Large* 487: "[I]n cases of murder or of rape . . . the jury may qualify their verdict by adding thereto 'without capital punishment;' and whenever the jury shall return a verdict qualified as aforesaid the person convicted shall be sentenced to imprisonment at hard labor for life." In capital cases Parker went to great lengths to fully instruct the jury on the meaning of such basic terms as willfulness, intent, malice aforethought, murder, manslaughter, mistake, accessory, etc. An example of his jury instruction is *United States v. Boyd*, 45 Fed. 851 (C.C. W.D. Ark. 1890), *rev'd*, 142 U.S. 450 (1892). He always believed in the soundness of the jury system, but stated publicly that the court has a duty to lead the jury. *Fort Smith Elevator*, September 18, 1896, 1.

39. R. H. Tuller, "'The Hanging Judge' and the Indians: Isaac C. Parker and U.S. Indian Policy, 1871–1896" (unpublished master's thesis, Texas Christian University, 1993), 43. Another case is described by Stolberg, "Politician, Populist, Reformer: A Reexamination of 'Hanging Judge' Isaac C. Parker," *Arkansas Historical Quarterly* 47 (1988): 21, where Parker wrote to President Arthur in 1881 seeking, and obtaining, clemency for Sequahnee, a full-blooded Sac and Fox Indian who was convicted of scalping and killing a white man in 1879.

40. *Annual Report of the Attorney General of the United States*, 1889, at xx. General Miller renewed his plea in 1891, *Annual Report*, at xxiii, and 1892, *Annual Report*, at xxii. Attorney General Richard Olney endorsed Miller's recommendation in 1893, *Annual Report*, 1893, at xxv. In 1896 Attorney General Judson Harmon stated:

> The increasing repugnance on the part of juries to inflict the death penalty, in connection with the fact that the law makes no degrees in murder, constantly leads to the entire acquittal of persons charged with capital crimes in cases where the facts proven not only warrant conviction for murder, but oblige the court to charge that they do not permit a conviction for mere manslaughter. This danger to society can be at least mitigated by the establishment by statute of different degrees of murder, with corresponding appropriate grades of punishment. Juries will not then be confronted with the alternative of a verdict of acquittal in cases where they think the accused guilty of murder but not deserving of the extreme punishment.

Annual Report, 1896, at xvii.

Congress finally acted in a major reform of federal criminal law in 1909, Act, March 4, 1909, ch. 321, §§ 273, 275, 330. The current law is at 18 U.S.C.A. § 1111. One irony in this history is the fact that the criminal codes of at least four of the five Civilized Tribes recognized degrees of murder in their own nations.

41. The entire interview with a reporter for the *St. Louis Republic*—reported on September 6, 1896, two months before Parker died—was reprinted in full in Fort Smith, *Fort Smith Elevator*, September 18, 1896, 1. Also see Shirley, *Law West of Fort Smith*, 146. The origin of the "flowers and jellies" language is probably an article—that appeared just prior to the first mass execution under Parker—in the *Western Independent*, September 1, 1875, 1. This Fort Smith newspaper reported extensively on Parker's first six executions held on September 3, 1875. In the September 1 article the paper reported on the religious instruction given to the six condemned killers and said:

> Much kindness and sympathy is manifested for the condemned. Many ladies visit the jail and furnish them an abundant supply of fruits, pastry

> and substantials. Bouquets of flowers adorn the cell windows, which the prisoners water with care, and they display sincere gratitude for the kind attentions of fair visitors whose pious exhortations have had a great influence in their reformation.

42. Judge Parker took great pride in the fact that in his entire tenure at Fort Smith only three lynchings had occurred in the vast jurisdiction of his court.

43. *Fort Smith Elevator*, September 18, 1896, 1.

44. See, for an example, the *Independent-True Democrat* (Fort Smith), June 27, 1883, 2. The newspaper reported the hanging of four would-be train robbers who killed a conductor near Mulberry, Arkansas. The execution was at Clarksville and attracted several thousand people: "The elevations about the scaffold, trees, house tops and cars, were literally covered with curious spectators." After 1881, federal hangings in Fort Smith were not open to the public, although many people attended with passes. Army personnel or deputy marshals were used to check admittance, and a stockade was built around the gallows to prevent public viewing of executions.

45. Luce, "'Hanging Judge' a Soft-hearted Man." Also see, Shirley, *Law West of Fort Smith*, 79: "On execution days he returned home and prayed. When he finished sentencing the first six men to the gallows, he bowed his head and wept."

46. Luce, "'Hanging Judge' a Soft-hearted Man." Court personnel frequently chided the judge for being "taken in" by fake widows who came to call at his house after a sentencing.

47. "In the 1880s Parker ran afoul of the attorney general when he ignored Justice Department mandates to send prisoners to facilities he disliked. He insisted on using prisons in Detroit, Michigan, and Chester, Illinois, because he said institutions closer to him in the West and South were run for profit rather 'than the good of the men sentenced.' In 1894 Attorney General Richard Olney chastised Parker for sending boys who were over the maximum age of sixteen to reformatories when they should have been going to prison. But Parker maintained he had done the right thing because most of the boys could be 'saved' with proper treatment. The following year, Parker complained to Attorney General Judson Harmon when three boys were not accepted by the reform school at Washington, D.C., because they were Indians." M. M. Stolberg, "The Evolution of Frontier Justice: The Case of Judge Isaac Parker," *Prologue* (Quarterly of the National Archives), 20, no. 1 (1988): 13–14. Also see Stolberg, "Politician, Populist, Reformer: A Reexamination of 'Hanging Judge' Isaac C. Parker," *Arkansas Historical Quarterly* 47 (1988): 22–23. Parker's prison sentences were usually short, one to three years, and he knew that someone sent to Detroit would come back literate and with some job skills. Harrington noted that the Detroit House of Correction had been run by the greatest warden of his day, Zebulon Brockway, and that one newspaper in Fort Smith, commenting on the fact that two Indian inmates, Buffalo Chips and White Bear had come back from Detroit, literate and with trades, wrote: "Moral—if you wish to become useful and high toned, steal something and pass one year at the model prison of the world, the House of Correction at Detroit, Michigan." Harrington, *Hanging Judge*, 98.

48. Luce, "'Hanging Judge' a Soft-hearted Man." Luce also states that Ed Hagin, former deputy clerk, said that this was only one of many instances of that kind.

49. *Annual Report of the Attorney-General of the United States*, 1885, 30.

50. While waiting for an appropriation for a new jail, Parker did as much as he

could to make the place more humane: "Lacking help from Washington, Parker did what he could alone. He checked bids for mattresses and blankets. He kept his eyes on food costs. (Fifty cents a day per prisoner would do the job, the Judge believed, if gouging contractors were eliminated.) Then, too, the Judge held down the jail population by dismissing minor cases and by letting many defendants out on bail." Harrington, *Hanging Judge*, 139.

51. 14 F.Cas. 353 (W.D. Ark. 1878).

52. Ibid., at 354.

53. Ibid.

54. Ibid., at 355.

55. *Oliphant v. Suquamish Indian Tribe*, 435 U.S. 191, 199 (1978). Rehnquist's reliance on the *Kenyon* case has been severely criticized; see R. W. Johnson and B. Martinis, "Chief Justice Rehnquist and the Indian Cases," *Public Land Law Review* 16 (1995): 10, 13. Also see, Note, "*Greywater v. Joshua* and Tribal Jurisdiction Over Nonmember Indians," *Iowa Law Review* 75 (1990): 685, 697–98. One of the difficult problems in Indian Territory was how to handle a crime committed in one nation against an Indian by an Indian of another nation. All of the nations had extradition treaties with each other, but the treaties were often ignored or evaded.

56. 20 F.Cas. 582 (W.D. Ark. 1879).

57. Ibid., at 585.

58. Ibid.

59. Ibid., at 585–86.

60. For example, in *Ex parte Kyle*, 67 Fed. 306 (W.D. Ark. 1895) Parker had to deal with a defendant who became a member of the Cherokee Nation by marriage. In 1894 he was indicted in a Cherokee court for larceny. After two hung juries, and about to face a third trial, Kyle filed a petition in the federal court in Indian Territory to be naturalized under an 1890 statute providing that "any member of any Indian Tribe or nation, residing in the Indian Territory, may apply to the United States court therein to become a citizen of the United States." After being naturalized, Kyle petitioned Parker's court for a writ of habeas corpus. Parker denied the writ on the ground that jurisdiction of the Indian court had vested prior to the naturalization and could not be divested; otherwise, reasoned Parker, "before the law can be vindicated, a party charged with a crime will swear himself away from their [Indian] courts by becoming a naturalized citizen of the United States."

61. 20 Fed. 298 (W.D. Ark., 1883).

62. Ibid., at 301.

63. Ibid., at 305–6.

64. B. W. Kidder, "Who Took the Trees? A Review of Timber Trespass Litigation in the Federal Court for the Western District of Arkansas Under the Administration of Judge Isaac C. Parker, 1875–1896" (unpublished master's thesis, University of Arkansas, 1996), 3–4.

65. Revised Statutes § 5388, 18 U.S.C.A. § 104.

66. 27 F.Cas. 742 (C.C. W.D. Ark. 1879).

67. Ibid., at 743.

68. Ibid., at 745.

69. Ibid., at 746.

70. *United States v. Payne*, 8 Fed. 883 (W.D. Ark. 1881).

71. 23 Fed. 658 (W.D. Ark. 1885).

72. 22 Stat. 400.

73. 23 Fed., at 666.

74. See Burton, *Indian Territory and the United States*, 171–237. The creation of Oklahoma Territory was by Act, May 2, 1890, 26 *Statutes at Large* 81. Many in Congress wanted to abrogate the Cherokee rights in the strip and add it to Oklahoma Territory, but the nation lobbied heavily to retain its lucrative property rights; in 1890 the government frustrated the Cherokee negotiations for the fifteen-year grazing lease that would have paid the nation $6.6 million, and in 1891, seeing the futility of resisting settlement of the Outlet, the Cherokees sold their interest to the United States for $8.6 million.

75. Burton, *Indian Territory and the United States*, 54–55.

76. In the first ten years of Parker's tenure—1875–1885—the records show 1,190 convictions for selling liquor in Indian country, 97 convictions for illegal distilling, and 124 convictions for violating internal revenue laws. Shirley, *Law West of Fort Smith*, 62.

77. *Fort Smith Elevator*, June 29, 1887, 5.

78. 51 Fed. 808 (W.D. Ark. 1892).

79. Ibid., at 809–10.

80. *Sarlls v. United States*, 152 U.S. 570, 572 (1894).

81. *Ex parte McClusky*, 40 Fed. 71 (C.C. W.D. Ark 1889) (larceny held to be an infamous crime); *Ex parte Brown*, 40 Fed. 81 (C.C. W.D. Ark 1889) (assault with intent to kill held to be an infamous crime; also aggravated assault, a misdemeanor, cannot be carved out of the greater crime).

82. *Ex Parte Farley & Wilson*, 40 Fed. 66 (C.C. W.D. Ark. 1889). Parker cited the language of David Culberson, chairman of the House Judiciary Committee, to the effect that the purpose of the Muskogee federal court was to try minor offenses and felonies were to remain in the jurisdiction of the federal courts in Texas, Kansas, and Arkansas. See Burton, *Indian Territory and the United States*, 138, for the history of the statute. These territorial courts operated from 1890 to 1895 when Congress terminated the jurisdiction of the federal courts in Arkansas, Kansas, and Texas and transferred the jurisdiction to federal courts in Oklahoma Territory. See note 2, above.

83. *In re Wolf*, 27 Fed. 606, 612 (W.D. Ark. 1886).

84. 26 F.Cas. 394 (W.D. Ark. 1881).

85. *Annual Report of the Attorney General of the United States*, 1894, at xx–xxi. Also see Harrington, *Hanging Judge*, 67–72.

86. See Harrington, *Hanging Judge*, 79–90.

87. *Annual Report of the Attorney General of the United States*, 1894, at xxii. Earlier, in 1878, a similar situation was noted:

> After a session of only five days this important court was necessitated for want of funds, to continue all criminal business till the next (February) term. This is for various and obvious reasons a serious misfortune to the district. Having occurred before, it is becoming decidedly monotonous, and strenuous efforts should be made to prevent its repetition. As the criminal docket was very large, a considerable number of witnesses and prisoners on bond were in attendance, many of whom came hundreds of miles from the different nations of the Indian Territory.

Fort Smith Elevator, November 15, 1878, 3.

88. *Annual Report of the Attorney General of the United States*, 1889, at 260.

89. Ibid. Marshal Yoes continues to explain that Judge Parker was determined to clear the docket, and "[n]ot a witness was kept a moment longer than actually necessary . . . Thus the accumulated work of nine months was disposed of in less than half that time. My disbursements for witnesses since July 1, to date, amounts to $64,113.55." Ibid. This situation was not unusual. In 1879 the newspaper reported in mid-term that "there are so many of them [witnesses] that there is scarcely any perceptible diminution. About 225 have been paid off. Court convenes at half past eight in the morning and at half past one in the afternoon, and the sessions are frequently prolonged till after candle light. Deputy marshals, frequently dispatched with attachments for witnesses, and still occasionally arriving with new prisoners. This is an almost continuous court the whole time." *Fort Smith Elevator*, November 21, 1879, 3.

90. Harrington, *Hanging Judge*, 129.

91. *Fort Smith Elevator*, May 8, 1896, 2. The *Elevator* called the Nowata piece an unvarnished lie.

92. See Shirley, *Law West of Fort Smith*, 71.

93. *Fort Smith Elevator*, May 8, 1896, 3.

94. H. Starr, *Thrilling Events: Life of Henry Starr* (Tulsa: R. D. Gordon, 1914), 32. This rare fifty-page autobiography was written by Starr while he was serving time in the Colorado State Penitentiary in 1913. It was printed in Tulsa, Oklahoma, and sold for fifty cents.

95. Shirley, *Law West of Fort Smith*, 73. Shirley reports that when the verdict of not guilty was announced, a roar of applause filled the courtroom and men threw their hats in the air. Judge Parker supposedly said, "Justice is justice—not chivalry!" and then ordered all those who had participated in the outburst fined for contempt.

96. *Annual Report of the Attorney General of the United States*, 1875–1896. The statistical tables in these reports show that the number of civil cases in the Western District of Arkansas in which the United States was a party totaled 609 for the period and the number of private civil cases totaled 853. Civil disputes between Indians and non-Indians arising in the territory fell into a jurisdictional limbo most of the time; the tribal courts shunned those cases and the Western District court only had jurisdiction over crimes in the territory, and jurisdiction based on diversity of citizenship did not apply.

97. 6 F.Cas. 313 (C.C. W.D. Ark. 1876).

98. Ibid., at 314.

99. Ibid., at 316.

100. *Pickett v. McGavick*, 19 F.Cas. 588 (W.D. Ark. 1876).

101. 14 F.Cas. 639 (C.C. W.D. Ark. 1876).

102. Ibid., at 640. Often Parker could not suggest an alternative to achieve justice. In *Bland v. Fleeman*, 29 Fed. 669 (W.D. Ark. 1887), a suit was brought against the administrator of an Arkansas estate for fraudulent dealings. The plaintiff heirs were residents of Tennessee and Mississippi. Unfortunately, two or three of the heirs were Arkansas residents, and the plaintiffs tried to keep the case in federal court by naming them as defendants. Judge Parker, saying—"It is with some degree of regret that I feel compelled to hold that the court has no jurisdiction, as, from the examination of the facts of the case, I am led to the conclusion that the acts of Fleeman . . . bristle with fraud,"—had to find that the joinder of parties was collusive.

103. 53 Fed. 410 (C.C. W.D. Ark. 1892).

104. *Vahlberg v. Keaton*, 51 Ark. 544, 11 S.W. 878 (1889).

105. 52 Fed. 618 (C.C. W.D. Ark. 1892).

106. Ibid., at 627. The bottom line was: "The relief that would meet this demand would be to decree the amount of the $30,000 advanced, with 6 per cent. interest on the same, less the year's interest already paid in advance, and to decree the foreclosure of the mortgage given to secure the payment of the debt, and to cancel the remaining part of the contract." Ibid.

107. 17 F.Cas. 1209 (C.C. W.D. Ark. 1879).

108. Ibid., at 1211.

109. 39 Fed. 7 (C.C. W.D. Ark. 1889).

110. Ibid., at 8. The Arkansas act in question provided in section 2 that persons having demands against counties must present them in county court for acceptance or rejection.

111. *Culver v. Woodruff County*, 6 F.Cas. 949 (C.C. W.D. Ark. 1878), citing *United States v. Dawson*, 56 U.S. 467 (1853).

112. See Burton, *Indian Territory and the United States*, 138–202.

113. 47 Fed. 561 (C.C. W.D. Ark. 1891) (annotated in 81 A.L.R. 497).

114. Ibid., at 565.

115. Burton states: "The presence in this Creek delegation of men as keenly opposed to one another as Porter and Isparhecher, and the Muskogee national council's prompt ratification of the agreement, suggest that the tribe was more united on this issue than on any other in its history. There was a dissident group whose leaders threatened to kill the whole delegation, but it never came out into the open and soon subsided into silence." Burton, *Indian Territory and the United States*, 149. The federal legislation directed that the balance of $2 million would be kept in the treasury at 5 percent interest, the interest to be paid annually to the Creek Nation.

116. President Harrison proclaimed that the central portion of Oklahoma would open to homesteaders on April 22, 1889, at noon. "At the appointed moment, cavalry trumpets and firearms signaled the start of 'Harrison's Horse Race' from various points along the perimeter of the Unassigned Lands. Simultaneously, in the heart of the district, thousands of men, mainly members or employees of Kansas townsite companies, crawled out of freight cars or swarmed out of the long grass by the railroad tracks to scoop the real prizes—the most promising town lots in Guthrie and Oklahoma City." Burton, *Indian Territory and the United States*, 155. This first land rush was rife with corruption. A number of those who emerged from the railroad cars were federal officials who wore deputy marshals' badges and acted as agents for the land-grabbers. One of them was Parker's chief prosecutor, W. H. H. Clayton, who lost his position after a Senate Judiciary Committee report that he had misused his office to buy up land before the territory was officially open for settlement. See Stolberg, "Politician, Populist, Reformer: A Reexamination of 'Hanging Judge' Isaac C. Parker," *Arkansas Historical Quarterly* 47 (1988): 25 n. 55.

117. Act, July 4, 1884, 23 Stat. 73. The line was to run from the Kansas border to Dennison, Texas.

118. 33 Fed. 900 (W.D. Ark. 1888).

119. 39 Fed. 174 (C.C. W.D. Ark. 1889).

120. Ibid., at 177.

121. 40 Fed. 273 (C.C. W.D. Ark. 1889).

122. Ibid., at 275. Act, July 4, 1884, 23 Stat. 73, § 8.

123. 40 Fed. 276 (C.C. W.D. Ark. 1889).

124. *Dwyer v. St. Louis & S. F. R. Co.*, 52 Fed. 87, 90 (C.C. W.D. Ark. 1892).

125. 47 Fed. 530 (C.C. W.D. Ark. 1891).

126. *James v. St. Louis & S. F. R. Co.*, 46 Fed. 47 (C.C. W.D. Ark. 1891).

127. *Payne v. Kansas & Ark. Valley R. Co.*, 46 Fed. 546 (C.C. W.D. Ark. 1891).

128. Ibid., at 561.

129. *Kansas & A. V. Ry. Co. v. Payne*, 49 Fed. 114 (C.C.A., 1892). The court determined that the footbridge was within the legislative grant and that if there were increased damages to the lands of the plaintiff a remedy at law for additional compensation was available.

130. Kidder, "Who Took the Trees? A Review of Timber Trespass Litigation in the Federal Court for the Western District of Arkansas Under the Administration of Judge Isaac C. Parker, 1875–1896" (unpublished master's thesis, University of Arkansas, 1996), 69.

131. *Ligget & Myer Tobacco Co. v. Hynes*, 20 Fed. 883 (W.D. Ark. 1884). Cf. The famous dissenting opinion of Judge Jerome Frank in *Triangle Publications, Inc. v. Rohrlich*, 167 F.2d 969, 976–77 (2d Cir. 1948), discussing the problem of how judges and courts of law can determine if there is actual confusion among products or confusion over names in the absence of independent scientific surveys.

132. 52 Fed. 81 (C.C. W.D. Ark. 1892).

133. 47 Fed. 544 (C.C. W.D. Ark. 1891).

134. 46 Fed. 52 (C.C. W.D. Ark. 1891).

135. Ibid., at 53.

136. After Parker was appointed, he attempted to get his brother-in-law appointed as a special attorney in the court, writing to the attorney general with fulsome praise for Thomas Burnett, the brother-in-law, who was a St. Louis attorney. Parker did not disclose the familial relationship in his correspondence. See Stolberg, "Politician, Populist, Reformer: A Reexamination of 'Hanging Judge' Isaac C. Parker," *Arkansas Historical Quarterly* 47 (1988): 13–14. Parker also sought and joined Senator Powell Clayton in securing a position as deputy prosecutor for Thomas Brizzolara. Ibid.

137. *Fort Smith Elevator*, September 18, 1896, 1. In 1889 President Harrison offered Parker an appointment to the Eastern District of Arkansas. Parker rejected the offer citing the important work he was doing in the Western District. Harrington, *Hanging Judge*, 192. A suggestion has been made that Parker was also under consideration for appointment to the Fourth Circuit Court of Appeals to replace Supreme Court justice David Brewer. Stolberg, "Politician, Populist, Reformer: A Reexamination of 'Hanging Judge' Isaac C. Parker," *Arkansas Historical Quarterly* 47 (1988): 28 n. 60.

138. H. P. Daily, "Isaac C. Parker," *Proceedings of the Bar Association of Arkansas* (1932): 88, 103.

139. Shirley, *Law West of Fort Smith*, 70.

140. Harrington, *Hanging Judge*, 59.

141. Professor Wigmore cited the example of Baron Brampton, of the Old Bailey, who told of the "after dinner trials" that had the judge sum up the evidence and tell the jury that he had no doubt the defendant was guilty. The entire trial might last less than five minutes. J. H. Wigmore, *Evidence* (Boston: Little, Brown & Co., 1970), vol.

3, § 769, citing Sir Henry Hawkins; Baron Brampton, *Reminiscences* (London: Edward Arnold, 1904), 1: 30.

142. This view is best expressed by Stolberg, "Politician, Populist, Reformer: A Reexamination of 'Hanging Judge' Isaac C. Parker," *Arkansas Historical Quarterly* 47 (1988).

143. *Fort Smith Elevator*, September 18, 1896, 1.

144. Tuller, "'The Hanging Judge' and the Indians: Isaac C. Parker and U.S. Indian Policy, 1871–1896" (unpublished master's thesis, Texas Christian University, 1993), 63–74.

145. *Fort Smith Elevator*, September 18, 1896, 1.

146. Harrington, *Hanging Judge*, 58.

147. Daily, "Isaac C. Parker," *Proceedings of the Bar Association of Arkansas* (1932): 97.

148. Ibid., at 107. Pleasant Porter was a Creek, not a Choctaw. This error was repeated in a book: H. Croy, *He Hanged Them High* (New York: Duell, Sloan & Pearce, Inc.-Little Brown & Co., 1952), 222. It was, unfortunately, restated by the United States Supreme Court in *Oliphant v. Suquamish Indian Tribe*, 435 U.S. 191, 199, footnote 10.

149. S. Greenleaf, *Law of Evidence* (Boston: Little Brown & Co., 1899), vol. 1, § 14 *p*, n. 25 (16th ed. Wigmore rev.).

12. John Henry Rogers (1896–1911)

1. Ch. 517, 26 *Statutes at Large* 826.
2. 25 *Statutes at Large* 655.
3. 82 Fed. 199 (1897).
4. In that time, the United States attorney had statutory power to designate the place of imprisonment, including state penitentiaries, and many defendants sentenced in the Western District went to Detroit.
5. *In re Christian*, 82 Fed. 885 (1897).
6. 82 Fed. 33 (1897).
7. 81 Fed. 977 (1897).
8. See, e.g., *Sheck v. Kelly*, 95 Fed. 941 (1899); *Johnson v. Southern Building & Loan Ass'n.*, 95 Fed. 922 (1899); *Bowman v. Harris*, 95 Fed. 917 (1899); *In re Rogers Milling Co.*, 102 Fed. 687 (1900).
9. 95 Fed. 434 (1899).
10. 158 U.S. 564, 15 S. Ct. 910 (1895)
11. 96 Fed. 353 (1899).
12. 1 Fed. Cas. 213 (Case No. 102, 1874).
13. 92 U.S. 275 (1875).
14. 183 U.S. 185, 22 S. Ct. 47, 46 L. Ed. 144 (1901).
15. 109 Fed. 603 (1901).
16. The case was appealed to the Eighth Circuit, sub nom. *Chauncy v. Dyke Bros.*, 119 Fed. 1 (1902), where in a 2–1 opinion Rogers's decision was modified (the dissenter would have reversed outright). The appellate court interpreted the Arkansas lien laws differently.
17. 139 Fed. 209 (1905).

18. 116 Fed. 419 (1902)

19. 124 Fed. 446 (1903). In 1902 the Harrison Division of the Western District was created, 32 *Statutes at Large* 72, and this was one of the early cases "on the circuit." The only other division Judge Rogers presided over was Texarkana, originally part of the Eastern District, but transferred to the Western District in 1897, 29 *Statutes at Large* 590.

20. 167 Fed. 389 (1908).

21. See *Arkansas Gazette*, January 20, 1985, 14A, for an account of the story about the late Judge J. Smith Henley, who, while a district judge in a moonshine case in the Harrison Division, faced a question about the authenticity of the clear liquid in evidence. According to Judge Oren Harris, who was telling the story, Henley allegedly took two or three swigs and announced to the jury, "That's moonshine." Judge Henley reportedly gave the true account: "I just put my thumb over the bottle and turned it up, licked my thumb and told the jury, 'In my opinion, which you are free to ignore, that's whiskey.'" Whether swigging or thumb licking occurred, in either case it is an interesting example of judicial notice.

22. 180 Fed. 1006 (1910).

23. 191 Fed. 673 (1911).

24. *Ex Parte Webb*, 225 U.S. 663 (1912), and *United States v. Wright*, 229 U.S. 226 (1913).

25. 93 Fed. 857 (1899).

26. 21 S. Ct. 917 (1899).

27. 110 Fed. 62 (1901).

28. In 1883 the western half of the Indian Territory was transferred to the Northern District of Texas and the District of Kansas, 22 *Statutes at Large* 400. In 1889 jurisdiction over the Choctaw and Chickasaw Nations was transferred to the Eastern District of Texas, 25 *Statutes at Large* 786; and as of September 1, 1896, all the authority of the Arkansas, Texas, and Kansas courts was transferred to the newly created District Courts for Indian Territory, 28 *Statutes at Large* 697.

29. In 1890 the total of crimes was 1,871; in 1891, 2,034; in 1892, 2,584; in 1893, 2,213; in 1894, 1,988; in 1895, 2,125; and in 1896, the last year of Parker's service, 1,482. Nearly half of those numbers represent misdemeanor liquor violations and simple assaults. See J. Burton, *Indian Territory and the United States, 1866–1906* (Norman: University of Oklahoma Press, 1995). "All told, therefore, more than 4,000 criminal cases from Indian Territory were settled by the Fort Smith and Paris courts between July 1, 1889, and June 30, 1893, at a cost to the United States of $1.7 million. Addition of the 6,841 civil and minor criminal cases that went through the Muskogee court and the $731,000 required for its upkeep produces a grand total of 11,000 cases of all classes and overall expenditure of nearly $2.5 million." Ibid., 196. Note that these are only the Indian Territory cases and the figures do not include criminal cases in the Western District of Arkansas proper. For the entirety of Parker's jurisdiction, July 1, 1875, to June 30, 1896, a total of 12,031 criminal prosecutions were closed. Ibid., 229–30.

30. Ibid., 190.

31. The lengthy report in the *Arkansas Gazette* began: "Beneath unruffled coverlets and surrounded by every indication of a passing away as peacefully as a child dropping off to sleep, the dead body of Judge John H. Rogers . . . was found in room 444 of the New Capital Hotel." *Arkansas Gazette*, April 18, 1911, 1. Another account describes Rogers's death: "On the evening of Easter Sunday (April 16, 1911), he retired

to rest apparently in good health and in good spirits, and fell asleep to awake no more on this earth forever. Friends found him the next morning, as if in slumber, with one hand beneath his head, and the other lying gently upon his breast. His eyes were closed and there was no trace of pain nor trouble on his noble face." *Memorial, John Henry Rogers*, July 31, 1911 (Meeting in memory of the late Honorable John H. Rogers, held at Fort Smith, Arkansas, July 31, 1911, in the United States Court room).

13. Frank Abijah Youmans (1911–32)

1. *Arkansas Democrat*, April 17, 1911:

> There is a well-defined movement already on foot to petition President Taft for the appointment of Judge Joseph M. Hill, former chief justice of the Arkansas Supreme Court, to succeed Judge Rogers. Judge Hill is regarded by members of the bar as one of the ablest jurists in the South, and it is believed that President Taft will not be unfriendly to the appointment of a Democrat to succeed the place made vacant by the untimely death of Judge Rogers.

2. Neither the *Arkansas Gazette* nor the *Southwest American* of Fort Smith mentioned the speculation about a successor in their lengthy articles on the death of Judge Rogers.

3. *Arkansas Democrat*, April 19, 1911, 1. The *Southwest American* reported the same resolution on April 20, 1911, 1. The latter story bore the subhead, "Well known Fort Smith attorney is boomed for United States judgeship says honor comes unsolicited."

4. "[I]t is a matter of considerable pride that the lawyers of Texarkana, Arkansas, unanimously endorsed me for the position in very flattering resolutions. This was repeated by the lawyers of Texarkana, Texas, also by the lawyers of Hope, Camden and other places. We thought that as Judge Rogers was a Democrat and the party rules somewhat relaxed in judicial matters that a Democrat might possibly be elected to succeed." W. H. Arnold, *The Arnold Family* (St. Paul: West Publ. Co., 1935), 182.

5. *Southwest American*, April 22, 1911, 1.

6. Ibid.

7. *Southwest American*, April 25, 1911, 1.

8. When Judge Rogers died, he had been hearing cases for Judge Trieber in Little Rock, so the death of Rogers undoubtedly created a severe burden for Judge Trieber.

9. *Southwest American*, May 20, 1911, 6.

10. *Southwest American*, May 30, 1911, 8.

11. After his elevation to the federal bench, Youmans continued to serve on the Fort Smith School Board until 1914.

12. Youmans told the Fort Smith newspaper, after his visit to the White House, that his meeting with President Taft in May 1911 was more of a "social call" than a serious discussion of the federal judgeship:

> It was just a nice social call in which the president chatted entertainingly about things in general and Arkansas in particular. In looking Mr. Youmans over, the president smiled broadly and asked:

> "How many children have you?"
>
> "Six," promptly replied the prospective federal judge.
>
> "Good," heartily rejoined Mr. Taft, and then he shook with good-natured laughter at the thought of the absence of race suicide in the Youmans family *Southwest American*, May 30, 1911, 8.

13. Interview with Pat Youmans Wagner, Stockton, California, December 15, 1997.

14. Ibid.

15. *Arkansas Gazette*, Sunday Magazine section, n.d.

16. Interview with Catherine Youmans Sandahl and Mary Youmans Udouj, December 6, 1997.

17. Interview with Pat Youmans Wagner, Stockton, California, December 15, 1997.

18. 189 Fed. 511 (1911).

19. Ibid., 515.

20. 192 Fed. 353 (1911).

21. 192 Fed. 608 (1911).

22. 197 Fed. 180 (1912).

23. 197 Fed. 216 (1912).

24. 197 Fed. 815 (1912), *aff'd*, 207 Fed. 338 (8th Cir. 1913).

25. Ibid., 820.

26. The cases Youmans relied on are *Chicago, B. & Q. Railway v. Drainage Commissioners*, 200 U.S. 561, 26 S.Ct. 341, 50 L.Ed. 596 (1906) and *Chicago, B. & Q. Railway Co. v. Bd. of Supervisors of Appanoose County*, 182 Fed. 291 (1910).

27. 197 Fed. at 823.

28. 199 Fed. 347 (1912).

29. *In re W. O. Craig Mfg. Co.*, 201 Fed. 548 (1912), *aff'd*, 211 Fed. 244 (8th Cir. 1914).

30. Under UCC § 9-313 (4) (a), the vendor of machinery would be protected if he files his security interest as a fixture filing in the real estate records.

31. 202 Fed. 581 (1912).

32. 206 Fed. 765 (1913), *rev'd*, 220 Fed. 863 (8th Cir. 1915).

33. *Doyle-Kidd Dry Goods Co. v. Sadler-Lusk Trading Co.*, 206 Fed. 813 (1913); *New Paddock-Hawley Co. v. Fayetteville Wagon Wood & Lumber Co.*, 207 Fed. 786 (1913).

34. *Municipal Waterworks v. City of Fort Smith*, 216 Fed. 431 (1914).

35. 216 Fed. 654 (1914).

36. Ibid., 672.

37. *Mardis v. Hines*, 258 Fed. 945 (1919), *aff'd*, 267 Fed. 171 (8th Cir. 1920).

38. *Hosler v. Ireland*, 219 Fed. 489 (1915); *Sauve v. Fleschutz*, 219 Fed. 542 (1915); *Atchison, T. & S.F. Ry. Co. v. DeSedillo*, 219 Fed. 686 (1915); *Sullivan v. Ellis*, 219 Fed. 694 (1915); *Himrod v. Ft. Pitt Min. & Mill. Co.*, 220 Fed. 80 (dissent) (1915); *Stanard v. Dayton*, 220 Fed. 441 (1915); *Rogers v. Hennepin County*, 220 Fed. 453 (1915); *Bishop v. Wight*, 221 Fed. 392 (1915); *Denver & R.G.R. Co. v. Mills*, 222 Fed. 481 (1915); *Newton Washing Mach. Co. v. Grinnell Washing Mach. Co.*, 222 Fed. 512 (1915); *Parsons v. Trowbridge*, 226 Fed. 15 (1915); *Smart v. Wright*, 227 Fed. 84 (1915); *Gilliland v. Adamson*, 227 Fed 93 (1915), *rev'd*, 242 U.S. 350, 37 S.Ct. 169, 61 L.Ed. 356 (1917).

39. *Waters-Pierce Oil Co. v. United States*, 251 Fed. 56 (1918); *Clarkson Coal & Dock Co. v. Northern Lakes S.S. Co.*, 251 Fed. 181 (1918); *Griggs v. Nadeau*, 250 Fed. 781 (1918); *Reynolds v. United States*, 252 Fed. 65 (1918), *rev'd*, 250 U.S. 104, 39 S.Ct. 409, 63 L.Ed. 873 (1919); *Privett v. United States*, 261 Fed. 351 (1919); *Kreibich v. United States*, 261 Fed. 168 (1919); *United States v. Lena*, 261 Fed. 144 (1919); *Missouri Pac. R. Co. v. Mette*, 261 Fed. 755 (1919); *Lane v. Equitable Trust Co. of New York*, 262 Fed. 918 (1919); *First Nat. Bank of Evanston, Wyo. v. Bank of Waynesboro*, 262 Fed. 754 (1919).

40. *Bingham Mines Co. v. Bianco*, 276 Fed. 513 (1921); *Davis v. Wilson*, 276 Fed. 672 (1921); *Deming Ladies' Hospital Ass'n v. Price*, 276 Fed. 668 (1921); *Rocky Mountain Fuel Co. v. Consolidated Coal & Coke Co.*, 276 Fed. 661 (1921); *United States v. Bothwell*, 277 Fed. 419 (1921); *Moore v. Gas Securities Co.*, 278 Fed. 111 (1921); *Bench Canal Drainage Dist. v. Maryland Casualty Co.*, 278 Fed. 67 (1921); *Nishimura v. Mansfield*, 277 Fed. 792 (1921).

41. *Sinclair v. Butt*, 284 Fed. 568 (1922); *Roberson v. United States*, 284 Fed. 503 (1922); *Wood County Grocer Co. v. Frazer*, 284 Fed. 691 (1922); *Clarke v. Boysen*, 285 Fed. 122 (1922); *Simonson v. Typer*, 285 Fed. 240 (1922).

42. *Weiderman v. United States*, 10 F.2d 745 (1926); *Clement v. Wilson*, 11 F.2d 355 (1926); *Logan v. Haynes*, 11 F.2d 369 (1926); *Mack v. Connecticut General Life Ins. Co.*, 12 F.2d 416 (1926); *Mayer v. White*, 12 F.2d 710 (1926); *Elbukan Oil Co. v. Lamb*, 12 F.2d 387 (1926).

43. *Lockhart v. United States*, 51 F.2d 732 (1931); *Drainage Dist. No. 17 v. Guardian Trust Co.*, 52 F.2d 579 (1931); *United States v. McLaughlin*, 53 F.2d 450 (1931).

44. 294 Fed. 102 (1923), *aff'd per curiam*, 270 U.S. 627, 46 S.Ct. 206, 70 L.Ed. 768 (1925).

45. Ibid., 108.

46. 18 F.2d 285 (1926).

47. Ibid., 287.

48. *Davis v. United States*, 15 F.2d 697 (1926).

49. Ibid., 698. Davis said that because of this misunderstanding he was not claiming allowance for the three and a half months served in that jail.

50. *In re Watson*, 22 F.2d 689 (1927).

51. 33 F.2d 158 (1929).

52. 25 F.2d 1007 (1928).

53. *United States v. One 1929 Model Ford Coupe*, 38 F.2d 520 (1930).

54. Ibid., 521.

55. 43 F.2d 179 (1930).

56. Ibid., 181.

57. Ibid., 183.

58. 3 F.Supp. 114 (1931), *appeal dismissed*, 64 F.2d 752 (8th Cir. 1933).

59. 44 F2d 403 (1930).

60. U.S. Constitution art. 4, § 2.

61. *Roberts v. Reilly*, 116 U.S. 80, 6 S.Ct. 291, 29 L.Ed. 544 (1885).

62. 2 F.Supp. 32 (1932).

63. Ibid., 33.

64. See, e.g., *Tracy v. Spitzer-Rorick Trust & Savings Bank*, 12 F.2d 755 (1926).

65. 206 Fed. 765 (1913), *rev'd*, 220 Fed. 863 (8th Cir. 1915).

66. 21 F.2d 912 (1928).

67. Ibid., 914.

68. 2 F.2d 574 (1924).

69. 19 F.2d 732 (1927).

70. 225 Fed. 1 (1916).

71. 258 Fed. 829, *rev'd, United Mine Workers v. Coronado Coal Co.*, 259 U.S. 344, 42 S.Ct. 570, 66 L.Ed. 975 (1922).

72. *United Mine Workers of America v. Coronado Coal Co.*, 259 U.S. 344, 42 S.Ct. 570, 66 L.Ed. 975 (1922).

73. 300 Fed. 965 (1924).

74. 39 F.2d 408 (8th Cir. 1930), *rev'd*, 283 U.S. 353, 51 S.Ct. 476, 75 L.Ed. 1112 (1931).

75. One of Youmans's granddaughters stated that serious health problems were not discussed in the family, but she speculated that the judge probably had prostate surgery. Interview with Pat Youmans Wagner, December 15, 1997.

76. However, a statement was made in the memorial services for Judge Heartsill Ragon to the effect that when Ragon ascended to the bench in 1933 the docket was very crowded because Judge Youmans "during the last years of his term had been forced by ill health to remain inactive for much of the time." Western District of Arkansas, May 21, 1941.

77. *Arkansas Gazette*, April 12, 1932, 2.

78. *Arkansas Democrat*, April 11, 1932, 1.

14. Heartsill Ragon (1933–40)

1. William H. Pruden III, "Hiram Heartsill Ragon 1885–1940," *Encyclopedia of Arkansas History and Culture*, www.encyclopediaofarkansas.net (Accessed September 13, 2015). Sources differ on Ragon's birth and marriage years.

2. *History of the Federal Judiciary*. http://www.fjc.gov. Website of the Federal Judicial Center, Washington, DC (Last visited October 24, 2010).

3. John C. Williams, "David Dickson Terry," the *Encyclopedia of Arkansas History and Culture*, www.encyclopediaofarkansas.net (Last visited October 24, 2010).

4. *United States v. Miller*, 26 F. Supp. 1002 (W.D. Ark. 1939).

5. *Futrall v. Bartee*, 28 F. Supp. 495 (D.C. 1939).

6. *Arkansas Louisiana Gas Company v. City of Texarkana, Arkansas*, 17 F. Supp. 447 (W.D. Ark. 1936).

7. *United States Fidelity & Guaranty Co. v. Pierson*, 21 F. Supp. 678 (W.D. Ark. 1937).

8. *United States Fidelity & Guaranty Co. v. Shrigley*, 26 F. Supp. 625 (W.D. Ark. 1939).

9. *King v. Shepherd*, 26 F. Supp. 357 (W.D. Ark. 1938).

10. *McCallum v. General American Oil Co. of Texas*, 21 F. Supp. 401 (W.D. Ark., 1937).

11. *Central United National Bank v. Fort Smith and W. RY. Company*, 32 F. Supp. 568 (W.D. Ark. 1940).

12. *Wood v. United States*, 20 F. Supp. 197 (W.D. Ark. 1937).

13. *U.S. v. Giger*, 26 F. Supp. 624 (W.D. Ark., 1939).

14. *In re Harris Bros.*, 5 F. Supp. 191 (W.D. Ark., 1933).

15. *In re Magness Bros.*, 5 F. Supp. 578 (W.D. Ark., 1934).

16. *In re Jackson*, 9 F. Supp. 717 (W.D. Ark., 1935).
17. *In re Cherokee Public Service Company*, 20 F. Supp. 195 (W.D. Ark., 1937).
18. *Harrod v. Missouri Pac. R. Co.*, 26 F. Supp. 619 (W.D. Ark., 1939).
19. *Yoes v. Continental Oil Company*, 5 F. Supp. 575 (W.D. Ark., 1934).

15. John Elvis Miller (1941–67)

1. *Arkansas Democrat*, Sunday, February 1, 1981; *Arkansas Gazette*, Sunday, February 1, 1981; *History of the Federal Judiciary*. http://www.fjc.gov. Website of the Federal Judicial Center, Washington, DC.
2. *History of the Federal Judiciary*. http://www.fjc.gov. Website of the Federal Judicial Center, Washington, DC.
3. Ibid; see also note 1.
4. Ibid.
5. Memorandum, "Selected opinions of John E. Miller," Susan Scafidi to Hon. Morris S. Arnold, November 30, 1994.
6. *Kempe v. United States*, 151 F. 2d 680 (8th Cir. 1945), *cert. denied*, 331 U.S. 843 (1946). Susan Scafidi prepared the case summary.
7. *Kempe v. United States*, 160 F. 2nd 406 (8th Cir. 1947). Susan Scafidi prepared the case summary.
8. *King v. Sweatt*, 115 F. Supp. 215 (W. D. Ark. 1953). Susan Scafidi prepared the case summary.
9. *Gibson v. Reynolds*, 77 F. Supp. 629 (W. D. Ark. 1948). Susan Scafidi prepared the case summary.
10. Ibid., 637.
11. *United States v. Owen*, 415 F. 2d 383 (8th Cir. 1969). Susan Scafidi prepared the case summary.
12. Ibid., 390.
13. *United States v. Bryant*, 293 F. Supp. 922 (W. D. Ark. 1968). Susie Margaret Ross prepared the case summary.
14. Memorandum, "Cases of Judge John E. Miller," BJN to MSA, November 30, 1994. Bradley J. Nicholson prepared the case summary.
15. *Aaron v. Cooper*, 143 F. Supp. 855 (E. D. Ark. 1956), *aff'd*, 243 F. 2d 361 (8th Cir. 1957). Bradley J. Nicholson prepared the case summary.
16. 347 U.S. 483 (1954) and 349 U.S. 294 (1955).
17. 143 F. Supp. 866. Bradley J. Nicholson prepared the case summary.
18. See *Aaron v. Cooper*, 156 F. Supp. 220 (E. D. Ark. 1957); *aff'd sub. nom. Faubus v. United States*, 254 F. 2d 797 (8th Cir.), *cert. denied*, 358 U.S. 829 (1958). Bradley J. Nicholson prepared the case summary.
19. *Aaron v. Cooper*, 163 F. Supp. 13 (E. D. Ark.) *cert. denied*, 357 U.S. 566, *rev'd*, 257 F. 2d 33 (8th Cir.), *aff'd*, 358 U.S. 1 (1958). Bradley J. Nicholson prepared the case summary.
20. *Aaron v. Cooper*, 261 F. 2d 97 (1958). Bradley J. Nicholson prepared the case summary.
21. *Aaron v. Cooper*, 169 F. Supp. 325 (E. D. Ark. 1959). Bradley J. Nicholson prepared the case summary.
22. *Aaron v. McKinley*, 173 F. Supp. 944 (E. D. Ark); *aff'd sub. nom. Faubus v. Aaron*, 361 U.S. 197 (1959). Bradley J. Nicholson prepared the case summary.

23. *Aaron v. Tucker*, 186 F. Supp. 913 (E. D. Ark. 1960), *rev'd sub nom. Norwood v. Tucker*, 287 F. 2d 798 (8th Cir. 1961). Bradley J. Nicholson prepared the case summary.

24. 186 F. Supp. at 932–33.

25. Ibid., 932.

26. Ibid., 933.

27. 287 F. 2d at 808. Bradley J. Nicholson prepared the case summary.

28. Interviews, Judge J. Smith Henley with Frances Mitchell Ross, Harrison, Arkansas, March 23–24, 1987, pp. 86, 110–11; April 24, 1987, p. 23. Available at UALR Center for Arkansas History and Culture, Arkansas Studies Institute, Little Rock, Arkansas.

29. *Arkansas Democrat*, Sunday, February 1, 1981; *Arkansas Gazette*, Sunday, February 1, 1981; *History of the Federal Judiciary*. http://www.fjc.gov. Website of the Federal Judicial Center, Washington, DC.

16. Harry Jacob Lemley (1939–58)

1. William H. Arnold to United States attorney general Frank Murphy, Texarkana, Arkansas, January 19, 1939.

2. *History of the Federal Judiciary.* http://www.fjc.gov. Website of the Federal Judicial Center (Accessed March 15, 2015).

3. See Fay Williams, "A National Authority on Indian Archeology: Federal Judge Harry Lemley Said to Have Largest Private Collection in U.S.," *Arkansas Democrat Magazine*, March 2, 1952, 6–7.

4. Ibid.

5. *Barksdale v. Ford, Bacon & Davis, Inc.*, 70 F. Supp. 690 (1947).

6. *Aaron v. Ford, Bacon & Davis, Inc.*, 174 F.2d 730 (8th Cir. 1949).

7. *Powell v. United States Cartridge Co.*, 339 U.S. 497 (1950).

8. *United States of America v. Miller*, 317 U.S. 192 (1942).

9. *Aaron v. Cooper*, 143 F. Supp. 855 (E.D. Ark. 1956).

10. *Aaron v. Cooper*, 163 F. Supp. 13 (E. D. Ark. 1958).

11. *Cooper v. Aaron*, 358 U.S. 1 (1958).

12. *Bryant v. Chicago Mill & Lumber Co.*, 120 F. Supp. 463 (E.D. Ark. 1954).

13. *Ussery v. Anderson-Tully Co.*, 122 F. Supp. 115 (E.D. Ark. 1954).

14. Philip Alston, "In Memoriam: Harry J. Lemley" (resolution presented at the Eighth Circuit Judicial Conference, St. Louis, Missouri, September 10, 1965), 3.

17. Jesse Smith Henley (1959–75)

1. History of the Federal Judiciary: http://www.fjc.gov. In Memoriam, Honorable J. Smith Henley, 168 F.3d 85, remarks of the Honorable Susan Webber Wright, January 14, 1998. Richard S. Arnold, "Judge J. Smith Henley, A Personal Reminiscence," *Arkansas Law Review* 52 (1999): 300.

2. Morris Sheppard Arnold, "A Tribute to Judge J. Smith Henley," *Arkansas Law Review* 52 (1999): 297; Judge J. Smith Henley, interview by Frances M. Ross, March 23–24, 1987, pp. 1–3, 8, 10, 14–17. The interview is available at the UALR Center for Arkansas History and Culture, Arkansas Studies Institute, Little Rock, Arkansas.

3. History of the Federal Judiciary: http://www.fjc.gov.; Morris Sheppard Arnold, "A Tribute to Judge J. Smith Henley," *Arkansas Law Review* 52 (1999): 297; Henley, interview by Ross, 21.

4. Garnett Thomas Eisele, "A Tribute to Judge J. Smith Henley," *Arkansas Law Review* 52 (1999): 305.

5. *Holt v. Sarver*, 309 F. Supp. 362, 381 (E.D. Ark. 1970).

6. Henley, interview by Ross, 144.

7. See, e.g., *Davis v. Board of Educ.*, 328 F. Supp 1197 (E.D. Ark. 1971); *Clark v. Board of Educ.*, 316 F. Supp. 1209 (E.D. Ark 1970); *Graves v. Board of Educ.*, 302 F. Supp. 136 (E.D. Ark. 1969); *Cato v. Parham*, 293 F. Supp. 1375 (E.D. Ark. 1968); *Brown v. Board of Educ.*, 263 F. Supp. 734 (E.D. Ark. 1966); *Dove v. Parham*, 196 F. Supp. 944 (E.D. Ark. 1961).

8. Garnett Thomas Eisele, "A Tribute to Judge J. Smith Henley," *Arkansas Law Review* 52 (1999): 305.

9. Henley, interview by Ross, 127–28.

10. Ibid., 118–21.

11. Richard S. Arnold, "Judge J. Smith Henley, A Personal Reminiscence," *Arkansas Law Review* 52 (1999): 300.

12. In Memoriam, Honorable J. Smith Henley, 168 F.3d 85, remarks of the Honorable Gerald Heaney, January 14, 1998.

CONTRIBUTORS

RICHARD S. ARNOLD graduated at the top of his class from Harvard Law School. After clerking for United States Supreme Court justice William J. Brennan, Arnold practiced law in Washington, DC, and then returned to Arkansas to practice in his family firm. He was later appointed United States district judge for the Eastern and Western Districts of Arkansas, then circuit judge of the United States Court of Appeals for the Eighth Circuit. Judge Arnold was a member of the Arkansas and District of Columbia Bars.

LYNN FOSTER is the Arkansas Bar Foundation Professor of Law at the University of Arkansas at Little Rock William H. Bowen School of Law, which awarded her the Law School Award for Outstanding Public Service in 2014.

GEORGE C. FREEMAN III is a Yale Law School graduate and former law clerk to Judge Richard S. Arnold and to Lewis F. Powell Jr., associate justice of the United States Supreme Court. Freeman is chairman, president, and CEO of Universal Corporation in Richmond, Virginia, and is a member of the Virginia Bar.

MORTON GITELMAN is Distinguished Professor of Law Emeritus at the University of Arkansas School of Law. In addition to teaching and contributing to law reviews, he has authored and edited several legal textbooks, and has been actively involved in Arkansas Bar Association work for many years.

GERALD W. HEANEY received his law degree from the University of Minnesota Law School in 1941. Following service in the United States Army during World War II, Heaney practiced labor law with Lewis, Hammer, Heaney, Weyl and Halverson in Duluth, Minnesota. He was also active in Democratic Party politics. Appointed and confirmed to the United States Court of Appeals for the Eighth Circuit in 1966, Judge Heaney served full time and later as senior judge until he retired in 2006.

MICHAEL B. HEISTER graduated summa cum laude from the University of Arkansas School of Law. He was law clerk to Judge Richard S. Arnold in 2002–3, practiced law in Washington, DC, and then returned to his hometown of Little Rock. He practices law with the firm of Quattlebaum, Grooms, Tull and Burrow PLLC focusing on complex civil litigation and appeals and is a member of the Arkansas and District of Columbia Bars.

BRADLEY J. NICHOLSON is a former law clerk to Judge Morris S. Arnold, United States district judge for the Western District of Arkansas and circuit judge of the United States Court of Appeals for the Eighth Circuit. Nicholson received a law degree from the University of Pennsylvania School of Law and clerked for Judge Arnold on both the district and circuit courts.

HEARTSILL RAGON III received his law degree from the University of Arkansas School of Law in 1982. He is the grandson of Judge Heartsill Ragon and is a third-generation lawyer. He served as corporate counsel for Fairfield Communities, Inc. and now practices with Gill Ragon Owen, PA in Little Rock where he specializes in corporate and commercial law. He has been active in Arkansas Bar Association work and as a member of the board of directors of the Arkansas Science and Technology Authority.

STEPHEN M. REASONER received a law degree with honors from the University of Arkansas School of Law in 1969 where he was editor-in-chief of the *Arkansas Law Review*. He practiced law in Jonesboro, Arkansas, with Barrett, Wheatley, Smith and Deacon until he was confirmed as United States district judge for the Eastern District of Arkansas in 1988. He was on the bench full time, serving seven years as chief judge, until he took senior status in 2002.

FRANCES MITCHELL ROSS is an emeritus member of the faculty at the University of Arkansas at Little Rock, where she served in the Department of History from 1963 to 2013. She is a past president of the Historical Society of the United States Courts in the Eighth Circuit and is a founding member and past president of the Arkansas Supreme Court Historical Society. She remains a board member of both societies.

SUSIE MARGARET ROSS is a former law clerk to Judge Morris S. Arnold, United States district judge for the Western District of Arkansas and circuit judge of the United States Court of Appeals for the Eighth Circuit. She received a law degree, cum laude, from Indiana School of Law-Bloomington and served as Judge Arnold's senior law clerk for sixteen years.

ELSIJANE TRIMBLE ROY was the daughter of Judge Thomas Clark Trimble III. She graduated from the University of Arkansas School of Law in 1939, the only female law student to graduate that year. Along with private practice, service as law clerk and as assistant attorney general for the state, she held three judgeships by appointment: as state circuit court judge, as associate justice of the Arkansas Supreme Court and as United States district judge for the Eastern and Western Districts of Arkansas. She was the first female in Arkansas to hold any of these judgeships, and as United States district judge she presided in the same courtroom her father had used.

SUSAN SCAFIDI is a former law clerk to Judge Morris S. Arnold, United States district judge for the Western District of Arkansas and circuit judge of the United States Court of Appeals for the Eighth Circuit. A graduate of Yale Law School, she is professor and founder of the Fashion Law Institute at Fordham Law School.

LOGAN SCOTT STAFFORD is Emeritus Professor of Law at the University of Arkansas at Little Rock William H. Bowen School of Law where he taught from 1982 to 2008. In 1999 he was a founding member of the Arkansas Supreme Court Historical Society, Inc. Stafford was the society's first president and remains a member of the board of directors. He has numerous publications in legal journals and magazines on topics of historical interest.

HENRY WOODS received a law degree from the University of Arkansas School of Law in 1940. His varied career included FBI special agent, referee in bankruptcy, campaign manager for Sid McMath's two successful bids for governor of Arkansas, executive secretary to Governor McMath and special associate justice of the Arkansas Supreme Court. He was also a delegate to two Democratic National Conventions and maintained an active law practice until 1980 when he was confirmed as United States district judge for the Eastern District of Arkansas.

SUSAN WEBBER WRIGHT received a law degree from the University of Arkansas School of Law and served as law clerk to Judge Jesse Smith Henley, circuit judge of the United States Court of Appeals for the Eighth Circuit. She then joined the faculty at the University of Arkansas at Little Rock School of Law and in January 1990 was confirmed as United States district judge for the Eastern and Western Districts of Arkansas. Judge Wright was recommissioned to the Eastern District when the position with the two districts was made solely an Eastern District position. She continues to serve as senior United States district judge for the Eastern District of Arkansas.

DAVID YOUNG is a nephew of Eastern District judge Gordon Young. Judge David Young retired as US magistrate judge in 2015. He has served as one of two members from the Eastern District of Arkansas on the Board of the Historical Society of the United States Courts in the Eighth Circuit.

INDEX

A

C

D

E

K

L

M

T

Y

Z